REGIONALISM IN WORLD POLITICS

Regionalism in World Politics

REGIONAL ORGANIZATION AND INTERNATIONAL ORDER

Edited by

LOUISE FAWCETT

and

ANDREW HURRELL

OXFORD UNIVERSITY PRESS

*This book has been printed digitally and produced in a standard specification
in order to ensure its continuing availability*

OXFORD
UNIVERSITY PRESS

Great Clarendon Street, Oxford OX2 6DP

Oxford University Press is a department of the University of Oxford.
furthers the University's objective of excellence in research, scholarship,
and education by publishing worldwide in

Oxford New York

Auckland Bangkok Buenos Aires Cape Town Chennai
Dar es Salaam Delhi Hong Kong Istanbul Karachi Kolkata
Kuala Lumpur Madrid Melbourne Mexico City Mumbai Nairobi
São Paulo Shanghai Taipei Tokyo Toronto

Oxford is a registered trade mark of Oxford University Press
in the UK and in certain other countries

Published in the United States
by Oxford University Press Inc., New York

ISBN 0-19-828067-X

ACKNOWLEDGEMENTS

THIS book forms part of the Research Programme on 'Developing States in a Changing World Order' supported by the John D. and Catherine T. MacArthur Foundation and based at the Centre for International Studies, Oxford. We would like to thank the MacArthur Foundation for its generous support of this work. Institutional support, hospitality, and secretarial assistance was also provided by Exeter College and Nuffield College. For their time and advice in helping us to organize this project we are especially indebted to Adam Roberts, Robert O'Neill, and Tim Barton.

L. F.
A. J. H.

October 1994

CONTENTS

NOTES ON CONTRIBUTORS

LOUISE FAWCETT is the Wilfrid Knapp Fellow in Politics at St Catherine's College, Oxford and University Lecturer in Politics at Oxford University. She was previously the MacArthur Scholar and Junior Research Fellow in International Relations at Exeter College, Oxford, working on a research project on 'The Developing States in a Changing World Order' supported by the MacArthur Foundation. Her publications include *Iran and the Cold War* (1992).

ROSEMARY FOOT is the John Swire Senior Research Fellow in the International Relations of the Far East and a Fellow of St Antony's College, Oxford. Her publications include *A Substitute for Victory: The Politics of Peacemaking at the Korean Armistice* (1990) and *The Practice of Power: U.S. Relations with China since 1949* (1995). She is currently Director of the Asian Studies Centre, St Antony's College.

ALAN HENRIKSON is Associate Professor of Diplomatic History at the Fletcher School of Law and Diplomacy, Tufts University, where he serves as Director of the Fletcher Roundtable on a New World Order. He teaches American diplomatic history, contemporary US–European relations, and international organization and negotiation. He is also an Associate of the Center for International Affairs at Harvard University. Among his publications are *Defining a New World Order: Toward a Practical Vision of Collective Action for International Peace and Security* (1991) and, as editor, *Negotiating World Order: The Artisanship and Architecture of Global Diplomacy* (1986).

ANDREW HURRELL is University Lecturer in International Relations at Oxford University and a Fellow of Nuffield College. He taught previously at the Johns Hopkins School of Advanced International Studies in Bologna, Italy. He has written on the theory of international relations and the international relations of Latin America. His publications include, as co-editor and contributor, *Latin America in Perspective* (1990) and, as co-editor (with Benedict Kingsbury), *The International Politics of the Environment* (1992).

JAMES MAYALL is Professor of International Relations at the London School of Economics. His publications include *Nationalism and International Society* (1990) and, as editor, *The End of the Post-war Era* (1980) and *The Community of States: A Study in International Theory* (1982).

CHARLES TRIPP is Senior Lecturer in Politics with reference to the Near and Middle East at the School of Oriental and African Studies, University of London. He is co-author (with Dr Shahram Chubin) of *Iran and Iraq at War* (1988), editor of *Regional Security in the Middle East* (1984), and co-editor (with Roger Owen) of *Egypt under Mubarak* (1988).

WILLIAM WALLACE is Walter F. Hallstein Fellow at St Antony's College, Oxford. From 1978 to 1990 he was Director of Studies at the Royal Institute of International Affairs in London. His books include *The Transformation of Western Europe* (1990), as editor and contributor, *The Dynamics of European Integration* (1990), and *Regional Integration: the West European Experience* (1995).

ANDREW WYATT-WALTER is University Lecturer in International Relations at Oxford and a Fellow of St Antony's College. His publications include a book on the relationship between hegemonic powers and the stability of the international financial system, *World Power and World Money* (1993), and various articles on international political economy. His current research interests include the policy implications of foreign investment in the OECD, and the regulation of international financial markets.

ABBREVIATIONS AND ACRONYMS

ACC	Arab Co-operation Council
AFTA	Asian Free Trade Area
AMU	Arab Maghreb Union (Union du Maghreb Arabe [UMA] in French)
ANZUS	Australia–New Zealand–USA Pact
APEC	Asia-Pacific Economic Co-operation forum
ARF	ASEAN Regional Forum
ASEAN	Association of South-East Asian Nations
CACM	Central American Common Market (MCCA in Spanish)
CAP	Common Agricultural Policy
CARICOM	Caribbean Community and Common Market
CBI	Caribbean Basin Initiative
CBM	Confidence Building Measure
CET	Common External Tariff
CENTO	Central Treaty Organization
CFE	Conventional Armed Forces in Europe (Treaty)
CIS	Commonwealth of Independent States
CMEA	Council for Mutual Economic Assistance (also known as COMECON)
CSCE	Conference on Security and Co-operation in Europe (became Organization for Security and Co-operation in Europe [OSCE] in December 1994)
CUSFTA	Canada–USA Free Trade Agreement
EAEC	East Asian Economic Caucus
EAI	Enterprise for the Americas Initiative
EC/EU	European Community (European Union from 1 January 1994)
ECO	Economic Co-operation Organization
ECOMOG	Economic Community of West African States Monitoring Group
ECOWAS	Economic Community of West African States
EDC	European Defence Community
EEA	European Economic Area

EFTA	European Free Trade Association
EU	European Union
EMU	European Monetary Union
EPC	European Political Co-operation
EPU	European Payments Union
EMS	European Monetary System
ERM	European Exchange Rate Mechanism
ECSC	European Coal and Steel Community
FDI	foreign direct investment
FTA	free trade area
G-77	Group of 77
GATT	General Agreement on Tariffs and Trade
GCC	Gulf Co-operation Council
GDP	gross domestic product
GNP	gross national product
IAEA	International Atomic Energy Agency
IMF	International Monetary Fund
ISI	import substitution industrialization
LAFTA	Latin American Free Trade Association (ALALC in Spanish)
LAIA	Latin American Integration Association (ALADI in Spanish)
LAS	League of Arab States
Mercosur	Common Market of the South (*Mercado Común del Sur*)
NACC	North Atlantic Co-operation Council
NAFTA	North American Free Trade Area
NAM	Non-Aligned Movement
NATO	North Atlantic Treaty Organization
NGO	non-governmental organization
NIC	newly industrialized country
NIE	newly industrialized economy
NIEO	New International Economic Order
NTB	non-tariff barrier
OAU	Organization of African Unity
OAS	Organization of American States
OECD	Organization for Economic Co-operation and Development
OEEC	Organization for European Economic Co-operation

OECS	Organization of East Caribbean States
OIC	Organization of the Islamic Conference
ONUCA	United Nations Observer Group in Central America
OPEC	Organization of Petroleum-Exporting Countries
PECC	Pacific Economic Co-operation Council
PfP	Partnership for Peace
PICC	Paris International Conference on Cambodia
SEA	Single European Act
SADC	Southern African Development Community (previously SADCC)
SAARC	South Asian Association for Regional Co-operation
SEATO	South-East Asia Treaty Organization
SPF	South Pacific Forum
UAE	United Arab Emirates
UAR	United Arab Republic
UN	United Nations
UNAMIR	UN Assistance Mission in Rwanda
UNAVEM	UN Angola Verification Mission
UNCTAD	United Nations Conference on Trade and Development
UNFICYP	UN Peacekeeping Force for Cyprus
UNIFIL	United Nations Interim Force in Lebanon
UNMIH	UN Mission in Haiti
UNOGIL	UN Observation Group in Lebanon
UNOMIL	UN Observer Group in Liberia
UNOSOM	UN Operation in Somalia
UNPROFOR	UN Protection Force (Croatia; Bosnia and Hercegovina; and Macedonia).
UNTAC	United Nations Transitional Authority in Cambodia
WEU	Western European Union
WTO	Warsaw Treaty Organization
WTO	World Trade Organization
ZOPFAN	Zone of Peace, Freedom, and Neutrality

1

Introduction

Louise Fawcett and Andrew Hurrell

THE period since the late 1980s has witnessed a resurgence of regionalism in world politics. Old regionalist organizations have been revived, new organizations formed, and regionalism and the call for strengthened regionalist arrangements have been central to many of the debates about the nature of the post-Cold War international order.[1] The revival of political and academic interest in regionalism has been associated with a number of developments, including: the end of the Cold War and the erosion of the Cold War alliance systems; the recurrent fears over the stability of the GATT and the multilateral trading order during the long-drawn-out (if ultimately successful) negotiation of the Uruguay Round; the impact of increasing economic integration and globalization; changed attitudes towards economic development in many parts of the developing world; and the impact of democracy and democratization. The political salience of regionalism rose significantly as a result of developments within Europe (the EC decision to press ahead with the completion of the Single Market, the negotiation of the Maastricht Treaty, and enlargement of the Union towards

---

[1] For many analysts, trends towards regionalism are well established. Dominick Salvatore, for example, believes that '[T]he world has already and probably irreversibly moved into an international trade order characterized by three major trading blocs': Dominick Salvatore, 'Protectionism and World Welfare: Introduction', in Salvatore (ed.), *Protectionism and World Welfare* (Cambridge: CUP, 1993), 10. Peter Drucker believes that the demands of what he calls the 'knowledge economy' 'makes regionalism both inevitable and irreversible': Peter F. Drucker, *Post-Capitalist Society* (London: Butterworth-Heinemann, 1993), 137. Aaron Friedberg argues that '[R]ecent rhetoric notwithstanding, the dominant trend in world politics today is towards regionalization rather than globalization, toward fragmentation rather than unification: Aaron L. Friedberg, 'Ripe for Rivalry. Prospects for Peace in a Multipolar Asia', *International Security*, 18/3 (Winter 1993–4), 5. See also W. W. Rostow, 'The Coming Age of Regionalism', *Encounter*, 74/5 (June 1990); Richard Rosecrance, 'Regionalism and the Post-Cold War Era', *International Journal*, 46 (Summer 1991); and Kenichi Ohmae, 'The Rise of the Region State', *Foreign Affairs* (Spring 1993).

Scandinavia and Central Europe); the successful negotiation and ratification of the North American Free Trade Agreement (NAFTA); and the increased momentum of co-operative efforts within ASEAN and continuing discussions within the Asia-Pacific region over new economic and security agreements (APEC, PECC, ARF). Inis Claude's remark of the early 1960s that '[T]he world is engaged in the process of organizing' is no less appropriate to the post-Cold War world with regionalism forming a central part of that process.[2] The recent wave of regionalist activity ranges from discussion of a world of regional trading blocs on the one hand, to increased emphasis on subregional co-operation and integration on the other.

Most recent academic discussion of regionalism seeks—quite naturally—to analyse a particular regionalist arrangement, be it the EU, NAFTA, or ASEAN. Again not unnaturally there has been a great deal of attention devoted to the economic issues associated with schemes for free trade and economic integration. There are, however, good reasons for taking a broader perspective: bringing together the many different institutions and ideas to be found under the label of 'regionalism'; seeking to place the revival of regionalism in a broader historical perspective; asking whether there are common factors behind the revival of regionalism in so many different parts of the world; and analysing the cumulative impact of different brands of regionalism on international order.

In the first place, the number, scope, and diversity of regionalist schemes have grown significantly since the last major 'regionalist wave' in the 1960s.[3] Writing towards the end of this earlier regionalist wave, Joseph Nye could point to two major classes of regionalist activity: on the one hand, microeconomic organizations involving formal economic integration; and on the other, macroregional political organizations concerned with controlling conflict.[4] Today micro-regional schemes for economic integration stand together with arguments for macroeconomic or 'bloc regionalism' built around the triad of Europe, the Americas, and Japan. In

---

[2] Inis L. Claude, *Swords into Plowshares* (London: University of London Press, 1964), 3.

[3] For quantitative data on increased involvement in regional organizations in the 1980s, see Paul Taylor, *International Organization in the Modern World. The Regional and Global Process* (London: Pinter, 1993), 24–8.

[4] Joseph S. Nye, *Peace in Parts: Integration and Conflict in Regional Organizations* (Boston: Little, Brown & Co., 1971).

the political field ageing regionalist dinosaurs such as the OAU and the OAS have re-emerged and have been joined both by a large number of micro-regional regional political bodies, and by what one might call meso-regional security groupings such as the Conference on Security and Co-operation in Europe (CSCE, now OSCE) or, more recently, the ASEAN Regional Forum. Some may be formal organizations, but many aim at informal political co-ordination or concertation. Indeed, an important characteristic of the new regionalism is the very wide variation in the level of institutionalization, with many regional groupings consciously avoiding the institutional and bureaucratic structures of traditional international organizations and of the regionalist model represented by the EC.[5] Finally, forming part of a broader resurgence of questions of identity and belonging, many parts of the world have seen a marked increase in regional awareness or regional consciousness, even if this is not always easily or unproblematically translated in concrete schemes for regional co-operation.

Second, the revival of interest in regionalism and regionalist projects needs to be seen within a global perspective. The fact that regionalist schemes have emerged in so many different parts of the world suggests that broad international forces may be at work and that a single-region focus is inadequate. Whilst intra-regional dynamics remain important, the re-emergence of regionalism needs to be related to changes in the global system: in a state system previously dominated by the struggle between the superpowers; in an economic system in which state policies are ever more shaped by the structure and dynamics of an increasingly (if very unevenly) globalized world economy; in a world political system in which, for many commentators, the boundaries between the 'domestic' and the 'international' have become increasingly blurred and in which transnational flows of ideas and values and transnational patterns of social mobilization become more powerful and more prevalent.

Third, the old divisions between patterns of regionalist organiz-ation in the industrialized world on the one hand and in the developing world on the other have been undermined. A central characteristic of many of the most important examples of the new

---

[5] The term 'new regionalism' has been used by several writers, including Norman D. Palmer, *The New Regionalism in Asia and the Pacific* (Lexington, Mass.: Lexington Books, 1991; and Björn Hettne, 'Neo-Mercantilism: The Pursuit of Regionness', *Cooperation and Conflict*, 28, 3 (Sept. 1993).

regionalism is that they span the divide between developed and developing countries. North–South regionalism is the most important innovative feature of the inclusion of Mexico within the North American Free Trade Area. But central to debates on regionalism in Asia is the relationship between Japan on the one hand and China and the developing economies of South-East Asia on the other. And in Europe the EC is wrestling with the difficulties of finding a stable relationship between the highly developed regionalist project embodied in the Community and the developing economies and often unstable polities of central Europe and the former Soviet Union.

Fourth, the dividing line between economic and political regionalism becomes ever harder to draw. A central characteristic of the new regionalism is its multidimensional character. If it is important to compare geographically, it is still more important to examine the interrelationship between political, economic, and security issues. Even if the outward form of regionalism is economic in nature (as with the EC, NAFTA, or APEC), the factors that underpin and sustain such projects are often far from solely economic and economic regionalism may carry with it important geopolitical or security consequences. As has been noted for Asia, 'security cannot be considered separately from the regional economy'.[6] The European example or 'model' has tended to focus too much attention on the specific question of economic integration—certainly very important, but only one part of the regionalist picture. Economic regionalism can often be a mechanism by which broader security and political goals can be pursued. Moreover, even if regionalism is to be built around economic considerations, it is unlikely to prove resilient if there are serious divergences over other issues.

Finally, the proliferation of regionalist arrangements raises complex and difficult questions concerning the character and maintenance of international order. The analysis of regionalism as a principle of international order, which formed such an important element of earlier writings, has only recently begun to reappear. Yet both in the politico-security and the politico-economic spheres questions of stability and order are closely bound with the relationship between regionalist institutions and arrangements on the one hand and global or multilateral bodies on the other.

[6] Yoichi Funabashi, 'The Asianization of Asia', Foreign Affairs, 72/5 (Nov./Dec. 1993), 81.

For all the legitimate scepticism about the prospects for regionalism in many parts of the world (reflected very strongly in several of the chapters in this book), the past decade has have seen both a striking reappearance of regionalist rhetoric, as well as evidence of concrete progress in various parts of the world. The analysis of regionalism, even of cohesive and effectively institutionalized regionalism, can no longer be confined to Europe. None of the authors in this volume suggests that there is some unstoppable momentum towards regionalism and several are deeply sceptical as to whether the revival of regionalist rhetoric is likely to be translated into effective and durable institutions. But all are agreed that regionalism is a political phenomenon that needs to be subjected to comprehensive and critical scrutiny and that there have been concrete developments that need to be explained.

This book concentrates on the politics and political economy of contemporary regionalism. As such it is intended to complement both the more narrowly economic literature and the growing number of detailed studies of specific examples of regionalism in different parts of the world. Taking a broad perspective will inevitably involve omissions and problems of selection. Partly for this reason, the book opens with two survey chapters. The first by Louise Fawcett places the new regionalism in historical perspective, provides an overview of the major forms of regionalism in the contemporary international system, and reviews the most important literature on the subject. The second chapter by Andrew Hurrell relates the revival of regionalism to contemporary debates in International Relations theory. It considers the perennial problem of defining regionalism and draws together some of the principal theories that may be deployed to explain the emergence of the new regionalism.

The following three chapters consider the links betweens regionalism and three broad issues in contemporary international relations. Andrew Wyatt-Walter considers the ways in which new regionalist trends are related to developments in the global political economy. He asks three questions: What do we mean by 'economic regionalism' and 'economic regionalization'? What explains the new economic regionalism? And is the world economy becoming more regionalized? Alan Henrikson sets the revival of regionalist groupings against the parallel revival of the most important global political organization, the United Nations. He analyses both the scope for a productive partnership between them and the tensions that may emerge. If regionalist projects are related to the powerful forces working towards globalization, they also face challenges from within. James Mayall considers the critical issue of the relationship between identity and political community and the various ways in which this may affect regionalism: on the one hand, the continued strength of national identity working to block any moves towards the dilution of national sovereignty; on the other, the fragmentation of identity and the growth of sub-national communities which may both challenge traditional regionalist structures and, paradoxically, increase the scope for effective regionalism.

The chapters in Part II examine regionalism in various parts of the world. Given the extent to which Europe and the European Community have so often been viewed as an example for regionalist projects elsewhere, this section begins with a chapter by William Wallace. This places the story of the EC within a broad historical perspective and discusses the ways in which it has become ever more problematic to view the European case as a 'model' for other parts of the world. It draws attention to the ways in which many of the same factors that have stimulated regionalism in other parts of the world have complicated the situation in Europe and undermined traditional assumptions and approaches. The two chapters that follow examine areas where region-building has been a central feature of the past few years and where forward momentum has been most apparent: Asia Pacific (Rosemary Foot) and the Americas (Andrew Hurrell). In contrast, the chapter by Charles Tripp examines the Arab Middle East which has by no means remained immune from the recent regionalist enthusiasm, but in which the obstacles and constraints are all too apparent. Finally, the Conclusion seeks to sketch out some of the ways in which contemporary regionalism is related to international order.

This book therefore examines recent developments in regional co-operation in different parts of the world and places them in their historical context. The contributors take a critical look at recent trends towards the new regionalism and regionalization, assessing their origins, their present and future prospects, and their place in the evolving international order.

PART I

2

Regionalism in Historical Perspective

Louise Fawcett

THE return of regionalism to the international agenda has produced a mixed reaction. Some regard it as a positive and permanent characteristic of the post-Cold War international order. Others are more sceptical and believe, that like the regionalism which flourished in the 1960s, this newer version will have a limited application and shelf life. However, both regional optimists and pessimists must agree that whatever its content, regionalism is on the increase. There is little doubt that the mid-1980s marked something of a turning-point in the fortunes of regionalism. If the passing of the Single European Act in 1986 was decisive, no less important was the impact of global economic change and, of course, the transformation of the international system occasioned by the end of the Cold War. These and other factors, for reasons that are explored in this chapter, have led both to a proliferation of new regional groupings and to a revival of older regional bodies. And in contrast to other regionalist waves, the new regionalism spans all issue areas and has a truly global reach.

Although Western Europe and the Americas stand out as the areas where institutionalized regionalism has made the most impressive advances, a growing sense of regional awareness has been universal, although this has manifested itself in different ways. Some countries have restated a commitment to greater unity within an existing organization—such as occurred first in the European Community but then in the Association of South-East Asian Nations (ASEAN), the Organization of African Unity (OAU), the Andean Pact or the Central American Common Market (CACM). Others—notably the East Europeans and former Soviet republics— have sought accommodation within existing economic and security arrangements such as the European Community, NATO, CSCE, or the Nordic Council. A third option has been the launch (or relaunch) of schemes such as the Southern Cone Common Market

(*Mercosur*), the Arab Maghreb Union (AMU) in North Africa, the Economic Co-operation Organization (ECO) among the Islamic countries of central and south Asia, and the Visegrad Pact and *Pentagonale* in former communist Europe. Other ventures remain at the conference and discussion stage: the Asia-Pacific Economic Co-operation (APEC) forum, East Asia Economic Caucus (EAEC), and a variety of schemes for promoting co-operation in the Black Sea, Balkan, Baltic, and southern Mediterranean regions are just a few examples.

What is the origin and significance of this new activity at the regional level? Will the regionalism of the 1990s prove more durable than the regionalism of the the 1960s, or will it too run the risk of becoming 'the latest international fad'.[1] Already some of the promise of the late 1980s had evaporated. That flagship of regionalism—the European Community, now European Union—has already demonstrated the difficulties of moving too fast in the direction of political and economic union, and floundered on the rock of foreign policy co-ordination. A more recent regional grouping like *Mercosur* has also run into difficulties in achieving its goal of balanced economic co-operation. The wide array of 'micro'- and 'macro'-regional options now available also makes it difficult for many countries to devise a rational policy towards regional co-operation. This chapter will look briefly at the history of regionalism, before turning to examine the origins of the present regionalist trend. It will then consider some of the strengths and weaknesses of the new regionalism, introducing some of the themes that will taken up elsewhere in the book.

1. REGIONALISM: A BRIEF HISTORY

When should a history of regionalism begin? Given the obvious difficulty involved in defining regions and regionalism, as discussed in the following chapter, there is no simple answer to this question. For just as there are no absolute or naturally determined regions, there is no single explanation that encompasses the origins and development of the regional idea. Clearly a sense of 'regional

[1] Joseph Nye (ed.), *International Regionalism* (Boston: Little, Brown & Co., 1968), p. xii.

awareness' and a desire by states to 'make the best of their regional environment' have long predated the existence of formal regional organizations. And in many parts of the world, where institutionalized regionalism is weak, such terms remain more appropriate in describing the state of regional co-operation today. However, such criteria are elusive, so it is also useful to consider the history of regionalism in terms of the rise of modern institutions. If we adopt Joseph Nye's definition of an international region as 'a limited number of states linked together by a geographical relationship and by a degree of mutual interdependence', regionalism may then be defined as 'the formation of interstate groupings on the basis of regions'.[2]

If formal organization, at the regional as opposed to the international level, is to be the yardstick by which we measure the onset of regionalism it is difficult to place its real origins much before 1945. With the notable exception of the Inter-American System very few regional groupings existed before the Second World War. It may be objected that of the international organizations which had proliferated since the early nineteenth century many were Eurocentric and therefore effectively regional in scope. However, as William Wallace argues in his chapter, the idea of Europe as a region within a broader global system would have seemed an anathema, and what in fact existed was a Europe-centred world order.

What did emerge in this period, however, were a growing number of international public and private associations, novel for their establishment of secretariats and holding of regular meetings. The General Postal Union and the International Law Association were just two examples of such functional associations which preceded the attempt by the victor states of the First World War to fashion an international organization on more ambitious lines.[3] Yet both these early organizations and the League system itself, inspired by the idealist thinking which was dominant at the time of its creation, were intended to be universal. To make war impossible, the primary task of the League of Nations, required the commitment of the entire international community, not selective parts of it. Regionalism, and this was a point stressed by the founders of universal organizations as well as by early functionalists like David

---

[2] Ibid., p. vii.
[3] Clive Archer, *International Organizations* (Routledge, London 2nd edn., 1992), 12–15.

Mitrany, was at odds with the principles of collective security and the idea of international government.[4]

By the Second World War, then, regionalism had still not entered the vocabulary of International Relations. That it did so at such rapid speed owes much to two factors: the great international upheavals of the 1930s and 1940s and the expansion and transformation of international society. The Second World War and its consequences demolished the old European order and crudely divided the world into two competing spheres where the new superpowers vied for influence. The region as a unit of analysis became important not only in a Cold War context, but increasingly as a result of the growing assertiveness and self-consciousness of regions themselves. 'One reality of post-war world politics', writes Stanley Hoffmann, was 'the division of a huge and heterogeneous international system into subsystems in which patterns of co-operation and ways of controlling conflicts are either more intense or less elusive than those in the global system.'[5]

All this was reflected in the creation of a new global organization designed to overcome the weaknesses of the League: the United Nations. While some of the idealism and internationalism that had surrounded the creation of the League was present at the early UN conferences, newer theories jostled for position in determining the nature of the world body. On the one hand regionalism made its appearance in the preliminary version of the UN Charter worked out at Dumbarton Oaks in 1944 which stipulated that 'the existence of regional bodies for dealing with peace and security matters should not be precluded'. And subsequent demands by states 'that had already made heavy political invesments in such arrangements as the Inter-American system, the Commonwealth and the Arab League', meant that the finalized Charter went further in stressing the role of regional bodies as 'agencies of the first resort in dealing with disputes among their own members'.[6] On the other hand, realism had now displaced idealism as the dominant philosophy of international relations. The realists, whose 'power-politics model'

---

[4] David Mitrany, A Working Peace System (Oxford: OUP for RIIA, 1944).

[5] Stanley Hoffmann, 'International Organization and the International System', in Janus and Minerva: Essays in the Theory and Practice of International Politics (Westview Press: Boulder, Colo., 1987), 293.

[6] Inis Claude, 'The OAS, the UN and the United States', in Nye (ed.), International Regionalism, 5–6. This question is dicussed in further detail in Chapter 5.

was designed to supplant the 'utopian model' of the interwar period, tended to view international organizations as no more than interstate institutions. For the realists, then, whether such institutions were global or regional was largely irrelevant. International relations was about the struggle for power in a world where 'international agencies can perform only modest services'.[7]

The experience of international co-operation in the early Cold War seemed to vindicate the realists' position. The UN was paralysed, its collective security system largely impotent. Regional agencies were subordinated to the broader purposes of the East–West conflict, indeed many were specifically designed to serve the interests of one of the two superpowers. Into the latter category fell the selective security pacts that mushroomed in the early Cold War years: NATO, the Warsaw Pact, the Rio Pact, SEATO, CENTO, and ANZUS. The Organization of American States (OAS), for its part, often became a vehicle for the promotion of US interests in the Cold War, albeit against the will of some of its members. The early European institutions too were part of a policy of securing Western Europe in an anti-Soviet alliance. Organizations like the Arab League and Organization of African Unity (founded in 1963) were to face somewhat different problems. In particular, the 'pan' movements whose interests such organizations claimed to uphold did not provide the desired basis of unity among their diverse memberships.

As the above picture suggests, the limitations of the early postwar regional organizations made obvious the attractions of the realist vision of international anarchy. Yet it soon became clear that with its excessive emphasis on power and interstate relations, realism had failed to explain other important factors at work in the international system. In particular the success of the early attempts at integration in Western Europe posed the 'new challenge of regionalism', spawning a new school of functionalist writers.[8] Neofunctionalism, which incorporated into its integrationalist logic the concept of political, as well as functional 'spillover', was attractive because of its strong predictive element and because 'it appeared to explain exactly what was happening in Western Europe'.[9] The neo-

[7] Stanley Hoffman, 'Hans Morgenthau: Limits and Influence of "Realism" ', in *Janus and Minerva*, 75.

[8] E. Haas, 'The Challenge of Regionalism', *International Organization*, 12/4 (Fall 1958), 441.

[9] Stephen George, *Politics and Policy in the European Community* (Oxford: OUP, 1991), 19.

functionalists furthermore had few qualms about the regional, indeed almost exclusively European basis, of their analysis. For them Europe was merely a starting-point for a further set of comparable experiments in integration. And on the heels of the European experience there duly came attempts to create common markets and free-trade associations in the Middle East, Africa, the Pacific, and the Americas: 'The world was indeed filled in the 1960s with proposals for NAFTA, PAFTA, LAFTA, and ever more.'[10] With the proliferation of regional institutions, the literature on regionalism flourished, as social scientists tried to describe, explain, and predict the consequences of this new regionalist trend.[11]

Yet as we know, the regionalist challenge of the 1960s fell far short of expectations. By the end of the decade, as other contributors to this volume have noted, there were few places outside Europe where the regionalist experiment had produced tangible results. And developments in Europe itself had led the neo-functionalists virtually to abandon their theory. As Haas wrote in 1975 regional integration theory was 'obsolete in Western Europe and obsolescent—though still useful—in the rest of the world'.[12] Liberals moved away from the problems of regionalism and focused instead on the broader challenges posed by transnationalism and interdependence and on the ways in which these phenomena challenged the state-centric paradigm thereby, undermining the foundations of realism. Much of this work concentrated on the analysis of interdependence within particular issue areas and on the role of international regimes.[13]

The 1960s and 1970s were marked by another regionalist challenge, this time from the Third World, and manifest in groupings such as the Non-Aligned Movement (NAM) or the Group of 77 (G-77). Dislike of the East–West conflict and of the state of North–

---

[10] Jagdish Bhagwati, The World Trading System at Risk (Princeton: Princeton UP, 1991), 71.

[11] Two important contemporary works are Nye (ed.), International Regionalism, and Louis J. Cantori and Stephen L. Speigel, The International Relations of Regions: a Comparative Approach (Englewood Cliffs, NJ: Prentice-Hall, 1970).

[12] E. B. Haas, The Obsolesence of Regional Intergration Theory (Berkeley, Calif.: Institute of International Studies, 1975), 1.

[13] Joseph Nye and Robert Keohane (eds.), Transnational Relations and World Politics (Cambridge, Mass.: Harvard UP, 1972); Power and Interdependence: World Politics in Transition (Boston: Little, Brown & Co., 1977). On their later refinements to this work see also Keohane and Nye, 'Power and Interdependence Revisited', International Organization 41/4 (Autumn 1987), 724–53.

South relations in general prompted the rise of this broad
'Southern' coalition in world politics, which in turn, generated a
school of writers advocating major structural reforms in the international system.[14] These Third World 'structuralists', many of the
dependency school, were interested in regionalism as a tool in the
struggle to end the exploitative and dependent relationship between
the developing countries (the South) and the industrialized countries (the North).

Although their writings[15] are divided between those who adopted
a rejectionist approach towards existing international organizations, and those who argued that such institutions can provide the
basis for a change in the condition of the South, structuralists
agreed on the utility of Third World regionalism in some form. Yet
their various attempts to promote such regionalism, whether in UN
forums through bodies like the United Nations Conference on
Trade and Development (UNCTAD) or the G-77, or through
groupings like the NAM, the OAU, or the Organization of
Petroleum Exporting Countries (OPEC), or indeed through the
fashioning of new indigenous organizations, were ultimately disappointing. The solidarity demanded of developing countries by
structuralist theorists has simply not materialized. Even the impact
of the achievements of OPEC in the early 1970s or the demands for
a New International Economic Order (NIEO) articulated later in
the decade failed to produce the desired effect in terms of uniting
developing countries behind a common goal.

The disappointing legacy of regionalist efforts and the return to
Cold War by the end of the 1970s seemed to reaffirm the conflictual
nature of international affairs, thus signalling yet another triumph
for the power politics model, now refined by a new school of realist,
or neo-realist, theorists. Although the neo-realists took note of
some of the changed features of the international system, acknowledging, in particular, a growing degree of economic interdependence, they saw no need to radically refine their views: about the
constraints of the international anarchy, the prevalence of conflict,
the relative unimportance of non-state actors, and the limits to
international co-operation.[16] And in many respects the evidence, at

[14] Peter Willits, *The Non-Aligned Movement* (London: Pinter, 1978), p. xiii.
[15] These are surveyed by Clive Archer in *International Organization*, 118–24.
[16] Kenneth Waltz, 'Political Structures', in R. Keohane, *Neorealism and its Critics*
(New York: Columbia UP, 1986), 89.

least until the mid-1980s, appeared to support their position. Both European, and particularly Third World regionalism had run off course, the UN had entered 'a period of acute crisis'[17], and older regional organizations, like the OAS, the OAU, or the Arab League, had all experienced serious difficulties in achieving a consensus among their members across a wide range of issues.

However, a newer set of regional arrangements was emerging which attempted to overcome the problems associated with the earlier indigenous bodies or the great-power-sponsored regional alliances and which were somewhat more successful. Informed by a consciousness of the geopolitical environment in which they were operating, such 'subregional security organizations' were free from any integrationist pretensions, and tended to be limited in terms of their goals and memberships. As such they were not inconsistent with much neo-realist thinking. An early example was ASEAN (1967); CARICOM and ECOWAS were formed in 1973 and 1975 respectively, but many emerged in the 1980s: the South African Development Co-ordination Conference (SADCC, 1980), the Gulf Co-operation Council (GCC, 1981) and the South Asian Association for Regional Co-operation (SAARC, 1985).[18] In the insecure environment of the 'Second Cold War' such organizations did represent a serious attempt to create a security consensus in a given area without the direct backing of a major external power.

Throughout the Cold War period, then, regionalism had remained on the international agenda, but its scope was limited, partly as a consequence of the continuing bipolar nature of the international system to which all regional arrangements were subordinate, but also because of the extreme tenacity with which states clung to their sovereignty, not only in most matters of high politics but in many matters of low politics as well.

It was the developments in the European Community in the mid-1980s, set against a broader pattern of global economic change, and followed by the radical transformation of Eastern Europe and the USSR at the end of the decade which led to revived interest in new, and more ambitious, forms of regionalism. It is to the new

---

[17] Maurice Bertrand, 'The Historical Development of Efforts to Reform the United Nations' in Adam Roberts and Benedict Kingsbury (eds.), *United Nations, Divided World* (Oxford: Clarendon Press, 1993), 426.

[18] William Tow, *Subregional Security Cooperation in the Third World* (Boulder, Colo.: Lynne Rienner, 1990).

regionalism and its origins that I now turn. What is it that distinguishes the new regionalism from the old, and what are its real chances of survival, not only in the Western world where it has already been tried and tested, and survived, but in the non-Western world where it has not?

2. ORIGINS OF THE NEW REGIONALISM

As the short history of regionalism offered above suggests, the 'new regionalism', if it is to survive, needs to rest on some more solid and enduring foundation than the old. The legacy of the past is of course important. If the picture painted in the first part of this chapter was demonstrably bleak, much of what is described as the new regionalism would be incomprehensible without reference to the experience of the past. Yet for regionalism to succeed, new conditions are clearly required. And writers on the new regionalist phenomena have indeed noted that both the international and domestic context of the 1990s is much more favourable than that of the 1960s.[19] The chapters of this book, in different ways, take a critical look at this assumption. What follows here is an attempt to identify some of the common factors behind the new regionalist wave.

(a) The end of the Cold War

The new regionalism had already taken root before the end of the Cold War thrust the region to the centre stage of international politics, in a way made possible only by the collapse of the old bipolar system. Significant, if less spectacular progress in the direction of increased regional co-operation had already been made in a number of areas from Western Europe to the Americas, South-East Asia, and the Middle East. Developments in the European Community and political and economic changes at the global level helped to account for these early changes, to be discussed further below. Yet in many ways it makes sense to start with the most dramatic and the most publicized reason for what has seemed to many to be a definitive return to regionalism: the end of the Cold War.

---

[19] Peter Robson, 'The New Regionalism and the Developing Countries', *Journal of Common Market Studies*, 31/3 (Sept. 1993), 335.

1. New attitudes towards international co-operation. The
collapse of the old bipolar system and easing of the antagonism
which characterized it provide one of the most obvious
explanations for the new interest in regional, and indeed in all
forms of international co-operation. Having emerged 'a little
battered but intact after their headlong trip down the primitive
Cold War roadways',[20] the UN and most other international
organizations initially benefited in some way from the improved
atmosphere brought about by a relaxation of East–West tensions.
Just as important as the end of the Cold War itself has been the
transformation in Soviet/Russian attitudes towards international
co-operation. Former Soviet President Gorbachev's much cited
September 1987 press article in which he spoke of the need to build
a 'comprehensive system of international peace and security'[21] was
but one example of a newfound preference to work through
international organizations and multilateral forums.

In this new international climate the United Nations itself was,
not surprisingly, the first international organization to profit directly from the winding down of the Cold War. It may still preside
over a 'divided world', but the fault lines have changed dramatically since the mid-1980s, while the increasing scope of the organization's activities represents a real sign of progress. Since that
'dazzling outburst of common sense among governments' which
Brian Urquhart dates from early 1987 when the UN Security Council decided, finally, to seek a ceasefire in the Iran–Iraq war, there
have been many cases of constructive Security Council involvement
in the trouble spots of the world: Afghanistan, Namibia, Cambodia,
and the Gulf, to name but a few examples.[22] While the notion of a
United Nations revival may be 'open to challenge' on a number of
counts[23], it cannot be denied that the organization enjoys a higher
profile than it did during the Cold War, and correspondingly its
members have increased expectations as to its capabilities.

[20] Frederick Lister, 'The Role of International Organizations in the 1990s and
Beyond', *International Relations*, 10/2 (Nov. 1990), 115.
[21] Cited in Brian Urquhart, *Decolonization and World Peace* (Austin, Tex.:
University of Texas Press, 1989), 85–6.
[22] B. Urquhart, 'The United Nations System and the Future', *International Affairs*, 65/2 (Apr. 1989), 226.
[23] Adam Roberts and Benedict Kingsbury, 'Introduction: The UN's Roles in
International Society since 1945', in Roberts and Kingsbury (eds.), *United Nations,
Divided World*, 4–5.

There is little doubt that the increase in both the number and activity of regional organizations is related to this 'more robust globalism'.[24] There has been a widespread upgrading of international co-operation and the organizations it has spawned. The latter have gained greater respectability, and are seen less as time-wasting debating chambers, and increasingly as useful forums where members can engage in a wide range of activities. It may seem paradoxical to some that part of the recent success of the regional idea can be explained in terms of the achievements of the UN. Yet there are few people today who would argue seriously that the potential of the UN is jeopardized by the growth of regionalism, or that regionalism is merely a 'halfway house between the nation-state and a world not ready to become one'.[25] The old controversy over the relative merits of regionalism and globalism has become increasingly obsolete. Indeed, as Alan Henrikson illustrates in his chapter in this volume, recent history is rich in examples of global–regional co-operation, and he sketches out a comprehensive rationale for a new global–regional partnership in peacemaking.

Regional organizations today then tend to be regarded as a natural outgrowth of international co-operation, compatible with the UN and indeed an 'indispensable element in its successful growth and functioning'.[26] Given the greatly increased burden placed upon the UN since the end of the Cold War, it makes good sense to advocate a greater role for regional bodies. And in some areas at least, the UN appears willing to concur with the old regionalist argument that 'smaller' may, in certain cases, be 'better' when it comes to regional problem-solving.[27] Certainly the idea—endorsed by UN Secretary General, Boutros-Ghali, in his 1992 report *An Agenda for Peace*—if not always the practice of greater burden-sharing has gained ground, most notably in Europe, but also in Africa, the Americas, and South-East Asia.[28] If the new international climate has greatly improved the prospects for inter-

---

[24] Kevin Clements (ed.), *Peace and Security in the Asia-Pacific Region* (Tokyo: United Nations UP, 1993), 10.
[25] Francis O. Wilcox, 'Regionalism and the United Nations', *International Organization*, 19/3 (Summer 1965), 789.
[26] Ibid. 811.
[27] See e.g. Joseph Nye, *Peace in Parts: Integration and Conflict in Regional Organization* (Boston: Little, Brown & Co., 1971).
[28] Adam Roberts, 'The United Nations and International Security', *Survival*, 35/2 (Summer 1993), 7–8.

national co-operation at all levels, the transformation of US–Soviet relations and the demise of the USSR itself have also directly affected the fortunes of regionalism in a number of other ways.

2. *Decentralization of the international system.* In a general sense the decentralization of the international system that has followed the end of the Cold War has strengthened the argument for regionalism. As Barry Buzan has noted the removal of old 'overlay' patterns of great power influence has encouraged multipolarity and contributed to an international system in which 'regional arrangements can be expected to assume greater importance'.[29]

Among the industrialized countries of the Western world where regionalism already enjoys a high profile, existing institutions have not only proved their ability to adapt and survive in the post-Cold War era, they have also demonstrated a potential for resurgence and reform.[30] Both the EU and NATO, for example, envisage expansion of their memberships as well as their spheres of activity as a result of international changes. The Western European Union (WEU) and the Conference on Security and Co-operation in Europe (CSCE, now CSCE), the latter bringing in a wider non-European membership, have also sought to consolidate their respective roles in supplying Europe with a more effective security framework.

Perhaps more significantly, both the former superpowers have also manifested a new interest in regionalism. US President Clinton's commitment to what he has called 'open regionalism' in the Americas and the Asia Pacific (discussed in the chapters by Andrew Hurrell and Rosemary Foot respectively) is indicative of this. On the Soviet side, Gorbachev repeatedly expressed his desire to end Russia's isolation from Europe through his vision of a 'common European home'.[31] And if the former Soviet premier's pan-European dream remains unrealized, subsequent Russian leaders have advocated the CSCE as the supreme regional grouping in

[29] Barry Buzan, *People, States and Fear* (London: Harvester Wheatsheaf, 1991), 208.
[30] On this issue, see Robert O. Keohane and Stanley Hoffman, 'Conclusion: Structure, Strategy and Institutional Roles', in Robert O. Keohane, Joseph S. Nye, and Stanley Hoffmann (eds.), *After the Cold War: International Institutions and State Strategies in Europe, 1989–1991* (Cambridge, Mass.: Harvard UP, 1993).
[31] M. S. Gorbachev, *Perestroika: New Thinking for Our Country and the World* (London: Collins, 1987), 194–5; Karen Dawisha, *Eastern Europe, Gorbachev and Reform* (Cambridge: CUP 2nd edn., 1990), 10–23.

Europe, while governments in Eastern Europe and former Soviet republics alike remain anxious to participate in structures of Western co-operation. No longer condemned as a 'bourgeois' concept, interdependence has thus become highly desirable for the former socialist states.[32] For some, association agreements with the European Union and NATO's North Atlantic Co-operation Council (NACC) and the 'Partnership for Peace' (PfP) proposals are seen as stepping-stones to full membership of these organizations.

Regionalism is no less a priority for countries outside the old East–West alliance systems. For the developing states in particular, decentralization has meant adjustment to the idea that regional affairs will no longer be conditioned by the exigencies of superpower politics. For many the end of the Cold War has brought about greater independence: as the old balance between the superpowers no longer dominates questions of regional security, local powers enjoy greater liberty than was previously possible in conducting their foreign policies and in determining their international alignments. In practical terms this may mean that foreign security concerns will be handled increasingly at the regional rather than at the global level.[33]

A desire for greater independence among developing countries predates, to some extent, the formal ending of the Cold War, and is related to a change in thinking among developing country élites about the desirability of home or region-grown structures as opposed to externally backed ones. The subregional security organizations which flourished in the 1970s an 1980s were early evidence of this trend. Characteristic of the post-Cold War period have been attempts both to strengthen such local alliances and if appropriate put them to use, but also to create new collective security mechanisms. The ECOWAS action in Liberia is one example of this trend, ASEAN's involvement in the Cambodian peace process is another, as have been the attempts to fashion CSCE-style arrangements in both the Mediterranean and Middle East regions.

If the end of the Cold War has helped promote a greater sense of independence for many parts of the world it has also led to a greater

---

[32] Colin W. Lawson, 'The Soviet Union in North-South Negotiations; Revealing Preferences', in Robert Cassen (ed.), *Soviet Interests in the Third World* (London: Sage, 1985), 177.

[33] See e.g. Doug Bandow, 'Avoiding War', *Foreign Policy*, 89 (Winter 1992–3), 173.

sense of vulnerability: the fashioning of new or more effective regional organizations has been seen as one way of combating the dangerous isolation in which many countries have found themselves. For former Soviet and Eastern bloc countries, regionalism has become the route for overcoming the economic and security vacuum left in the region with the winding up of COMECON and the Warsaw Pact. For many developing countries regionalism has, quite simply, been seen as a way of overcoming marginalization.

This sense of marginalization has been widespread. Developing countries have lost their value as bargaining chips in a world where the USA and Soviet Union had once courted them for their favours. Neither aid, nor trade, nor security are assured in the post-Cold War order. The developing countries must compete with the newly emerging states of Eastern Europe and the former USSR for loans, markets, and even humanitarian assistance. They must demonstrate a capacity to liberalize their economies and political systems or perhaps face what they fear may be permanent relegation to the 'periphery of world politics'.[34] Promoting regional co-operation would appear then to be a rational policy choice for developing countries, both in terms of strengthening links with the advanced industrialized countries but also demonstrating greater independence and self-sufficiency. In Latin America, the fear, perhaps exaggerated, of 'Africanization' has prompted a new search for regional initiatives.[35] Caribbean and African states also share the view that 'bold local solutions' such as 'regional co-operation in a form never before attempted' may provide at least a partial solution to their predicament.[36] Prior to South Africa's entry into the Organization of African Unity and readmission to the Commonwealth (in June 1994), President Nelson Mandela called for a revival of regional and subregional organizations, promising that 'a democratic South Africa [would] bring to an end an important chapter in Africa's

[34] John Chipman, 'Third World Politics and Security in the 1990s', *Washington Quarterly* (winter 1991), 151. The concept of peripherality is developed by Christopher Clapham in *Third World Politics: An Introduction* (London: Routledge, 1985), 3–5.

[35] Jorge G. Castañeda, 'Latin America and the End of the Cold War', *World Policy Journal*, 7/3 (Summer 1990), 491; for a more recent view on the prospects of Latin American integration, see Alberto van Klaveren, 'Latin America and the International Political System of the 1990s', in Jonathan Hartlyn, Lars Schoultz, and Augusto Varas (eds.), *United States and Latin America in the 1990s* (Chapel Hill, NC: University of North Carolina Press, 1992), 39–41.

[36] Franklin W. Knight, *The Caribbean* (Oxford: OUP, 1990), 330.

efforts to achieve unity and closer co-operation.'[37] Even in Asia Pacific, where the concept of marginalization is less appropriate, changes in the international system have raised the profile of regionalism as evident in the Malaysian-led initiative to create an exclusively East Asian economic grouping in the form of the EAEC, and in ASEAN's efforts to upgrade its efforts at regional co-operation.

(b) Economic changes

If the end of the Cold War and its consequences have contributed to a raised level of regional awareness, this has been accentuated by a process of global economic change that long predated the turbulent period of the late 1980s. For many countries economic marginalization represents a greater threat than does the sense of security marginalization that has accompanied the end of the bipolar system. Thinking regionally at the economic level is thus no less important than thinking regionally at the strategic level. Indeed the two processes often complement and reinforce each other. A number of reasons, many of which are discussed in greater detail elsewhere in this book, account for this change. Here I will merely touch on a few of the most important ones.

1. *The example of the European Community.* Recalling the earlier history of regionalism, it is perhaps not surprising to discover that the origins of the most recent regionalist wave date from the mid-1980s when the European Community unveiled its plans to initiate a single market by the end of 1992. This decision, itself the result of a determination to reinvigorate the European idea in an increasingly competitive global economy, had a dramatic impact. Indeed, there are few regions of the world where the apparently spectacular progress of the European Community towards economic and political union has failed to evince a response. While serving as an example, developments in the Community have also sounded a note of warning in countries beyond the Twelve. Fears, perhaps once overstated, of a 'fortress Europe', encouraged other areas of the world also to rethink their policies towards economic regionalism. Perhaps most strikingly, developments in Europe—in combination with a range of other

[37] Nelson Mandela, 'South Africa's Future Foreign Policy', *Foreign Affairs*, 72/5 (Nov./Dec. 1993), 90–1.

factors—have contributed to a US (and Canadian) shift from multilateralism to a support of regional arrangements. This has been evidenced not only in its promotion and ultimate ratification of the North American Free Trade Area, but in its support for an Asia Pacific trading bloc also.

For much of the world for whom the option of joining a trading bloc is neither attractive nor immediately available, and for whom the long-drawn-out Uruguay Round of GATT negotiations gave rise to serious concern, the EC, NAFTA, and APEC processes have been closely observed. And just as the first successful wave of European integration inspired the creation of common markets and free-trade areas throughout the world, so has this second wave of European-led integration produced the further launching of ambitious schemes borrowing heavily from the Europe 1992 idea.

The impact of the European project can be clearly seen in groupings like the Arab Maghreb Union, the Andean Pact, *Mercosur*, and ASEAN. All have committed themselves, at least on paper, to the creation of common markets within a certain time frame. Even that most fragile of regional groupings—the Commonwealth of Independent States—has agreed in principle to the creation of an economic union. It is not difficult to see how, for the Arab Maghreb Union countries for example, which have traditionally conducted some 75 per cent of the trade with the European Community, the creation of a regional trading bloc was seen as a means of providing an economic lifeline. Other such groupings have reached similar conclusions. In Latin America, the example of the European Community and fear of exclusion from the NAFTA bloc have inspired the Andean Pact, the Group of Three (G-3), and *Mercosur* to sign free-trade agreements scheduled to become effective around 1995. Similarly concern among Caribbean states has led to a CARICOM initiative to unite with the G-3 to devise an action plan on economic co-operation.[38] Formerly a neglected part of the ASEAN agenda, economic integration has come to occupy a more prominent place. It has also been elevated on the agendas of once security-orientated groupings like the Gulf Co-operation Council.

Even in parts of the world where economic regionalism has long been discredited, local leaders have called again for the creation of effective groupings. Denouncing the 'ridiculously large number of

[38] Graham Norton, 'Concern in the Caribbean', *World Today* (March 1994), 56–60.

often economically unviable states in Africa', former Nigerian head of state Olusegun Obasanjo urged African countries to look to European-type integration and pool capacities.[39] If action may be slow to follow rhetoric, the influence of the European Community could not be clearer, and its example is no less powerful than in the 1960s. While it may be true that many of the organizations mentioned above have merely restated older commitments to greater economic integration, there is evidence that the prospects for economic regionalism are in fact better than during the last regionalist wave. The reasons for this lie in the political and economic changes that have taken place in many countries as well the gradual transformation that has taken place at the level of the global economy since the 1970s.

2. *Global trends.* The developments in the European Community referred to above took place against a background of economic and political changes which together have arguably created a more favourable climate for regionalism. In his chapter, Andrew Wyatt-Walter outlines some of the common factors that might explain the trend towards economic regionalism: the effects of the end of the Cold War on the global political economy, the shifting balance of world economic power, and the shift towards outward-orientated policies in many parts of the developing world.

The effects of these changes have included the shift away from multilateralism on the part of North America, the rise of new trading blocs, and a new interest in regionalism in general. For some countries an interest in economic regionalism reflects the same fear of isolation brought on by a post-Cold War world of exclusive trading blocs. And if this were the only reason for the new economic regionalism, it might well be condemned to a similar fate as its predecessor. Yet the process of economic (and political) liberalization that has taken place since the 1980s, at a more gradual pace in the developing states and more dramatically in the former Soviet bloc countries, has made economic regionalism a more serious long-term possibility than before. Trade liberalization accompanied by the intense competition to gain access to Western markets has made more urgent the search for regional partners— the 'Euro-banana' crisis, in which Latin American producers have

---

[39] Quoted in O. Aluko, 'The Foreign Policies of the African States in the 1990s', *The Round Table*, 317 (1991), 37.

struggled to enter the Caribbean-dominated European market is one case in point. The broader consequences of 'globalization', and the long period of uncertainty over the final outcome of the Uruguay Round of GATT talks helped to accelerate this move towards regionalism.

In Africa, Latin America, and elsewhere there is an unmistakable trend towards regionalization if not always to institutionalized regionalism. Indeed, as various commentators have observed, the regionalization of the world economy has been fuelled in part by the opposition of states to what are perceived to be the damaging consequences of globalization, as well as the concentration of economic activity around four poles: the European Union, North America, Asia, and the Pacific Rim.[40]

(c) The end of Third Worldism?

If regionalism benefited from the collapse of old economic orthodoxies in the 1980s, it has also been assisted, in developing countries at least, by the decline of the myth of 'collective solidarity' in the Third World. This, like the demise of collective solidarity in the Second World has opened greater space for the promotion of new co-operative ventures at the regional or subregional level. It is difficult to argue with Robert Gilpin's statement that the Third World 'no longer exists as a meaningful entity'.[41] As already noted, the show of strength by the developing countries as manifested in forums such as the G-77, the NAM, or the OPEC proved to be short-lived. Any collective bargaining power that the South may once have possessed has been drastically reduced since the 1970s which saw the climax of Third World efforts at international economic reform with the launch of demands for a New International Economic Order.[42]

In retrospect, examples of successful South–South co-operation seem few and far between, while perhaps more significantly, the Third World has lost much of the homogeneity it once appeared to possess. Given its wide and growing diversity in terms of wealth

[40] See e.g. David Held and Anthony McGrew, 'Globalization and the Liberal Democratic State', in *Government and Opposition*, 28/2 (Spring 1993), 270.
[41] Robert Gilpin, *The Political Economy of International Relations* (Princeton: Princeton UP, 1987), 304.
[42] James Mayall, *Nationalism and International Society* (Cambridge: Cambridge UP, 1990), 124, 141.

and power—arguably it is of little use as an analytical category, except in a negative, residual sense[43]—it is hardly surprising that truly collective action of any kind has been difficult to achieve except in certain limited areas. Indeed the very survival of any cohesive Third World coalition, the continued existence of institutions such as the NAM notwithstanding, is in doubt.[44] Various alternative regionalist scenarios have been suggested as means of improving the position of the developing countries in the international political arena. One rather original proposal was contained in Rajni Kothari's book *Footsteps into the Future*, published in the early 1970s, which advocated the organization of developing countries, not into a single southern coalition, but into a variety of different regional coalitions.[45] In general, given the wide disparity among developing states in terms of wealth and power, the trend in the 1990s would appear to be moving away from broad coalitions and towards more viable subregional groupings of like-minded members. This might explain the relative success of subregionalism in Latin America, with its plethora of mini-groupings.

(d) Democratization

The obsolescence of much structuralist thinking about Third World reform reflects the processes of economic and political change, whose, impact has been felt far beyond the developing world. The political liberalization or 'democratization' that has swept through many countries has also helped to produce an environment which is more hospitable to interdependence at the regional and global level. Eastern Europe is an obvious case in point. Now among the most ardent advocates of regionalism, the earlier weak commitment of member countries to institutions like the Warsaw Pact or COMECON demonstrates how the absence of democracy or any real equality among members makes genuine and deep-rooted regional co-operation difficult to achieve.[46]

[43] For a useful discussion of the problems of categorization of the Third World, see Clapham, *Third World Politics*, 1–4.
[44] For a contrary view, see e.g. Marc Williams, 'Re-articulating the Third World Coalition: The Role of the Environmental Agenda', *Third World Quarterly*, 14/1 (1993), 7–29.
[45] Rajni Kothari, *Footsteps into the Future* (New Delhi: Longman, 1974).
[46] On the limitations of integration in the socialist system, see Margot Light, *The Soviet Theory of International Relations* (Brighton: Wheatsheaf, 1988), 188–9.

From the point of view of the European Community it might be argued that democratization in Eastern Europe has, in the short term, greatly complicated the process of integration by increasing the potential number of aspiring members and by contributing to the ethno-nationalistic uprisings in the continent. It might be recalled, however, that the European Community has, in the past, played an important role in helping to consolidate democracy in southern Europe: 'In Greece, Spain, and Portugal, the establishment of democracy was seen as necessary to secure the economic benefits of EC membership, while Community membership was in turn seen as a guarantee of the stability of democracy.'[47] Viewed thus regionalism and democracy become mutually reinforcing processes: the EU could play a central and vital role in stabilizing democracy in Eastern Europe, and indeed in other countries seeking membership, like Turkey.

Will democratization promote regionalism (or will regional institutions promote democracy) in other parts of the world where comparable structures to the EU, to lead and inspire regionalism, do not exist? Of course democracy is not a necessary condition for regionalism. Regional co-operation is not limited to countries where democracy has taken root: it has long taken place among countries where democratic institutions are weak or non-existent. The fragility of Mexican democracy did not prevent that country's accession to the NAFTA treaty. And voices in some countries—one thinks in particular of parts of South-East Asia or the Middle East—would argue that while regionalism is desirable, Western-style democracy is not its necessary accompaniment, nor indeed appropriate in their own regional context.[48] Yet it remains difficult to refute the argument that regionalism has so far enjoyed the greatest success among liberal, like-minded states.[49] Certainly, as Charles Tripp points out in his chapter in reference to the weakness of regional bodies in the Middle East, leaders who are unwilling to

[47] Samuel P. Huntinton, 'Democracy's Third Wave', in Larry Diamond and Marc F. Plattner (eds.), *The Global Resurgence of Democracy* (Baltimore: Johns Hopkins UP, 1993), 5.
[48] See e.g. the regionalist arguments advanced by Iran, set out in John Calabrese, *Revolutionary Horizons. Regional Foreign Policy in Post-Khomeini Iran* (London: Macmillan, 1994). On the emerging 'Asian world view', see e.g. Yoichi Funabashi, 'The Asianization of Asia', *Foreign Affairs*, 72/5 (Nov./Dec. 1993), 75–85.
[49] Stanley Hoffman, *Janus and Minerva: Essays in the Theory and Practice of International Politics* (Boulder, Colo.: Westview Press, 1987), 380.

make compromises with domestic constituencies appear similarly unwilling to make compromises with neighbouring states.

Yet in the Middle East, from the Gulf states to North Africa, there have been widespread 'rumblings of political liberalism and even democratization'.[50] In Africa too, most countries have been affected by 'the wind from the East that is shaking the coconut trees', and have gone some way towards adopting the trappings of multiparty politics and the holding of competitive elections.[51] In both cases though it is clearly too early to assess what impact such developments will have on different efforts at regional co-operation. Certainly, the history of these regions suggests that the lack of political stability and/or representative institutions does not provide the foundations on which regionalism can thrive.

If the evidence from the Middle East and Africa remains patchy and incomplete the picture may look somewhat different elsewhere. In the Americas, for example, there is evidence that political change has a positive effect on efforts to promote regional co-operation. In South America the recent trend towards greater integration has been influenced not only by external factors already mentioned but also by internal political liberalization. It was no coincidence that the *Mercosur* agreement was negotiated in the wake of the return of civilian governments to power in both Argentina (1983) and Brazil (1985). By the same token, Chile, under President Frei (1964–70), was an ardent advocate of regional co-operation, a position that was reversed by the Pinochet regime.[52] And under the post-Pinochet administrations of Presidents Aylwin and Frei, Chile has moved closer to the APEC process, a logical step given its trade interests in the Pacific, and become an associate member of *Mercosur* reflecting also its burgeoning trade relationships with a number of states within its own region.

Finally, there is a sense in which regionalism (like political and economic liberalization) has become fashionable, even desirable. Leaders both from the newly emerging states of Eastern Europe and

[50] M. C. Hudson, 'After the Gulf War: Prospects for Democratization in the Arab World', *Middle East Journal*, 45/3 (Summer 1991), 408. On this theme see also Tim Niblock and Emma Murphy (eds.), *Economic and Political Liberalization in the Middle East* (London: British Academic Press, 1993).

[51] Samuel Decalo, 'The Process, Prospects and Constraints of Democratization in Africa', *African Affairs*, 91/362 (Jan. 1992), 7.

[52] Joseph Grunwald *et al.*, *Latin American Economic Integration and US Policy* (Washington, DC: Brookings Institution, 1972), 8–9.

the former USSR as well as from many developing countries have been quick to perceive that a commitment to regionalism is likely to receive the approval of the international community, notably the advanced industrialized countries, and is therefore a policy worth pursuing. A good example of this was the effort by certain Middle Eastern states (the six Gulf Co-operation countries plus Egypt and Syria), through the Damascus Declaration of 1991, to fashion a more effective regional security arrangement in the wake of the Gulf War: a move to which the outside world probably attached more importance than the regional powers themselves. Similarly, waiting in the queue to join NATO or the EU, East European powers have sought to demonstrate their regionalist credentials through their commitment to revived regional groupings such as the Visegrad Pact or the *Pentagonale*. This may be to take a rather cynical view of the new regionalism but it would be wrong to discount the power of example and the example and influence of the powerful as additional factors in motivating the desire for co-operation.

3. SOME COMMON OBJECTIONS

The above outline of the main motivating factors behind the new regionalism has been deliberately optimistic as to its future prospects. It has been argued that at the regional and global level there seem to be more forces operating to make regionalism work than ever before. Yet a note of caution is also needed. Regionalism, in any or all of its present forms, can offer no miracle cure for the evils of the world, and very many objections can, and have been raised as to its real value. Indeed, many of the chapters in this book will take issue with the assumptions made here. In the last part of this chapter I will briefly sketch out some of the most common objections to the new regionalism. We will return to some of these themes in the conclusion.

How, for example, will the relationship between regional organizations and the United Nations evolve? The fact that regional organizations have generally benefited so far from the enhanced reputation of the United Nations does not necessarily mean that the world body will always promote their activities. Secretary-General, Boutros-Ghali's report, *An Agenda for Peace*, while underlining the new importance of regional agencies, was perhaps intentionally ambiguous both in describing their future role and their relationship with the United Nations. The difficulties encountered by regional organizations in dealing with certain post-Cold War crises, perhaps most strikingly the European Community's failure to bring an end to the civil war in Yugoslavia, brings their efficacy into doubt. In such cases where deference to regional organizations could prove both costly, the UN might rightly question its utility.[53]

Has the end of the Cold War really brought about an end to great power rivalries, thus leaving regions relatively free to determine their own security and foreign policies? Before the disintegration of the USSR, different scholars predicted that competition in some form would continue, and that the immediate inability of the USSR to 'mold the international environment' did not preclude further conflict or even 'modest involvement' in the Third World.[54] Events since the summer of 1991 have obviously constrained any attempts by Russia or the Commonwealth of Independent States, from pursuing a too ambitious foreign policy in the short term. But the many sources of instability in the Third World, to say nothing of Eastern Europe or the former Soviet republics themselves, demonstrate a number of areas of possible conflict.[55] Great power disputes in these areas may re-emerge even if the intensity of the Cold War years may be lacking. The prevalence of conflict in the post-Cold War era, and the continuing dependence of weaker states on external security guarantees, means that the risk of outside intervention—and therefore competition—will remain, especially in geopolitically sensitive areas.[56] And paradoxically the very fashioning of regional structures to deal with such conflicts may be the cause of tension. The admittance of East European countries to NATO is an example of one way in which regionalism might provoke Russia's relationship with the West.

[53] Andrew Bennett and Joseph Lepgold, 'Reinventing Collective Security after the Cold War and the Gulf Conflict', *Political Science Quarterly*, 108/2 (1993), 232.

[54] Fred Halliday, *Cold War Third World* (London: Hutchinson Radius, 1989), 163; R. E. Kanet, 'From New Thinking to the Fragmentation of Consensus in Soviet Foreign Policy: The USSR and the Developing World', in R. E. Kanet *et al.* (eds.), *Soviet Foreign Policy in Transition* (Cambridge: Cambridge UP, 1992), 122, 137, 140.

[55] Steven R. David, 'Why the Third World still Matters' *International Security*, 17/3 (Winter 1992/3), 127–59.

[56] This argument is developed by Amitav Acharya in 'Regional Military-Security Cooperation in the Third World: A Conceptual Analysis of the Relevance and Limitations of ASEAN', *Journal of Peace Research*, 29/1 (Feb. 1992), 15–19.

Even if the risk of superpower competition in local conflicts is reduced overall, the consequently greater autonomy of regional actors may not, of course, always have benign consequences, and this raises new questions about regionalism. On the one hand the removal of great-power overlay has been shown to increase rather than decrease the likelihood of regional conflicts. As Gaddis writes, the system of 'accommodating regional crises within a structure of global stability', which depended on the existence of two functioning superpowers, has now broken down, making conflict at once more dangerous and more difficult to contain.[57] This has been borne out by the proliferation of post-Cold War crises of ethnic, religious, or nationalist origin. On the other hand it may give rise, or encouragement to aspiring new hegemons. Many regions and regional organizations are exposed to the dangers of one country seeking to play a dominant role.[58] The preponderance of US power in the Organization of American States is an obvious example, India's position in SAARC is another, but there is also Saudi Arabia in the GCC, Japan (or China) in any possible East Asia grouping, or South Africa in the SADC or the OAU.[59] Aspirations to regional leadership can, of course, have a devastating effect on regional bodies, as the damage wreaked on both the Arab League and the short-lived Arab Co-operation Council following Iraq's invasion of Kuwait clearly showed. Such aspirations may not always be malign, but while regional leadership remains the goal of rich and powerful states, regional organizations are in danger of losing the element of consensus upon which any workable grouping must be based. The prospect of pernicious regionalism, reminiscent of the 1930s may return. Certainly this fear has held up schemes for promoting regionalism in East Asia.[60]

The European Community (or indeed NAFTA) as a model for regionalism also raises some serious problems as both William Wallace and James Mayall argue in their contributions to this book. There are few, if any, comparable organizations in a position

[57] J. L. Gaddis, The United States and the End of the Cold War (Oxford: OUP, 1992), 204.
[58] On this theme see Iver Neumann (ed.), Regional Great Powers in International Politics (London: Macmillan, 1992).
[59] See Graham Evans, 'Myths and Realities in South Africa's Future Foreign Policy', International Affairs, 67/4 (1991), 716–19.
[60] Frank B. Gilnsney, 'Creating a Pacific Community', Foreign Affairs, 72/5 (Nov./Dec. 1993), 21.

to embark on a similar programme, and even the Community has faced great obstacles in its drive to achieve higher levels on integration. For example, despite some changes in recent years, the high levels of inter-regional trade which help account for the relative success of the EU, remain unmatched elsewhere.[61] This is particularly true of Africa and the Middle East, less so for Latin America and parts of East Asia. Yet, as Rosemary Foot points out in her chapter, the growing levels of inter-regional trade in East Asia may be deceptive indicators: most developed states in the area remain more concerned with global than regional connections.[62] Moreover the setting of ambitious goals and rigid timetables to achieve common markets may be quite unrealistic for many groupings. Both ASEAN and *Mercosur*, for example, have repeatedly rescheduled the proposed dates for completion of their own FTAS. Commentators on the African case have been particularly dismissive of the applicability of European-style integration to unindustrialized African states: 'Any set of prescriptions for integration which does not start from an appraisal of the political and economic structure of African states . . . is built on sand.'[63]

In the short term at least, it does not seem that many Third World countries, or indeed the newly emerging democracies of Eastern Europe, will fit easily into moulds shaped on the basis of European and North American experiences.[64] Their economies may be better suited to integrationalist schemes than they were a couple of decades ago (although the road to economic liberalization has not always been a smooth one). Their political climates too may be somewhat more favourable, though they still have a long way to go before embarking on any EC-type arrangement. Yet critically they lack one ingredient that was vital to the early and continuing success of the Community: the presence of a powerful parallel security organization. As yet no other region of the world has been able to rely on the backing of an institution of the calibre of NATO.

Region building then is a task to which many countries still need to address themselves. They could be assisted in this task by the

---

[61] Robson, 'The New Regionalism', 334.
[62] See also Barry Buzan and Gerald Segal, 'Rethinking East Asian Security', *Survival*, 36/2 (Summer 1994), 12.
[63] Christopher Clapham, 'Africa's International Relations', *African Affairs*, 86/345 (Oct. 1987), 578–9.
[64] Joel Migdal, *Strong Societies, Weak States* (Princeton, Princeton UP, 1988), 37.

United Nations or the European Community, both of whom have, to a greater or lesser degree, committed themselves to the promotion of successful regional groupings elsewhere. Yet it has to be said that the present preoccupations of both organizations make it unlikely that they will supply the assistance and expertise that is required to promote successful regional co-operation. This initiative must come from within. And in much of the Third World in particular the tasks of nation building, promoting political stability or economic development are of more immediate importance and indeed are prerequisites to greater integration. The widely held view that a key aim of regional co-operation should be not the weakening but the strengthening of national autonomy remains a serious obstacle to effective regionalism.

On a similarly pessimistic note it may be argued that the absence of collective solidarity among the developing countries may not necessarily encourage more limited co-operative ventures at the regional level. Many of the problems inherent in the collective Third World approach exist also at the regional level where the forces making for unity remain weak. As J. D. B. Miller wrote in 1966: 'Given that the Afro-Asian countries find difficulty in uniting other than in declaratory statements at the United Nations and its surrounding bodies, and that national interests continue to make themselves evident, we may ask whether a more harmonious spirit is shown at regional meetings of Third World states.'[65] In the case of the G-77, for example, as James Mayall has pointed out, there have been enormous difficulties encountered in putting together a package of demands according to the principle of the 'highest common denominator', offering something for everyone. The more successful European Community has tended to operate according to the contrary principle of the 'lowest common denominator' with integration traditionally proceeding only at the pace of the slowest member. Many of the forces making for a lack of co-operation in the 1960s and 1970s relating to disparities in size, development, culture, and language as well as a host of other factors are no less relevant today, and apply equally to broader Southern coalitions as well as to more selective regional groupings.[66] Even in areas of relative linguistic and cultural homo-

[65] J. D. B. Miller, *The Politics of the Third World* (Oxford: OUP, 1966), 26.
[66] Mayall, *Nationalism and International Society*, 141.

geneity like the Arab world or South America the record of regional organizations is mixed. As one commentator on the Latin American case has observed: 'the experience of the last decades indicates the need to base any new initiatives on concrete common interests, rather than on grandiose and all-embracing projects that invariably end in frustration .'[67] This is a lesson that could well be applied to other areas.

Equally much scepticism has been expressed about the democratization process and whether or not it will contribute towards the creation of more viable regional structures. While its effects have been widely felt, its progress in many developing areas is likely to be painfully slow, full of false starts, reversals, and disappointments. The statement that democratization is 'sweeping parts of the Arab world' seems both exaggerated and premature.[68] As Charles Tripp demonstrates in his chapter, the weak commitment to democracy in most Middle Eastern countries remains a considerable obstacle to regional co-operation. In Africa too, it may be unreasonable to hope that countries can 'suddenly reverse course and institutionalize stable democratic government simply by changing leaders, constitutions and/or public mentalities; [the process] is likely to be gradual, messy, fitful and slow.'[69] Outside South Africa democratization is likely to have little short-term impact on the regional process. It seems clear that for Africa as for much of the developing world, real progress towards regional co-operation will require a much sturdier foundation of political cohesion and economic progress.[70]

Clearly, an evaluation of the new regionalism presents a number of problems. In particular the view that regionalism is riding on the crest of a wave is open to serious challenge. In this introductory chapter, I have merely attempted to set the scene for the discussion that follows on the nature and meaning of regionalism in the contemporary world, and to introduce some of the themes that will be picked up and developed in later chapters. It should be plain

[67] Van Klaveren, 'Latin America and the International Political System', 41.
[68] As'ad Abu Khalil, 'A New Arab Ideology?', *Middle East Journal*, 46/1 (Winter 1992), 22–36.
[69] Decalo, 'Process, Prospects and Constraints of Democratization in Africa', 35.
[70] On this theme see Robert O'Neill, 'Western Security Policy towards the Third World', in Robert O'Neill and John Vincent (eds.), *The West and the Third World* (London, Macmillan, 1990), 220.

from the outset that there is no commonly accepted view of the 'new regionalism' nor indeed of its place in any evolving international order. The debate on regionalism remains very much an open one.

3

Regionalism in Theoretical Perspective

Andrew Hurrell

THIS chapter addresses two very basic questions: first, what do we mean when we talk of regionalism and what are the principal varieties of regionalism? And second, what are the major sets of theories that may be deployed to explain the dynamics of regionalism? Theory, of course, is not everything. But it is central to the creation of the definitions, concepts, and categories around which the analysis of regionalism is necessarily conducted; it brings to the surface assumptions that remain explicit and unquestioned in purely descriptive or historical work on regionalism; it sharpens our understanding of the main explanatory variables and causal mechanisms; and it provides a coherent framework for systematically comparing different forms of regionalism in different parts of the world. The purpose of this chapter, then, is to open up a series of theoretical perspectives on the study of contemporary regionalism and to highlight the close connections that exist between the analysis of contemporary regionalism and the major theoretical debates in the academic study of International Relations. The theoretical literature on regionalism is enormous, but it is also uneven and fragmented. Moreover, leaving aside the ongoing theoretical debates about the European Community, the amount of explicitly theoretical or conceptual work on the resurgence of regionalism since the late 1980s has been relatively modest. This chapter, then, draws together some of the principal elements of the theoretical literature, first in terms of the *process* by which different forms of regional arrangements may emerge, and, second, in terms of the *character* of those arrangements. It does not press the theoretical strengths of any one school of thought, but rather tries to give an idea of what the theoretical landscape looks like and to provide a framework for understanding and assessing the arguments that appear in subsequent chapters.

1. VARIETIES OF REGIONALISM

Both 'region' and 'regionalism' are ambiguous terms. The terrain is contested and the debate on definitions has produced little consensus. Although geographical proximity and contiguity in themselves tell us very little about either the definitions of regions or the dynamics of regionalism, they do helpfully distinguish regionalism from other forms of 'less than global' organization. Without some geographical limits the term 'regionalism' becomes diffuse and unmanageable. The problem of defining regions and regionalism attracted a good deal of academic attention in the late 1960s and early 1970s but the results yielded few clear conclusions. Regionalism was often analysed in terms of the degree of social cohesiveness (ethnicity, race, language, religion, culture, history, consciousness of a common heritage); economic cohesiveness (trade patterns, economic complementarity), political cohesiveness (regime type, ideology), and organizational cohesiveness (existence of formal regional institutions).[1] Particular attention was given to the idea of regional interdependence.[2]

Nevertheless, attempts (such as those by Bruce Russett) to define and delineate regions 'scientifically' produced little clear result.[3] The range of factors that may be implicated in the growth of regionalism is very wide and includes economic, social, political, cultural, or historic dimensions. There are no 'natural' regions, and definitions of 'region' and indicators of 'regionness' vary according to the particular problem or question under investigation.

Moreover it is how political actors perceive and interpret the idea of a region and notions of 'regionness' that is critical: all regions are

[1] See e.g. Bruce M. Russett, 'International Regimes and the Study of Regions', *International Studies Quarterly*, 13/4 (Dec. 1969); Louis J. Cantori and Steven L. Spiegel (eds.), *The International Politics of Regions: A Comparative Approach* (Englewood Cliffs, NJ: Prentice-Hall, 1970); William Thompson, 'The Regional Subsystem: A Conceptual Explication and a Propositional Inventory', *International Studies Quarterly*, 17/1 (1973); and Raimo Väyrynen, 'Regional Conflict Formations: An Intractable Problem of International Relations', *Journal of Peace Research*, 21/4 (1984).

[2] A good example is Joseph S. Nye (ed.), *International Regionalism: Readings* (Boston: Little, Brown & Co., 1968).

[3] Bruce Russett, *International Regions and the International System* (Chicago: Rand McNally, 1967). For a discussion of the difficulties of classifying regional systems, see David Grigg, 'The Logic of Regional Systems', *Annals of the Association of American Geographers*, 55 (1965).

socially constructed and hence politically contested. This makes it especially important to distinguish between regionalism as description and regionalism as prescription—regionalism as a moral position or as a doctrine as to how international relations ought to be organized. As with the more general idea of interdependence, there is often a strong sense that the states of a given region are all in the same 'regional boat', ecologically, strategically, economically; that they are not pulling together; but that, either explicitly stated or implicitly implied, they should put aside national egoisms and devise new forms of co-operation. In much of the political and academic debate, then, there is a strong implication that regionalism is a naturally good thing.

Even a cursory glance at recent debates suggests that the broad term 'regionalism' is used to cover a variety of distinct phenomena. Indeed rather than try and work with a single, very broad overarching concept, it is helpful to break up the notion of 'regionalism' into a five different categories. These are analytically distinct although the ways in which they can be related to each other lie at the heart of both the theory and practice of contemporary regionalism.

(a) Regionalization

Regionalization refers to the growth of societal integration within a region and to the often undirected processes of social and economic interaction. This is what early writers on regionalism described as informal integration and what some contemporary analysts refer to as 'soft regionalism'. The term lays particular weight on autonomous economic processes which lead to higher levels of economic interdependence within a given geographical area than between that area and the rest of the world. Although seldom unaffected by state policies, the most important driving forces for economic regionalization come from markets, from private trade and investment flows, and from the policies and decisions of companies. The growth of intra-firm trade, the increasing numbers of international mergers and acquisitions, and the emergence of an increasingly dense network of strategic alliances between firms are of particular importance. For many commentators '[T]hese flows are creating inexorable momentum towards the further integration of economies within and across regions.'[4] Such regionalization processes have become a particularly important feature of Asia-Pacific regionalism, driven by complex, market-based imperatives of international specialization and organized around transnational (and especially Japanese) firms and regional business networks.

Regionalization can also involve increasing flows of people, the development of multiple channels and complex social networks by which ideas, political attitudes, and ways of thinking spread from one area to another, and the creation of a transnational regional civil society. Regionalization is therefore commonly conceptualized in terms of 'complexes', 'flows', 'networks' or 'mosaics'. It is seen as undermining the monolithic character of the state, leading to the creation of cross-governmental alliances, multi-level and multi-player games and to the emergence of new forms of identity both above and below existing territorially defined states.[5]

Two points should be stressed. First, that regionalization is not based on the conscious policy of states or groups of states, nor does it presuppose any particular impact on the relations between the states of the region.[6] And second, that patterns of regionalization do not necessarily coincide with the borders of states. Migration, markets, and social networks may lead to increased interaction and interconnectedness tying together parts of existing states and creating new cross-border regions. The core of such 'transnational regionalism' may be economic as in the development of transborder growth triangles, industrial corridors, or the increasingly dense networks linking major industrial centres. Or it can be built around human interpenetration, for example the transnational economic role played by overseas Chinese in East Asia or the dense societal linkages that now exist between California and Mexico.[7]

---

[4] Robert D. Hormats, 'Making Regionalism Safe', *Foreign Affairs* (Mar./Apr. 1994), 98.

[5] For a discussion of these trends in the European case, see William Wallace, *The Transformation of Western Europe* (London: Pinter for RIIA, 1990).

[6] The distinction between conscious political direction and autonomous market processes is developed in Andrew Wyatt-Walter's chapter. See also Christopher Bliss's definition of an economic bloc: '[Yet] co-ordination of policy, whether with regard to trade or exchange rates, is at the heart of the idea', Christopher Bliss, *Economic Theory and Policy for Trading Blocks* (Manchester: Manchester UP, 1994), 14.

[7] For a fascinating study of this phenomenon, see Abraham F. Lowenthal and Katrina Burgess (eds.), *The California–Mexico Connection* (Stanford, Calif: Stanford UP, 1993).

(b) Regional awareness and identity

'Regional awareness', 'regional identity', and 'regional consciousness' are inherently imprecise and fuzzy notions. Nevertheless they are impossible to ignore and, for many commentators, have become ever more central to the analysis of contemporary regionalism. All regions are to some extent subjectively defined and can be understood in terms of what Emmanuel Adler has termed 'cognitive regions'.[8] As with nations, so regions can be seen as imagined communities which rest on mental maps whose lines highlight some features whilst ignoring others. Discussions of regional awareness lay great emphasis on language and rhetoric; on the discourse of regionalism and the political processes by which definitions of regionalism and regional identity are constantly defined and redefined; and on the shared understandings and the meanings given to political activity by the actors involved.

Regional awareness, the shared perception of belonging to a particular community can rest on internal factors, often defined in terms of common culture, history, or religious traditions. It can also be defined against some external 'other' which may be understood primarily in terms of a security threat (Europe's self-image defined as against the Soviet Union or Latin American nationalism defined against the threat of US hegemony); or an external cultural challenge (the long tradition by which 'Europe' was defined in opposition to the non-European and, especially, Islamic world; or, more recently, the revival of notions of an Asian identity in contradistinction to the 'West').[9] Although concerns with the 'idea' of Europe, the Americas, or Asia are indeed striking features of the 'new regionalism', they are framed by historically deep-rooted arguments about the definition of the region and the values and purposes that it represents—although, again as with nationalism, there is a good deal of historical rediscovery, myth-making, and invented traditions.

---

[8] Emanuel Adler, 'Imagined (Security) Communities', Paper presented at 1994 Annual Meeting of the American Political Science Meeting, New York, 1–4 Sept. 1994. See also Anthony D. Smith, 'National Identity and the Idea of European Unity', *International Affairs*, 68/1 (Jan. 1992), and Wallace, *The Transformation of Western Europe*, ch. 2.

[9] For an example of these perspectives, see Iver B. Neumann and Jennifer Welsh, 'The Other in European Self-Definition: An Addendum to the Literature on International Society', *Review of International Studies*, 17/4 (Oct. 1991).

(c) Regional interstate co-operation

A great deal of regionalist activity involves the negotiation and construction of interstate or intergovernmental agreements or regimes. Such co-operation can be formal or informal and high levels of institutionalization are no guarantee of either effectiveness or political importance. As Oran Young correctly pointed out: 'Though all regimes, even highly decentralized private-enterprise arrangements, are social institutions, they need not be accompanied by organizations possessing their own personnel, budgets, physical facilities and so forth.'[10] It was this awareness that led those concerned with international co-operation to move away from the study of formal organizations and to focus instead on the broader concept of 'regime': 'explicit or implicit principles, norms, rules and decision-making procedures around which actors' expectations converge in a given area of international relations'.[11] Regional co-operation may therefore entail the creation of formal institutions, but it can often be based on a much looser structure, involving patterns of regular meetings with some rules attached, together with mechanisms for preparation and follow-up.

Such co-operative arrangements can serve a wide variety of purposes. On the one hand, they can serve as a means of responding to external challenges and of co-ordinating regional positions in international institutions or negotiating forums. On the other, they can be developed to secure welfare gains, to promote common values, or to solve common problems, especially problems arising from increased levels of regional interdependence. In the security field, for example, such co-operation can range from the stabilization of a regional balance of power, to the institutionalization of confidence-building measures, to the negotiation of a region-wide security regime. Unlike some brands of regional integration, such co-operative arrangements are very clearly statist, designed to protect and enhance the role of the state and the power of the government. They involve a reassertion and extension of state authority as part of a process by which states are increasingly willing to trade a degree of legal freedom of action for a greater degree of practical

---

[10] Oran Young, *International Cooperation: Building Regimes for Natural Resources and the Environment* (Ithaca, NY: Cornell UP, 1989), 25.

[11] Stephen D. Krasner, 'Structural Causes and Regime Consequences: Regimes as Intervening Variables', in Krasner (ed.), *International Regimes* (Ithaca, NY: Cornell UP, 1983), 1.

influence over the policies of other states and over the management of common problems.[12]

(d) State-promoted regional integration

An important subcategory of regional co-operation concerns regional economic integration. Regional integration involves specific policy decisions by governments designed to reduce or remove barriers to mutual exchange of goods, services, capital, and people. Such policies have generated an enormous literature: on the processes of integration, on the paths which it might take, and on the objectives that it might fulfil.[13] As Peter Smith points out, regional economic integration can be compared along various dimensions: scope (the range of issues included); depth (the extent of policy harmonization); institutionalization (the extent of formal institutional building); and centralization (the degree to which effective authority is centralized).[14] Early stages of integration tend to concentrate on the elimination of trade barriers and the formation of a customs union in goods. As integration proceeds, the agenda expands to cover non-tariff barriers, the regulation of markets, and the development of common policies at both the micro- and macro-levels. Dominated by the European 'model', regionalism is all too often simply equated with regional economic integration, even though this is only one aspect of a more general phenomenon.

[12] Although designed to reinforce state power, there may still be an important difference between *intention* and *outcome*. The mushrooming of co-operative arrangements may set in motion changes that ultimately tie down states in a process of 'institutional enmeshment'. On the ways in which cumulative institutionalization may be changing the dynamics of world politics see Mark W. Zacher, 'The Decaying Pillars of the Westphalian Temple: Implications for Order and Governance', in James N. Rosenau and Ernst-Otto Czempiel (eds.), *Governance without Government: Order and Change in World Politics* (Cambridge: Cambridge UP, 1992).

[13] Some of this literature is surveyed in Andrew Walter's chapter. One of the most important classic works is Bela Balassa, *The Theory of Economic Integration* (London: Allen & Unwin, 1961). For an up-to-date analysis of the evolving process of European integration see Loukas Tsoukalis, *The New European Economy. The Politics and Economics of Integration* (Oxford: OUP, 2nd edn., 1993).

[14] Peter H. Smith, 'Introduction: The Politics of Integration: Concepts and Themes', in Peter H. Smith (ed.), *The Challenge of Integration: Europe and the Americas* (New Brunswick, NJ: Transaction, 1992), 5.

(e) Regional cohesion

Regional cohesion refers to the possibility that, at some point, a combination of these first four processes might lead to the emergence of a cohesive and consolidated regional unit. It is this cohesion that makes regionalism of particular interest to the study of international relations. Cohesion can be understood in two senses: (i) when the region plays a defining role in the relations between the states (and other major actors) of that region and the rest of the world; and (ii) when the region forms the organizing basis for policy within the region across a range of issues.

As we have seen, regionalism is often defined in terms of patterns or networks of interdependence. But political significance derives not from some absolute measure of interdependence, but from the extent to which that interdependence (and the possibility of its disruption) imposes significant potential or actual costs on important actors. For those outside the region, regionalism is politically significant to the extent that it can impose costs on outsiders: whether through the detrimental impact of preferential regional economic arrangements (so-called malign regionalism that diverts trade and investment) or through causing a shift in the distribution of political power. It is also politically significant when outsiders (again including both states and non-state actors) are forced to define their policies towards individual regional states in regionalist terms. For those inside the region, regionalism matters when exclusion from regional arrangements imposes significant costs, both economic and political (such as loss of autonomy or a reduction in foreign policy options) and when the region becomes the organizing basis for policy within the region across a range of important issues. An important indicator of regional cohesion is the extent to which, as is increasingly the case in Western Europe, regional developments and regional politics come to shape and define the domestic political landscape.

It is extremely important to recognize that there are different paths to regional cohesion. The early theorists of European integration were obsessed by a particular end-goal (the formation of a new form of political community) and by a particular route to that goal (increased economic integration). Their concern was with the possible transformation of the role of nation states via the pooling of sovereignty, leading to the emergence of some new form of political community.

Yet regional cohesion might be based on various models. One might indeed be the gradual creation of supranational regional organization within the context of deepening economic integration. A second model might involve the creation of series of overlapping and institutionally strong interstate arrangements or regimes. A third model (perhaps visible in the current status of the European Union) might derive from a complex and evolving mixture of traditional intergovernmentalism and emerging supranationalism. A fourth might involve the development of 'consociationalist' constitutional arrangements of the kind discussed by Paul Taylor.[15] Fifthly, regional cohesion might be conceived of in terms of a 'neo-medieval' order in which the principles of territoriality and sovereignty are replaced by a pattern of overlapping identities and authorities.[16] Finally, cohesion might be based on a strong regional hegemon which, with or without strong regional institutions, both polices the foreign policies of states within its sphere of influence and sets limits on the permissible range of domestic policy options.[17]

2. EXPLAINING REGIONALISM IN WORLD POLITICS

The theoretical analysis of regionalism conventionally begins with those theories that were developed explicitly to explain the creation and early evolution of the European Community.[18] This literature

[15] Paul Taylor, *International Organization in the Modern World. The Regional and Global Process* (London: Pinter, 1993), esp. ch. 4.

[16] John Ruggie, for example, describes the EC as a 'multiperspectival polity' 'in which the process of unbundling territoriality has gone further than anywhere else': 'Territoriality and Beyond: Problematizing Modernity in International Relations', *International Organization*, 47/1 (Winter 1993), 171–2. The notion of 'neo-medievalism' (and the parallel idea of a 'Grotian moment') was developed by Hedley Bull, *The Anarchical Society* (London: Macmillan, 1977), 264–76.

[17] On the multiple roles played by regional powers, see Iver B. Neumann (ed.), *Regional Great Powers in International Politics* (London: Macmillan, 1992).

[18] Most surveys tend to focus overwhelmingly on Europe, e.g. Carole Webb, 'Theoretical Perspectives and Problems', in Helen Wallace, William Wallace, and Carole Webb (eds.), *Policy-making in the European Community* (Chichester: Wiley, 2nd edn., 1983); Charles Pentland, *International Theory and European Integration* (London: Faber & Faber, 1973); or more recently Simon Hix, 'Approaches to the Study of the EC: The Challenge to Comparative Politics', *West European Politics*, 17/1 (Jan. 1994). For a broader survey, see Clive Archer, *International Organizations* (London: Routledge, 2nd edn., 1992), esp. ch. 3. For an excellent reader, see Friedrich Kratochwil and Edward D. Mansfield (eds.), *International Organization. A Reader* (New York: HarperCollins, 1994).

was dominated by liberal theorists who focused on the changing character of intra-regional relations, on the conditions that were likely to promote or to hinder the movement towards regional economic integration, and on the relationship between deepening economic integration on the one hand and the prospects for peace and political community on the other. Yet the strongly Eurocentric character of this work and and its dominant concern with processes of economic integration suggest the need for an alternative focus. In order to escape from the theoretical shadow of the European Community, this section will start with the relevance of systemic theories to the analysis of contemporary regionalism, and then move on to consider, first, those theories which focus on the impact of regional interdependence, and, second, those theories which highlight the importance of domestic factors.

(a) Systemic theories

In the modern world there can be no wholly self-contained regions, immune from outside pressures.[19] Systemic theories underline the importance of the broader political and economic structures within which regionalist schemes are embedded and the impact of outside pressures working on the region.[20] Two sets of systemic or structural theories are especially significant: first, neo-realist theory that stresses the constraints of the anarchical international system and the importance of power-political competition; and second, theories of structural interdependence and globalization which emphasize the changing character of the international system and the impact of economic and technological change.

1. Neo-realism. On one level regional co-operation has often seemed to pose a direct challenge to realism. The appearance of 'islands of peace and co-operation' in what was commonly viewed as an inherently conflictual world dominated by the struggle for power was widely seen in the 1950s as an anomaly that realism was incapable of explaining. Indeed, much of the early work on

[19] For a useful discussion of the concept of regionalism in Geography, see Paul Cloke, Chris Philo, David Sadler (eds.), *Approaching Human Geography: An Introduction to Contemporary Theoretical Debates* (London: Paul Chapman Publishers, 1991), 8–13.

[20] The useful distinction between 'outside-in' and 'inside-out' approaches to regionalism has been developed by Iver B. Neumann, 'A Region-Building Approach to Northern Europe', *Review of International Studies*, 20/1 (Jan. 1994).

regionalism and regional integration can be seen as an attempt to shed light on this apparent anomaly. Yet, neo-realism can in fact tell us a number of very important things about regionalism. *Regionalism, Power Politics, and Mercantilism.* Both classical realism and its more recent neo-realist variants stress the importance of external configurations of power, the dynamics of power-political competition, and the constraining role of the international political system considered as a whole.[21] For the neo-realist, the politics of regionalism and the emergence of regionalist alignments have much in common with the politics of alliance formation.[22] Regionalism is understood by looking at the region from the outside in and by analysing the place of the region in the broader international system. Regional groupings form in response to external challenges and there is no essential difference between economic and political regionalism.

Proponents of such a view, for example, emphasize the fundamental importance of the geopolitical framework within which the moves towards European integration took place.[23] As William Wallace's chapter argues, the ending of the Cold War makes it easier to understand the extent to which the dramatic shift within Europe in the 1940s and early 1950s from war and competition to regional co-operation and then to the promotion of regional integration depended on a very particular set of geopolitical circumstances: the erosion and then collapse of the colonial empires on which the power of Britain and France had been built; the immense physical destruction and psychological exhaustion of the thirty-year European civil war; the perception of a burgeoning threat from the Soviet Union; the long-predicted transformation in the scale of power and the emergence of a new class of super-powers (with whom the traditional nation states of Western Europe acting alone could no longer hope to compete); and the powerful pressure from the USA to move towards greater regional co-operation.

[21] The most influential statement of the structural realist position has been Kenneth Waltz, *Theory of International Politics* (Reading, Mass.: Addison-Wesley, 1979).

[22] See, in particular, Stephen M. Walt, *The Origins of Alliances* (Ithaca, NY: Cornell UP, 1987).

[23] For a strong restatement of the realist position, see John Mearsheimer, 'Back to the Future: Instability in Europe after the Cold War', *International Organization*, 15 (Summer 1990).

For the neo-realist, US hegemony was especially important. Neo-realists highlight the degree to which integration was spurred by direct US encouragement and pressure (for example, the conditions attached to Marshall Aid leading to the formation of the OEEC (Organization of European Economic Co-operation) and EPU; or the determination of Washington to press ahead with the rearmament of West Germany following the start of the Korean War, thus forcing Europe to find a way of living with the rehabilitation of German power. They also stress the extent to which European integration—which was in reality subregional integration—was embedded within a transatlantic security framework. This meant that the immensely difficult tasks of politico-military co-operation and security could be left to one side. The acceptance of security dependence was therefore one of the essential compromises on which European co-operation and integration was built—a fact that makes it vital to examine the relationship between economics and security issues in other parts of the world.

Neo-realism focuses attention both on power-political pressures and on the dynamics of mercantilist economic competition. This suggests to the neo-realist that 'outside-in' pressures have continued to influence the path of European integration, but that these have had ever more to do with mercantilist economic rivalry. Thus already in the 1960s de Gaulle placed great weight on European co-operation (albeit in the form of a *Europe des patries*) as a means of countering *le défi americain* and reducing what he saw as the 'exorbitant privilege' of the USA. Equally, the relaunch of European integration in the 1980s can be interpreted as a response *au défi japonais* and the loss of competitiveness, especially in strategically (*sic*) important high-technology industries. From this perspective the economic objectives of regional integration do not derive from the pursuit of welfare, but from the close relationship that exists between economic wealth and political power and from states' 'inevitable' concern with relative gains and losses.

Economic regionalism can therefore be seen as a strategy in the game of neo-mercantilist competition. It can also be deployed as a bargaining chip in the negotiations that determine the shape of the international economic order. From this perspective, for example, growing US interest in economic regionalism in the mid-1980s was both a response to its declining competitiveness and its relative loss of economic power *vis-à-vis* Europe and Japan, and a negotiating ploy or bargaining tool (NAFTA as a 'stick' to increase pressure on Japan to open its markets; APEC as a means of applying pressure on the EU in the final stages of the negotiations on the Uruguay Round of GATT).

The same neo-realist logic can also be applied to the policies of smaller states outside Europe. On this view many regionalist groupings are basically the natural response of weak states trapped in the world of the strong. Thus much regionalist activity through the Cold War years involved, in essence, schemes for diplomatic and political co-operation designed to improve their region's position in the international system, either by increasing its bargaining strength or by attempting to seal off the region and reduce the scope for outside intervention. Equally, the revival of regionalism that gathered pace in many parts of the developing world in the 1980s followed logically from the erosion of alternative, cross-regional coalitions. As Louise Fawcett argues in her chapter, the erosion of the Third World coalition on which so many hopes had been pinned in the 1970s, combined with a fear of marginalization and vulnerability, pressed developing countries in Africa, Latin America, and the Middle East towards 'group-solidarity' of a more limited, regional character.

Neo-realism also brings out the extent to which regional economic and security arrangements created by relatively weak states remain contingent upon the policies and attitudes of the major powers. Thus during the Cold War both superpowers favoured those regionalist arrangements that reinforced the strength of their respective alliance systems or provided support for important clients. But where regionalism went against their geopolitical interests it was firmly opposed—as, for example, in the US opposition to subregional co-operation in Latin America in the early 1950s, or to numerous proposals for 'zones of peace' or nuclear-free zones; or the Soviet ambivalence towards European regionalism. Although much has changed as a result of the end of the Cold War, the neo-realist would expect this pattern to continue—for example, that the success of subregional co-operation will be contingent upon the policies of either major powers acting unilaterally, or of the macro-regional groupings which those powers will naturally come to dominate. In Asia Pacific, for example, it is the evolving character of the Chinese–Japanese–US balance that will ultimately determine the fate of existing subregional groupings such as ASEAN, as well as broader co-operative schemes such as APEC or the ASEAN Regional Forum.

Hegemony. Although a vast amount of effort has been expended in analysing the general relationship between hegemony and co-operation, links between hegemony and regionalism remain undertheorized. Clearly the existence of a powerful hegemon within a region may undermine efforts to construct inclusive regional arrangements involving all or most of the states within a region. India's position in the subcontinent and the chequered history of SAARC provides a powerful illustration. But the picture is far more interesting and complex than this. There are at least four ways in which hegemony may act as a powerful stimulus to regionalism and to the creation of regionalist institutions.

First, subregional groupings often develop as a *response* to the existence of an actual or potential hegemonic power. Thus in many parts of the world there is a tendency for subregional groupings to form as a means of improving the balance of power *vis-à-vis* a locally dominant or threatening state. Although varied in scope and character, ASEAN (against Vietnam), the Gulf Co-operation Council (against Iran), SADC (against South Africa), the Contadora Group, the Rio Group and *Mercosur* (against the USA) cannot be understood except against the background of their respective regional balances of power and the policies of the regionally dominant power.

Second, regionalism can emerge as an attempt to restrict the free exercise of hegemonic power through the creation of regional institutions. Many would see the position of Germany within the European Community as the classic illustration of this 'regionalist entrapment'. If European integration was pressed from outside by the threat of the Soviet Union on the one side and by the hegemonic leadership of the USA on the other, it was also explicitly promoted as a means of managing German power. Although the division of Germany mitigated the fears of other Europeans, it certainly did not remove them. Europe needed German economic power to fuel post-war recovery and German military power to counter the Soviet threat. Indeed, the specific project of regional *integration* arose precisely as the preferred means of dealing with this problem: permitting rearmament and economic rehabilitation by tying a semi-sovereign Germany into an integrated network of institutions in both the economic field (the EC) and the military (NATO/WEU).

From Germany's perspective, regionalism has provided the essential multilateral cover under which it could first of all re-establish its position and recover its sovereignty and, more recently, re-establish its influence.[24] In the Far East, by contrast, the containment of Japanese power was achieved by undermining macro-regionalism and relying instead on extra-regional bilateral alliances with the USA.

Although the end of the Cold War has altered the context, the idea of using institutionalized regionalism as a means of tying down or constraining the potentially disruptive effects of unequal power remains an important factor in the international politics of both Europe and Asia Pacific.[25] In addition, the relationship between institutions and unequal power can serve as a plausible starting-point for theorizing about the different character of regionalism in different parts of the world. Consider, for example, the contrast between the relatively highly institutionalized structures of NAFTA on the one hand, and the loose character of APEC on the other. In both cases the USA has a clear set of economic objectives that it has only been partially able to promote through the GATT. For Mexico and the relatively weak states of South America, outright opposition would be dangerous and costly. The balance of incentives therefore favours a rule-constrained hegemonic order in which acceptance of major US objectives is traded for more secure access to the crucial US market and in which relatively high levels of institutionalization will (hopefully) restrict their vulnerability to the unilateral exercise of US power. In Asia Pacific, by contrast, the far stronger states of the region have successfully resisted US efforts to promote APEC as an alternative formal vehicle for pressing its foreign economic agenda. From their perspective a loose regional arrangement is a way of keeping the USA involved in the security of the region, whilst at the same time restricting its ability to press its economic agenda.

This kind of behaviour is often closely linked to a third possibility, namely the tendency of weaker states to seek regional

---

[24] On the multiple uses of the idea and institutions of Europe, see Timothy Garton Ash, *In Europe's Name: Germany and the Divided Continent* (London: Vintage, 1994).

[25] Attempts at institutional 'taming' or 'entrapment' do not of course always succeed, as illustrated by repeated attempts in the Middle East to use regionalism to restrict e.g. Iraq or Libya.

accommodation with the local hegemon either in the hope of receiving special rewards ('bandwagoning' in the realist jargon). Neorealist theory predicts that this kind of behaviour is most likely when power differentials are very great, when there are few external alternatives to accommodation with the hegemon, and when the small state finds itself in close geographic proximity. Although prompted by actual or potential vulnerability such a strategy offers the smaller state the possibility of material benefits. Participation in a great-power-dominated military coalition may, for example, be the most viable means of acquiring modern weapons systems. Clearly the greater the degree to which the dominant power is prepared to accept a rule-constrained hegemonic order, the more acceptable is a strategy of bandwagoning for the weak states.[26]

Fourth, the hegemon itself may seek to become involved actively in the construction of regional institutions. Interestingly the logic here is at variance with the argument that the emergence of co-operation and the creation of international institutions are linked with hegemonic ascendancy. Looking almost exclusively at non-regional institutions, theorists of hegemonic stability argued that the creation of institutionalized co-operation depends very heavily on unequal power and on the existence of hegemony. Yet, if the hegemon is in an extremely dominant position, the very extent of that power may make institutions, and in this case, institutionalized regionalism unnecessary or at best marginal. Declining hegemony, however, may well press the hegemon towards the creation of common institutions to pursue its interests, to share burdens, to solve common problems, and to generate international support and legitimacy for its policies. This combination of still marked inequality but declining overall levels of power may be particularly conducive to the creation of regionalist arrangements. On the one hand, the core state is strong enough to provide effective leadership and, if

---

[26] On traditional realist accounts in which states will always be fearful of unequal *power*, bandwagoning will be an exception. However, if, as Stephen Walt argues, states seek to balance *threats* rather than simply power and if factors such as ideological commonality and institutionalization play a role, then accommodation with the hegemon becomes a less anomalous policy. For Walt's modification of traditional balance of power logic, see *The Origins of Alliances*, esp. ch. 1. For a restatement of the view that states will always balance unequal power, see Kenneth Waltz, 'The Emerging Structure of International Politics', *International Security* 18/2 (Fall 1993).

necessary coercion. On the other, this is balanced by the perception that declining power makes co-operation ever more necessary.[27]

Neo-realism, then, has little interest in *regionalization* or *regional economic integration*, believing so called 'autonomous market processes' to be ultimately determined by the structures of the international political system and the policies of major states. *Regional cohesion* is indeed possible, but as the result of either the power of a regional hegemon or of a sustained convergence of material interests and incentives. Little weight is given to the notion of *regional awareness*. Within its own limits, neo-realist theory still has a good deal to tell us both about the importance of 'outside-in' pressures and about the importance of hegemony. It is helpful in unravelling the ways in which external constraints and the structure of the international system shape the regionalist options of all states, but especially of relatively weak states. It is also good at explaining the logic of strategic interaction when the identity of the actors and the nature of their interests is known and well understood.

Neo-realism, however, says little about the character of regional co-operation once established and the ways in which the habits of sustained co-operation may involve institutional structures very different from the traditional idea of a coalition, alliance, or traditional international organization. The workings of such institutions may lead to a new definition of self-interest, and perhaps to new conceptions of 'self'. Neo-realism also says very little about the impact of domestic factors. It talks a great deal about states as self-interested actors competing in an anarchical world but leaves the identity of the 'self' and the nature of the interests unexplained, or simply assumed. Moreover, if there are limitations regarding both domestic factors and the workings of regional institutions, there are also major difficulties on the external side, and it is to these that we now turn.

2. *Structural interdependence and globalization.* One of the most consistent and telling criticisms of neo-realism has been its mischaracterization of the international system. On this view sys-

---

[27] This argument has recently been made in relation to the Asia-Pacific region by Donald Crone, see 'Does Hegemony Matter? The Reorganization of the Pacific Political Economy', *World Politics* 45/4 (July 1993). In relation to Latin America, see Andrew Hurrell, 'Latin America and the New World Order: A Regional Bloc in the Americas?', *International Affairs*, 68/1 (Jan. 1992).

temic factors are extremely important, but neo-realism provides a grossly oversimplified account of the nature of the system and one which neglects the ways in which the competitive dynamics of the system change over time. In particular, its picture of the international system misses out entirely the ways in which both the nature of political and economic competition and the consequent definition of state interests are affected by changes in the global economic system.

Criticisms of this kind grew out of the work in the 1970s on interdependence and modernization associated with writers such as Joseph Nye, Robert Keohane, and Edward Morse. Yet the structural or systemic focus of this work became blurred (and all too often disappeared entirely) as attention shifted to the links between interdependence and state power, and to the nature and role of regimes for managing interdependence within a specific-issue area;[28] and as the initial concern with transnationalism and non-state actors was replaced by a strongly state-centric perspective. Although the focus on issue-specific regimes is undoubtedly significant, it is also extremely important to revive the idea of interdependence as a systemic or structural phenomenon and to set contemporary regionalism against what many see as powerful trends towards ever deeper interdependence and globalization.

'Globalization' has become an important theme of the post-Cold War discussion of the nature of international order. Although rarely tied to any very clearly articulated *theory*, it has become a very powerful *metaphor* for the sense that a number of universal processes are at work generating increased interconnection and interdependence between both states and societies. The increasingly common image is of a global flood of money, people, images, values, and ideas overflowing the old system of national barriers that sought to preserve state autonomy. The result is that territorial boundaries are becoming decreasingly important, that traditional understandings of sovereignty are being undermined, and that individual regions must be viewed within a broader global context.

---

[28] Thus in *Power and Interdependence*, which largely set the agenda for this scholarship, Keohane and Nye write that they 'sought to integrate realism and liberalism *using a conception of interdependence which focused on bargaining*' (my emphasis). Robert O. Keohane and Joseph S. Nye, *Power and Interdependence*, 2nd edn. (Glenview, Ill.: Scott, Foresman & Co., 1989), 251.

Such perspectives are well captured by such catchphrases as the 'borderless world' or the 'end of geography'.[29]

Most contemporary arguments in favour of globalization rest on some combination of the following arguments. First, that we are witnessing a dramatic increase in the 'density' and 'depth' of economic interdependence; second, that information technology and the information revolution is playing an especially critical role in diffusing knowledge, technology, and ideas; third, that these developments create the material infrastructure for the strengthening of societal interdependence. This, together with the integrating and homogenizing influence of market forces, facilitates increased flows of values, knowledge, and ideas, and increases the ability of like-minded groups to organize across national boundaries, creating a transnational civil society that includes both transnational policy communities and transnational social movements; and fourth, that this is leading to an unprecedented and growing consciousness of 'global problems' (such as global environmental change) and of belonging to a single 'human community'.

But how do these ideas relate to regionalism? The answer is complex and ambiguous. On one side, there are a number of ways in which globalization works against the emergence of regionalism. In the first place, increasing levels of economic interdependence, together with the rise of new global issues (such as environmental degradation, refugees, responding to humanitarian disasters), create powerful 'demand' for non-regionally based, issue-specific international institutions designed to solve common problems and to manage the many new sources of friction to which interdependence gives rise. Indeed it was precisely increased concern with patterns of interdependence that transcended any single region that persuaded many of those involved in the study of regional integration to turn their attention to a broader stage.[30]

Second, the expansion of economic interdependence and the growth of political, economic, and security co-operation across the OECD world has created powerful elements of 'Western' rather than specifically regional cohesion. Although these institutional

---

[29] Richard O'Brien, *Global Financial Integration: The End of Geography* (London: Pinter for RIIA, 1992); Kenichi Ohmae, *The Borderless World* (London: Fontana, 1991).

[30] See Keohane and Nye, *Power and Interdependence*, 247–51; and Ernst Haas, *The Obsolescence of Regional Integration Theory* (Berkeley: Institute of International Studies, 1975).

structures have been diffuse (the Bretton Woods institutions, the OECD, the Group of Seven, transatlantic and transpacific security systems), taken together they have represented (and continue to represent) an important constraint on the growth of coherent regional groupings. Third, as the following chapter analyses in more detail, the balance between the globalization and regionalization of economic activity is a complex one. Although there has been some shift in the balance towards regionalization, there is much ambiguity in the data and there are powerful integrative forces, especially in the areas of global finance, of global production structures involving state/firm alliances that cut across regions.

Nevertheless there are also a number of ways in which globalization may act as a stimulus to regionalism. In the first place, ever-deepening integration creates problems which demand collective management and, more specifically, particular forms of management and regulation that bite ever more deeply into the domestic affairs and sovereign prerogatives of states. This is a stimulus to regionalism to the extent that it is politically more viable to construct such institutions at the regional rather than the global level. On this view, commonality of culture, history, homogeneity of social systems and values, convergence of political and security interests, and the character of domestic coalitions all make it far easier to accept the necessary levels of intrusive management, both in terms of standard-setting and regulation, but even more of enforcement and effective implementation.

Second, the 'global' character of many issues is often exaggerated. Although there are undoubtedly genuinely global issues (such as climate change or the loss of biodiversity) and although many other issues (such as the problems of environmental refugees) do indeed constitute a global issue when aggregated, their effects are likely to be felt most directly within particular regions and it is on a regional, rather than a global, level that the balance of interests and incentives is likely to press states to seek some policy response. Thus, although in an abstract sense the logic of co-operation may point towards globalism, there are powerful practical arguments in favour of regionally based contributions to solving global problems, and of the regional enforcement of globally agreed standards or measures.

Third, there is the related argument that regionalism represents the most viable level at which to reconcile the integrative market and techological pressures towards globalization and integration on the one hand, and the equally visible trends towards fission and fragmentation on the other. Liberals recognize the strains involved but see this process of reconciliation as a necessary adjustment to new technological opportunities which will in the long run enhance global welfare. Radical theorists, by contrast, highlight the extent to which the general shift in authority from states to markets is driven by the changing corporate strategies of transnational capital.[31] They argue that the reduction in the domestic regulatory role of the state and its replacement by politically weak international institutions at both the regional and global levels have important implications for the balance of wealth and power among social groups within and across regions. The politics of regionalism are therefore centrally about issues of inequality and redistribution.

Fourth, global integration may have acted as a powerful stimulus to economic regionalism by altering and intensifying patterns of mercantilist economic competition. Changes in technology, in communications, in the operation of global markets, and in the growth of global systems of production have certainly had a profound impact on the ways in which governments have defined the two most important goals of foreign policy—economic development and political autonomy—and the range of acceptable trade-offs between them. On the one hand, globalization means that states are facing powerful pressures towards the homogenization of economic policies, in order to attract foreign investment and technology and to compete in an ever more closely linked market-place. These systemically driven pressures towards market-liberal policies have increased the importance of export expansion and trade liberalization at *both* global *and* regional levels. On the other hand, the nature of competition presses towards the formation of larger units, both for economic efficiency and to ensure the political power necessary to bargain effectively over the rules and institutions that govern the world economy. Within this picture, states cease to be the only important actors. Economic regionalization may be driven by transnational companies and the politics of regional integration

---

[31] See e.g. 'Papers from the International Conference on the NAFTA, Mexico City, March 1993', *Review of Radical Political Economics*, 25/4 (Dec. 1993). For arguments linking regionalism to 'a crisis of global economic order', see Stephen Gill, 'Restructuring Global Politics: Trilateral Relations and World Order "After" the Cold War' (York University, CISS Working Paper, Sept. 1992).

can be understood in terms of a convergence of interests between state élites and firms in response to changes in the international economic structure.

Thus, for example, whilst at one level it may be true to see the relaunch of European integration in the 1980s as promoted by fears of 'Eurosclerosis' and of falling behind in the competitive battle with the USA and Japan, this picture is too simple. We need to ask what changed in the period from the 1960s to the 1980s that made previous foreign economic policies decreasingly viable. The answer cannot be gleaned from the parsimonious but barren world of neo-realist theory. Changes in the global economy (in technology and production systems, but especially the impact of information technologies and the second industrial revolution) meant that national industrial policies and the promotion of national champions were no longer considered adequate. A changing global environment had undermined the possibility of successful national-level responses to the challenges of international competition, as well as putting in doubt the reliance on Keynesian and welfarist policies on which domestic political bargains had so heavily depended.[32] As a result we have seen the growth of European-level programmes of technological development, the promotion of European 'champions', and a complex pattern of deregulation, collaboration, and strategic alliances.

(b) Regionalism and interdependence

In contrast to these 'outside-in' approaches which start with the system as a whole, a second cluster of theories sees a close link between regionalism and regional (as opposed to global) interdependence. The first two variants view regionalism as a functional response by states to the problems created by regional interdependence and stresses the critical role of institutions in fostering and developing regional cohesion. They stand full square in the liberal camp with their emphasis on rationality, welfare goals, scientific and technical knowledge, and their generally pluralist view of inter-

---

[32] On the importance of changes in the international structure for understanding the 1992 process in Europe, see Wayne Sandholtz and John Zysman, '1992: Recasting the European Bargain', *World Politics*, 42/1 (Oct. 1989). See also Margaret Sharp, 'Technology and the Dynamics of Integration', in William Wallace (ed.), *The Dynamics of European Integration* (London: Pinter for RIIA, 1990).

national society. The third lays greater emphasis on the relationship between material interdependence and understandings of identity and community.

1. *Neo-functionalism.* Neo-functionalism has played a central, although much criticized, role in the development of theories of European integration.[33] Neo-functionalists argued that high and rising levels of interdependence would set in motion an ongoing process of co-operation that would lead eventually to political integration. Supranational institutions were seen as the most effective means of solving common problems, beginning with technical and non-controversial issues, but 'spilling over' into the realm of high politics and leading to a redefinition of group identity around the regional unit.

The central prediction of neo-functionalism was that integration would become self-sustaining and that the central metaphor was that of 'spillover'. There were two sorts of spillover, each of which would deepen integration by working through interest-group pressure, public opinion, and élite socialization. First, functional spillover whereby partial small initial steps down the integration road would create new problems that could only be solved by further co-operation. Partial integration and the increased complexity of interdependence meant that co-operation in one area would force governments to expand their co-operative endeavours into further areas. Pressure groups would press for further integration in order to capture greater economic benefits. Second, political spillover, whereby the existence of supranational institutions would set in motion a self-reinforcing process of institution building. On this view the management of complex interdependence requires centralized technocratic management. Once created, institutions generate an internal dynamic of their own (hence the great attention to the role of the Commission in articulating goals, proposing and brokering bargains).[34] The end-result would be a

---

[33] The classic texts are Ernst B. Haas, *The Uniting of Europe: Political, Social and Economic Forces* (London: Stevens, 1958), pp. xv–xvi; and Leon N. Lindberg, *The Political Dynamics of European Economic Integration* (Stanford, Calif.: Stanford UP, 1963).

[34] More recently there has been a good deal of attention given to the dynamics of legal integration and the idea of 'legal spillover'. See e.g. J. H. H. Weiler, 'Journey to an Unknown Destination: A Retrospective and Prospective of the European Court of Justice in the Arena of Political Integration', *Journal of Common Market Studies*, 31/4 (Dec. 1993).

shift in loyalties. For Ernst Haas, integration was: 'the process whereby actors in several distinct national settings are persuaded to shift their loyalties, expectations, and political activities towards a new centre whose institutions possess or demand jurisdiction over the pre-exisiting national states.'[35]

Neo-functionalism therefore laid great emphasis on the unintended consequences of previous (and often small) decisions; on the idea of learning how to adapt to new situations; on the extensive interbureaucratic penetration of the EC; and on the capacity of supranational officials to provide leadership. Yet, as the EC developed in ways that were often at variance with the predictions of the theory, criticisms grew: that the theory failed to predict evolution of the EC; that it underestimated the resilience of nation states and of loyalties at the national level; that it ignored the great differences that exist between matters of 'low politics' which may be subject to technocratic management and matters of 'high politics' that remain essential to national sovereignty; that it ignored the changing role of external factors, political, economic, and security (and also the influence of shifts in the economic cycle); and that it was overly deterministic, technocratic, and apolitical with little ability to explain the nature of power-political and distributional conflicts between member states and the choices between different means of managing them. Yet the core idea that enhanced interstate co-operation and moves towards formal integration are essentially responses to increased social and economic interdependence has remained an important element in the European debate and the renewed momentum of integration in the late 1980s prompted a reconsideration of the relevance of the theory.[36]

Despite its influence on both the theory and practice of European regionalism, its relevance to contemporary regionalism elsewhere is rather less clear. In the first place, neo-functionalism has always had more to say about the ongoing role of institutions than about the factors that explain the birth of regionalist schemes. Second, its

---

[35] Haas, *The Uniting of Europe*, pp. xv–xvi.
[36] See e.g. Andrew Moravcsik, 'Preferences and Power in the European Community: A Liberal Intergovernmentalist Approach', *Journal of Common Market Studies*, 31/4 (Dec. 1993), esp. 474–80; Robert O. Keohane and Stanley Hoffmann, 'Conclusions: Community Politics and Institutional Change', in Wallace (ed.), *The Dynamics of European Integration*; and Jeppe Tranholm-Mikkelsen, 'Neo-functionalism: Obstinate or Obsolete? A Reappraisal in the Light of the New Dynamism of the EC', *Millennium*, 20/1 (1991).

expectations about the declining role of the state in relation to central institutions seem radically at variance with the very heavily statist orientation of most regionalist arrangements outside the EC. Third, (in contrast to both neo-liberal institutionalism and Deutsch's concept of security community) neo-functionalism views institutions as fundamental and is thus difficult to relate to the relatively low levels of institutionalization found in many regionalist schemes. It is, however, possible that neo-functionalist insights may become more relevant in the future as regional co-operation deepens and as regional institutions become more firmly established. Thus, for example, recent institutional developments in *Mercosur* or the wide-ranging and often highly technical provisions of NAFTA may lead to the kinds of social and political processes that have been so central to neo-functionalist thinking about European integration: the process of institutional growth and spillover across different sectors; the leading role for technical élites and international bureaucracies; and the extent to which the institutionalized structure of the complex negotiating process opens the way for transnational interest group mobilization.

2. *Neo-liberal institutionalism.* Neo-liberalism institutionalism has been the most influential theoretical approach to the recent study of international co-operation and represents a highly plausible and generalizable theory for understanding the resurgence of regionalism.[37] Institutionalists base their analysis on a number of core arguments. In the first place, increasing levels of interdependence generate increased 'demand' for international co-operation. Institutions are viewed as purposively generated solutions to different kinds of collective action problems. As Robert Keohane puts it:

Institutionalists do not elevate international regimes to mythical positions of authority over states: on the contrary, such regimes are established by states to achieve their purposes. Facing dilemmas of coordination and collaboration under conditions of interdependence, governments demand

---

[37] The literature is enormous. See e.g. Robert O. Keohane, *International Institutions and State Power* (Boulder, Colo.: Westview, 1989); Keohane, *After Hegemony: Cooperation and Discord in the World Political Economy* (Princeton: Princeton UP, 1984); David A. Baldwin (ed.), *Neorealism and Neoliberalism* (New York: Columbia UP, 1993); Volker Rittberger (ed.), *Regime Theory and International Relations* (Oxford: OUP, 1993); Helen Milner, 'International Theory of Cooperation among Nations: Strengths and Weaknesses', *World Politics*, 44 (Apr. 1992).

international institutions to enable them to achieve their interests through limited collective action.[38]

Norms, rules, and institutions are generated because they help states deal with common problems and because they enhance welfare.

Second, neo-liberal institutionalism is heavily statist, concerned with ways in which states conceived of as rational egoists can be led to co-operate.[39] In contrast to the pluralist networks stressed by the neo-functionalists, the state is viewed as the effective gatekeeper between the domestic and international. Indeed, this approach emphasizes how the successful collaborative management of common problems strengthens the role of the state. Thus the dominant strand of rationalist institutionalism has sought to retain neo-realist assumptions but to argue that they do not preclude co-operation. The aim is to analyse and isolate the particular constellations of power, interests, and preferences likely to explain the sources and constraints of co-operative behaviour.

Third, institutions matter because of the benefits that they provide, and because of their impact on the calculations of the players and the ways in which states define their interests. They achieve this through the provision of information, the promotion of transparency and monitoring, the reduction of transaction costs, the development of convergent expectations, and facilitating the productive use of issue-linkage strategies. Particular attention is paid to the number of players; the extent to which states are involved in an ongoing process of co-operation (the idea of repeated games or 'iteration' and the importance of lengthening the shadow of the future'); and the effectiveness of mechanisms to discourage cheating (it is cheating or defection that is considered the main obstacle to co-operation rather than, as neo-realists argue, distributional conflict and concern for relative gains).

Institutionalist theories, then, concentrate on the ways in which strategic interaction may lead to the emergence of co-operation in a given area of international relations. As noted earlier, the domin-

---

[38] Robert O. Keohane, 'Institutionalist Theory and the Realist Challenge After the Cold War', in Baldwin (ed.), *Neorealism and Neoliberalism*, 274.

[39] Because it takes states as central, this is often seen as a realist theory (e.g. by Hix, 'Approaches to the Study of the EC'). Unlike realism, however, institutionalism accords a major role to institutions and accepts that sustained co-operation is possible.

ant trend in the 1970s and 1980s was to apply this approach to non-region-specific questions (mainly in the economic and environmental fields, but with some emphasis on security regimes). However, institutionalists have increasingly turned their attention to the EC, highlighting the extent to which even institutionally complex regional arrangements rest on an evolving set of intergovernmental bargains between the major states; and pointing to the reassertion of the control of European national governments after the early moves in the direction of supranationalism and the creation or strengthening of intergovernmental practices and institutions.[40]

Applied to other examples of regionalism, institutionalist theory would seek to identify the ways in which processes of *regionalization* and *regional economic integration* create, first, material problems and what Richard Cooper has called 'international policy externalities' that require collective management; and, second, incentives for reducing transaction costs and facilitating intra-regional linkages.[41] It is expected that both lead to the expansion of formal or informal *interstate co-operative institutions*. Thus, for example, the choice facing the USA and Mexico in the NAFTA process was not whether to move closer to each other; but rather whether the management of the increasingly complex and dense economic, environmental, and societal interdependencies that had emerged over the past forty years should be formalized and institutionalized, or left to *ad hoc* political bargaining. Equally, for institutionalist theory, the increased emphasis on political regionalism in Asia Pacific reflects the need to 'manage' the increased levels of economic interdependence that have grown up across the region. As Peter Petri has argued:

The importance of a particular partner in a country's transactions is likely to be closely related to the country's investments in linkages with that partner. It is thus not surprising that a wide array of regional initiatives have recently emerged to address the new issues generated by East Asian interdependence. From an analytical perspective, these initiatives can be seen as attempts to reduce transaction costs in regional trade, manage

[40] See e.g. Robert O. Keohane and Stanley Hoffmann (eds.), *The New European Community: Decisionmaking and Institutional Change* (Boulder, Colo.: Westview, 1991).
[41] Richard N. Cooper, 'Interdependence and Co-ordination of Policies', in Cooper, *Economic Policy in an Interdependent World: Essays in World Economics* (Cambridge, Mass.: MIT Press, 1986).

intraregional trade frictions, and marshal regional economic forces against external economic challenges.[42]

From an institutionalist perspective, the emergence of regional security regimes (such as CSCE or the ASEAN Regional Forum, or the network of confidence-building measures in South America) should not be viewed in terms of the balance of power or alliance formation. Rather they have been created and will survive because of the benefits they provide: by facilitating communication, information, transparency; by reducing mutual threat perceptions and worst-case thinking; and by undercutting the self-fulfilling prophecies that lie at the heart of the security dilemma.

Finally *regional cohesion* would emerge, on this view, not from grand proposals to create new federal structures but from the way in which individual or issue-specific co-operation comes to form an increasingly dense network where co-operation on each new issue becomes embedded in a larger and more complex whole.

3. *Constructivism.* Constructivist theories focus on *regional awareness* and regional identity, on the shared sense of belonging to a particular regional community, and on what has been called 'cognitive regionalism'. They stress the extent to which *regional cohesion* depends on a sustained and durable sense of community based on mutual responsiveness, trust, and high levels of what might be called 'cognitive interdependence'.

There are two main variants that are relevant to the study of regionalism.[43] The first derives very centrally and directly from Deutsch's original work on integration. It involves a view of evolving community that stresses two central ideas: first, that the *character* of interstate (or more accurately for Deutsch, inter-societal)

---

[42] Peter A. Petri, 'The East Asian Trading Bloc: An Analytical History', in Jeffrey A. Frankel and Miles Kahler (eds.), *Regionalism and Rivalry. Japan and the United States in Pacific Asia* (Chicago: University of Chicago Press, 1993), 42–3. See also Stephan Haggard's comment on Petri, pp. 48–52.

[43] Nicholas Onuf used the term 'constructivism' in his study of rules in international relations (*World of Our Making. Rules and Rule in Social Theory and International Relations* (Columbia, SC: University of South Carolina Press, 1989). Its more general use has arisen out of the critique of both Waltzian structural realism and rationalist theories of co-operation. For a particularly clear account of constructivism see Alexander Wendt, 'Collective Identity Formation and the International State', *American Political Science Review*, 88/2 (June 1994). See also Keohane's distinction between rationalist and reflectivist approaches: 'International Institutions: Two Approaches', in *International Institutions and State Power* (Boulder, Colo.: Westview, 1989), ch. 7.

relations within such a community can (and should be) understood in terms of a sense of community, 'we-ness', mutual sympathy, loyalty, and shared identity. This in turn is likely to be based on shared principles, on collectively held norms, and on common understandings, rather than on expediency or a temporary conjunction of short-term interests. And second, that the *process* by which such a community emerges is related in some way to the compatibility of major societal values (especially capitalism and liberal democracy); and to processes of social communication based on an increase in the level of transactions between two or more societies (hence the label 'transactionalism').

The second variant rejects the rigidity of the linkage in Deutsch's work between transactions and identity, but upholds the fundamental importance of understanding the processes by which new communities are created and sustained.[44] This involves a number of central ideas: first, that, in contrast to rationalist theories, we need to pay far more attention to the processes by which both interests and identities are created and evolve, to the ways in which self-images interact with changing material incentives, and to the language and discourse through which these understandings are expressed; second, that it matters how actors interpret the world and how their understandings of 'where they belong' are formed; and third, that both interests and identities are shaped by particular histories and cultures, by domestic factors, and by ongoing processes of interaction with other states.

Instead of focusing solely on material incentives, constructivists emphasize the importance of shared knowledge, learning, ideational forces, and normative and institutional structures. They claim that understanding intersubjective structures allows us to trace the ways in which interests and identities change over time and new forms of co-operation and community can emerge. As Wendt puts it: 'Constructivists are interested in the construction of identities and interests, and, as such, take a more sociological than economic approach to systemic theory. On this basis, they have argued that states are not structurally or exogenously given but constructed by historically contingent inter-

---

[44] For a discussion of the weaknesses of Deutsch's views and the contemporary relevance of the concept of 'security community', see Emanuel Adler and Michael Barnett, 'Pluralistic Security Communities: Past, Present and Future', *Working Paper Series on Regional Security*, 1 (University of Wisconsin, 1994).

actions.'[45] To their neo-realist and rationalist critics, however, they overestimate the importance of regional identities and the discourse of regions and region-building. Instead neo-realists repeatedly point out that violent conflict has often occurred within highly integrated communities sharing values and beliefs (not least as part of civil wars), and highlight the malleability of identity and the fluidity of regionalist rhetoric.

The revival of interest in such approaches reflects a strong belief that the constant and confused eddying of contemporary claims to identity has become more important and more contentious. Thus the present difficulties facing regionalism in Europe need to be set against the erosion of the apparently solid and durable myths around which the EC was born and developed.[46] In Europe, the Americas, and Asia, the politics of regionalism may be complicated by the existence of different *national* conceptions of the region, and there may be deep conflicts over the geographical scope of the region and the values which it is held to represent.[47]

(c) Domestic-level theories

A third cluster of theories focuses on the role of shared domestic attributes or characteristics. Such an emphasis is not new. Those seeking to define regions have often highlighted the importance of commonalities of ethnicity, race, language, religion, culture, history, and consciousness of a common heritage. Writers such as Karl Deutsch stressed the importance of 'the compatibility of major values relevant to political decision-making' in the emergence of security communities. Neo-functionalists believed that the dynamics of the 'spillover' depended on certain domestic prerequisites, above all the pluralist nature of modern industrialized societies and the particular role played by élites in redefining

---

[45] Wendt, 'Collective Identity Formation', 385. As this quotation indicates, constructivism can be seen as a systemic theory. Whilst perceptions of a non-regional 'other' can indeed reinforce regional identity, it is constructivism's analysis of strategic interaction and cognitive interdependence within the region that is most relevant for our purposes.

[46] See Tony Judt, 'The Past is Another Country: Myth and Memory in Postwar Europe', Daedalus, 121/4 (Fall 1992).

[47] Ole Waever, 'Three Competing Europes: German, French and Russian', *International Affairs*, 66/3 (1990), and 'Territory, Authority and Identity', Paper for EUPRA Conference on European Identity, Florence, 8–10 Nov. 1991.

interests on a broader than national basis. There are three ways in which domestic factors can be related to contemporary regionalism.

1. *Regionalism and state coherence.* Regionalism is often seen as an alternative to the state or as a means of going 'beyond the nation state', and it has been common (and perhaps rather too easy) for regional enthusiasts in Europe to talk about the end of sovereignty or the unimportance of national frontiers (conveniently forgetting the case of Yugoslavia and the Balkans). Yet the possibilities of regional co-operation and integration are likely to depend very heavily on the coherence and viability of the states and state structures within a given region. It is becoming a truism that many of the most serious problems of the post-Cold War world result not from the lack legitimacy between states, but from the still greater lack of legitimacy within them. In many parts of the post-colonial world political instability, civil war, economic mismanagement, and environmental degradation interact to undermine the cohesion of state structures, to erode the economic base and social fabric of many weak states, and to produce a deadly downward spiral leading towards disintegration and anarchy.

The absence of viable states (both in terms of effective state apparatuses and mutually accepted territorial boundaries) makes the process of region-building difficult, if not impossible. If the state collapses it is all too likely that the warlords and the drug barons will move in. These problems already stand as major obstacles to the development of effective regionalism in parts of Africa and South Asia; and, as Charles Tripp's chapter argues, the instability of regimes, their intolerance of all opposition, and the erosion of projects of state-dominated economic development work powerfully to undermine sustained interstate co-operation in the Middle East. It is, therefore, no coincidence that the most elaborate examples of regionalism (the EC, NAFTA, ASEAN, *Mercosur*) have occurred in regions where state structures remain *relatively* strong and where the legitimacy of both frontiers and regimes is not widely called into question (although territorial disputes might continue to exist). Whilst regionalism may over time lead to the creation of new forms of political organization, regionalism and state strength do not stand in opposition to each other and states remain the essential building-blocks with which regionalist arrangements are constructed.

2. *Regime type and democratization.* A great deal of theoretical attention has been devoted over the past few years to reevaluating the importance of domestic factors and the impact of democracy and democratization. This has formed part of the broader attack on neo-realism and its emphasis on the overriding importance of systemic pressures and dynamics. Substantial theoretical momentum has developed around the proposition that democracy does indeed make a fundamental difference and, in particular, that democracies do not go to war with each other.[48] Much of this work is concerned with general propositions about the behaviour of liberal states. Equally many would seek to identify 'liberal zones' that cross geographical regions (the North Atlantic area in Deutsch's classic study, or Daniel Deudney and John Ikenberry's picture of continued co-operation across the OECD world, or Anne-Marie Burley's analysis of legal dynamics of liberal zones).[49] Nevertheless, the possible existence of *regional pacific unions* is clearly of major potential importance for understanding the dynamics of contemporary regionalism. Indeed, as Raymond Cohen argues, the robustness of the link between democracy and peace within regional clusters of states that have historically been willing and able to fight each other is central to assessing the overall theory.[50]

The importance of democracy was easy to overlook in the early phases of the European community. Whilst the commitment to multiparty democracy was an explicit feature of the Treaty of Rome, the success of democratization in West Germany and Italy meant that the founding fathers could accept a common commit-

---

[48] The literature is expanding very rapidly. But see esp. Melvin Small and J. David Singer, 'The War Process of Democratic Regimes', *The Jerusalem Journal of International Relations*, 1 (1976); R. J. Rummel, 'Libertarian Propositions on Violence within and between Nations', *Journal of Conflict Resolution*, 29 (1985); Michael W. Doyle, 'Kant, Liberal Legacies, and Foreign Affairs', *Philosophy and Public Affairs* 12/3 and 4 (1983); Zeev Maoz and Bruce Russett, 'Normative and Structural Causes of Democratic Peace, 1946–1986', *American Political Science Review*, 87 (1993); and Bruce Russett, *Grasping the Democratic Peace* (Princeton: Princeton UP, 1993).

[49] Deutsch, *Political Community in the North Atlantic Area*; Daniel Deudney and G. John Ikenberry, 'The Logic of the West', *World Policy Journal*, 10/4 (Winter 1993/4); Anne-Marie Burley, 'Law among Liberal States: Liberal Internationalism and the Act of State Doctrine', *Columbia Law Review*, 92 (Dec. 1992).

[50] Raymond Cohen, 'Pacific Unions: A Reappraisal of the Theory that 'Democracies do not Go to War with Each Other', *Review of International Studies*, 20/3 (July 1994).

ment to democracy as given, and theorists could relegate pluralist democracy as a background factor. However, this situation was not to last and each round of enlargement has made the difficult issue of the political criteria for admission ever more pressing.[51] In part these questions have to do with confidence in the processes of democratic consolidation in the would-be member states. In part they have to do with more diffuse, volatile, but very powerful questions of boundaries (who is European?) and of identity (what is it to be European?).[52] Such questions also suggest the need to reassess the degree to which the past success of economic integration depended upon the subregional character of the Community and on the existence of common democratic institutions, common culture, and common history.

As the previous chapter discussed, there are certainly cases where the wave of democratic transitions that swept the world in the 1980s can be plausibly implicated in the revival of regionalism. Moves towards subregional co-operation in South America occurred against the background of a region-wide shift away from military and bureaucratic-authoritarian regimes. Yet it is also clear that the relationship between regionalism and democracy is complex. Thus even in cases where democratization did play a role, its relative weight needs to be assessed with some precision and on the basis of more detailed studies than have yet been undertaken. In Latin America, for example, the consistent relatively pacific character of interstate relations in this century cannot be easily related to the often extremely illiberal and violent character of many of the domestic regimes that have governed in this same period. Moreover, as Chapter 9 argues, there are numerous other factors that have been important in the revival of subregional co-operation. Equally, there are other important examples of contemporary regionalism in which democracy has clearly not played a major direct

---

[51] For a comparative treatment of this issue, see Laurence Whitehead, 'Requisites for Admission', in Peter H. Smith (ed.), *The Challenge of Integration: Europe and the Americas* (New Brunswick, NJ: Transaction Publishers, 1992).

[52] They also reinforce and complicate a problem that has become increasingly central to the European debate but remains marginal elsewhere, namely the question of democracy and legitimacy within the the EC itself. Liberal theorists of integration (indeed liberal economic thought more generally) had a deeply apolitical view of what integration involved. From the perspective of the early 1990s, however, it is clear that any theory of integration has to pay far greater attention to the relationship between the institutions by which states have sought to manage interdependence and issues of representation, accountability, and political legitimacy.

role—for example, the creation of NAFTA in which the limitations of political democracy in Mexico have threatened to become an obstacle to integration; or the case of ASEAN, in which increased regional interaction and institutional deepening in both the security and economic spheres has occurred despite the fact that only one ASEAN member can be considered democratic and despite the explicit rejection of Western-style liberalism and democracy.[53] Unravelling the complexity of these connections will involve paying more attention to a number of difficult issues: the precise meaning of 'liberal democracy', 'liberal regimes', and the ways in which different components of democracy might contribute in different ways to the creation and maintenance of a democratic peace; whether it is political democracy *per se* that contributes to regional peace or whether analysis should concentrate on underlying factors or prerequisites that sustain *both* democratic forms of government *and* pacific foreign policies; the relationship between *processes of democratization* and regional peace (as opposed to the emphasis in the existing literature on the behaviour of fully consolidated democracies); and the relationship between democratization and forms of social violence and instability that fall short of formal interstate war. Yet, however these issues are resolved, the links between democratization and regionalism are likely to remain of great theoretical and practical interest.

3. *Convergence theories.* Convergence theories understand the dynamics of regional co-operation and especially regional economic integration in terms of converging domestic policy preferences among regional states. Thus revisionist writings on the European Community have emphasized the extent to which the political mythology of European integration was deeply misleading. It was not pursued as part of a grand project of moving 'beyond the nation state', but rather as the best means of sheltering or protecting a particular domestic project built around Keynesian economics, social welfare, and corporatist social arrangements. Integration therefore emerged from the pursuit of quite narrowly focused national policies and parochial rather than internationalist visions and could result in a strengthening, not a weakening in the role of

---

[53] In both cases, however, domestic factors may still play an important role: changes in societal values and attitudes towards the USA in the case of Mexico; increased awareness of common social, economic, and political values in the case of ASEAN.

the state.[54] Similarly, the revival of integrationist momentum in the mid-1980s can be seen in terms of the convergence of national economic policy preferences, centred around economic liberalization and deregulation.[55]

Domestic policy convergence has undoubtedly been an important factor in the resurgence of regionalism, especially the widespread shift in the developing world towards market-liberal policies that stress trade liberalization and export expansion. Moreover, in some cases, regional integration becomes a way of consolidating market-liberal policies. Thus, for example, the importance of NAFTA does not rest on trade liberalization (much of which had already taken place) but on the ways in which the treaty locks Mexico into the particular set of domestic economic policies and insulates its economic reforms from future domestic political interference. The confidence created by this 'locking in' is central to the economic expectations (securing continuing flows of foreign capital), but is also intended to cement the political power of those groups that have benefited from reform.

3. CONCLUSION   *regionalism heavily tied to roots of IR*

This chapter has argued that debates over the revival of regionalism are deeply connected with the broader theoretical debates that have dominated International Relations and that much is to be gained by exposing and exploring the nature of these connections. It has also argued that the theories of regional integration that have dominated the analysis of the EC provide only a partial and incomplete guide to understanding contemporary regionalism. It has analysed three separate clusters of theories on three levels of analysis: the systemic, the regional, and the domestic. Yet, again as in International Relations more generally, a great deal hangs on how these levels are to be related to each other. There are three broad strategies.[56]

[54] As Alan Milward writes: '[D]omestic policy was not in the end sustainable unless this neo-mercantilism could be guaranteed by its Europeanization'; *The European Rescue of the Nation-State* (London: Routledge, 1992), 134.
[55] See Hix, 'Approaches to the Study of the EC', 7–8.
[56] For relevant discussions of the 'levels of analysis' problem, see R. B. J. Walker, *Inside/Outside: International Relations as Political Theory* (Cambridge: Cambridge UP, 1993), esp. 130–40; and Andrew Moravcsik, 'Introduction. Integrating Inter-

In the first place, the theorist can claim that primacy should be given to one level of analysis. Neo-realists, for example, argue for the primacy of the international political system. Their claim is not that systemic or structural theory can explain everything, but that, as Kenneth Waltz argues, it explains a small number of big and important things.[57] Other theories can be left to fill in the rest of the picture, to explain 'residual variance'. Similarly institutionalist theory focuses on intra-regional interactions, downplaying the importance of both domestic-level factors and the geopolitical context. Much is to be gained from such bold claims to primacy, particularly when theory is used to map the political landscape, to raise important questions about individual regionalist schemes, and to illuminate historical developments. But there are two difficulties. First, it is far from clear that even the main lines of any historical example of regionalism can be plausibly understood by focusing on a single level of analysis. And second, as Andrew Moravscik argues, assumptions about other levels of analysis are often smuggled in surreptitiously and then modified to explain anomalies in the theory.[58]

A second path is therefore to explore the nature of the interaction between the different logics that we see at work in contemporary regionalism. Thus constructivism provides a theoretically rich and promising way of conceptualizing the interaction between material incentives, inter-subjective structures, and the identity and interests of the actors (although there remains a considerable gap between conceptual sophistication and empirical application). Liberal theorists are increasingly seeking to link institutionalist ideas about interstate co-operation with domestically rooted theories of preference formation.[59] And finally much greater attention needs to be

national and Domestic Theories of International Bargaining', in Peter B. Evans, Harold K. Jacobsen, and Robert D. Putnam (eds.), *Double-Edged Diplomacy* (Berkeley and Los Angeles: University of California Press, 1993).

[57] See Kenneth Waltz, 'A Response to my Critics', in Robert O. Keohane (ed.), *Neorealism and its Critics* (New York: Columbia UP, 1986), 329.

[58] Moravscik, 'Introduction', 6–17. A good example is Stephen Walt's modification of neo-realist alliance theory, noted earlier (see n. 26). His argument that states seek to balance against threats and perceived intentions, rather than unequal power is certainly plausible. However, enquiring into such perceptions leads unavoidably to an analysis of domestic-level political and cognitive factors, thereby vitiating the much vaunted parsimony of neo-realist theory.

[59] For an important move in this direction see Moravscik, 'Preferences and Power'.

given to the tradition of dependency and radical political economy which has long stressed the need to unpack the 'state' and to examine the changing domestic political coalitions and 'state–society complexes' on which many examples of the new regionalism have come to rely.

Thirdly, one can adopt a phased or 'stage-theory' approach to understanding regionalism. Although theoretically somewhat unsatisfying, it is historically often very plausible. Thus, it might be argued that the early phases of regional co-operation may be the result of the existence of a common enemy or powerful hegemonic power; but that having been thrown together, different logics begin to develop: the functionalist or problem-solving logic stressed by institutionalists; or the logic of community highlighted by the constructivists. Thus, neo-realists may be right to stress the importance of the geopolitical context in the early stages of European unity, and yet wrong in ignoring the degree to which both informal integration and successful institutionalization altered the dynamics of European international relations over the following forty years. This kind of 'staged' approach has a great deal to offer in sharpening our understanding of the moves towards economic integration in the case of NAFTA, of the evolving pattern of co-operation within ASEAN, or of the growth of subregional co-operation in South America.

4

Regionalism, Globalization, and World Economic Order

Andrew Wyatt-Walter

THERE are two, apparently contradictory, metaphors which pervade contemporary commentary on the nature and trajectory of the world political economy. First, there is the view of the world economy as increasingly defined by three macro-regions or blocs which are largely self-sufficient (though marked by high levels of intra-regional interdependence) and increasingly competitive or even 'warring'. Second, there is a more benign but equally powerful and popular metaphor of the 'globalization' of economic activity. This presents a picture of a world in which economic agents, particularly transnational firms, are increasingly indifferent to political boundaries, competing in 'global markets' and satisfying the demands of consumers whose tastes are increasingly homogeneous.

The regionalization metaphor is one in which politics predominates over economics, in which 'Europe', 'North America', and 'East Asia' battle for economic and ultimately geopolitical predominance.[1] In contrast, the globalization metaphor is one in which rational economics triumphs over the irrational, old-fashioned, international politics of the struggle for power. Both views are founded upon the presumption that the world political economy after the Second World War was characterized by a hierarchical, statist structure founded upon American hegemony, though each differs fundamentally in its view of the structure which is replacing this hegemonic order. The regionalization metaphor implies that

I would like to thank Andrew Hurrell and Bryce Harland for comments on an earlier version of this chapter.

[1] See Lester Thurow, *Head to Head: The Coming Economic Battle among Japan, Europe and America* (London: Nicholas Brealey, 1992), and Jeffrey A. Hart, *Rival Capitalists: International Competitiveness in the United States, Japan, and Western Europe* (Ithaca, NY: Cornell UP, 1992).

the balance of forces in the world political economy is shifting away from 'multilateralism', underpinned by a global American hegemony, towards a system based upon competing regional blocs, each dominated by a regional hegemon. Globalization implies that there is a general shift underway which has favoured markets and firms rather than states, and that the hegemony of one or a few states is unlikely to constitute an adequate basis for world economic order.

Given the wealth of data that is used to support each of these metaphors, it is increasingly difficult to discern which of them, regionalization or globalization, better describes our present situation. According to the GATT, 52 per cent of world trade in 1990 was intra-regional, or within trading blocs.[2] In the United Nation's *World Economic Survey 1991*, it is argued that:

> The most noteworthy example of this trend is to be found in the trade pattern of the European Community. Intra-trade between Canada, Mexico and the United States is greater than this area's exports to any other region and the intra-trade of the Asia-Pacific area is at least as large as its interregional flows. Today the question is not whether these blocs will be formed, but rather how encompassing they will be and how to ensure that they will not harm the trading system.[3]

In contrast, the UN's *World Investment Report 1992* suggests that the increasingly central role of transnational firms in the world economy necessitates that we do away with our state-centric understanding of the world economy.[4] The globalization metaphor differs fundamentally from the regional one in suggesting that political geography, far from becoming more important in the structure of the world economy, is gradually being eroded as transnational firms and a global market-place increasingly operate irrespective of national boundaries. As Kenichi Ohmae writes:

> The nation state has become an unnatural, even dysfunctional, unit for organizing human activity and managing economic endeavor in a borderless world. It represents no genuine, shared community of economic interest; it defines no meaningful flows of economic activity.[5]

[2] GATT, *International Trade 90–91*, vol. ii (Geneva: GATT, 1992), 8.
[3] United Nations, *World Economic Survey 1991* (New York: UN, 1991), 60.
[4] United Nations, *World Investment Report 1992* (New York: UN, 1992), 6.
[5] Kenichi Ohmae, 'The Rise of the Region State', *Foreign Affairs*, 72/2 (Spring 1993), 78. For further examples of the globalization literature, see his *The Borderless World: Power and Strategy in the Interlinked Economy* (London:

Good metaphors are aids to the understanding of a reality which is always complex and untidy.[6] The metaphors of globalization and regionalization usefully point to certain forces at work in the contemporary world political economy. In important respects, however, as this chapter will argue, they are misleading as representations of a broader reality. On the one hand, the regionalization literature focuses excessively upon the supposed regionalization of international trade, overlooking the growing dominance of short- and long-term international capital movements over trade flows and the ways in which this has reinforced economic interdependence between regions more than within them. On the other hand, the globalization literature focuses largely upon firms and the way in which they structure economic relationships, including trade and technology flows, in responding to market demand. As a result, this literature often underplays the various ways in which the existence of political boundaries influences the flows of economic activity.

Second, both regionalization and globalization are slippery and imprecise concepts, reducing their value as metaphors. For example, writers in the globalization school such as Ohmae do not always reject regionalist forces out of hand, but rather tend to focus on the way in which natural, global-orientated, economic micro-regions rather than the big three macro-regions are emerging. Examples of these economic micro-regions include Baden-Württemberg, Silicon Valley, Hong Kong and Southern China, and the 'growth triangle' between Singapore, Jahore, and Indonesia, areas which may or may not fall within the boundaries of existing nation states.[7] As for globalization, the notion of an all-encompassing process is contradicted by the fact that of the 25 per cent of world investment flows which go to the developing world, fully two-thirds goes to just ten developing countries.[8] A large proportion of the world's population remains more or less untouched by the forces of globalization said to characterize our time.

Evid

Where you live still matters

Fontana, 1992); OECD, *Globalisation of Industrial Activities* (Paris: OECD, 1992); Richard O'Brien, *Global Financial Integration: The End of Geography* (London: RIIA/Pinter, 1992).

[6] On the use of metaphors in economics and the social sciences in general, see Donald N. McCloskey, *The Rhetoric of Economics* (Madison: University of Wisconsin Press, 1986).

[7] Ohmae, 'Rise of the Region State', 79–81.

[8] UN, *World Investment Report 1992*, 2.

Third, this chapter will argue that while regionalizing and globalizing tendencies are both at work in the contemporary world, these tendencies are at present more symbiotic than contradictory. In many ways, the protectionism and macro-regional posturing that is clearly visible in recent times is a response, if inadequate, to many of the changes underway in the world economy associated with globalization. Regionalism increases the necessity for large firms to become 'insiders' in other regions, promoting globalization. In turn, increased foreign competition across a broad range of industries has prompted the USA and EC to pursue regional alternatives in an effort to alleviate problems of adjustment and to promote non-economic regional objectives. The biggest and most important change has been in US policy. For the first time since the Second World War, the USA is actively pursuing its own regional policy, rather than playing its traditional post-war role of ensuring that the regionalism of others, particularly Europe's, remains reasonably compatible with multilateralism in international economic relations. Whether this shift in US policy will tilt the balance dramatically towards regionalism in a manner not seen since the 1930s will be discussed in the final section.

The structure of this chapter is as follows. First, in keeping with the broader theme of this book, I will consider what the concepts of 'economic regionalism' and 'economic regionalization' might mean. Second, I will briefly outline what I consider to be the main factors behind the new economic regionalism. Third, I will discuss whether the world economy is in fact becoming more regionalized, or whether the concept of globalization is a more adequate description of the changes underway. Finally, I will consider the impact of these changes upon the management and stability of the world economy.

1. 'ECONOMIC REGIONALISM' AND 'ECONOMIC REGIONALIZATION'

A basic distinction that needs to be made is between economic regionalism as a *conscious policy* of states or sub-state regions to co-ordinate activities and arrangements in a greater region, and economic regionalization as the *outcome* of such policies or of 'natural' economic forces.

The most common definitions of economic regionalism focus attention on the formation of preferential trading arrangements between groups of countries within a geographic region. Such arrangements are commonly termed 'trading blocs'.[9] However, in principle, economic regionalism extends from goods and market integration between neighbours (in the form of preferential trade areas, free-trade areas, and customs unions) to goods and factor market integration (common markets), to market and policy integration (economic and monetary unions), to complete economic (and political) union.[10] The working definition of economic regionalism I will use here is *the design and implementation of a set of preferential policies within a regional grouping of countries aimed at the encouragement of the exchange of goods and/or factors between members of the group.* The goals at which such arrangements aim will vary. Also left ambiguous is the extent to which such groups are intended to provide definition to the economic relations of members with third countries. Where regional arrangements provide for the development of common policy tools such as common external tariffs, monetary union, and so on, the possibility of acting as a unified whole in international economic relations becomes a possibility.

Although economic regionalism is by definition discriminatory *vis-à-vis* the rest of the world and hence opposed to the principle of non-discrimination which is the basis of multilateralism, *malign* and *benign* forms of regionalism are commonly distinguished (even if the distinction may depend upon the eye of the beholder). Benign regionalism might be defined as regional arrangements which, in the process of the voluntary swapping of mutual preferences between the group's members, do not at the same time increase barriers to economic exchange with the outside world. The basic point is that the intent is not consciously to reduce the welfare of outsiders (or indeed insiders). Malign regionalism is often associ-

---

[9] e.g. Jeffrey J. Schott, in his 'Trading Blocs and the World Trading System', *The World Economy*, 14/1, (Mar. 1991), 1–2, defines a trading bloc as 'an association of countries that reduces intra-regional barriers to trade in goods (and sometimes in services, investment and capital as well) . . . seek[ing] to (1) generate welfare gains through income and efficiency effects and trade creation; (2) augment negotiating leverage with third countries; and (3) sometimes promote regional political co-operation.'

[10] The classic work in this field is Bela Balassa, *The Theory of Economic Integration* (London: Allen & Unwin, 1961).

Malign
+
Benign

ated with the policies of Germany and Japan in the 1930s of forcing bilateral economic agreements upon weaker countries in order to establish a discriminatory trade and financing network in which they would dominate. However, there is no reason why malign regionalism should involve involuntary behaviour, since, if a large trading group were to raise tariffs *vis-à-vis* the outside world at the same time as reducing barriers to internal trade so as to exploit their increased market power, we would presumably also want to call this malign regionalism. Malign regionalism may be a consciously beggar-thy-*non*-neighbour policy amongst a group of countries within a geographic region.

Tolerance and even support for benign regionalism was an important part of the post-war international economic order. Although Article I of the GATT established the principle that member states should accord unconditional most-favoured nation status (i.e. non-discrimination) upon all other members, the founders of the GATT went so far as to build regionalism into the post-war rules on international trade in the form of Article XXIV. In part because of the example of apparently benign customs unions like Benelux (negotiated in 1944), it was felt that customs unions and free trade areas (FTAs) ought to be an exception to the general principle of non-discrimination, recognizing 'the desirability of increasing freedom of trade by the development, through voluntary agreements, of closer integration between the economies of the countries parties to such agreements'. Article XXIV contained clauses that were meant to ensure that GATT-sanctioned regionalism was of a benign rather than malign form. Customs and free-trade areas should be completed 'within a reasonable length of time', should cover 'substantially all the trade' between the parties, and should not raise barriers to the trade of non-members.[11]

Regionalism in the Western world economy was entrenched in practice by American support of the first moves towards Western European integration. After US attempts to establish the Bretton Woods system in the early post-war years failed, the USA promoted a solution more in keeping with its security objective of anchoring

[11] See John H. Jackson, *The World Trading System: Law and Policy of International Relations* (Cambridge, Mass.: MIT Press, 1989), 141, and Jagdish N. Bhagwati, 'Regionalism versus Multilateralism', *The World Economy*, 15/5 (Sept. 1992), 535–55. Article XXIV 3(*a*) also noted that 'Advantages accorded by any contracting party to adjacent countries in order to facilitate frontier traffic' was allowable.

Western Europe in a firmly anti-Soviet alliance. The European Payments Union (EPU) and the European Coal and Steel Community (ECSC), both established at the beginning of the 1950s, represented the first major steps on the road towards regional integration. Although EPU was necessarily portrayed to American critics as a 'stepping-stone' towards the return of the European currencies to full convertibility rather than an abandonment of Bretton Woods, the ECSC clearly represented permanent discrimination, and the US supported a GATT waiver in the face of substantial criticisms by European non-members.[12]

Economists have usually been less enamoured of regional economic agreements than foreign policy makers. This is particularly true of regional trading arrangements, where economists have tended to see regional trading blocs as, at most, a second-best alternative to world-wide, multilateral trade liberalization. Some staunch supporters of multilateralism see Article XXIV as having allowed the entry of the beast of regionalism into the temple of multilateralism.[13] In terms of economic theory, the question of what is benign (welfare-increasing) and what is malign (welfare-decreasing) is less straightforward than in the common-sense formulation outlined above. The theory of customs unions and FTAs which emerged in the 1950s began from the point that since customs unions involved both reduced protection (within the group) and increased relative protection (towards non-members), it was not clear that a presumption that this would be welfare-enhancing was justified. The seminal work in this field was Jacob Viner's *The Customs Union Issue*, which established that the desirability of customs unions or FTAs depended on the circumstances.[14]

Further work suggested that much depended upon whether the countries involved in a preferential economic grouping were 'natural' trading partners, due to complementarity of production structures and a large share of world trade.[15] In such a case, *trade creation* might be significant, whereby a reduction in intra-union tariffs increases efficiency and growth as demand shifts from less

---

[12] Gardner Patterson, *Discrimination in International Trade: The Policy Issues 1945–1965* (Princeton: Princeton UP, 1966), 75–90.

[13] Kenneth W. Dam, *The GATT: Law and International Organization* (Chicago: University of Chicago Press, 1970), 290.

[14] Jacob Viner, *The Customs Union Issue* (London: Stevens & Sons, 1950).

[15] See Willem Molle, *The Economics of European Integration* (Aldershot: Dartmouth 1990), ch. 5.

efficient domestic production towards more efficient partner-country production. A customs union or FTA was also more likely to increase global welfare if initial levels of protection between partner countries were high, and subsequent levels of protection *vis-à-vis* the outside world were low. On the other hand, *trade diversion* could also occur whereby the increase in relative protection *vis-à-vis* the rest of the world was sufficient to shift demand away from imports from efficient third countries to imports from a less efficient partner country. Whether such arrangements would raise or lower overall world welfare would depend upon the balance of these two effects. The subsequent literature built on the distinction between trade creation and diversion, although the consensus remained that trading blocs were a second-best option, with the ideal bloc being the whole world since there would be no scope for trade diversion.

The issue of whether economists should favour higher forms of regional monetary and policy integration was less clear-cut. As Cooper has noted, economic theory has been able to say relatively little about the size of the 'optimal geographic area' of policy jurisdiction.[16] Arguments were made that externalities and economies of scale meant that optimal jurisdictional areas are greater than the borders of existing countries for some public goods, though the likelihood of significant diseconomies of scale after some point suggested that the optimal area was likely to be smaller than the world economy. Much would depend upon the particular area of policy; the optimal jurisdiction for policing or environmental policy may be very different from that for monetary policy, for example. To take the example of monetary union, states within a geographic region might form an 'optimal currency area' if they have similar economic structures (and hence are less likely to suffer asymmetrical economic shocks), and if they enjoy a high degree of intra-area factor mobility (and hence are more able to adjust to asymmetrical shocks if they occur).[17]

There are also some political economy reasons why regional

[16] Richard N. Cooper, 'Worldwide Regional Integration: Is there an Optimal Size of the Integrated Area?', in *Economic Policy in an Interdependent World* (Cambridge, Mass.: MIT Press, 1986), 123–37.
[17] It is arguable that the EMS countries perform better on the first criterion than the USA, though less well on the second. It has been argued, however, that economic diversity can actually favour monetary union, as shocks are neutralized as they hurt one part of the region while favouring others.

arrangements might be more optimal for some purposes. First, the interaction of history and geography may favour the emergence of regional cultural, economic, legal, and political commonalities, which may help neighbouring countries to reach agreement over difficult issues, particularly those related to regulation and the distribution of costs and benefits. There may also be a history of co-operation on non-economic issues which could facilitate the emergence of regional economic institutions, and redistribution mechanisms to compensate losers. Security factors may also play a major role in underpinning regional co-operation; certainly, in the presence of severe security dilemmas, regional economic relations are likely to be very uncooperative. It might also be argued, against the grain of a discipline that has become used to the notion that co-operation in international relations tends to derive from hegemony, that large inequalities in the power and economic weight of countries in a region may not favour *regional* economic co-opera-tion. Smaller states may be concerned that economic integration will lead to loss of sovereignty and identity, and they may be more likely to pool sovereignty if they are not concerned about the potential for the dominance of one particular country within the bloc (although fear of the dominance of a non-member may pro-vide an incentive towards integration).

Second, since distributional issues are likely to be more acute the larger the difference in income levels between countries, the fact that the pattern of global wealth tends to have a strong regional bias may mean that regional groupings are less likely to suffer from such problems. Third, transportation and communications costs are significant, which over time leads to the emergence of important complementarity of economic structure amongst neighbours, and which give important natural advantages to neighbours as trading partners. Fourth, as Kenneth Oye points out, regional agreements might mobilize domestic interest groups which favour open trade, creating a momentum towards inter-regional or multilateral liberalization.[18]

There is a final consideration. We have been discussing regional-ism as public policy, working through a legal or institutional frame-work within a regional grouping. As noted earlier, this must be distinguished from the idea of the *regionalization of markets*, some-

[18] Kenneth A. Oye, *Economic Discrimination and Political Exchange* (Princeton: Princeton UP, 1992).

thing which may result from regional policies but which may also have no necessary connection to government policies. The spatial aspects of market activity *within* a country such as the USA, for example, could be said to have an identifiable regional pattern. The mid-West specializes in agricultural products, California in high technology, entertainment, and defence, the North-East in manufacturing and finance, and so on. While such regional specialization is affected by the location of different layers of government and by various government policies, much is due to natural forces such as transportation and communication costs, historical accident, externalities, and economies of scale.[19] Furthermore, as Ohmae suggests, there is no necessary reason why such regional patterns should coincide with existing international borders. Therefore, it is important to note that while regionalism as a policy might be said to aim at encouraging the regionalization of economic activity, natural market regions might exist even in the absence of such policies. This point will be taken up in Section 3.

2. WHAT EXPLAINS THE NEW REGIONALISM?

Since the mid-1980s, economic regionalism has made a come-back after a long period of retreat since the late 1960s. Its initial manifestations were in the North, with the beginning of negotiations on an FTA between the USA and Canada in 1986 and the passing of the Single European Act in the same year. It then spread out to the developing world, with the reinvigoration of long-stagnant regional economic schemes in Latin America and Africa. The momentum continued in the North, with the prospective eastward and northward widening of the EC and the creation of a European Economic Area (EEA) with EFTA, and the extension of the Canada–USA FTA (CUSFTA) to Mexico to create NAFTA. Finally, after a long period of dormancy, the stirrings of an Asia-Pacific economic regionalism began to be heard, largely in reaction to developments elsewhere.

It is tempting to see this new phase of economic regionalism as representing a fundamental shift in the world political economy that has deep underlying causes. However, some argue that the

---

[19] For an interesting development of the spatial aspects of international and interregional trade and specialization, see Paul R. Krugman, *Geography and Trade* (Leuven and Cambridge, Mass.: Leuven University Press/MIT Press, 1991).

use for paper

appearance of a new phase is little more than coincidence. For example, Ostry has argued that 'The [US–Canadian] FTA and Europe 1992 are very different in both genesis and nature. Indeed, their coincidence in timing is accidental, not planned.'[20] While Ostry accepts that 'coincidence' could have an important cumulative impact on the shape of the world economy, this would represent a secondary effect rather than a shift in underlying factors. Are there common factors behind the new regionalism? In order to consider this question, it is first necessary to outline very briefly the main variations of the new economic regionalism. The discussion will be confined largely to Western Europe, the Americas, and Asia Pacific, partly for reasons of space but also because what happens in these regions will be crucial for determining the strength of regionalist forces in the world political economy as a whole.

(a) The Western Hemisphere

1. *North America.* The most novel aspect of regionalism amongst developed countries in the 1980s was the turn to regionalism on the part of two of the staunchest traditional supporters of multilateralism in the West, Canada and the USA. Until the 1980s, regional initiatives by other countries were either tolerated by the USA or, in the case of Europe, promoted for specific (largely political) reasons. The implicit conventional wisdom was that the USA, as the champion of multilateralism and the GATT, ought not itself to indulge in a practice which was widely held to be at odds with the spirit of non-discrimination. Regionalism in an economically and politically 'unviable' Europe was one thing, but regionalism for the free world's superpower was out of the question. For both Canada and Mexico, the political arguments against economic integration with the USA have always been strong, given these countries' concern to protect their cultural and economic independence. Such fears, combined in Canada's case with its self-perception as a middle power supporting multilateralism, helped ensure that since the GATT was established, bilateral initiatives towards the USA were largely eschewed.[21] In the course of the 1980s, the policies of all three countries changed direction.

Evid

[20] Sylvia Ostry, *Governments and Corporations in a Shrinking World* (New York: Council on Foreign Relations, 1990), 12.
[21] The exception was the 1965 automobile pact with the USA.

The origins of a regional policy on the part of the USA lay partly in the debt crisis of the early 1980s, when the USA acted quickly in the Mexican crisis of August 1982 to ensure that a Mexican default did not materialize and thereby jeopardize US financial stability. However, it was the combination of policies which led to the appreciation of the dollar and the associated dramatic deterioration in the US trade deficit in the first half of the 1980s which created a real ground-swell for change in US policy. The pressure upon the Reagan administration to shift course became intense during the summer of 1985, and what emerged was a 'multi-track' policy which combined multilateral with bilateral and unilateral initiatives.[22] The administration continued to push hard for the initiation of a new GATT trade round, but at the same time signalled its intention to utilize 'fair trade' legislation to press for changes in the trade practices of some of its most important partners, above all Japan. Along with such unilateral measures, the USA embarked on a series of bilateral measures which marked a more activist approach to trade policy than in the early 1980s.

In such a climate, the Reagan administration responded favourably to a Canadian proposal for a CUSFTA, using the bilateral, fast-track authorization contained in the 1984 Trade and Tariffs Act that had enabled the negotiation of an FTA with Israel.[23] CUSFTA was concluded in 1988. In 1990, the Bush administration also accepted Mexico's initiative to negotiate a bilateral FTA, leading to negotiations from 1991 which Canada decided to join, and which in summer 1992 led to the NAFTA agreement. Dominated by the USA, NAFTA involves the creation of the world's largest FTA, with a combined GNP of $6.3 trillion and a population of 363 million in 1990.[24] From the US perspective, it was perceived that this might place additional pressure upon the recalcitrant Europeans and East Asians to make trade concessions to the USA which has not so far been forthcoming through the GATT process.

For Canada, a similar shift towards a twin-track policy was essentially a defensive one. Faced with growing US resort to administered protection, particularly in the form of the anti-dumping and

[22] I. M. Destler, *American Trade Politics* (New York: Twentieth Century Fund and Institute for International Economics, 2nd edn., 1992), 124–5.

[23] Destler, *American Trade Politics*, 96.

[24] Nora Lustig, Barry P. Bosworth, and Robert Z. Lawrence (eds.), *North American Free Trade: Assessing the Impact* (Washington, DC: Brookings Institution, 1992), 4.

countervailing duties contained in US fair trade legislation, Canada became increasingly concerned during the 1980s about the ability of GATT to protect the access of its exporters to their major market. Once the USA decided to open talks with Mexico on an FTA, it was inevitable that Canada would ask to join, since a bilateral US–Mexican FTA could undermine some of aspects of the CUSFTA and encourage a migration of footloose, US-orientated manufacturing industry from Canada to low-wage Mexico without any compensation for Canada.

Mexico, like Canada, also wanted to safeguard access to its major market, particularly important because of Mexico's shift towards export-orientation in the later 1980s. In addition, the Salinas government wanted to underline the extent and enhance the credibility of its economic reform programme by attaching itself to a reciprocity-based treaty with its powerful northern neighbour. Mexico's accession to the GATT in 1986 and its Framework Agreement with the USA in 1989 were steps in this direction, but the binding agreement involved in an FTA with the USA would provide a much more credible constraint against the reversal of reforms.[25] Naturally, there were fears in Mexico that free trade (or even significantly liberalized trade) with the USA could lead to major adjustment costs for large sections of Mexico's inefficient industry. However, Mexico's programme of unilateral trade liberalization since the second half of the 1980s had already led to considerable adjustment, so that the economic impact of NAFTA can be exaggerated.[26] The main source of gain to Mexico was expected to be increased foreign direct investment (FDI), due to the consequent attractiveness of Mexico as an export platform.

The recession of the early 1990s reduced support for NAFTA within the USA and Canada, though the Salinas government in Mexico seemed to be more dependent than ever upon the ratification of NAFTA as a key element in its economic strategy. This gave key lobby groups in the USA, particularly organized labour and environmental groups, the ability to insist upon revisions to the

[25] From 1970 to 1990, the share of Mexico's total imports coming from North America increased from 19½ to 45½ per cent (from 51½ to 64 per cent for manufacturing imports), while the share of Mexico's total exports to North America increased from 25 to 52 per cent (GATT, *International Trade 90–91*, 15).

[26] See, in general, Lustig *et al.*, *North American Free Trade*, and John Whalley, 'CUSTA and NAFTA: Can WHFTA be far behind?', *Journal of Common Market Studies*, 30/2 (June 1992), 125–41.

NAFTA. With the electoral success of President Clinton at the end of 1992, and growing concern about the threat of a loss of manufacturing jobs to Mexico as a result of NAFTA, the USA initiated two major 'side-agreements' to NAFTA. Agreements on labour and environmental protection standards were reached in August 1993, including disputes-settlement procedures for the enforcement of such standards.[27] In the end, these were sufficient to reduce the influence of the powerful anti-NAFTA lobbies in the USA and Canada, allowing the final ratification of the agreement by the US congress in December 1993.

The novelty of NAFTA is that this is the first time that fair trade provisions on labour and environmental standards have been built into a regional trade agreement, and may well presage similar future US demands in other forums. NAFTA is also unprecedented because of the extent of the disparities in income between the partners. Unlike the EC, NAFTA has no redistribution mechanism to cope with the adjustment problems of poorer states and intra-regional regions; Mexico clearly understood that this would be unacceptable to the USA and Canada. Given the USA's more important extra-regional interests, and Mexico's and Canada's concerns about loss of sovereignty and identity, it is difficult to agree entirely with Schott that 'the North American trading bloc exhibits most of the basic characteristics of a successful trading bloc.'[28]

2. *Latin America.*   While it might be argued that free-trade agreements with Canada and Mexico were simply responses to requests from neighbours that were difficult to refuse, President Bush's Enterprise for the Americas speech of 22 June 1990, with its vision of Western hemispheric regionalism, underlined the new departure from previous US policy.[29] The USA offered to proceed by negotiating 'framework agreements' to serve as a basis for improved trading and investment relations.[30] Moves towards creating or renewing existing regional economic arrangements in Latin America have been driven by considerations which echo the motivations of Mexico and Canada. In essence, much of Latin

---

[27] See 'Side Deals on Nafta give accord "Bite"', *Financial Times*, 14/15 Aug. 1993, and 'Negotiators End Impasse on American Trade Pact', *International Herald Tribune*, 14/15 Aug. 1993.
[28] Schott, 'Trading Blocs', 8.
[29] For further details, see Chapter 9 below.
[30] By early 1992, 29 such agreements had been signed since 1987, though this included groups like *Mercosur* and extra-regional countries like Singapore.

America has hoped to gain similar benefits from preferential access to the US market as Mexico, but they are driven by the additional concern that any country that is left behind could suffer considerably. The US market absorbs about 40 per cent of Latin America's total exports, but US market-access is particularly crucial for countries like Mexico, Venezuela, and those in the Caribbean and Central American areas. In addition, the Bush initiative gave and added impetus to a flurry of regional activity already underway in the late 1980s, including *Mercosur* and a range of subregional free-trade agreements.[31]

(b) Europe   -> best example of regionalism

Europe was by far the most successful example of economic regionalism in the 1950s and 1960s, largely because it was underpinned by broader, political goals. Even so, it hardly lived up to the strictures of Article XXIV of the GATT, and was mainly confined to trade in goods. Progress towards 'the abolition, as between Member States, of obstacles to freedom of movement of persons, services and capital' [Article 3 (c) of the Treaty of Rome] was very limited. Most of the 'integration' which occurred in the EEC during the 1950s and 1960s came in the form of high rates of growth in intra-industry trade in manufactures. Significant non-tariff barriers (NTBs) to trade remained, often related to government industrial policy, which included the promotion of national champions across a wide range of industries. This prevented a deeper kind of integration from emerging, in particular the development of significant levels of cross-border ownership and control of corporations in Europe. Furthermore, the increase in non-tariff barriers to intra-European trade in the 1970s associated with the economic crisis partly undermined the achievements of the 1960s.

In the mid-1980s, however, the EC embarked upon a new and vigorous phase of integration which did much to raise both hopes and fears of a powerful trend towards renewed regionalism in Europe. The Delors Commission's 1985 White Paper on *Completing the Internal Market* marked the beginning of this new phase, envisaging the removal of remaining barriers to the free movement of goods, services, persons, and capital by the end of 1992. A major

[31] Edward Best, 'Latin American Integration in the 1990s: Redefinition amid Uncertainty', *International Review of Administrative Sciences*, 57 (1991), 611–40.

motivating force was the declining competitiveness of European industry relative to American and Japanese rivals, especially in technology-intensive sectors, with associated problems of high structural unemployment. With the signing of the Single European Act in February 1986, both self-sustaining economic recovery and renewed market integration gradually set in.[32] In addition, what had begun as a deregulatory, supply-side programme eventually created a momentum for 'positive' integration that overturned, for a time, the pessimism of the 1970s and early 1980s.

An effect of the inward orientation of the debate over the Single Market was to raise fears abroad that the Single Market would be complemented by a 'Fortress Europe'; aimed at preventing third countries from enjoying the benefits of liberalization within Europe. Such fears were enhanced by comments made by the then Commissioner for External Affairs, Willy de Clerq, to the effect that foreign firms would not automatically receive the benefits of the liberalizing measures of the 1992 programme *unless* their countries offered 'reciprocal' access for EC firms.[33] While this position was later softened, the damage was done. Soon after, a debate over Economic and Monetary Union (EMU) ensued which led to revived prospects of monetary integration, resulting in the establishment of a timetable for monetary union at the Maastricht summit of December 1991. Meanwhile, the EEA agreement between the EC and EFTA in 1991 reinforced the perception of a solidifying economic bloc encompassing the whole of Western Europe. Events in the East soon led to the signing of Association Agreements between the EC and its eastern neighbours and appeared to hold out the long-term prospect of an even more radical widening of the Community.

However, 1991 proved to be the high point of the latest cycle of European integration, and the recession that set in over 1992–3 brought with it a swathe of major reversals. First, the limited popular support throughout Europe for the Maastricht Treaty, reflected in the débâcles of Danish and French referendums and the divisive debate in the UK, weakened the position of the pro-integ-

[32] Loukas Tsoukalis, *The New European Economy: The Politics and Economics of Integration* (Oxford: OUP, 2nd edn., 1993), ch. 3.
[33] Stephen Woolcock, *Market Access Issues in EC–US Relations* (London: RIIA/ Pinter, 1991), 13–16; Gary Clyde Hufbauer (ed.), *Europe 1992: An American Perspective* (Washington, DC: Brookings Institution, 1990).

ration élites in the Commission and certain governments. Second, the growing inappropriateness of German monetary policy in the wake of reunification as the basis of interest-rate policy in the rest of Europe resulted in an ongoing crisis within the EMS from summer 1992 which culminated in the virtual collapse of the system in July 1993. The *de facto* floating of the French franc within wider 15 per cent bands, in combination with the earlier exit from the system of the Italian lira and pound sterling, underlined the extent of economic divergence within Europe, calling into question the viability of EMU and even the future of Franco-German economic co-operation.[34] The Swiss rejection in a referendum of the EEA agreement only further underlined the extent to which the momentum of the late 1980s and early 1990s had so rapidly dissipated, bringing with it a further period of Euro-pessimism. Whether this increased or decreased the tendencies towards a Fortress Europe, however, was unclear.

(c) Asia Pacific   ⟶ *reaction to Europe*

For those East Asian countries which had concentrated upon exporting to rich Western markets in the post-war period, the sight of revived regionalism in Europe and the Americas, with its perceptible anti-Japanese tones, was a threatening one. This has led to a series of rather confused manœuvrings, some of which point to a regionalist impulse in the Asia-Pacific area. Indeed, some commentators have become fond of referring to 'Asia Pacific' as a coherent economic region which is coming to challenge Western Europe as the major regional grouping in the world economy. For example, Elek has written:[35]

This diverse, but correspondingly complementary group of economies accounts for more than half of world GNP and almost 40 per cent of world trade. Close to 65 per cent of their exports are to each other; this is higher than the corresponding share for the European Community.

[34] The latter received another blow when only months earlier, the German government refused to follow the rest of the EC in retaliating against US restrictions on European firms bidding for telecommunications contracts, citing a German–US treaty which preceded the 1957 Treaty of Rome.
[35] Andrew Elek, 'Trade Policy Options for the Asia-Pacific Region in the 1990s: The Potential of Open Regionalism', *American Economic Review, Papers and Proceedings*, 82/2 (May 1992).

Such an impression, however, can be highly misleading.[36] Given the size of the Pacific and the undoubted dynamism of the economies which surround it, it is hardly surprising that the region accounts for such large proportions of world trade and output. Also, effective economic regionalism in the area has been almost completely absent in the post-war period, a legacy of Japanese imperialism before and during the Second World War and the continuing security problems which the region faces. Only ASEAN attempted to create a preferential trading arrangement after 1967, but this turned out to be totally ineffective.[37] The very success of Japan, the NICs, and even mainland China in penetrating markets in North America and Western Europe gives these countries an overwhelming interest in the multilateral trading system from which they have benefited. Their vulnerability to developments in Europe and North America has prompted a serious debate about how they ought to respond.

Unsurprisingly, recent calls for an East Asian economic bloc of substance have attracted little firm support. In the wake of the December 1990 breakdown of the Uruguay Round negotiations and moves towards regionalism in Europe and North America, Malaysia called for the establishment of an economic bloc in the form of an East Asian Economic Caucus, to include Japan but not the USA, Canada, Australia, or New Zealand. However, US hostility to the idea has made it difficult for important countries in the region to support the EAEC. The USA has also held out the possibility of reaching bilateral FTAs with particular countries in East Asia and Australasia. As a result, the most that has been possible is a joint Australia–Japan initiative to create the all-inclusive Asia-Pacific Economic Council (APEC) in 1989, which has confined itself to declarations of support for the GATT, for a continuing US–Japanese dialogue on trade problems, and the sharing of information across a wide range of areas. This initiative received a boost in November 1993 when President Clinton affirmed his commitment to the APEC process at the Seattle APEC summit.

Hopes for an equivalent of the OECD for the Pacific (OPTAD) or a Pacific FTA (PAFTA) have not materialized. At a high-profile

---

[36] On this theme, see Gerald Segal, *Rethinking the Pacific* (Oxford: OUP, 1991), esp. 'Conclusions', 369–91, and Rosemary Foot's chapter in this volume.

[37] Marcus Noland, *Pacific Basin Developing Countries: Prospects for the Future* (Washington, DC: Institute for International Economics, 1990), 140–1.

regional conference in Indonesia in August 1993, for example, delegates could reach little agreement as to whether future co-operation should take place within the context of an East Asian grouping or a broader Asia-Pacific context, which would include North America. Suspicions of the intentions of the USA, Japan, and China on the part of other countries would seem to preclude significant progress within a wider forum.[38] In spite of the agreement at the Bogor APEC summit of November 1994 to create an FTA by 2020, considerable disagreement over the specifics of trade liberalization remains. The only real sign of movement has been in the limited grouping of ASEAN, which in 1991 reached agreement to create a FTA in manufactures over fifteen years, but this is unlikely to have more than a limited impact on trading patterns.

What, if any, are the common factors behind this apparent trend towards economic regionalism in the Americas, Europe, and, to a very limited extent, Asia Pacific? There are at least four main factors which might be identified: the end of the Cold War, the shifting balance of world economic power, economic reform in developing countries, and the growing importance of non-tariff barriers to trade.

1. *The end of the Cold War.* The end of the Cold War is a general factor behind the shifting patterns of the global political economy in recent years, though its complex effects are often difficult to discern.[39] First, and most obviously, it is eroding the common security linkages which helped to underpin post-war economic co-operation between Western Europe, the USA, and Japan. Second, the end of the Cold War has increased the salience and the visibility of conflict between different forms of capitalism in Europe, East Asia, and America.[40] The Cold War facilitated economic co-operation between the USA, Western Europe, and East Asia and emphasized what they had in common; these two factors have combined to reduce the likelihood of economic co-operations at the global or inter-regional level. Third, the collapse of the Soviet threat has pushed traditional and non-traditional security threats arising from political and economic instability *within regions* up the agenda. These include weapons proliferation, mass migration,

---

[38] 'East Asia Disputes the Road to Growth', *Financial Times*, 13 Aug. 1993.
[39] See also Louise Fawcett's chapter in this volume.
[40] See e.g. Thurow, *Head to Head.*

and threats arising from poverty, drugs, and environmental disasters—illustrated, for example, by the importance of migration and environmental issues in US policy towards Mexico.

Finally, assessing the impact of the end of the Cold War upon the European integration project is highly speculative, though in Europe it has already raised particular concerns about the long-term role of Germany. In the short run, it has concentrated attention upon the region and in the eyes of other countries raised the prospect of a much wider European Community than has ever been contemplated. For many developing countries, who traditionally feared marginalization during the Cold War, the creation of the European Bank for Reconstruction and Development and the focus upon problems of transition in the former Eastern bloc have exacerbated such fears.

2. *The shifting balance of world economic power.* The long-heralded retreat from globalism on the part of a declining America can be seen as another fundamental cause of the new regionalism. Consistent with this view is the idea that the post-war world economy was constructed and managed by the American hegemon, and that US decline brings with it increasingly powerful centrifugal forces which push the world political economy towards the kind of competitive disorder which reigned in the interwar period.[41] Whatever the shortcomings of the theory of hegemonic stability, there has been an undeniable trend in US policy since the early 1970s towards disenchantment with 'free-riding allies' and multilateral institutions such as the GATT, and towards unilateralism and bilateralism in US trade and macroeconomic policies.[42] The shift to a multi-track trade foreign economic policy by the USA enables it to use the leverage available to it to greater effect, which means more 'balanced' outcomes and an enhanced ability to enforce compliance. At the same time, the threat of US unilateralism has increased the incentive for smaller countries of regional groupings highly dependent upon the USA to secure preferential access to the American market through bilateral agreements. Most importantly,

[41] For a critique of this theory, see Andrew Wyatt-Walter, *World Power and World Money: Hegemony and International Monetary Order* (Hemel Hempstead/ New York: Harvester Wheatsheaf/St Martin's Press, 2nd edn., 1993).

[42] See Jagdish Bhagwati, 'Aggressive Unilateralism: An Overview', in J. Bhagwati and Hugh T. Patrick (eds.), *Aggressive Unilateralism: America's Super 301 Trade Policy and the World Trading System* (Ann Arbor: University of Michigan Press, 1990).

American decline, in combination with the end of the Cold War, has led the USA to depart from its post-war policy of encouraging economic regionalism in Europe while refraining from regionalism itself.

The other side of the coin of American decline has been the rise of Japan and East Asia. The economic threat from Japan and the NICs is felt acutely in both North America and Europe. This competitive threat and the large bilateral trade surpluses Japan and East Asia enjoy with North America and the EC have increased pressures for protection and measures to enhance the competitiveness of and increase market-access for American and European firms. As Paul Krugman has noted, the widespread notion that Japan is an unfair trader 'has done a great deal to undermine the perceived effectiveness and legitimacy of the GATT in the USA and Europe. So the great advantage of regional pacts is that they can exclude Japan.'[43] While this is an exaggeration, since both the USA and EC have used the threat of protection to induce Japanese firms to substitute local production in Western markets for exports from Japan, one objective of regionalism in the West (and even in East Asia) has been to increase pressure upon Japan to make various market-opening concessions. Such pressure, given the limited importance of tariff barriers, has come primarily in the form of rules of origin, local content rules, dumping and countervailing duties, about which Article XXIV is silent.[44]

3. *The shift towards 'outward orientation'.* The failure of debt-financed import-substitution policies in much of Latin America, South Asia, and Africa, and the striking success of the outward-orientated policies of East Asia, has led to a generalized shift in the developing world towards favouring rather than discriminating against exports. This has increased the need to gain access for their manufactured exports in Western markets, at a time when protectionist pressures in the West have been growing and when Central and Eastern European countries are attempting to do the same. In turn, this has led to a greater willingness to negotiate bilateral or regional deals with the largest trading partners.

[43] Paul R. Krugman, 'The Move to Free Trade Zones', Paper presented to a symposium sponsored by the Federal Reserve Bank of Kansas City, 'Policy Implications of Trade and Currency Zones', 23 Aug. 1991, 36.
[44] See John H. Jackson, 'Regional Trade Blocs and the GATT', *The World Economy*, 16/2 (Mar. 1993), 121–31.

Second, access to large markets is also crucial for attracting export-orientated foreign direct investment, another area in which developing-country attitudes have undergone a major shift in recent years. This has also led to a growing perception of the dominance of American, German, and Japanese multinational firms in foreign-investment flows to lower-wage countries within their respective regions. At the end of 1991, 63 per cent of Mexico's stock of inward investment was owned by American firms, with the UK and Germany at 6 per cent each being the next most important investors.[45] The gradual erosion of the legacies of the Second World War have perhaps been most important for Japanese and German foreign investment. There is a strong perception that Japanese firms are carving out a *de facto* regional economic division of labour through foreign direct investment, taking advantage of lower wage costs in other countries to ensure the competitiveness of the labour-intensive parts of the manufacturing process, while retaining higher value-added activities in Japan. Similarly, in countries such as the Czech Republic and Slovakia in Central Europe, there was growing concern after 1989 that German firms would dominate foreign ownership of important parts of their industries. A regional bias to outward investment might over time increase the regional orientation of German and Japanese foreign policy.

Third, due to the often acute credibility problems of economic reform in many developing and transforming economies, reciprocal and binding regional economic arrangements with more powerful partners can often signal greater commitment to a path of economic reform than can other gestures such as joining the GATT.[46] Finally, regional agreements between developing countries can also be a means of increasing their limited bargaining power in bilateral negotiations with larger countries. For many export-orientated countries, however, regional solutions may at best constitute a form of minimal insurance policy should multilateral trade break down.

4. *The growing importance of non-tariff barriers to trade.*   The

---

[45] Lustig *et al.*, *North American Free Trade*, 7.

[46] In the GATT, the concession to developing countries which relieved them of the obligation of reciprocity actually helped to marginalize them and to reduce the credibility of economic reform programmes. Regional agreements, being based upon reciprocity and with greater scope for enforcement on the part of more powerful members, have the benefit of 'tying one's hands'. For a general discussion, see Dani Rodrik, 'Credibility of Trade Reform: A Policy Maker's Guide', *World Economy*, 12 (Mar. 1989), 1–16.

success of the GATT in reducing tariff barriers to manufacturing trade to very low levels in major countries has focused attention on remaining non-tariff barriers (NTBs) to trade since the end of the Kennedy Round. The widely perceived failure of the GATT to deal adequately with rising levels of NTBs in the 1970s, despite the codes negotiated during the Tokyo Round, has eroded support for multilateralism, especially in the USA. This failure owes much to the fact that the problem of NTBs often goes to the heart of the role of the modern state in the economy, such as government procurement practices, subsidies, standards-setting, and increasingly to basic social organization and practice (as with Japanese *keiretsu* corporate relationships, for example). Not surprisingly, cultural and philosophical differences between the USA, East Asia, and Europe on such issues have often been significant, which has hampered agreement. While the agenda of the Uruguay Round explicitly aimed at increasing the relevance of GATT rules and enforcement mechanisms to contemporary trade problems, the slow rate of progress and broken deadlines reinforced pessimism about the future of multilateralism.

It is sometimes claimed that within regions, greater cultural and historical affinities can sometimes facilitate agreement on such issues, the Single Market programme in Europe being the prime example.[47] In Europe and North America, countries have looked to regional arrangements where the problem of the lowest common denominator may be less acute. Yet this argument can be overdone, since affinities between countries do not always coincide with geographical propinquity, and it betrays a tendency to overgeneralize the European example. The greater importance of non-tariff barriers has also increased the tendency to bilateralism in trade policy, the Structural Impediment Initiative talks between the USA and Japan being an example. American officials also claim that through NAFTA the USA obtained better intellectual property protection from Mexico than they had been able to obtain through the GATT, but this owes less to regional affinities than to an asymmetry of bargaining power which the USA does not enjoy in the multilateral forum. Higher common denominators may also be found within the OECD, between the USA and EC on a number of issues,

---

[47] Albert Bressand, 'Beyond Interdependence: 1992 as a Global Challenge', *International Affairs*, 66/1 (Jan. 1990).

Counter

and between countries such as the Cairns Group of agricultural exporters.

There are therefore a number of important factors behind the rise of the new economic regionalism, most of which appear to be structural in nature and which are unlikely to disappear in the foreseeable future. While this has not undermined completely the forces in favour of multilateral approaches to international economic co-operation, Bhagwati is probably correct in his assessment that: 'As the key defender of multilateralism through the postwar years, [the US] decision now to travel the regional route (in the geographical and the preferential senses simultaneously) tilts the balance of forces away at the margin from multilateralism to regionalism.'[48] However, it ought to be added that part of the US objective in pursuing such policies has been to increase its bargaining power in multilateral forums—possibly successfully in the case of the Uruguay Round of the GATT. Although this twin-track strategy suggests that regionalism and multilateralism may not be mutually incompatible, there is an obvious danger that it could reinforce the temptation in the USA and elsewhere to pursue regional policies at the expense of multilateral ones.

3. THE WORLD ECONOMY: REGIONALIZATION OR GLOBALIZATION?

If there is a discernible trend towards economic regionalism as a policy, to what extent has the world economy become more regionalized? In addition, how do present claims as to the regionalization of the world economy sit with other claims about the powerful forces of globalization at work? Since the regionalization of the world economy is crucially dependent upon what happens in the three most important regions, North America, Europe, and East Asia, the discussion that follows will focus upon these three areas. This is largely because of the economic weight of these regions in the world economy; as in the 1950s and 1960s, regionalism in Latin America and Africa is unlikely to have a major impact on the shape of the world political economy and is in many ways a response to regionalism elsewhere.

---

[48] Bhagwati, 'Regionalism versus Multilateralism', 540.

It is important to point out at the beginning that one of the hazards of the literature in this area is the difficulty of agreeing upon standard definitions of different regional groupings. The GATT places Mexico in 'Latin' rather than 'North' America, while the UN does the reverse. The UN talks of 'Asia Pacific' mainly in terms of Japan, the NICs, and ASEAN, while 'Asia' for the GATT stretches from Afghanistan to North-East Asia to Australasia. Such variations can produce very different results, and there is a tendency to use definitions that support particular arguments. In the tables that follow, inconsistencies are avoided where possible but are noted where they are forced by the availability of data.

(a) Trade

As has already been noted, the idea that the 1980s saw a significant regionalization of international trade is widespread. Table 1 shows that on the face of it, this is justified, particularly in the case of the EC and East Asia, where intra-regional trade jumped significantly in the second half of the 1980s. However, this phenomenon is less sinister than at first it might appear. For the EC, the second half of the 1980s saw a vigorous investment boom after a long period of stagnation, which provided large benefits to an already highly integrated group of trade partners, but also to the rest of the world. In the 1973–84 period, when the European economy's performance was much poorer than in the 1950s and 1960s, intra-EC trade grew more slowly than imports from third countries.[49] The strengthening of the European economy in the second half of the 1980s led to the re-emergence of the trend towards growing intra-regional trade ratios, a trend which had always been consistent with increased trade with the rest of the world.

As for East Asia, an interesting pattern that has emerged since 1955 is that while the share of Japan's exports going to the East Asian region has not shown a general tendency to increase, its regional imports have grown particularly rapidly since 1970.[50] However, this is related to Japan's post-war structure of trade, importing raw materials from developing countries while exporting

---

[49] Alexis Jacquemin and André Sapir, 'European Integration or World Integration?', *Weltwirtschaftliches Archiv*, 124 (1988), 131.
[50] Albert Fishlow and Stephan Haggard, *The United States and the Regionalisation of the World Economy* (Paris: OECD, Mar. 1992), tables 3 and 3a.

TABLE 1. *Regional trade patterns: EC12, North America, and East Asia ($bn.)*

	1980	(%)	1985	(%)	1991	(%)	% of regional GNP (1991)
EC12							
Total trade [(X+M)/2]	731.9	100	656.8	100	1,413.6	100	25
Of which:							
Intra-regional	383.3	52	351.4	54	842.1	60	15
Trade with ROW	348.7	48	305.4	46	571.6	40	10
Trade with North America	62.5	9	69.0	11	116.5	8	2
Trade with East Asia	32.8	4	36.0	5	111.0	8	2
North America							
Total trade [(X+M)/2]	319.0	100	380.5	100	637.4	100	10
Of which:							
Intra-regional	104.9	33	143.2	38	241.0	38	4
Trade with ROW	214.1	67	237.3	62	396.4	62	6
Trade with East Asia	60.4	19	97.7	26	172.6	27	3
Trade with EC12	58.6	18	69.7	18	112.2	18	2
East Asia							
Total trade [(X+M)/2]	252.9	100	324.4	100	737.7	100	16
Of which:							
Intra-regional	89.1	35	124.5	38	332.0	45	7
Trade with ROW	163.9	65	199.9	62	405.7	55	9
Trade with North America	56.3	22	93.1	29	169.2	23	4
Trade with EC12	30.1	12	36.7	11	112.5	15	2

Note: North America = USA, Canada, Mexico; East Asia = Japan, Singapore, Taiwan, Hong Kong, South Korea, Indonesia, Malaysia, Philippines, Thailand, China (mainland).

Source: GATT, *Direction of Trade Statistics Yearbooks;* Republic of China (Taiwan), *Statistical Yearbook 1991* (Executive Yuan, 1992).

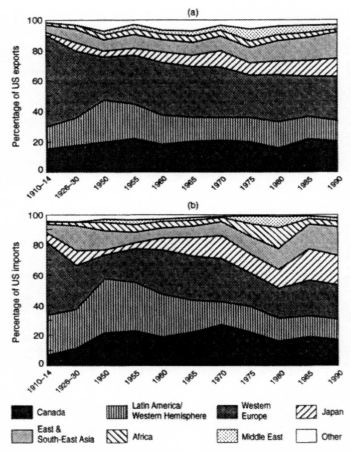

FIG. 1.   US Merchandise (a) exports and (b) import, by region,
1910–1990
Source: US Dept. of Commerce, Statistical Abstract of the United States
(various years)

manufactures mainly to OECD markets, particularly the USA. Although this is now changing, the region's manufacturing exports continue to be especially focused on the North American market. This is particularly true for Japan, but also the four NICs: the USA and Canada took on average 30 per cent of the NICs' exports in 1989, while Japan took only 11 per cent. The general lack of enthusiasm for a regional trading bloc in East Asia is therefore understandable even on purely economic grounds, despite the growing levels of intra-industry trade in the region.

For North America, Figure 1 shows how the importance of US trade with Canada has stayed reasonably constant since 1950, while intra-hemispheric trade with Latin America (particularly imports from Latin America) has declined over the past four decades. Trade with Europe has declined since the beginning of this century (though only marginally since 1950), while trade (particularly imports) with Japan and East Asia has shown rapid growth. This has prompted some to talk of the USA becoming a Pacific rather than an Atlantic economy. Rather, it seems that the US trading pattern has become more broadly diversified over the course of the century, with no one region playing a dominant role in US exports or imports—a feature confirmed by the ratification of NAFTA and the US support for APEC in late 1993. What has remained striking for the North American region as a whole is the extent to which it remains dependent upon extra-regional trade. However, this masks an important asymmetry: Canada and Mexico send about 70 per cent of their exports to the USA while the USA only sends about 25 per cent of its exports to Canada and Mexico. Thus, while Canadian and Mexican moves to secure FTAs with the USA are understandable, the USA's newfound interest in regional economic arrangements is a more complex phenomenon.

A final point is worth making about the supposed regionalization of international trade. Most trade in the world economy is driven by income: the big importers are the richest countries. A crude illustration of this is shown in Table 2. What it shows, however, is how much geography matters as well. Countries that are neighbours tend to trade with each other much more than does the rest of the world.[51] When this is taken into account, European trade does not look excessively regionalized compared to the trade of

---

[51] Clearly, other factors such as complementarity of economic structure and trade policy regimes will also affect trading patterns.

TABLE 2. *Network of world trade (1990) with 'gravity' calculations*

Destination region

Origin region	North America	G NA (%)	USA (%)	G USA (%)	Latin America	G LA (%)	Mexico	G Mex (%)	Western Europe	G WE (%)	Germany	G Ger (%)	Eastern Europe/ USSR	G EEU (%)	Africa (%)	G Afr (%)
North America	178.0	191	93.7	498	55.8	272	18.6	442	125.0	51	25.7	50	5.3	22	9.0	66
USA	83.0	594			54	351	18.2	578	112.9	62	22.9	59	4.24	24	5.7	56
Latin America	68.6	261	64.7	307	19.8	342	1.5	155	33.4	49	9.3	64	8.5	127	1.7	44
Mexico	19.1	401	18.9	496	1.8	216			3.6	29	0.6	23	0	0	0.1	14
Western Europe	127.7	45	110.8	48	28.8	46	5.1	39	1164.2	155	233.1	199	45.4	62	54.0	129
Germany	32.1	43	29.2	49	8.0	49	1.5	44	294.9	191			32.3	17	10.0	91
Eastern Europe/ USSR	2.9	9	2.5	10	6.9	97	0.2	14	62.3	74	13.6	76	76.9	939	3.5	74
Africa	13.2	79	12.2	92	1.7	46	0.1	13	50.8	117	10.3	112	2.9	69	5.9	242
Middle East	19.0	81	18.2	97	7.9	153	0	0	34.2	56	4.1	32	4.2	71	6.9	3.293
Asia	210.4	150	193.7	172	15.4	50	2.4	38	148.4	40	45.8	59	13.8	39	13.3	65
Japan	97.7	192	89.5	219	7.2	64	1.1	48	63.7	48	20.4	72	3.3	26	4.3	58
World	619.7	100	495.8	100	136.3	100	27.9	100	1618.2	100	341.9	100	157.1	100	90.5	100
% World imports	17.8		14.2		3.9		0.8		46.4		9.8		4.5		2.6	

TABLE 2. (cont.)

Origin region	Destination region						World	% World exports	Intra -trade (%)	Extra -trade (%)	(%) World GNP
	Middle East	G ME (%)	Asia (%)	G Asia (%)	Japan	G Jap (%)					
North America	12.10	87	133.0	126	61.3	173	525.3	15.1	33.9	66.1	27.0
USA	13.31	128	119.1	150	52.8	200	393.1	11.3	21.1	78.9	24.5
Latin America	1.80	46	13.7	46	9.4	94	148.0	4.2	13.4	86.6	4.3
Mexico	0.30	42	1.9	35	1.9	105	26.8	0.8	6.7	93.3	1.0
Western Europe	44.80	105	119.8	37	42.7	39	1612.8	46.3	72.2	27.8	30.4
Germany	9.40	84	33.2	39	10.8	38	421.1	12.1	70.0	30.0	6.6
Eastern Europe/ USSR	2.40	50	20.6	56	4	33	181.7	5.2	42.3	57.7	12.1
Africa	2.10	85	5.7	30	3.8	60	93.7	2.7	6.3	93.7	0.8
Middle East	7.00	200	52.1	196	31	349	132.0	3.8	5.3	94.7	2.8
Asia	22.30	106	358.1	224	82.4	243	791.2	22.7	45.3	54.7	22.1
Japan	9.10	120	98.2	255		100	286.9	8.2	34.2	65.8	14.2
World	92.40	100	703.0	100	234.6	100	3485.0	100.0	0.0	100.0	
% World imports	2.7		20.2		6.7		100.0				

Notes: 1. Mexico is included in Latin America; Turkey and Yugoslavia in Western Europe; Oceania in Asia.

2. 'Gravity' calculations ('G' columns) show each region's (country's) share of its total exports to another region as a percentage of the destination region's (country's) share of world imports.

3. 'Germany' means West Germany.

Source: GATT, *International Trade 90–91*, ii (Geneva, 1992); UN, *World Development Report, 1992*, table 1; IMF, *Direction of Trade Statistics Yearbook, 1992*; UN, *World Economic Survey, 1992*.

other regions. Western Europe (essentially the EEA) does 1.5 times more trade with itself than one would expect from its weight in international trade. However, Europe's major trading nation, Germany, does not look out of line if we compare it in this respect with Japan (Germany exports 1.9 times more to Western Europe than expected, but Japan exports 2.5 times more to Asia than expected). The USA exports 6 times more to Canada than expected, and 5.8 times more to Mexico, a much greater regional trade bias than Germany or Japan.

This point also accounts for much of the increase in the regionalization of trade flows in East Asia over the 1980s. That is, as the share of the region in world output has grown, we would expect its intra-regional trade ratio to increase without any increase in the regional 'bias' of its trade. Indeed, once account is taken of the growth in the region's share of world output, it appears to be the case that East Asia's regional trade bias (as opposed to that of the EC) actually fell over the 1980s.[52] As regards Europe, the figures on trade as a percentage of GNP also suggest that the EC is much more open than the USA (Table 1). Extra-regional trade as a percentage of GNP is higher for the EC than for either the USA or Japan. However, this difference is largely eliminated if Western Europe is seen as a whole, since the EC's major trading partner is EFTA. It is also interesting that the oft-noted extra-regional trade dependence of developing countries is primarily due to their lesser weight in the world economy rather than an absence of regionalization. For example, Africa trades with itself more than two times what would be expected, suggesting a regional trade 'bias' greater than that of the EEA though much less than that of CUSFTA. This is also true for Latin America and Asia.

(b) Investment

Flows of foreign direct investment (FDI) have grown much more rapidly than trade in the 1980s and have thereby acted as an increasingly important motor for rising levels of economic inter-

[52] Jeffrey A. Frankel, 'Is a Yen Bloc Forming in Pacific Asia?', in Richard O'Brien (ed.), *Finance and the International Economy: 5* (Oxford: OUP/Amex Bank Review, 1991), 7–9.

TABLE 3. *FDI outflows for the USA, Germany, and Japan*

USA: Foreign Investment Outflows by Region, 1960–90 (%)

	1960–5	1965–70	1970–5	1975–80	1980–5	1985–7	1988	1989	1990	1960–90 Cumulative
Canada	24	22	21	15	12	13	25	8	6	15
Latin America	11	6	11	24	−71	23	18	32	19	17
Mexico	0	0	0	7	−6	−0	4	4	4	2
Western Europe	41	43	50	51	60	54	34	50	56	51
Japan	2	3	4	3	20	8	12	2	5	5
Other Asia	2	3	7	3	46	2	8	7	7	6
Africa	4	4	−0	1	5	−0	−1	−1	−0	1
Middle East	2	0	−11	7	16	−1	−1	1	1	1
Other	13	18	19	−12	17	2	2	−4	3	2
Total ($bn.)	17.6	26.0	48.6	91.3	14.9	84.1	19.2	36.6	51.4	389.6

Germany: Foreign Direct Investment Outflows by Region, 1985–90 (%)

	1985	1986	1987	1988	1989	1990	1985–90 Cumulative
US	59	55	70	52	25	14	40
Japan	1	1	1	1	1	1	1
France	4	3	7	6	10	7	6
Italy	9	8	2	6	3	4	5
UK	20	7	11	9	25	21	16
Netherlands	0	12	1	6	9	9	7
Benelux	4	2	1	6	11	17	8
Austria	2	1	2	4	2	2	2
Switzerland	0	3	1	5	−1	8	3
Ireland	0	0	0	0	6	13	5
Spain	0	8	3	5	8	6	5
Total (DMbn.)	13.0	14.6	10.7	16.3	18.0	26.4	99.0

Japan: Foreign Direct Investment Outflows by Region, 1980–9 (%)

	1980	1985	1986	1987	1988	1989	1980–9 Cumulative
US & Canada	34	45	47	46	48	50	47
Asia	25	12	10	15	12	12	12
Europe	12	16	16	20	19	22	19
UK	4	3	4	7	8	8	7
Other	28	28	27	20	21	16	20
Total ($bn.)	4.7	12.2	22.3	33.4	47.0	67.5	187.1

Sources: USA—US Bureau of the Census, *Statistical Abstract of the United States*, various years; Germany—Institut der Deutschen Wirtshaft, *IW-Trends*, 19(2), 1992; Japan—OECD, *Economic Survey; Japan 1989/90* (OECD, Paris).

dependence.[53] If there is only limited evidence for a regionalization of international trade, has FDI played a major role in the regionalization of the world economy?

What is clear is that the global distribution of income also weighs heavily in the pattern of FDI, though more so for manufacturing and services industries than for the extractive industries. As for the distribution of US trade flows, there has been a tendency over time for the distribution of US foreign investment stock to become less rather than more regionally orientated. In 1960, 68 per cent of US foreign investment stock was concentrated in North and South America, 21 per cent in Western Europe, and only 4 per cent in Asia. By 1990, this had changed to 33 per cent in the Americas, 48 per cent in Western Europe, and 11 per cent in Asia. Only in the later 1980s did flows to Mexico and Latin America begin to grow rapidly again, after a period of volatility and decline (Table 3). What is striking is the importance of Western Europe as a destination for US FDI flows, where local sales by US affiliates are much greater than US exports to Europe. As Table 4 shows, there is a lesser regional bias to US FDI compared to US trade, and Western Europe and Japan attract relatively more FDI than trade from the USA. The US penetration of the European economy is therefore much greater than trade figures alone suggest.

Looking at Japanese investment outflows in the 1980s, what is clear is how they have been increasingly concentrated upon North America and Europe rather than its region, in spite of the much faster growth of the East Asian economies (Table 3). The idea that Japanese corporations have concentrated upon carving out a regional sphere of economic influence in East Asia, facilitated by Japanese government aid, can be exaggerated, although it is true that over 80 per cent of Japanese FDI to developing countries in the late 1980s went to East Asia, contributing to the rapid industrialization of these countries. The most important factor in Japanese foreign investment has been in ensuring market-access to the major markets of North America and Europe (where Japanese firms have been underrepresented). The growing concentration of Japan's outflows to developing countries in its region is hardly anomalous when compared to the regional bias of US FDI (see Table 4). Also,

---

[53] UN, *World Investment Report 1992*, and DeAnne Julius, *Global Companies and Public Policy: The Growing Challenge of Foreign Direct Investment* (London: Pinter/RIIA, 1990).

TABLE 4. USA, Germany, and Japan: FDI stock by region (%) (with gravity calculations for FDI and trade)

Destination region	Origin region								
	USA			Germany			Japan		
	USA FDI stock by region, 1990	USA: ratio of FDI share to region's share of world FDI	USA: ratio of trade share to region's share of world imports	Germany FDI stock by region, 1990	Germany: ratio of FDI share to region's share of world FDI	Germany: ratio of trade share to region's share of world imports	Japan FDI stock by region, 1991	Japan: ratio of FDI share to region's share of world FDI	Japan: ratio of trade share to region's share of world imports
North America	16	225	594	27	40	43	44	26	192
USA	NA	NA	NA	24	88	49	42	156	219
Latin America	17	336	351	6	93	49	12	265	64
Mexico	2	109	578	1	58	44	1	30	48
Western Europe	48	120	62	60	147	191	20	52	48
Germany	7	112	59	NA	NA	NA	2	27	72
Eastern Europe/USSR	ND	ND	24	ND	ND	170	0	NA	26
Middle East	1	59	128	1	32	84	1	58	120
Africa	1	44	56	1	65	91	2	89	58
Asia	11	73	150	3	18	39	22	269	255
Japan	5	405	200	2	164	38	NA	NA	NA
World	100	100	100	100	100	100	100	100	100

Notes: NA = not applicable; ND = not disclosed.
Source: US Bureau of the Census, Statistical Abstract of the United States, various years; Deutsche Bundesbank, Kapitalverflechtung mit dem Ausland, June 1993; Japan, Ministry of Finance.

it may be due in part to the economic problems of Latin America during the 1980s, and this previously favoured destination may once again become attractive for Japanese corporations in the 1990s.[54] Finally, Fishlow and Haggard argue that growing penetration of East Asian countries by Japanese corporations only increases the concerns of smaller countries regarding Japanese economic domination, and may work against regionalism in East Asia.[55] This too is debatable, since the growth that has flowed from Japanese FDI might also serve to assuage concerns about Japanese intentions in the region.

In the EC, the combined effects of London's 'Big Bang' financial deregulation, the Single European Act, and EC enlargement spurred a considerable increase in cross-border mergers and acquisitions in the later 1980s.[56] This can be seen in the pattern of German FDI flows in the 1980s. In the mid-1980s, German investment flows were directed largely towards the USA, even more so than for Japan, though a strong regional pattern emerged in the late 1980s. However, European investment flows to the USA remain very important, and the dominant trend of the 1980s as a whole was investment by European (and Japanese) companies in America, hitherto a market in which foreign firms played a relatively limited role. This is particularly true for the EC's largest foreign investor, the UK, which far outstrips Germany in this regard.

Overall, then, flows of FDI have enhanced inter-regional more than intra-regional linkages in the world economy, which is somewhat at odds with the regionalization hypothesis. As so much recent management-studies literature has suggested, companies competing in global markets were increasingly likely to establish a local presence in the three main markets of the 'triad' during the 1980s. However, Japan as a destination for FDI remains, even more than in its trade, the big anomaly.[57]

[54] On this subject, see Barbara Stallings and Gabriel Szekely (eds.), *Japan, the United States and Latin America* (Baltimore: Johns Hopkins UP, 1993).
[55] Fishlow and Haggard, *United States and the Regionalisation of the World Economy*, 34.
[56] See Stephen Thomsen and Stephen Woolcock, *Direct Investment and European Integration: Competition among Firms and Governments* (London: Pinter/RIIA, 1993), chs. 2–3.
[57] On this, see Robert Z. Lawrence, 'Japan's Low Levels of Inward Investment: The Role of Inhibitions on Acquisitions', *Transnational Corporations*, 1/3 (Dec. 1992), 47–75.

(c) *Money and finance*

There has been some degree of regionalization in the structure of the international monetary system since the breakdown of the Bretton Woods system in the early 1970s, which was based primarily upon the dollar. The main development in this regard is that despite limited periods of unilateral floating, a growing number of West European countries gradually came to peg their currencies to the Deutschmark rather than the dollar. Although the 'Snake' and subsequently the EMS have provided only very limited insulation from periodic dollar crises since the early 1970s, they have created a zone of relative monetary stability in Europe, at least until 1992.

However, it is important not to exaggerate this shift. Although the mark has become the world's second reserve currency after the dollar, in part the result of the expansion of intra-EMS intervention by European countries, mark assets accounted for only 18 per cent of world foreign-exchange reserves at the end of 1991, while dollar assets represented 56 per cent (the share of the ECU in official reserves was only 5 per cent.[58] Even within Europe, the dollar remains by far the most important reserve currency. The recent breakdown of the EMS also suggests that there are important limits to the possibility and desirability of fixed exchange-rate systems in the context of continued economic divergence between countries and high levels of short-term capital mobility.

There has been no equivalent emergence of a so-called 'yen zone' in East Asia. It is true that smaller countries in East Asia increased their holdings of yen foreign reserves from 14 per cent of their total reserves in 1980 to 17½ per cent in 1989, above the current world average of 10 per cent.[59] In addition, many have accepted the logic of growing trade dependence upon Japan and pegged their currencies to a basket in which both the dollar and the yen play an important role. The proportion of borrowing in yen for the region has also increased significantly, though in part this is due to dollar depreciation. However, the high level of trade dependence of the NICs on the US market and the limited political and economic integration in East Asia has prevented the emergence of an East

---

[58] Bank for International Settlements, *62nd Annual Report, 1991–1992* (Basle: BIS, 1992), 101.
[59] Frankel, 'Is a Yen Bloc Forming?', 16.

Asian version of the EMS. Hence, while the influence of Tokyo upon interest rates in the region has increased over time due to the liberalization of East Asian financial markets, 'overall its influence is as yet no greater than that of New York'.[60]

In addition, the continuing dominance of the dollar in the international monetary system and of US financial markets and dollar instruments in the global financial system suggests that the regionalization of money and finance has been very limited.[61] The gradual removal of exchange controls has particularly promoted inter-regional short-term capital mobility, mainly between the USA, Japan, and Europe (and there, mainly the UK). The three main financial centres, London, New York, and Tokyo, are much more connected to each other than to other regional financial centres. Short-term international capital flows are concentrated upon dollar–mark and dollar–yen cross-rates and much less upon intra-regional exchanges. Indeed, the argument has been made that geography is of decreasing importance in an increasingly global financial market, due to the role of modern technology and communications.[62] However, the agglomeration of financial industry in the big three international financial centres suggests that geography remains crucially important, even though these centres are increasingly interlinked. It is also a major reason why direct investment flows in services industries such as banking and insurance (which even for the Japanese came to constitute the majority of outward FDI in the 1980s) are primarily inter-regional, focused on the major financial centres in different time-zones. Indeed, financial services are probably the best example of an industry in which the major firms do indeed tend to have a major presence in all three areas of the triad.

We have seen that the evidence in favour of the simple regionalization hypothesis is not strong. Economic interdependence has continued to rise in recent decades, increasingly driven by short- and long-term capital flows rather than trade. However, at the macro-level, this if anything has enhanced *inter*-regional economic linkages rather than intra-regional ones. The possible exception to this trend is Western Europe, where the regionalization of markets is more pronounced. However, Europe is not exceptional

[60] Frankel, 'Is a Yen Bloc Forming?', 17.
[61] Wyatt-Walter, *World Power and World Money*, ch. 7.
[62] O'Brien, *Global Financial Integration*.

on trade if viewed as a bloc; is a major host for foreign multi-nationals; and, like Japan, has enjoyed a rapidly expanding owner-ship stake in the US economy in the 1980s. Furthermore, the long-term trend for the US economy has been towards increased openness *vis-à-vis* the rest of the world and increased importance of extra-regional linkages. Thus it might be argued that the globalization of the US economy, to the extent that it has been associated with growing concern about American decline, has been a cause of the USA's newfound enthusiasm for regionalism.

Nor, however, is the metaphor of globalization entirely helpful. The continued importance of geography for investment patterns belies superficial views of the globalization process, with the bulk of countries effectively marginalized from this process. The simple fact is that the world's big economies are located in North America, Europe, and East Asia, and the large firms that dominate economic activity emanate from and gravitate towards these economies. However, the growing importance of FDI as a motor of economic interdependence varies considerably by industry. As we have seen, international competition in the wholesale financial services indus-try is largely of an inter-regional kind. The bulk of activity is located in the large 'global' centres of London, New York, and Tokyo, each of which plays a regional role (this is least true, perhaps, of Tokyo). In general, the rise of inter-regional FDI is partly due to the increasing importance of services in the world economy, since a local presence in services often necessitates mar-ket penetration through FDI rather than through exports. The trend since the 1970s towards the deregulation of important service industries from banking to telecommunications has also contrib-uted significantly.

A further factor which tends to be underestimated in the litera-ture is the implications of greatly increased exchange-rate instabil-ity since the early 1970s. This has been a major stimulant to the wholesale financial services industry, with consequent effects upon foreign investment in this sector. In manufacturing industry, the risk of sustained misalignment of currencies, against which financial hedging techniques are inadequate, increases the value to firms of foreign production and supply networks in major markets. To the extent that the key exchange-rate risks have been of an inter-regional kind (between the dollar, the yen, and the European cur-rencies), this has encouraged a 'triadic' pattern of investment by multinational firms. In 1993–5, large Japanese manufacturing firms, which remain on average much more dependent upon exports than upon foreign production as a means of accessing foreign markets than their US and European counterparts, have been highly vulnerable to the exceptional strength of the yen. This has increased considerably the relative attractiveness of foreign over domestic investment.[63]

Even apart from exchange-rate considerations, for much manufacturing industry such as automobiles and machinery, the importance of transport costs and proximity to important customers often means that FDI is more efficient as a strategy for market entry than exports. More generally, the inter-regional orientation of FDI flows also results from the oligopolization of so many of the important industries in the major economies, as Alfred Chandler has pointed out. The existence of very high barriers to entry in many of the US industries in which large firms came to dominate domestic and often international production by mid-century meant that it was unsurprising that challengers to US firms usually came from outside the USA, often because foreign governments provided them with initial protection from US competition. Having achieved adequate economies of scale and scope, these European and Japanese firms then came to challenge US firms across a range of markets, including the American market. FDI could also provide an important means of pursuing oligopolistic strategies, placing pressure upon and reducing the profits of major competitors in key markets. Thus, the 1970s saw not only substantial increases in import penetration of the US economy, but also much more rapidly growing inward investment into the USA.[64]

Of course, inter-regional investment flows may also be encouraged by protectionism, as has apparently been the case with Japanese investment in the USA and EC in recent years. In addition, foreign firms may gain important leverage with foreign governments by investing within their political jurisdictions, facilitating the participation of affiliates in R & D programmes, in government procurement contracts, and in greater equality of treatment vis-à-vis domestic firms. An important element in this is that Europe (excep-

---

[63] 'Coping with Yen Shock', *International Business Week*, 30 Aug. 1993, 16–18.
[64] See Alfred D. Chandler, Jr., *Scale and Scope: The Dynamics of Industrial Capitalism* (Cambridge, Mass.: Harvard UP, 1990), 599–620.

tionally) has increasingly engaged not only in regional trade protection but also 'regional technonationalism'.[65] That is, the increasing perception in Europe of a need for a common response to the challenge presented by US and Japanese firms in high-technology sectors has led to the adoption of publicly subsidized, collaborative R & D programmes aimed at enhancing the competitiveness of European firms. The foreign (i.e. non-European) firms which have gained substantial access to such programmes are those, like IBM and Ford, which have important manufacturing and R & D facilities within Europe.

While investment outflows from the major economies has tended to be more inter-regional than intra-regional, we have also seen that there remains a substantial bias to FDI within regions. There are a number of reasons for this. For industries in which transport costs are considerable, such as raw materials, there is an obvious incentive to locate mines and processing plants close to major markets (where there is a choice). This probably accounts for the regional orientation of much US and Japanese FDI in primary industry, though the high levels of investment in the oil-rich Middle East are an obvious exception. Also, barriers to entry in manufacturing and service industries, particularly those of a cultural or social kind, may sometimes be less within regions. American manufacturing firms, having established themselves in a particular (micro-) region of the US economy, usually expanded first to other regions within the USA, before venturing abroad, typically in the first instance to the UK. Another factor has been the growing demand for just-in-time delivery in manufacturing industries since the 1970s, which favours the geographical proximity of supplier to customer firms, promoting an intra-regional network of investment.

While trade protectionism has tended to promote inter-regional flows of investment, other forms of government interference can promote intra-regional investment patterns. For example, states often react to the increasing ease of firms establishing 'transplant' operations within their territory (so as to avoid trade protection) by imposing constraints such as rules of origin and of local content. Such investment-related forms of protection are increas-

[65] Candice Stevens, 'Technoglobalism vs. Technonationalism: The Corporate Dilemma', *Columbia Journal of World Business* (Fall 1990), 42–9.

ingly, at least for the EC and NAFTA, defined on a regional basis, which can allow firms to take advantage of intra-regional wage differentials while satisfying host-region demands concerning sourcing and production. As has been clear in the electronic and automobile industries in the EC, this can encourage firms to establish local value-added production and sourcing arrangements more quickly or more extensively than they might otherwise do for purely commercial reasons. Traditional suppliers to large Japanese car firms have often followed the assemblers to the USA and Europe. Of course, central to such convergence of regional policies and corporate strategy, given the importance of intra-firm trade to the modern industrial corporation, is regional trade liberalization itself. For example, US affiliates in Mexico account for nearly 40 per cent of Mexico's total trade with the USA.[66]

Thus, while access to major markets seems to be the most important incentive for FDI, as confirmed by surveys of multinational firms,[67] this seems to produce both a predominance of inter-regional FDI flows in the world economy as well as a clear tendency for firms to establish *intra*-regional production and sourcing networks. Good examples of this are the regionalized networks operated by Japanese and American multinational automobile companies in the USA and Europe. Increasing competition and the rising fixed costs of certain corporate activities such as R & D increases the incentives for firms to access foreign markets, while the communications revolution due to digital technology may increase the ability of managers to control multinational operations.[68] Nevertheless, no industries are completely 'footloose' or global in orientation, and the realities of business and politics work to ensure that strong inter- and intra-regional patterns of trade and investment emerge. Above all, it is important to emphasize the way in which corporate strategy and regional policies interact to produce both 'globalization' and 'regionalization' in the patterns of trade and investment.

---

[66] UN, *World Investment Report 1992*, 2.
[67] See e.g. Emergency Committee for American Trade, *Mainstay II: A New Account of the Critical Role of U.S. Multinational Companies in the U.S. Economy* (Washington, DC: ECAT, July 1993), 7, and the evidence presented in Thomsen and Woolcock, *Direct Investment and European Integration*, chs. 3–4.
[68] See OECD, *Globalisation of Industrial Activities*.

4. IMPLICATIONS FOR THE MANAGEMENT AND STABILITY OF THE WORLD ECONOMY

The conclusion that trends towards regionalization and globalization are symbiotic more than contradictory raises an important question about how this affects the management and stability of the world economy. In particular, there was a growing concern in the early 1990s that despite evidence of growing inter-regional linkages in the world economy, regionalism might nevertheless develop a cumulative momentum. This raised the spectre that for the first time since 1945, regionalism and multilateralism threatened to operate in divergent directions. Even though this fear has been reduced with the eventual success of the Uruguay Round, we need to assess the likelihood of this outcome, and to ask whether it would represent such a negative development.

As already suggested, the experience since 1945 has been that regionalism and multilateralism for the most part have coexisted reasonably successfully. The most important reason for this was that US leadership during the Cold War period limited the negative tendencies of the most important manifestation of regionalism, that in Western Europe. Where the USA was unwilling to push the Europeans towards rough compatibility with the GATT, such as in agriculture during the 1950s and 1960s, the result was severely negative. When the European Community was taking shape in the early 1960s, US pressure and the existence of the GATT helped to tip the balance in favour of Western European countries inside the EEC (such as Germany and Benelux) and those who had decided for the time being to remain outside (above all, the EFTA countries), who favoured the creation of a Community relatively open to the rest of the world.

European regionalism in the 1960s and early 1970s implied more than just a damage-limitation exercise for multilateralism, however. The emergence of a powerful European trade grouping armed with a Common External Tariff prompted the US itself to offer much deeper cuts in its own tariff protection than it would otherwise have done, leading to the successful Kennedy Round outcome which substantially reduced the diversionary effects of the CET.[69] Similarly, the USA initiated both the Tokyo and Uruguay Rounds

[69] John W. Evans, *The Kennedy Round in American Trade Policy* (Cambridge, Mass.: Harvard UP, 1971).

when the EC was embarking upon new phases of enlargement. Finally, the trade and investment boom that integration helped to maintain led to considerable benefits for third-country exporters of manufactures, though especially for the large number of American multinational firms that established a local presence in the Community.

The boom in Western Europe in the second half of the 1980s coincided with the latest liberalizing phase of European integration and finally enabled the EC to accept US proposals in 1986 for an extremely ambitious agenda for the Uruguay Round. The EC found it difficult to contain the liberalization measures of the Single Market Programme fully within the borders of Europe, again in part because of American pressure. For example, the reciprocity provisions of the Second Banking Directive of 1989, largely responsible for the talk about Fortress Europe, prompted discussions with the USA which led to a watering down of the provisions.[70] The EC's recent Utilities Directive, which envisages an open market for government utilities procurement within the Community, also prompted a major dispute with the USA which ultimately led to a market-opening compromise. Although American pressure has helped to reduce the cost of European integration perhaps mainly for US firms, the benefits to others have been considerable, perhaps in part because intra-regional liberalization creates domestic political coalitions which can also favour and encourage broader liberalization. Also, a powerful European bloc helps to constrain tendencies towards unilateralism in the USA.

It has been during periods of slow growth that European integration has been weakest and the tendencies to protectionism strongest. The period from the first oil shock to the early 1980s saw both a stagnation of regionalism as well as major world recessions, slow growth of international trade, and rising protectionism. The weak state of the world economy in the depths of recession in 1982 created both pessimism in Europe about economic 'sclerosis' and an EC refusal to embark upon the new GATT 'Reagan Round' that the Americans were proposing. In difficult times, the EC tends to become cautious and introspective and finds it difficult to embark upon either multilateral or regional liberalization. The response is usually the opposite in the USA, where the executive branch tends

[70] Carter H. Golembe and David S. Holland, 'Banking and Securities', in Hufbauer, *Europe 1992*.

to take export-promotion initiatives to deflect rising demands for import protection. Thus, the USA tends to meet European resistance to trade liberalization at the time when the American political system needs it most.

Hence, it is not entirely surprising that as the pressures of protectionism have risen within the USA since the 1980s, frustration with the EC has grown to the point where the USA now pursues trade liberalization on a number of fronts simultaneously. Yet European recalcitrance and introspection is not the only cause of this shift in US strategy. In contrast to Europe, where regionalism in the form of the Community was seen as an antidote to perceived German and Soviet aspirations to hegemony and could therefore be actively promoted, in East Asia after 1945 the containment of Japanese power was achieved by the undermining of macro-regionalism. US economic and political hegemony in East Asia ensured that Japan and other East Asian countries were integrated into the world economy primarily through their exporting to the US market. This has had some important negative consequences in the longer term.

First, the rise of Japan has considerably complicated the management of the world economy, since its relationship with the USA and Europe is highly unbalanced compared with the US–European relationship. The low levels of foreign penetration of the Japanese economy led to growing tension with Japan's major trading partners and a weakening of their commitment to the GATT, as well as making for an asymmetrical dependence that only increases Japanese resentment of Western pressure. Second, unlike in Europe where the promotion of regional integration forced Germany and its neighbours to come to terms with the past and to seek solutions, Japan's rise has complicated relations with its region. The smaller countries simultaneously resent the relative closedness of the Japanese economy and yet fear the consequences of dependence upon Japanese capital and technology.

In summary, it may be difficult to extrapolate from the experience of a positive and largely reinforcing relationship between regionalism and multilateralism after 1945 to a general principle. That is, this positive relationship was essentially the product of the unique circumstances surrounding the European–American relationship during the Cold War era. There is no necessary reason to suppose, as have many American writers, that regionalism might be a building-block to multilateralism when it is also pursued in East

Asia and North America.[71] Much depends upon events in the Pacific-Asia region as the balance of the world economy shifts further away from the US–European axis to the North American–Asian axis. It may be true that the perceived success of the APEC summit in Seattle in December 1993 prompted the necessary movement for agreement in the GATT Uruguay Round negotiations later that month.[72] However, it is unclear that a positive relationship between regionalism and multilateralism can be maintained in the longer term, outside of the constraints of a common Cold War alliance and in presence of deep economic asymmetries. At present, most countries in East Asia favour the continued economic and political engagement of the USA in the region, as a counterweight to real or perceived Japanese and/or Chinese hegemonic aspirations. But the debate over 'open vs. closed' regionalism in East Asia is not yet resolved, and the potential effects of any further US attempts to prevent regionalism in Asia through either APEC or a divide-and-rule strategy of selective FTA agreements are difficult to discern.

While supporters of US regional policy claim that NAFTA can help reinforce US demands for GATT reform and promote multilateral liberalization, it is also apparent that it has allowed important lobby groups to increase protectionist measures in important areas. For example, under NAFTA, the minimum local content ratio for automobile production in North America will be increased from 50 per cent (as under CUSFTA) to 62.5 per cent. Also, given the difficulty of achieving progress within the Uruguay Round, it is unclear as to how effective the threat of regionalism by the USA was in pushing other countries towards multilateral trade liberalization. Regionalism also strikes a chord with isolationist and nationalist elements in the USA, who equate the US support of multilateral institutions such as the GATT with the exploitation of America by its erstwhile allies in Europe and Asia. US regionalism is confusing precisely because it can appeal to both protectionists and free-traders, who support it as a means to different goals.

[71] See e.g. the argument of Robert Z. Lawrence, 'Emerging Regional Arrangements: Building Blocks or Stumbling Blocks?', in O'Brien, *Finance and the International Economy: 5.*
[72] C. Fred Bergsten, 'Sunrise in Seattle', *International Economic Insights* (Jan./Feb. 1994).

Therefore, it is debatable whether NAFTA is much more useful than as part of a new relationship with Mexico. As we have seen, the US is a global trader and investor, with a great stake in multilateral agreement on the treatment of trade in goods and services, of multinational firms, and of intellectual property. Nor can regionalism be seen as an easier option, as the tortuous negotiations with Mexico and Canada have shown. Moreover, since most of the USA's regional neighbours are developing countries, there are severe limits to the possibilities of American regionalism. The political difficulties involved in closer integration in the presence of large income disparities have been demonstrated in the case of NAFTA, while no other countries enjoy the political profile that Mexico does in US policy. As a result, any US 'regional' strategy would be likely to degenerate into a series of bilateral FTAs that have limited overall coherence, either geographical or economic.

The limitations of regionalism as a strategy for the USA do not ensure its demise, particularly as it increases the possibility of protective regionalism elsewhere. But would the further tipping of the scales away from multilateralism towards regionalism really be so detrimental to the management and stability of the world economy, as liberal international economists claim? International relations theory says little about this, though it is generally held to be negative in its impact. Liberals naturally favour the promotion of global economic interdependence as a means of promoting international order, while realists presume that order typically derives from the hegemony of one country in the international political economy. Accordingly, regionalism is generally perceived as a fracturing of the post-war international economic order, raising the prospect of a destabilizing conflict between three competing, great-power-dominated blocs.

The literature on co-operation suggests that agreement between states is more likely in small groups, which has implications for the assessment of regionalism. We saw earlier that the European model suggested that non-tariff barriers might be best dealt with, at least initially, in a regional context. However, the lowest-common-denominator problem associated with the GATT and other multilateral bodies does not necessarily imply the superiority of regional forums *per se*. In fact, there is no good reason why optimal jurisdictions have to be regional in nature, since similar levels of economic development might be much more important as a facilitator of international agreement than neighbourliness. Larger forums can also overcome problems of large numbers through coalitions; the GATT is essentially dominated by the USA and EC, with other countries forming coalitions to gain leverage (as with the developing countries or the Cairns Group).

A further shift away from multilateralism towards regionalism would be likely to promote further defensive behaviour on the part of multinational firms, who would continue to strive to improve their local or regional credentials as a means of limiting the impact upon their market access. If such firms become less dependent upon inter-regional exports as a result, this might reduce their incentives to lobby for open trade (and for policies to promote exchange-rate stability) between regions. However, most major corporations remain wedded to the principle of open markets because of their high propensity to engage in international trade and their desire for flexibility. Inter-regional trade can sometimes help such firms to defuse protectionist pressures, as non-traditional exports by Japanese affiliates from the USA and Europe back to Japan eventually might. The real danger is that the proliferation of national and regional rules of origin and local content will lead to a competitive scramble between the regions for the high value-added parts of the development and production chains of multinational firms. Hence there is a strong case for the considerable reinforcement of Article XXIV of the GATT, as discussed, to limited effect, within the Uruguay Round.[73] The shift in US policy towards the pursuit of regionalism markedly reduces the chances that this will be achieved.

The biggest losers in any such shift towards regionalism would be the Japanese, and the poorer countries in general, who remain much more dependent upon exports as a source of accessing the larger economies. Of all the large countries, the Japanese are most dependent upon extra-regional exports for their continued prosperity. The problem is of course much more acute for developing countries. Most of the contemporary regionalism in the developing world is a response to the growing difficulties of penetrating the increasingly protected big markets in the North.[74] If this access is increasingly denied, the rapid progress many developing countries

[73] See Jackson, 'Regional Trade Blocs', 129–30.
[74] Rolf J. Langhammer, 'The Developing Countries and Regionalism', *Journal of Common Market Studies*, 30/2 (June 1992), 211–31.

have made in recent years towards externally orientated economic policies will be jeopardized. For most developing countries and for developed countries outside of the major regions like Australia and New Zealand, regionalism is no substitute for multilateral trade liberalization. It is inevitable that Mexican-style opportunities will only be extended to the lucky few.

5

The Growth of Regional Organizations and the Role of the United Nations

Alan K. Henrikson

THE United Nations, particularly the Security Council, has re-asserted itself as the 'nerve-centre' of international decision-making in the field of peace and security.[1] However, the changes that took place during the Cold War probably will preclude any recentralization of world authority as conceived by some universalists at the time of the 1945 San Francisco Conference. An entirely new inter-organizational 'balance' will have to be struck between the UN Organization and what were then called by some 'regional councils'.[2] The novel possibility today is that *both* the universal body—the United Nations—and the regional institutions that have come into existence will become stronger and gain in acceptability as producers of international peace and security. The stock of both kinds of multilateral enterprise has risen more or less simultaneously as superpower unilateralism has declined. In consequence, the UN, on the one hand, and regional groupings, on the other, are no longer so likely to be regarded as rivals, or even

[1] The 'nerve-centre' image, implying a quasi-organic system of communication and decision, is that of R. A. Akindele in *The Organization and Promotion of World Peace: A Study of Universal–Regional Relationships* (Toronto: University of Toronto Press, 1976), p. xii.

[2] The principal Second World War proponent of 'regional councils' was Winston Churchill, who reasoned that only those countries directly affected by a dispute 'could be expected to apply themselves with sufficient vigour to secure a settlement'. To be sure, Churchill also favoured a 'Supreme World Council' which would have 'the last word': Winston S. Churchill, *The Second World War*, iv. *The Hinge of Fate* (Boston: Houghton Mifflin, 1950), 802–7. Most Latin American governments were unwilling to subject their existing system of international co-operation within the western hemisphere to possible veto action by the great powers within a centralized UN Security Council and therefore strongly defended the regional principle. See Ruth B. Russell, assisted by Jeanette E. Muther, *A History of the United Nations Charter: The Role of the United States, 1940–1945* (Washington, DC: Brookings Institution, 1958), 688–712.

as alternatives to one another, in international decisions for peace and security. They may come to work together in partnership.

Regional arrangements or agencies—the ones generally recognized as such by the UN community—include the Organization of American States (OAS), the Organization of African Unity (OAU), the League of Arab States (LAS), and, more recently, the Organization for Security and Co-operation in Europe (OSCE) and also the Commonwealth of Independent States (CIS). The UN and these various regional entities increasingly may be viewed as parts of the same overall assemblage of institutions. Even regionally centred pacts for mutual defence, not traditionally thought of by the UN as regional bodies, particularly the Western European Union (WEU), founded on the 1948 Brussels Treaty, and the North Atlantic Treaty Organization (NATO), established on the basis of the 1949 Washington Treaty, are becoming friends of the world institution. As will be seen, they are becoming less alliance-like and more 'multilateral' organizations.

The ill-feeling of the Cold War years is surrendering to a new tolerance, even appreciation, on the part of the UN of what regional institutions of all kinds might be able to do. 'For dealing with new kinds of security challenges, regional arrangements or agencies can render assistance of great value', as Secretary-General Javier Pérez de Cuéllar stated in his 1990 report to UN members. 'This presupposes the existence of the relationship between the UN and regional arrangements envisaged in Chapter VIII of the Charter. The defusion of tensions between states and the pacific settlement of local disputes are, in many cases, matters appropriate for regional action.' Though qualified by the important 'proviso' that the efforts of regional agencies 'should be in harmony with those of the United Nations and in accordance with the Charter', Pérez de Cuéllar's observation suggested the possible transition to a new era, a period of global–regional balance and comity.[3] This chapter addresses a central question: what are the prospects for inter-organizational co-operation in the field of peace and security, for what Tommy Koh has called a 'new partnership' between regional

---

[3] Quoted in Benjamin Rivlin, 'Regional Arrangements and the UN System for Collective Security and Conflict Resolution: A New Road Ahead?', *International Relations*, 11/2 (Aug. 1992), 97.

and subregional organizations on the one hand and the UN on the other?[4]

The traditional obstacle to co-operation between the UN and 'regional arrangements or agencies', as they are termed in Article 52(1) of Chapter VIII of the UN Charter, has been the basic issue of the primacy of the one or the other. This general question of rank can be expressed in several ways. First, there is the issue of which has *priority*—that is, which is the initial recourse, has the right of regard, takes logical precedence, and, in general, is expected to come first. A second is the issue of *supremacy*— that is, which is higher in terms of legal, political, and moral authority or status, and thus can bestow more legitimacy, implying greater international acceptability. A third is the issue of their relative *ascendancy*—that is, which tends to predominate, actually possessing more power and influence, and thus is able to accomplish more.

A different axis of analysis concerns what might generally be termed the personality of organizations. The first issue concerns the organization's *individuality* or separateness of identity—that is, how distinct is it in membership and purpose, organizational type and style, or current policy and activity. A second question is the degree of the organization's *autonomy*—that is, how sufficient and self-directing is it, or independent of other organizations (or major individual countries), in terms of initiative and direction. A third question concerns the organization's *capability*—that is, how resourceful, competent, and effective is it in solving problems in comparison with other international organizations. The weight of this chapter will be placed more on the attributes of organizational personality rather than on the formal or other indicia of institutional primacy. The vital question is whether the UN and regional organizations are sufficiently alike to be able to work together and not whether in some sense (precedence, authority, or power) the global or the regional organization is 'above' or 'below' the other.

In the sections that follow, I shall first set out the existing constitutional relationships between the UN and regional arrangements and agencies. Next I shall relate the main lines of the history of

---

[4] Tommy Koh, 'Summary and Conclusion', *The Singapore Symposium: The Changing Role of the United Nations in Conflict Resolution and Peace-keeping*, 13–15 Mar. 1991 (New York: United Nations, 1991), 82.

global–regional relations in international peacemaking.[5] This historical foundation is intended to establish the pattern of global–regional relations from the Second World War through the Cold War years. This is followed with a more detailed consideration of leading recent cases of peacemaking which have increasingly come to involve both the UN and regional organizations. These highlight the central argument of the chapter: *that at least some UN action is always necessary, if not to elicit regional-organizational efforts then to make them more fully accepted and effective; yet, without direct and deep regional involvement, international peacemaking is likely to lack continuity and consistency.* The chapter then analyses current proposals for improving global–regional co-operation, including, most notably, the relevant recommendations of *An Agenda for Peace*.[6] Finally, the chapter offers a comprehensive rationale for a new global–regional 'system' or practical partnership in international peacemaking.

1. THE UN CHARTER AND 'REGIONAL ARRANGEMENTS OR AGENCIES': LEGAL MANDATES AND INSTITUTIONAL RELATIONSHIPS

The bedrock is Chapter VIII on Regional Arrangements. This records an international consensus regarding the global–regional problem that was formulated, though not fully worked out substantively, at the Dumbarton Oaks Conference in late 1944 and the San Francisco Conference on International Organization early the next year. The new United Nations was intended to be the paramount institution, having supremacy over all others. 'In the event of a conflict between the obligations of the Members of the United Nations under the present Charter and their obligations

---

[5] Peacemaking is defined here, inclusively, to mean most kinds of international action for peace and security from military peace-enforcement through peacekeeping operations to pacific settlement via diplomacy. In current UN parlance, 'peacemaking' is defined, more narrowly, to refer to international action to bring hostile parties to agreement through peaceful means—specifically those outlined in Chapter VI (Pacific Settlement of Disputes) of the Charter. However, in contemporary journalistic usage, the word sometimes is contradistinguished with 'peacekeeping,' thus suggesting pacification by the use of military force.

[6] Boutros Boutros-Ghali, *An Agenda for Peace: Preventive Diplomacy, Peacemaking and Peace-keeping*, repr. in Adam Roberts and Benedict Kingsbury (eds.), *United Nations, Divided World* (Oxford: OUP, 2nd edn., 1993).

under any other international agreement', Article 103 unequivocally states, 'their obligations under the present Charter shall prevail.'[7] None the less, three 'fundamental concessions', as they have been characterized, were made to the idea of regionalism and regional peacemaking. The essential purpose of these provisions of the Charter was to give a regional entity the 'elbow-room' it needed in order to deal with local disputes, as the institutional forum of first instance.[8] Part of the Charter authors' thinking was that regional organizations might serve as a buffer—making it less necessary for the UN itself to deal with local problems.

The first so-called concession, stated in Article 33(1) of Chapter VI on the Pacific Settlement of Disputes, is the provision that parties to any dispute endangering international peace and security 'shall, first of all, seek a solution by ... resort to regional agencies or arrangements', by direct negotiation, third-party mediation, arbitration, or some other means of their own choosing. In addition, the region-focused Chapter VIII stipulates that nothing in the Charter is to preclude 'the existence of regional arrangements or agencies for dealing with such matters relating to the maintenance of international peace and security as are appropriate for regional action' (Article 52(1)). Chapter VIII states that UN members entering into such arrangements or constituting such agencies shall 'make every effort to achieve pacific settlement of local disputes through such regional arrangements or by such regional agencies before referring them to the Security Council' (Article 52(2)). Thus we find evidence of logical or temporal priority being given to regional consideration.

Such regional efforts were actively to be promoted, and employed, by the UN Organization. The Security Council 'shall encourage the development of pacific settlement of disputes through such regional arrangements or by such regional agencies either on the initiative of the states concerned or by reference from the Security Council', Article 52(3) of Chapter VIII states. But against this, the Charter carefully reserves to the Security Council, in Chapter VI on Pacific Settlement, the Council's independent authority

---

[7] The text of the UN Charter is reprinted in Roberts and Kingsbury (eds.), *United Nations, Divided World.*
[8] Francis O. Wilcox, 'Regionalism and the United Nations', in Norman J. Padelford and Leland M. Goodrich (eds.), *The United Nations in the Balance: Accomplishments and Prospects* (New York: Praeger, 1965), 427.

and also its organizational autonomy in the investigation of all disputes or situations that might threaten peace (Article 34). Moreover, Article 35 assures to any country, even countries that do not belong to the UN, the opportunity to come directly to the UN—either the Security Council or the General Assembly—provided such non-members accept the obligations of pacific settlement set forth in the Charter. The scope of the UN's willingness to act for peace was thus in principle universal. None the less, overall the priority accorded to regional organizations in dispute settlement is clear.

The second concession to regionalism is the allowance made in the Charter for the continued operation of existing mutual assistance pacts—perhaps most significantly, the 1942 Anglo-Soviet Treaty of Alliance against Nazi Germany and its European associates. Article 53(1) of Chapter VIII declares pointedly that measures against 'enemy states', defined in Article 53(2) as those that during the Second World War had been enemies of any Charter signatory, could be taken immediately, without prior authorization of the Security Council. These actions could continue until the UN itself assumed responsibility on the request of the government involved. Article 53(1) makes clear that these exceptional measures of enforcement against former enemy states might result from 'regional arrangements directed against renewal of aggressive policy on the part of any such state'. Chapter XVII on Transitional Security Arrangements similarly carries over the authority of the victors of the Second World War into the unsettled postwar situation. Pending the coming into force of 'special agreements' between the Security Council and UN members or groups of members to make available to the Organization armed forces, assistance, and facilities provided for in Chapter VIII, Article 43, the Four-Power Declaration signed in Moscow in October 1943 would remain in effect. Under this agreement, the Republic of China, the Soviet Union, the UK, and the USA could, with the addition of France, consult with one another and other UN members with a view to 'such joint action on behalf of the Organization as may be necessary for the purpose of maintaining international peace and security' (Article 106).

The third and most important concession to regionalism is the recognition of Article 51 at the end of Chapter VII on Action with respect to Threats to the Peace, Breaches of the Peace, and Acts of Aggression of 'the inherent right of individual or collective self-defence'. This right, which as 'inherent' was natural or inalienable, could be exercised regionally. Article 51 usually has been understood to allow for treaties of mutual assistance for the purpose of collective defence—that is, alliances. There is no reason why these defensive pacts could not be among the 'regional arrangements' referred to in Article 52 at the beginning of Chapter VII. Article 53(1) of that chapter contains the otherwise limiting (except for the right of self-defence assured in Article 51) provision that the Security Council 'shall, where appropriate, utilize such regional arrangements or agencies for enforcement action under its authority'. It further stipulates that, except for anti-enemy state measures, which would be virtually automatic, 'no enforcement action shall be taken under regional arrangements or by regional agencies without the authorization of the Security Council'. Yet regional groups constituted as alliances, using Article 51, could not be so constrained.[9] The early examples of regionally based, though not formally 'regional', mutual defence pacts were the Inter-American Treaty of Reciprocal Assistance completed at Rio de Janeiro in 1947, The Brussels Pact of 1948 focused on Western Europe, and the Washington Treaty of 1949 which was transatlantic in strategic scope.[10] All of these agreements for common defence refer to Article 51, and thus can be said to avoid the restraints on 'regional arrangements or agencies' in Chapter VIII, and perhaps even the more general limitations imposed by the Charter on the resort to force by UN members.[11]

   [9] This reasoning, emphasizing the autonomy of 'Article 51' organizations, follows Hans Kelsen, The Law of the United Nations: A Critical Analysis of Its Fundamental Problems (London: Stevens & Sons, 1950), 792–7.
   [10] Both US Secretary of State Dean Acheson and British Foreign Secretary Ernest Bevin made statements to the effect that the arrangement based on the North Atlantic Treaty was not an regional organization within the meaning of Art. 52 in Chapter VIII of the UN Charter. Ambassador E. N. van Kleffens, the Dutch representative to the USA, did evidently consider the Atlantic Pact to be a regional arrangement, however. See his 'Regionalism and Political Pacts with Special Reference to the North Atlantic Treaty', American Journal of International Law, 43 (1949), 666–78. From the Soviet perspective, the Atlantic Pact was an illegitimate 'conspiracy' against the UN Charter. The USSR already had a comparable network of defensive arrangements of its own, of course. See Boleslaw Adam Boczek, 'The Eastern European Countries and the Birth of the Atlantic Alliance', in Ennio Di Nolfo (ed.), The Atlantic Pact Forty Years Later: A Historical Reappraisal (Berlin: Walter de Gruyter, 1991), 171–3.
   [11] There should be noted, however, the often-overlooked qualification in Art. 51 that the right of individual or collective self-defence could be exercised 'until the Security Council has taken measures necessary to maintain international peace and

The individual UN member's right of self-defence, exercised alone or in concert with other UN members of similar interest and outlook and perhaps in a regional setting, and the prerogative of leadership held by the Security Council for the purpose of preserving international peace and security thus were delicately balanced. Neither, according to the Charter, was unmistakably supreme—or at least clearly dominant. Yet there was no concrete plan for enabling the world and regional organizations to function together and to act jointly. One of the US delegates at San Francisco, Senator Arthur H. Vandenberg, declared hopefully that 'we have found a sound, a practical formula for putting regional organizations into effective gear with the global institution.' What Vandenberg meant was that Article 51, with its explicit recognition of the right of collective self-defence, permitted the formation of a regionally based inter-American security arrangement, the Rio Treaty, which would preserve America's freedom under the Monroe Doctrine. This US-controlled mechanism could become incorporated into the larger UN system only nominally. The world organization was 'infinitely strengthened' by enlisting 'the dynamic resources of these regional affinities', Vandenberg asserted. 'We weld these regional king-links into the global chain.'[12]

This loosely constituted dual arrangement was intended by its designers to enable the UN and all present and future regional bodies to function in theoretical if not practical union. Despite the roominess of the Charter structure, there subsequently developed considerable tension, even contention, between the world body and regional entities. As shown, there exist the competing claims of, on the one hand, Articles 33(1) and 52(2), which seem to allow regional organizations priority of action with regard to managing disputes essentially of a 'local' character; and, on the other, Articles 34 and 35 which, together with the powerful general

security', at which point the need for such self-defensive measures, presumably, no longer would exist. The signatories of the San Francisco Charter conferred on the United Nations Organization, specifically the Security Council, 'primary responsibility' for maintaining international peace and security (Art. 24(1)). Furthermore, Art. 39 at the beginning of Chapter VII establishes that it is the Security Council that 'shall determine the existence' of threats to the peace, breaches of the peace, or acts of aggression, and then 'shall make recommendations, or decide what measures shall be taken'.

[12] Arthur H. Vandenberg, Jr. (ed.), with the collaboration of Joe Alex Morris, *The Private Papers of Senator Vandenberg* (Boston: Houghton Mifflin, 1952), 366.

Charter authorizations of Articles 24 and 39, appear to give the UN, specifically the Security Council, the pre-eminent role and supremacy if not ascendancy. The vagueness of this division of responsibility between the global organization and regional groupings has conditioned the history of all subsequent dealings between them.

As for regional organizations, because of the strong impression conveyed especially by Chapter VIII that 'regional arrangements or agencies' are to be subordinate to the UN at least in the matter of 'enforcement action', it matters a great deal whether these organizations consider themselves to be Chapter VIII entities or not. The OAS's 1948 Bogotá Charter expressly states that, 'within the United Nations, the Organization of American States is a regional agency' (Article 1). The preparatory materials of the Addis Ababa Charter of 1963 indicate that the Organization of African Unity also was intended to be a 'regional arrangement'. The League of Arab States, though established in 1945 shortly before the San Francisco Conference (April–June), none the less clearly was meant by its founders to be a regional part of a global structure.[13] In July 1992 the forerunner of the OSCE, the Conference on Security and Co-operation in Europe (CSCE), established at Helsinki in 1975, designated itself a regional organization in the sense of Chapter VIII.[14] In March 1994 the successor organization of the Soviet

[13] Although the UN General Assembly did not acknowledge the Arab League's intended relationship to the United Nations when it invited it to send an observer, the League's own resolutions, and the subsequent actual practice of UN organs, leave little doubt about the League's Chapter VIII orientation. On this issue of the qualification of the OAS, OAU, and Arab League as UN Charter 'regional' bodies, see Erkki Kourula, 'Peace-keeping and Regional Arrangements', in A. Cassese (ed.), United Nations Peace-keeping: Legal Essays (Alphen aan den Rijn: Sijthoff & Noordhoff, 1978), 102–6. It might be noted that on three early occasions the General Assembly 'avoided passing judgment' on whether these three organizations were 'arrangements or agencies' in the context of Art. 52 of Chapter VIII. See Akindele, The Organization and Promotion of World Peace, 11, citing Leland M. Goodrich, Edvard V. Hambro, and Anne P. Simons, Charter of the United Nations: Commentary and Documents (3rd edn., New York: Columbia UP, 1969), 356–7.

[14] During the opening and closing of the 1975 Helsinki Conference itself, the participants were addressed by the UN Secretary-General, Kurt Waldheim, attending as a guest of honour. The Final Act, though not a treaty and therefore not eligible for registration under Art. 102 of the UN Charter, none the less was transmitted to the Secretary-General for circulation to all UN members as 'an official document of the United Nations': 'Conference on Security and Cooperation in Europe: Final Act', The Department of State Bulletin, 73/188 (1 Sept. 1975), 323–50.

Union, the Commonwealth of Independent States, rather surprisingly registered itself as a regional arrangement, winning observer status from the UN General Assembly.

Formalistic and declaratory self-qualification along the lines of the UN Charter's Chapter VIII does not, of course, establish actual working relationships with the world body. The proferred OAS, OAU, LAS, OSCE, and CIS associations with the UN do give them, however, the appearance of consistency with the central organization, a kind of family resemblance to it. They qualify *structurally*, so to speak, to be regional counterparts and potential close accessories of the UN. Moreover, as relatively general-purpose formations, often the leading ones within their respective large geographical spheres, they have a presumptive role in maintaining peace and security there, as well as in handling other matters of common regional concern.

A test, although by no means a conclusive one, of whether these and other possible Chapter VIII entities actually do exercise responsibilities in the peace-and-security field in conjunction with the UN is whether they fulfil the reporting requirement of Article 54. This article in Chapter VIII stipulates that, 'at all times', the Security Council is to be 'kept fully informed of activities undertaken or in contemplation under regional arrangements or by regional agencies for the maintenance of international peace and security'.[15] Non-performance of this timely reporting requirement, of course, would not itself prove that the actions taken by regional organizations were at variance with the basic purposes and principles of the Charter of the United Nations. It would, however, suggest that the individuality, autonomy, and capability of a regional grouping were such that it felt it could ignore the world organization.

Controversy regarding the compatibility of regional or subregional security structures with the UN Charter has focused mainly on NATO. Similar to it, as alliances or collective-defence schemes, are the WEU, the Australia–New Zealand–United States (ANZUS) Pact, the South-East Asia Treaty Organization (SEATO), and the Warsaw Treaty Organization (WTO). Although some of these bodies (viz. SEATO and the WTO) are defunct and others

[15] Art. 51, of the preceding non-regionally related Chapter VII, stipulates that measures taken in exercise of the right of self-defence be 'immediately reported' to the Security Council—after the fact.

(e.g. ANZUS) perhaps moribund, all of these treaty-based security relationships contributed substantially to the Cold War bipolar international order. They had important international stabilizing effects, and in some cases even peacemaking influence. Other, newer regional and subregional formations, such as the ASEAN Regional Forum (ARF), may also serve to promote international order and cannot be ignored in any account of global–regional relationships in the field of peace and security, whatever their formal relationship to the UN.

In addition to the structural, or formal-institutional, criteria that may need to be satisfied by a region-based organization, there can be other, more practical tests. If met, these could *functionally* legitimize regional groups' peacemaking actions. As R. A. Akindele has rightly emphasized, 'relations of a regional organization to the United Nations are determined and defined not by the character of the regional organization, but by the function it is performing at a particular time'.[16] The critical fact is not what the organization is, but what it does. Thereby, UN compatibility can be earned by a regional body.

2. GLOBAL–REGIONAL COMPETITION IN INTERNATIONAL PEACEMAKING: THE EVOLVING HISTORICAL PATTERN

During most of the Cold War period the UN and regional bodies tended to grow apart. Paradoxically, certain regional entities, particularly the alliances, assumed some of the broad security responsibilities of the global body, while the UN itself, though retaining its world-wide mandate, in fact involved itself mostly in local peacekeeping duties. The net effect was to reduce the world's reliance on the UN and to de-emphasize the need for regional organizations to co-ordinate their actions with the UN. 'Rightly or wrongly, the emphasis is less on teamwork and more on independent action.'[17] This shift in the inter-organizational balance had important political and legal consequences. 'The constitutional history of the United Nations shows', wrote Akindele in the mid-1970s, 'that there has been a *de facto* revision of the Charter law of

---

[16] Akindele, *The Organization and Promotion of World Peace*, 63.
[17] Wilcox, 'Regionalism and the United Nations', 428 and 430.

universal–regional relationships in favour of greater autonomy for regional organizations.'[18]

There was during the Cold War, therefore, a kind of cross-over between regionalism and universalism. Some regional organizations, notably NATO, assumed the main responsibility for maintaining international security, almost world-wide.[19] Denied its ostensibly central role by the superpower division within it, the UN assumed, *faute de mieux*, the useful but marginal role of keeping peace whenever cease-fires and truces could be worked out in regions. This was not intended. Peacekeeping was an improvisation of the UN—'discovered, like penicillin'.[20] Only during the Korean conflict in 1950 was the UN Security Council, owing to a temporary absence from the Security Council of the Soviet delegate, able to assume its Charter-assigned primary responsibility for peace and security under Chapter VII. Even that exceptional episode, however, was dominated strategically by regional-alliance concerns, including NATO's worry about a possible Russian offensive on the European front.

Chapter VIII-based regional organizations (as distinct from alliances) played a much smaller role than the authors of the Charter had planned. They were not used either as 'shock absorber' or as 'forum of first resort'—at least by the UN Organization. This was not only because of their own weaknesses but also because the proper strength, authority, and credibility of the UN Security Council had not been built up. 'One can only hazard a guess,' Wilcox speculates, 'but in all likelihood if the Security Council had been able to discharge effectively its responsibility for the maintenance of peace, many more disputes of a local character would have been settled at the regional level.'[21]

With this suggestion in mind—namely that effective regional

---

[18] Akindele, *The Organization and Promotion of World Peace*, pp. xi–xii.

[19] On the geographical scope of consultation under the North Atlantic Alliance, see Sir Nicholas Henderson, *The Birth of NATO* (Boulder, Colo.: Westview Press, 1983), 100–5. On NATO's *de facto* extended influence, see Alan K. Henrikson, 'The North Atlantic Alliance as a Form of World Order', in Alan K. Henrikson (ed.), *Negotiating World Order: The Artisanship and Architecture of Global Diplomacy* (Wilmington, Del.: Scholarly Resources Inc., 1986), 111–35; also Elizabeth Sherwood, *Allies in Crisis: Meeting Global Challenges to Western Security* (New Haven: Yale UP, 1990).

[20] Brian Urquhart, 'The United Nations, Collective Security, and International Peacekeeping', in Henrikson (ed.), *Negotiating World Order*, 62.

[21] Wilcox, 'Regionalism and the United Nations', 431.

dispute-settlement depends on effective UN Security Council peace-making—we can now consider the inherited pattern of global–regional relations in the field of peace and security. The story, alas, is mainly one of inter-organizational competition.

(a) The Western Hemisphere

The primordial international-legal formulation of the relationship between the western hemisphere (and indeed all other geopolitical 'regions') and the world organization of the time is Article 21 of the Covenant of the League of Nations. 'Nothing in this Covenant', that article declares, 'shall be deemed to affect the validity of international engagements, such as treaties of arbitration or regional understandings like the Monroe doctrine, for securing the maintenance of peace.' Principally out of deference to the non-member USA, the Geneva-based League generally stayed out of western hemisphere territorial and other disputes. When both the League and the pan-American system did become involved, as during the Bolivian–Paraguayan conflict over the Gran Chaco, the very 'multiplicity of agencies' was regarded as one cause of the failure of peacemaking.[22]

Later, the UN also engaged in contests with the pan-American system. Divergences were partly a function of the inter-American community's sense of its own unique mission, its separate historical personality, but they were also a reflection of the failure of peacemaking at the global level. 'Many of the world-wide institutions under the aegis of the United Nations have become only pale shadows of what their founders . . . expected them to be', as a former OAS Secretary-General from Argentina, Alejandro Orfila, explained. 'In these circumstances, during the Cold War between the two superpowers, the vision of regional order in the Americas gained in attractiveness.'[23] In the western hemisphere the OAS became the organization of choice.

The UN and the OAS engaged in a jurisdictional struggle, in a pattern-setting way, over Guatemala in 1954. The government

[22] See Cordell Hull, *The Memoirs of Cordell Hull*, 2 vols. (New York: Macmillan, 1948), i. 336; F. P. Walters, *A History of the League of Nations*, 2 vols. (London: OUP, 1952), ii. 526.

[23] Alejandro Orfila, 'The Organization of American States and International Order in the Western Hemisphere', in Henrikson (ed.), *Negotiating World Order*, 139.

there under Jacobo Arbenz appealed to both the OAS and the UN in what became, in the words of the President of the Security Council at the time, US Ambassador Henry Cabot Lodge, Jr., a 'fundamental question of venue'.[24] The Soviet Union, supporting the left-wing Guatemalan government, maintained that the issue was one of 'aggression', rather than a 'local dispute' appropriate for a regional organization, and therefore that action by the Security Council under Article 24 (emphasizing the Security Council's 'primary responsibility') was called for. A compromise course (but in effect favouring the American side) was to argue that regional-organizational consideration took priority (Articles 33(1) and 52(2)) but to assert the unaffected legal authority, or supremacy, of the UN. This was the view that in the end prevailed.[25]

The regional–universal dilemma—essentially, a choice between power and law—was posed again in the autumn of 1962. Facing the threat of Soviet nuclear missiles in Cuba, the members of the OAS 'recommended' (for that is all its Charter enables the OAS to do) the collective 'quarantine', or blockade, of Cuba. This autonomous action by the OAS, a Chapter VIII regional organization, was questionable. The US government-promoted doctrine of the OAS as a regional surrogate for the United Nations, rather than a mere local-dispute-settlement mechanism, represents probably the greatest inroad of a UN Charter-based regional organization against the primary jurisdiction of the UN in the field of international peace and security.[26] Although the USA argued that the American republics had 'primary' responsibility, and a corresponding duty to act, the UN was not ignored; and, in accordance with Article 54 of the UN Charter, the OAS duly forwarded its 'quarantine' resolution to the UN. Yet Secretary-General U Thant left no doubt that he believed the US–OAS naval measures to be organ-

[24] UN doc. SCOR/675 of 20 June 1954, 1.
[25] Akindele, *The Organization and Promotion of World Peace*, 80–1. See also Brian Urquhart, *Hammarskjöld* (New York: Harper Colophon Books, 1972), 92–3.
[26] On this question and on US efforts to overcome the suspicion of illegality, see Akindele, *The Organization and Promotion of World Peace*, xii. 110–15; Abram Chayes, 'The Legal Case for the US Action on Cuba', *The Department of State Bulletin*, 47/1221 (Nov. 1962), 763–5. See also Abram Chayes, *The Cuban Missile Crisis: International Crises and the Role of Law* (New York: OUP, 1974); and Dean Rusk, as told to Richard Rusk, *As I Saw It*, ed. Daniel S. Papp (New York: Penguin Books, 1991), 232–3.

izationally *ultra vires*, however strategically warranted they might have been. [27]

The crisis in 1965 in the Dominican Republic very slightly reconciled the two organizations when, for the first time, a hemispheric organization fielded a military unit of its own. As nominally a 'peacekeeping' exercise rather than an 'enforcement' action, the dispatch of the Inter-American Peace Force by the OAS allegedly did not require prior approval by the Security Council (the 'authorization' mandated by Article 53(1)) but only the Security Council's being 'kept fully informed' (Article 54). After this event it would be generally understood that the UN would be able to increase its political involvement in the Americas only if regional action under OAS auspices were to fail.[28] UN Secretary-General U Thant, to be sure, did send a representative to the Dominican Republic to seek a cease-fire, observe, and report; and the first real cease-fire in the situation was in fact negotiated by that representative, the Venezuelan diplomat José Mayobre. It historically 'bears mentioning' that, as U Thant noted, the Dominican episode was the first one in which the.UN and the OAS acted concurrently, going in 'side by side'.[29] The relationship, however, remained strongly competitive.

(b) Africa

The global–regional balance with regard to peace and security in Africa was also tilted heavily in favour of the regional body, the OAU, despite that organization's lack of effectiveness. Its institutional disability for peacemaking purposes is partly a function of independent-Africa's consensus, embodied in the 1963 Addis

[27] U Thant, *View from the UN* (Garden City, NY: Doubleday & Co., 1978), 163–4 and 172. The UN Security Council refused a Cuban request that the Council request of the International Court of Justice an advisory opinion regarding, *inter alia*, whether the OAS had the right to take enforcement action against a UN member state without authorization by the Security Council. This refusal was described by Thant as 'a tragedy'. 'By this *nonaction* the Security Council implicitly endorses "Monroe Doctrines" everywhere on earth', ibid. 160 and 173.

[28] The US Ambassador to the UN, Adlai Stevenson, expressed the view that 'the purposes of the United Nations Charter will hardly be served if two international organizations are seeking to do things in the same place with the same people at the same time': UN doc. S/PV 1217 of 22 May 1965, 21, quoted in Linda B. Miller, *World Order and Local Disorder: The United Nations and Internal Conflicts* (Princeton: Princeton UP, 1967), 159.

[29] Thant, *View from the UN*, 371–3.

Ababa Charter establishing the OAU, that the territorial frame-work of boundaries inherited from the European colonial powers was not to be changed, and partly of the reluctance of outside powers again to become involved there.[30] OAU regional diplomacy therefore normally predominated. For example, when hostilities broke out in 1963 between Morocco and Algeria, Morocco's King Hassan II was doubtful that the OAU would take an open-minded approach to his revisionist boundary claims against Algeria and instead brought the matter to the attention of the UN Secretary-General. Algeria, relying on the Addis Ababa Charter, sought OAU mediation. The major Western countries, wishing to avoid en-tanglement, persuaded the Moroccan monarch to accept regional management of the issue. This finally was resolved in 1972 accord-ing to the territorial status quo guideline of the OAU Charter. The Moroccan–Algerian precedent established what has been termed the 'Try OAU First' principle.[31]

The OAU claimed precedence again in 1964 when Somalia, accusing Ethiopia and also Kenya of holding lands it believed were Somali, asked for UN Security Council consideration of its charge of aggression. Other African countries counselled withdrawal of the request and Somalia soon complied, informing the Security Council that it no longer wished to raise the issue 'while the problem is in the hands of the OAU'.[32] The pressures of regional conformity were simply too strong. As Akindele comments: 'no African state has adamantly insisted on ignoring the OAU and on having direct access to the world body.' This also then reflected the reluctance of UN members, especially the most powerful states, 'to be drawn into African disputes which were not perceived as raising fundamentally critical issues of global strategic signifi-

[30] See Samuel Chime, 'The Organization of African Unity and African Bound-aries', in C. G. Widstrand (ed.), *African Boundary Problems* (Uppsala: Scandin-avian Institute of African Studies, 1969), 65–79, and Boutros Boutros-Ghali, *L'Organisation de l'Unité Africaine* (Paris: Librairie Armand Colin, 1969). Art. III of the OAU Charter proclaims 'respect for the sovereignty and territorial integrity of each State and for its inalienable right to independent existence'.
[31] Berhanykun Andemicael, 'The Organization of African Unity and the United Nations: Relations in the Peace and Security Field', in Berhanykun Andemicael (ed.), *Regionalism and the United Nations* (Dobbs Ferry, NY: published for UNITAR by Oceana Publications, 1979), 238 and 254–6. Also see Wellington W. Nyangoni, *Africa in the United Nations System* (Cranbury, NJ: Associated University Presses, 1985).
[32] UN doc. SCOR s/5542 of 14 Feb. 1964, 65–6.

cance'.[33] Cold War divisions usually precluded the Organization's united action.

The UN did, to be sure, become deeply involved in the civil war in the Congo although this was a somewhat different category of problem, centring not on differences over boundaries but on the basic question of political and administrative control. In 1960, when the Belgian mercenary-assisted breakaway of Katanga Province occurred, the Congolese government urgently requested UN assistance. On the basis of a resolution by the Security Council, UN peacekeeping units and also a Reconciliation Commission were sent.[34] The UN wanted to insulate the Congo as much as possible from the risk of great-power intervention and encouraged maximum African participation. The formation of the OAU, in part a response to the Congo crisis, introduced a new regional player in the situation. It tried its best to 'Africanize' the process of bringing of peace to the Congo. An Ad Hoc Commission of ten OAU members under Jomo Kenyatta consulted, but could not prevent, an American–British–Belgian rescue operation that took place in Stanleyville in November 1964. The OAU joined in international requests for a meeting of the UN Security Council to condemn this extra-regional intervention. Ultimately, the Security Council passed a resolution placing the problem of peace promotion in the Congo 'in the lap of the OAU'.[35] The UN was not drawn into the Nigerian civil war of 1967–70, because it recognized that the majority of African states supported the Nigerian federal government in Lagos rather than the independence-seeking Biafra.

The OAU, though generally ineffective, did achieve a noteworthy, if minor, success with a peacekeeping operation in Chad during the war of 1981–3. OAU diplomatic and military efforts helped to 'erect a cordon' around that conflict, helping to prevent the collapse of the Chadian state, and underlining the African policy against outside involvement by the former European colonial states, by the superpowers, or even by the UN. 'The OAU fears the

[33] Akindele, *The Organization and Promotion of World Peace*, 96–8.
[34] Ralph J. Bunche, 'The United Nations Operation in the Congo', in Andrew W. Cordier and Wilder Foote (eds.), *The Quest for Peace: The Dag Hammarskjöld Memorial Lectures* (New York: Columbia UP, 1965), 126. On the juridical position of the UN Operation in the Congo (ONUC), see R. Simmonds, *Legal Problems Arising from the United Nations Military Operations in the Congo* (The Hague: Martinus Nijhoff, 1968).
[35] Akindele, *The Organization and Promotion of World Peace*, 98–102.

internationalization of African conflicts, and seeks to contain these conflicts within the continental jurisdiction'.[36]

(c) The Middle East

Organized diplomatic contact between regionalism and globalism for peace-and-security purposes in the Middle East has been minimal. A rare early case, showing the difficulty as well as the promise of co-ordinated peacemaking by a regional body and the world organization, concerned Lebanon. In May 1958 that country's President, Camille Chamoun, appealed to the League of Arab States and then also to the UN to put an end to what he considered foreign intervention in his country—armed subversives allegedly backed by the newly combined Egyptian—Syrian United Arab Republic (UAR). Because of the temporal priority of the request to the Arab League, and also because of the view that the regional organization ought to be allowed at least to try to promote peace, the Security Council suspended its own consideration of the issue. Although the Council of the Arab League sought exclusive control of the matter, the Government in Beirut exercised its right under Article 35 to return to the Security Council and it obtained, owing to the Soviet Union's abstention, a neutral Swedish resolution calling for dispatch of what became the UN Observation Group in Lebanon (UNOGIL). Because of the intrusion of extra-regional forces (underlined by the pre-emptive landing of US troops in Lebanon), the Arab League had to attempt to regain a measure of regional influence by acting within the UN. Ten Arab governments successfully proposed that the UN General Assembly call upon Secretary General Dag Hammarskjöld to arrange for an early withdrawal of foreign troops. Arab diplomacy, though not the Arab League *per se*, thus played a critical role, the UN being the context for it.[37]

Other situations in which there has been some Arab League– United Nations contact, occasionally also through the Arab group at the UN, include the Kuwait–Iraq border dispute of 1961, civil

---

[36] Bamayangay Joseph Massaquoi, 'Conflict Resolution: The OAU and Chad', *Transafrica Forum*, 7/4 (Winter 1990/1), 83–99.

[37] Urquhart, *Hammarskjöld*, 261–92; Akindele, *The Organization and Promotion of World Peace*, 89–92; Hussein A. Hassouna, 'The League of Arab States and the United Nations: Relations in the Peaceful Settlement of Disputes', in Andemicael (ed.), *Regionalism and the United Nations*, 310.

strife in Yemen in 1962, and, a decade later, a border conflict between North and South Yemen. In dealing with the first of these, which was largely managed by Arab diplomacy, an Arab League Security Force was actually organized and sent. At the time the machinery of the UN Security Council was veto-blocked, and the Arab League's action probably saved Kuwait. In 1976 an even larger Arab peacekeeping force went into Lebanon, which was increasingly beset by the Israeli–Palestinian struggle as well as by its own internal wrangling.[38] The UN did not become involved there until March 1978 when it augmented the Syrian-dominated Arab regional force with a more widely gathered UN Interim Force in Lebanon (UNIFIL). The interplay of the UN and the Arab League was beginning to become regularized.

(d) Europe

The prime example of peace-and-security action in the European strategic theatre and its environs is, of course, the defence and deterrence offered by NATO. Although US Secretary of State John Foster Dulles made it plain that 'NATO has not been organized as a regional association, nor has it any policy or jurisdiction to deal with disputes as between the members', the North Atlantic Treaty Organization, being a political alliance as well as a military force, actually has exercised a peacemaking influence. In late 1956, following the Suez débâcle, a NATO Committee of Three composed of the foreign ministers of Canada, Italy, and Norway recommended that the Alliance improve its consultation capabilities. The NATO member governments reaffirmed their obligation to settle disputes by peaceful means (a UN Charter commitment repeated in Article 1 of the North Atlantic Treaty). Moreover, they agreed to submit internal disputes among themselves to good-offices procedures *within* their Alliance—'before resorting to any other agency'.[39] NATO thus gained organizational priority, if not juridical supremacy, and the UN was scarcely thought of as an alternative.

[38] Hassouna, 'The League of Arab States and the United Nations', 319–21.
[39] *The Department of State Bulletin*, 34/884 (4 June 1956): 925–6, and 'Non-Military Co-operation in NATO: Text of the Report of the Committee of Three', *NATO Letter*, 5, special suppl. to no. 1 (1 Jan. 1957), 8, quoted in Wilcox, 'Regionalism and the United Nations', 431–2.

The major historical achievement of regional peacemaking by NATO as an organization surely has been its management of French–German differences, including the Saar dispute. NATO also institutionally mediated the British–Icelandic 'cod war' and moderated the British–Spanish Gibraltar question. The most notable case of inter-organizational pacific diplomacy, involving the UN as well concerns the issue of Cyprus. In 1956 the first Secretary-General of NATO, Britain's Lord Ismay, suggested to the North Atlantic Council that a committee be formed to mediate the Cyprus conflict, which divided the NATO allies Greece and Turkey.[40] When civil war broke out on the island in 1963, the British government, with the support of Washington, proposed sending in a NATO-recruited peacekeeping force of ten thousand men. This plan was rejected, however, by Archbishop Makarios, President of Cyprus, who insisted that the UN Security Council, and not NATO, was the proper venue. A revised British plan which tied the NATO force fairly closely to the UN ('linking' it to the UN by 'reports'), was also refused by Makarios, even though the Greek and Turkish governments were willing to participate. The eventual outcome was the establishment in 1964 of the United Nations' Peacekeeping Force for Cyprus (UNFICYP) with NATO forces remaining in the background.[41]

When in 1974 the Turkish government, responding to appeals from Turkish Cypriots, landed on Cyprus with a large-scale armed force and set up the Republic of Northern Cyprus, NATO as an organization failed to react as it could and should have done. Despite the long-lasting deadlock on that island, it can at least be said, however, that the structure of NATO, together with the organization's military power and latent political influence, probably has helped to keep the problem of Cyprus (and perhaps other European subregional problems) contained. But without a diplomatically active and effective United Nations, a regional alliance formation cannot by itself easily transform stability into peace.

[40] Robert S. Jordan, with Michael W. Bloome, *Political Leadership in NATO: A Study in Multinational Diplomacy* (Boulder, Colo.: Westview Press, 1979), 37.
[41] Miller, *World Order and Local Disorder*, 116–48; Karl Th. Birgisson, 'United Nations Peacekeeping Force in Cyprus', in William J. Durch (ed.), *The Evolution of UN Peacekeeping: Case Studies and Comparative Analysis* (New York: St Martin's Press, 1993), 219–36.

3. INTER-ORGANIZATIONAL CO-OPERATION IN PEACEMAKING: RECENT CASES

The end of the Cold War and the proliferation of ethnic and other conflicts have made it necessary, as never before, for regional organizations and the UN to work together—actually to co-operate, rather than merely to coexist. Although there is evidence that both categories of organization are becoming stronger, it remains to be seen whether they will become more united in action. Some involvement by the UN is clearly necessary for regional efforts, some of them unprecedented and innovative, to be made fully acceptable and practically effective. Organizational personalities, however, are not easily fused. Recent cases make the possibilities, as well as the difficulties, clear.

(a) Central America and the Caribbean

In the final phases of the East–West conflict in the 1980s, two phenomena stood out. The first was that the Organization of American States, which had been fairly effective in dealing especially with small Central American pacification problems, was for a time eclipsed.[42] The 'awkward absence', as it has been called, of the main regional organization in managing the internal and international conflicts centred on Nicaragua and El Salvador is an indication of the disqualifying 'structural problems' of the OAS. The organizational genius, or individuality, of the OAS has existed mainly in the field of economic and social development. It was not equipped to quell a big-power-supported 'proxy' guerrilla war in its midst. It lacked the needed capability for that purpose.

A second surprise of the 1980s was the 'appearance' of *ad hoc* subregional formations, notably the four-power Conta:Jora group (Mexico, Venezuela, Colombia, and Panama), the Lima Support Group (Argentina, Brazil, Peru, and Uruguay), and the combined Rio Group. This further detracted from the peacemaking com-

---

[42] Jack Child, *The Central American Peace Process: Sheathing Swords, Building Confidence* (Boulder, Colo: Lynne Rienner, 1992), 9. For background, see Alan K. Henrikson, 'East–West Rivalry in Latin America: "Between the Eagle and the Bear" ', in Robert W. Clawson (ed.), *East–West Rivalry in the Third World: Security Issues and Regional Perspectives* (Wilmington, Del.: Scholarly Resources Inc., 1986).

petence of the OAS.[43] As the OAS Secretary-General, Alejandro Orfila, frankly acknowledged: 'I believe that the OAS has paid a terrific price in terms of public opinion within the hemisphere, and also outside it, because of the existence of the Contadora group.'[44]

According to Orfila, the OAS was not considered by some to be a forum 'in which to win—to get complete support for partisan positions'.[45] Regional groups, it has been noted, have often made some intra-regional parties feel that they are 'outsiders', ostracized by the rest.[46] The Nicaraguan Sandinista government, no doubt, did consider the US-dominated OAS to be hostile toward it. As the USA 'contributes the lion's share of the OAS budget', that country easily could prevent the organization from dealing independently or in a positive and substantive way with conflicts it did not wish the body to address. Moreover, there is the relative 'paucity of experience' of the OAS in the field of reconstructing international peace and security. All of these considerations pointed to the relative superiority of the UN even in dealing with the traditional OAS preserve of Central America.[47]

At first the challenge was met by the Contadora partners and then by a new process of Central American presidential summit meetings initiated by Costa Rica's President Oscar Arias Sánchez, who sought to restore responsibility for resolving the crisis to Central Americans themselves.[48] The UN Security Council initially only 'nibbled around the edges' of the Central American problem by, for example, endorsing the ongoing efforts of the Contadora

[43] S. Neil MacFarlane and Thomas G. Weiss, 'Regional Organizations and Regional Security', *Security Studies*, 2/1 (Fall 1992), 21.

[44] Orfila, 'The Organization of American States and International Order in the Western Hemisphere', 141. The OAS was also slighted when, in Oct. 1983, the small subregional Organization of Eastern Caribbean States (OECS) was the body that acted to deal with the disturbed situation in Grenada. The OECS requested US military intervention and also sent in an improvised Caribbean Defense Force.

[45] Ibid.

[46] On this point, see Oscar Schachter, 'Authorized Uses of Force by the United Nations and Regional Organizations', in Lori Fisler Damrosch and David J. Scheffer (eds.), *Law and Force in the New International Order* (Boulder, Colo.: Westview Press, 1991), 86–9.

[47] This is the argument of MacFarlane and Weiss, 'Regional Organizations and Regional Security', 22.

[48] Luis G. Solís, 'Collective Mediations in the Caribbean Basin', in Carl Kaysen, Robert A. Pastor, and Laura W. Reed (eds.), *Collective Responses to Regional Problems: The Case of Latin America and the Caribbean* (Cambridge, Mass.: American Academy of Arts and Sciences, 1994), 110, 112.

group. Yet the UN Secretariat gradually became more active. At a low point in the talks in 1986, the Peruvian Secretary-General Pérez de Cuéllar made 'a gingerly *démarche*' to the Central American countries—in conjunction with his OAS counterpart, João Baena Soares—pointing out that the UN and the OAS, 'separately or jointly', could provide a number of useful services. This co-operative step, as his assistant for the Central American matter, Alvaro de Soto, reflects, had 'a catalytic effect'.[49]

The outcome (the Arias-designed Esquipulas Agreement on regional democratization and pacification), followed by the creation of an impartial UN verification mechanism (the United Nations Observer Group in Central America (ONUCA)) and also establishment of an OAS mechanism (the International Commission of Support and Verification (CIAV/OAS)), was a diplomatic achievement of the first order. The UN engaged in peacekeeping in the western hemisphere for the first time. The OAS, reinforced by its partnership with the UN and also by the recent addition of Canada to OAS membership, gained a measure of independence from the USA and a renewed sense of its own mission. Despite their different procedures and the strains that occasionally resulted, the two organizations basically worked well together, and also with a variety of non-governmental organizations. The UN shared with the OAS the tasks of monitoring elections and of demobilizing military forces in and near Nicaragua. They also combined efforts in supervising the complex reconciliation process in El Salvador. On 15 January 1992, after more than twelve years of fighting, a ceremony of completion and rededication to peace was held in Santa Elena, El Salvador, with both OAS Secretary-General Baena Soares, and the new UN Secretary-General, Boutros Boutros-Ghali, prominently participating.[50]

The UN and the OAS have also been institutionally involved in dealing with instability in Haiti. The UN at first held itself aloof from the Haitian problem, which did not clearly raise issues of international peace and security. An open invitation from Haiti's

---

[49] Alvaro de Soto, 'Case Study: The Peace Process in Central America', *Singapore Seminar*, 42–6.

[50] 'The United Nations Role in the Central American Peace Process', UN Focus, DPI/1036R-01201 (Feb. 1991); Terry Lynn Karl, 'El Salvador's Negotiated Revolution', *Foreign Affairs*, 71/2 (Spring 1992), 147–64; David Holiday and William Stanley, 'Building the Peace: Preliminary Lessons from El Salvador', *Journal of International Affairs*, 46/2 (Winter 1993), 415–38.

provisional President, Ertha Pascal-Trouillot, to both the UN and the OAS to observe that country's election in December 1990, however, posed the question of their participating together. After lobbying by a former US President, Jimmy Carter, and a number of Caribbean area leaders, the UN finally acceded to her request, and Election Day (16 December) was witnessed by representatives of both world and regional organizations.

It was partly because of this early electoral involvement that, when a military coup on 30 September 1991 overthrew the recently elected President Jean-Bertrand Aristide, the UN could not easily treat the Haitian problem as being 'essentially within the domestic jurisdiction' of a state (Article 2 (7)) and thus beyond the reach of the UN Charter. The OAS already seemed to have overcome its inhibitions regarding active 'domestic' interference to support constitutional government. The hemisphere (except for Cuba) was then, unprecedently, composed of democracies. At a historic meeting in Santiago, Chile, in June 1991, the participating members of the OAS had resolved that any 'sudden or irregular interruption of the democratic political institutional process' in any one of their countries would result in the calling of an emergency meeting of foreign ministers to decide what to do.[51] Invoking the so-called Santiago Commitment when the coup in Haiti occurred on 30 September, the OAS foreign ministers collectively urged: a mission to Port-au-Prince; the 'diplomatic isolation' of Lieut.-Gen. Raoul Cédras and the others who had illegally seized power there; and, except for humanitarian assistance, the suspension of economic, financial, and commercial ties with Haiti. Some OAS members even suggested an 'OAS force', to be mainly civilian but to have some lightly armed personnel along to provide protection.[52] The idea of military enforcement, however, did not fit with the OAS's organizational personality, and nothing was done.

[51] For further details, see Chapter 9.
[52] Robert A. Pastor, *Whirlpool: U.S. Foreign Policy toward Latin America and the Caribbean* (Princeton: Princeton UP, 1992), 247–50; Richard J. Bloomfield, 'Making the Western Hemisphere Safe for Democracy? The OAS Defense-of-Democracy Regime', *Washington Quarterly*, 17/2 (spring 1994), 157–69; 'OAS Resolutions on Haiti', texts of 'Support to the Democratic Republic of Haiti', MRE/RES. 1/91 (3 Oct. 1991), and 'Support for Democracy in Haiti', MRE/RES. 2/91 (8 Oct. 1991), *US Department of State Dispatch*, 2/41 (14 Oct. 1991), 760–1; Thomas L. Friedman' 'A Regional Group Moves to Isolate Haiti's New Junta', *New York Times*, 3 Oct. 1991, and id., 'Regional Group Plans to Increase Penalties on Haiti', *New York Times*, 9 Oct. 1991.

A further reason for that organization's inability to follow through more effectively at that time was the merely supportive role of the UN. The UN then was 'outrun' by the regional organization, candidly admits Dante Caputo, a former Argentine Foreign Minister who, remarkably, was appointed Special Envoy for the Haitian situation by UN Secretary-General Boutros-Ghali and subsequently by OAS Secretary-General Baena Soares as well. The UN General Assembly, for its part, did pass a resolution which requested that the Secretary-General lend his OAS opposite number collegial support, condemned the coup led by General Cédras, and called upon all UN member states 'to emulate the OAS example' (i.e. by applying sanctions), as Caputo described this non-binding and hortatory action. Some extra-hemispheric countries, including members of European Community, continued to trade with Haiti, even by exporting oil to it, thus effectively 'nullifying' the OAS-recommended sanctions.[53]

On the initiative of a new informal group—the Friends of the Secretary-General for Haiti (Canada, France, USA, and Venezuela)—the UN Security Council, invoking Chapter VII, in Resolution 841 (16 June 1993) did finally act to 'make universal and mandatory' the trade embargo previously recommended by the OAS and endorsed by the UN General Assembly. These measures required 'all States' and also 'all international organizations' (read: the European Community) to act strictly in accordance with their provisions, which were binding globally. This co-operative UN–OAS action made it possible that Haiti might be one case, in Dante Caputo's hopeful prediction, 'in which such sanctions could actually work'.[54] The sanctions regime later was tightened through Resolution 917 (6 May 1994). When even these stringent measures did not work to unseat the *de facto* government under Cédras, the USA persuaded the Security Council on 31 July to authorize 'a

---

[53] 'UN General Assembly Resolution 46/7 on Haiti', 12 Oct. 1991, *US Department of State Dispatch*, 2/41 (14 Oct. 1991), 762; Dante Caputo, 'Haiti: Un Cri de Cœur', *Global Action* (Newsletter of Parliamentarians for Global Action), 5/3, (Sept. 1993), 7 and 10. The European Community was handicapped somewhat by its Lomé Convention relationship with Haiti.

[54] 'UN Security Council Resolution 841 on Crisis in Haiti', 16 June 1993, *US Department of State Dispatch*, 4/26 (28 June 1993), 469–70; Caputo, 'Haiti', 10. The global–regional co-operative theme is explicit in SC Res. 841: 'Recalling . . . the provisions of Chapter VIII of the Charter of the United Nations and stressing the need for effective co-operation between regional organizations and the United Nations.'

multilateral force under unified command and control . . . to use all necessary means'.[55]

Owing to this sequence of events there has arisen some anxiety within the inter-American community lest the OAS fall into 'hierarchical' bondage to the UN.[56] Nevertheless, it had gradually become clear that, as a practical matter, the actions taken by the OAS to isolate the *de facto* regime in Haiti could not succeed without the constitutional authority and political backing of the UN. The actual forces used, however, were those of the USA, a hemispheric power, supplemented by personnel from a number of Caribbean Community (CARICOM) states with support from Argentina, Great Britain, and various other individual countries around the world. On 18 September 1994 the Cédras Government was persuaded to give way and the US-led Multinational Force made it possible for President Aristide to return to office. The OAS was essentially a bystander, although a combined UN–OAS International Civilian Mission (MICIVIH) was enabled to resume its human-rights monitoring role. The subsequent post-restoration phase of the Haiti crisis was to be handled mainly by a UN peacekeeping mission (UNMIH) and President Clinton made it clear that 'the coalition will pass the baton to the United Nations', which it did.[57]

(b) West Africa, the African Horn, Southern Africa, and Central Africa

It would seem impossible for any one organization to police the whole African continent. The structural weaknesses of the Organization of African Unity, which has plainly lacked the capability of handling conflicts located around that vast continent, and some-

[55] 'Shared Resolve in Restoring Democracy in Haiti', statement by Madeleine K. Albright and SC Res. 940, 31 July 1994, *US Department of State Dispatch*, 5/33 (15 Aug. 1994), 554–6.

[56] Brazil, as an elected member of the UN Security Council in 1993, pressed for a 'security'-based resolution to deal with Haiti partly in order to keep the UN out of other sensitive inter-American affairs, including not only human rights and democracy but also the realm of environmental protection: Bloomfield, 'Making the Western Hemisphere Safe for Democracy?', 165.

[57] 'The Crisis in Haiti', *US Department of State Dispatch*, 5/38 (19 Sept. 1994), 610. An extraneous, though strategically important, political reason behind the Clinton administration's turn to the UN, rather than the OAS, was its wish to set a precedent for close UN supervision of Russian-controlled CIS military peacekeeping intervention in the Caucasus region and Central Asia.

times even the political interest to do so, have contributed to peacekeeping experiments both at the subregional level and through the involvement of the UN.

The most remarkable case in point is the *ad hoc* military intervention carried out in Liberia in 1990 by ECOMOG—the 'Monitoring Group' of the Economic Community of West African States (ECOWAS). With offshore assistance from the US Navy and Marine Corps, ECOWAS, through this improvisation (at odds with its basic organizational personality as an economic-integration instrument) succeeded temporarily in bringing about a modicum of peace in that country, at least in its capital, Monrovia. To some sceptical Africans the ECOMOG forces provided by Nigeria and other English-speaking countries mostly served local hegemonic and partisan purposes—a recurrent complaint against regionally originated military interventions.[58] 'They came in there as a neutral party, hoping to bring about a mediation. But they're now one of the combatants', as the then US Assistant Secretary of State for African Affairs, Herman J. Cohen, admitted. This was one reason why it seemed to Cohen that the UN would have to take over as intermediary in the Liberian situation.[59]

The UN did send a representative, Trevor Gordon-Somers of Jamaica. Yet the Liberian state had effectively collapsed, and there seemed little to repair. As one commentator noted, even the UN was 'not collectively in a position to intervene in that kind of a situation'.[60] Partly for that reason, the UN Security Council initially backed the ECOWAS peacekeeping operation by imposing a Chapter VII arms embargo against the rebel forces in Liberia and by calling on all parties there to respect a cease-fire that was negotiated. This action (Security Council Resolution 788 of 19 November 1992) is 'the first major UN effort to promote peacekeeping by a regional organization'.[61]

Subsequent negotiations conducted in Geneva under the joint auspices of ECOWAS, OAU, and the UN produced a peace agreement; this was signed at an ECOWAS summit meeting in Cotonou,

---

[58] MacFarlane and Weiss, 'Regional Organizations and Regional Security', 18–21.
[59] Steven A. Holmes, 'U.S. Tries to Blunt Harm of Remark on Liberia Peacekeepers', *New York Times*, 15 Nov. 1992.
[60] *The Singapore Symposium*, 19.
[61] Peter James Spielmann, 'UN Approves Use of Force to Cut Off Liberia Rebels', *Boston Globe*, 20 Nov. 1992.

Benin, on 25 July 1993. The agreement called for ECOMOG to continue its peacekeeping function and for the UN to play a monitoring role through what became the UN Observer Mission in Liberia (UNOMIL). An advance group of UN military observers participated in a Joint Cease-fire Monitoring Committee that was set up. Without this technical and political support authorized by the UN Security Council, and also without the substantial humanitarian assistance extended by other parts of the UN system, these pioneering West African peacemaking efforts in Liberia could not have had much chance of success.[62] Even with additional support from the UN, they still have not brought stability to that country.

The uncivil conflict in Somalia on the Horn of Africa has put the principle of regional-organizational priority—specifically that of the OAU—to an embarrassingly severe test. Boutros-Ghali, being an Egyptian and formerly himself active in the Organization of African Unity as his country's Foreign Minister, was personally affected by the Somalian tragedy—as Pérez de Cuéllar was by the conflict in Central America. He therefore followed his predecessor's lead in directly taking up the Somali issue. Calling together in Cairo regional leaders from the OAU, the Arab League, and the Organization of the Islamic Conference (OIC), Boutros-Ghali pointed out their responsibilities (no doubt reflecting upon Chapter VIII, as well as Chapter VI) and sharply enquired as to their plans. Talks also were held in New York under UN, OAU, LAS, and OIC auspices with the contending Somali parties also present.

However, as none of the regional organizations asserted primacy in the situation, the UN increasingly stepped in. The first physical measure taken by the UN, in April 1992, was to assign some fifty unarmed military observers to Somalia. The ineffectuality of that action, long-delayed in actual execution, led to the Security Council's later authorization of an airlift. The Security Council resolution expressly welcomed 'the cooperation between the United Nations, the Organization of African Unity, the League of Arab States and Organization of the Islamic Conference in resolving the situation in Somalia'. This had little practical effect. On 3 December 1992 the Security Council authorized (via SC Res. 794) the UN membership, with the USA leading the way, to intervene with force in Somalia in order to deliver the needed assistance. This was an important precedent for the UN, as the first time the Security Council authorized military intervention 'for strictly humanitarian purposes'.[63] The UN thereafter found itself virtually responsible for reconstructing civic order—'painting nations blue', in Douglas Hurd's memorable phrase.[64]

Yet to the new Clinton administration, 'nation-building' seemed increasingly an impossible task and American forces, the vanguard and main body of the Unified Task Force, were therefore soon scheduled for complete withdrawal. The UN operation (UNOSOM II) that replaced it did not seem any more likely to be successful. In early 1995 it, too, was withdrawn. It can plausibly be argued, in retrospect, that had early regional intercession, mainly diplomatic, occurred rather than extra-continental military intervention, some kind of internal political arrangement might have been worked out. That, at any rate, is the assessment of Mohamed Sahnoun, the Algerian diplomat (formerly a Deputy Secretary-General of the OAU as well as Deputy Secretary-General of the Arab League) who served for a time as UN Secretary-General Boutros-Ghali's Special Representative for Somalia. 'The first stage should be regional,' Sahnoun has said. 'In Somalia, the OAU should have done it.'[65]

The priority of regional response, with the UN providing mainly substantive support, seems so far to have been the dominant lesson learned from the Somalian catastrophe. To the US government, wishing to distance itself from a disaster (not involving any vital national interest), the critical contribution required from the outside seemed to be 'reinforcement of Africans' own ability to resolve their internal and regional conflicts'. Given the limited financial resources available to and from the UN Organization, much of this help would have to come through US and other national foreign-aid programmes. Such assistance could build up

[63] Boutros Boutros-Ghali, *Report on the Work of the Organization from the Forty-seventh to the Forty-eighth Session of the General Assembly*, Sept. 1993 (New York: United Nations, 1993), 148.

[64] Paul Lewis, 'Painting Nations Blue: Somalia Mission May Become Model for the U.N. in Other Failed Countries', *New York Times*, 9 Dec. 1992.

[65] Interview with Mohamed Sahnoun, ' "It's difficult to point to a situation where armed intervention represented a solution" ', *Middle East Report*, 24/2–3 (Mar.–June 1994), 30. See also his *Somalia: The Missed Opportunities* (Washington, DC: US Institute of Peace Press, 1994).

the 'conflict-resolution capacity' of existing organizations in Africa, notably the OAU.[66] The UN could co-ordinate efforts as needed.

In situation after situation throughout Africa—from Angola and Mozambique in Southern Africa to Burundi and Rwanda in Central Africa—it usually has been, however, the UN that has assumed the primary responsibility. The OAU, though in 1993 it did finally begin to develop a permanent conflict-handling instrument (the Central Organ of the Mechanism for Conflict Prevention, Management, and Resolution), has often been 'the dog that did not bark'.[67] It was thus the UN that fielded the Angola Verification Mission (UNAVEM), which verified the departure of Cuban troops in 1988 and subsequently monitored elections in that country. It was the UN Operation in Mozambique (ONUMOZ) that has worked to implement a peace agreement between the Government and resistance movement there. It was the UN (with African countries lobbying at UN Headquarters in New York as well as working through the OAU) that for so long applied effective international pressure against the former apartheid regime in South Africa. It was the UN that sent a team into Burundi and has taken the lead, though not with constant effort or effect, in dealing with horrifying conditions of genocide in Rwanda.

The Rwandan case clearly presents the need for close global—regional co-operation in Africa. The effort of the UN and OAU are mutually dependent. Secretary-General Boutros-Ghali recalls: 'I have written a letter to the Secretary-General of the OAU [Salim Ahmed Salim], to the President of the OAU [Egyptian President Hosni Mubarak], asking them, please send troops, announce that you are ready to participate in the peacekeeping operation in Rwanda, and this will help me to obtain from the Security Council and from the donor countries the financial assistance necessary to reinforce the United Nations presence on the ground.' Without such a commitment from African countries, Boutros-Ghali feared, donor countries would say, 'Why must we be more royalist than the king?' At the same time, the UN Secretary-General emphasized the supremacy, ascendancy, and capability of his organization by noting that 'the leadership is supposed to be the Security Council. They

---

[66] Herman J. Cohen, 'Peace-keeping and Conflict Resolution in Africa', *US Department of State Dispatch*, 4/16 (19 Apr. 1993), 270–2.
[67] MacFarlane and Weiss, 'Regional Organizations and Regional Security', 15.

decide it, they have the mandate, they have the power, they have the financial capacity to send force.'[68]

If the West African countries could get together subregionally to send a force to Liberia, Boutros-Ghali and others have reasoned, then the countries of East and Central Africa ought to be able to co-operate within their area to assist Rwanda. The experience gained by Ghanaian troops in ECOMOG, if shared through joint action and training, could strengthen such an East-Central African effort. The OAU, with its new Mechanism for Conflict Prevention, Management, and Resolution, could take responsibility for fostering a durable peace settlement in the locale, if not for mustering an all-African peacekeeping force. Transportation and other technical support would have to come from wealthy outside countries such as France, Great Britain, the USA, and Japan. On 13 May 1994 the UN Security Council did finally agree to a plan which, though confined in purpose to shielding civilian refugees and protecting aid workers, was designed eventually to send as many as 5,500 peace-keeping troops to Rwanda.[69] Since early 1994 the organizational mainstay in the tragic Rwandan situation, apart from the militarily victorious Rwandan Patriotic Front, has been the UN Assistance Mission in Rwanda (UNAMIR), led by a Canadian and made up of African as well as non-African personnel.

(c) *South-East Asia and North-East Asia*

Probably the most ambitious UN-sponsored regional peacemaking project of all, involving the actual supervision of a nation's administration as well as management of its elections, has been the work of the UN Transitional Authority in Cambodia (UNTAC). Based on the October 1991 Paris Peace Agreements on Cambodia among the five Permanent Members of the UN Security Council together with interested states from Asia and the Pacific and the major factions inside Cambodia itself, the comprehensive UNTAC operation, headed by the UN Secretary-General's Special Representative Yasushi Akashi, supervised elections in May 1993 which established a new government for Cambodia.

[68] *ABC News Nightline*, 4 May 1994.
[69] Paul Lewis, 'U.N. Chief Seeks an African Peace Force for Rwanda', *New York Times*, 5 May 1994; id., 'Security Council Agrees on Plan to Send Peace Force to Rwanda', *New York Times*, 14 May 1994.

UNTAC, as Akashi has described it, was 'a genuine global effort', but it also had 'significant regional input'. Members of the Association of South-East Asian Nations (ASEAN) and other governments in Asia that were actively involved all sent contingents.[70] The so-called UN plan for Cambodia was actually not a UN proposal. It originated with the Paris International Conference on Cambodia (PICC), co-chaired by ASEAN-member Indonesia and France. From the early 1980s, however, the UN kept in close touch with the continuing South-East Asian regional discussions. UN Under-Secretary-General Rafeeuddin Ahmed, for example, was invited every year to meet with the ASEAN Foreign Ministers at the time of their annual ministerial meetings.[71] The culminating accomplishment in Cambodia—the May 1993 elections—was thus truly a combined global–regional diplomatic effort. That has been a factor in ensuring its continued success.

The other trouble spot in the Asian-Pacific region that has posed a major threat to international peace and security has been Korea. The North Korean government under President Kim Il-Sung, now deceased, appeared to be developing a nuclear-weapons capacity. It was the International Atomic Energy Agency (IAEA), an autonomous functional intergovernmental agency, that took the lead in meeting this challenge, which in 1994 was nearly brought to the UN Security Council for the possible application of sanctions. No Chapter VIII regional arrangement or agency exists for North-East Asia, although various suggestions for a 'multilateral dialogue' regarding the stabilization of the area have been offered over the years. Through the new ASEAN Regional Forum (ARF) which though based on the Association of South-East Asian Nations grouping also involves South Korea as well as Japan, China, Russia, the USA, New Zealand, Australia, and Europe, an inter-regional approach to Asian Pacific security issues might increasingly be taken. Eventually, the Asia-Pacific Economic Co-operation (APEC) grouping might also be able to act in a political way, although

[70] Yasushi Akashi, 'UNTAC in Cambodia: Lessons for U.N. Peace-keeping', text of Third Charles Rostov Lecture, Paul H. Nitze School of Advanced International Studies, Johns Hopkins University, Washington, DC, 14 Oct. 1993; Muthiah Alagappa, 'Regionalism and the Quest for Security: ASEAN and the Cambodian Conflict', *Journal of International Affairs*, 46/2 (Winter 1993), 439–67.
[71] Rafeeuddin Ahmed, 'The United Nations Peace Plan for Cambodia', *Singapore Seminar*, 65.

presumably it will remain chiefly concerned with trade, investment, and development issues.

Rejecting the need for a unitary defensive pact, President Clinton, sharing a general view, has argued that '[T]he challenge for the Asian Pacific in this decade, instead, is to develop multiple new arrangements to meet multiple threats and opportunities.' These could 'function like overlapping plates of armour, individually providing protection and together covering the full body of our common security concerns.'[72] To the extent that such subregional 'plates of armour' actually are forged for Asia and the Pacific, they probably will resemble alliances more than international organizations. They are not likely to displace the UN which, as a law-making and action-warranting body, is a sceptre as well as a shield.

(d) South-Eastern Europe, the Caucasus, and Central Asia

The establishment of Western relations with the countries of the collapsed Soviet bloc constitutes a heroic inter-organizational task and a profound diplomatic puzzle. There are more organizations in the wider European sphere than in any other part of the world and, in consequence, there has been a good deal of duplication and resulting mutual irritation. In close co-operation with the USA and Canada, the nations of Western Europe have in recent years joined together with members of the disbanded Warsaw Pact to form the twin foundations—NATO plus the OSCE—for something beginning to approximate what some have conceived of as a 'European security order'.[73] In addition, the Maastricht Treaty of December 1992 committed the European Community members to an 'ever closer Union' in foreign policy and also to formation of an identity in dealing with security and defence issues. Subsequently, together with the existing Western European Union, the new European

---

[72] Fundamentals of Security for a New Pacific Community', address by President Clinton before the National Assembly of the Republic of Korea, Seoul, 19 July 1993, US Department of State Dispatch, 4/29 (19 July 1993), 509–12.

[73] See e.g. Loïc Bouvard (France) and Bruce George (United Kingdom), Co-Rapporteurs, and Jacek Szymandershi (Poland), Associate Rapporteur, 'Draft Interim Report: Working Group on the New European Security Order', Political Committee, North Atlantic Assembly, AI 263, PC/ES (91) 2, International Secretariat, Oct. 1991, and Hans Binnendijk, 'The Emerging European Security Order', Washington Quarterly, 14/4 (Fall 1991), 67–81.

Union (EU) has begun to develop new capabilities. The Franco-German Eurocorps, a EU-sponsored stability pact on frontiers and ethnic disputes, and the NATO-endorsed plan for 'separable, but not separate' Combined Joint Task Forces can all be seen as working towards a European security and defence identity. A further consolidated and expanding European Union could in time become a foundation for not only Western security but also for a wider Eurasian stability. The notional Vancouver-to-Vladivostok reach of the OSCE, with NATO and the EU/WEU working solidly within it, is virtually hemispheric in scope.[74]

The deficiency of many such pan-regional, Euro-Atlantic security schemes is their relative lack of normative and, more specifically, legal-juridical content, and the fact that new peacemaking roles seem to depend of necessity on the international legitimacy provided by the UN. The CSCE's 1992 designation of itself as a Chapter VIII 'Regional Arrangement' is one move in that direction. It seems an attempt to gain more acceptability as a possible mandating authority, even though Article 53(1) clearly states that 'no enforcement action' at least is allowed without Security Council authorization. The increasing practical co-operation between the UN and NATO, from the level of their Secretaries-General down to operating levels in the field, is a comparable global-regional *rapprochement*. NATO Secretary-General Manfred Wörner, with colleagues in and outside the Alliance, developed in the early 1990s a doctrine of 'interlocking institutions' partly in order to ensure NATO's international licence to act. Yet he readily acknowledged: 'The UN or the CSCE would retain overall authority'.[75]

The UN–NATO institutional relationship, as Secretary-General Wörner envisioned it, would be basically complementary—the strengths of the one offsetting the weaknesses of the other. The two organizations' capabilities, however, like their organizational personalities (almost mutually allergic) are very different. Even the

[74] On the development of the US–EU 'Transatlantic Declaration' relationship, emphasizing its broad geographic and political span, see Alan K. Henrikson, 'The New Atlanticism: Western Partnership for Global Leadership', *Revue d'intégration européenne/Journal of European Integration*, 16/2–3 (Winter–Spring, 1993), 165–91.

[75] Manfred Wörner, speech at the 38th General Assembly of the Atlantic Treaty Association, Brussels, 30 Oct. 1992; 'Interlocking Institutions: The Conference on Security and Cooperation in Europe (CSCE)', *Basic Fact Sheet* (NATO Office of Information and Press), 6 (Sept. 1993).

most extraordinary personal dedication of UN Secretary-General Boutros-Ghali, Wörner frankly pointed out, could not solve the basic problem that the UN 'lacks the infrastructure, the logistics, and the command and control facilities for major military operations'. Only NATO could offer those assets, 'at least in the European theatre'. Yet Wörner also recognized that action by NATO would require legitimization. Co-operation with the UN 'facilitates the Alliance's new role in crisis management' by placing NATO's efforts 'in a broad, internationally accepted context' and also by increasing 'public awareness and acceptance of crisis management'. The future, he hoped, 'may well see frequent and close co-operation between the UN and NATO'.[76]

This prophecy has been borne out, most particularly in the area of the former Yugoslavia. Following the attack on a market-place in Sarajevo in Bosnia-Hercegovina on 5 February 1994, the UN through Secretary-General Boutros-Ghali asked NATO, even though not a Chapter VIII regional organization and therefore not capable of being 'utilized' (under Article 53(1)), to prepare for carrying out air strikes against the Bosnian Serb gun positions around Sarajevo, should such acts be asked for. Clearly, however, the Secretary-General and the Security Council-authorized Protection Force (UNPROFOR) did not wish to surrender UN operational control over the situation. Nonetheless the UN-NATO exchange seemed to demonstrate, at least formally, that, as US Permanent Representative on the Security Council Madeleine Albright said, 'the United Nations and the alliance can co-operate together'.[77]

The actual execution of UN–NATO co-operation following the so-called Sarajevo ultimatum has proved to be far more difficult than their rhetorical solidarity would suggest. On the one hand, the threat of NATO air strikes to force the Bosnian parties' compliance undeniably has given UN officials on the ground, the senior-most being the Secretary-General's representative, Yasushi Akashi, an increased practical credibility. Yet, on the other, his reputation for

[76] Manfred Wörner, 'A New NATO for a New Era', speech at that National Press Club, Washington, DC, 6 Oct. 1993. Cf. the careful reciprocating statement of the UN Under-Secretary-General for Peacekeeping Operations, Kofi Annan, 'UN Peacekeeping Operations and Cooperation with NATO', *NATO Review*, 41/5 (Oct. 1993), 3–7.

[77] Paul Lewis, 'UN Asks NATO to Prepare for Air Strikes Against Bosnian Serbs', *New York Times*, 7 Feb. 1994.

impartiality suffered. Akashi has acknowledged: 'It's very tough to reconcile the UN's traditional role as a peacekeeper with the use of force, in this case air power from NATO.'[78] The one organization was attempting to remain fair-minded while the other was trying to prove itself forceful. Wörner's successor as NATO Secretary-General, Belgium's Willy Claes, observed: 'The UN is trying to balance itself between opposing forces as a peacekeeping operation, while NATO is an efficient military machine wanting quick reprisals for any breaches of agreement.'[79] The UN-NATO 'dual-key' approach was difficult to maintain in such circumstances. However, the two organizations desperately needed and have had to depend on each other in containing the spread of chaos in southeastern Europe.

The European Union has intermittently been another organizational partner in Balkan diplomacy. After a surprising start in late 1991 when, without any institutional preparation for doing so, Brussels quickly dispatched some EC 'monitors', the organization failed to follow through, not least because it does not itself have any peacekeeping capability. As UN Secretary-General Boutros-Ghali recalled, 'The whole operation was begun by the European Community.' He further explained: 'According to Article 52 of the UN Charter, regional disputes are supposed to be solved at the regional level, so we abstained from intervening because there already was a regional organization involved.' When, later, the UN also became directly involved in the Yugoslav imbroglio, 'we decided to make a kind of clear division of labour'. The Europeans were dealing with 'the peace process', so the United Nations confined its role to 'maintaining a cease-fire'. The UN and EC became intertwined when they together convened in London the International Conference on the Former Socialist Federal Republic of Yugoslavia. This created 'a new framework', Boutros-Ghali notes. It was a joint, global–regional production. The Conference had 'co-chairs' and demonstrated the two organizations' 'equal responsibility'.[80]

Yet another peace partner, the Conference on Security and Co-

[78] Roger Cohen, 'Man in the Middle Calls on Confucius', *New York Times*, 26 Apr. 1994.
[79] Jonathan Clayton, 'UN Backs NATO on Bosnia', *Boston Globe*, 23 Oct. 1994.
[80] Boutros Boutros-Ghali, 'Setting a New Agenda for the United Nations' (interview), *Journal of International Affairs*, 46/2 (Winter 1993), 295–6.

operation in Europe, appeared even better suited, theoretically, to try to resolve the Yugoslav conflict. The CSCE did, for example, send a symbolically important monitoring mission to Kosovo, inside Serbia-Montenegro. Yet the crisis exposed its structural weaknesses, not least of these being its requirement of consensus in decision-making. (The government of the rump state of Yugoslavia, which for a time still participated in the CSCE, was in a position to block action—a circumstance giving rise to the formula, promoted by German Foreign Minister Hans-Dietrich Genscher, of 'consensus minus one'.) Clearly, a more authoritative, consolidated, and competent Europe-wide approach to peacemaking was needed. Many lamented the institutional incapacity of Europe as an actor in its own region.

The main responsibility for bringing about a settlement of the Bosnia-Hercegovina problem has fallen to an *ad hoc* Contact Group, a team of foreign ministers comprising the troika of the European Union together with the foreign ministers of France, Great Britain, the USA, and the Russian Federation, plus the co-chairmen of the Steering Committee of the International Conference on the Former Yugoslavia. With the UN Security Council holding itself quietly in reserve to authorize either a tightening or a lifting of sanctions against the Yugoslav parties, the Contact Group continued to try to move the combatants toward 'an equitable and balanced overall settlement' by dividing territory, with 'incentives and disincentives' to be brought into play as needed.[81]

Other 'inter-European crises' extending across the vast expanse of Eurasia—Moldova, Nagorno-Karabakh, Georgia/Abkhazia, and Tajikistan, to name only a few—will require either solitary organizational sufficiency, assumed by the newly renamed OSCE (whose Minsk Group has taken the diplomatic lead in dealing with Nagorno-Karabakh), by the UN (which is trying to lead the peacemaking activity in Georgia/Abkhazia), or combined organizational action, perhaps involving NATO. The Western allies, still reluctant to offer full NATO-integration to the countries of the former Eastern bloc, have sought to extend a securing influence through their November 1991 North Atlantic Co-operation Council (NACC) scheme and, from January 1994, also the Partnership for

[81] 'Foreign Ministers Contact Group Meeting on Bosnia', communiqué, 30 July 1994, US *Department of State Dispatch*, 5/33 (15 Aug. 1994), 553–4.

Peace (PfP). The new Government and parliament of Russia, lacking enthusiasm for either of these NATO-sponsored projects, none the less have in principle accepted them. In the view of Russian Defence Minister Pavel Grachev, the fifty-two-nation OSCE instead should be developed, and be granted 'permanent leadership and co-ordination' over both NATO and the European Union/WEU, as well as over the Russian Federation's proto-regional Commonwealth of Independent States.[82] Russia's signature of a Partnership for Peace agreement with NATO, the Russian Foreign Minister Andrei Kozyrev has made clear, should not lead to the 'juxtaposition' of NATO against other institutions but, rather, to 'co-ordination' under OSCE auspices. Of course, this would not mean establishing the OSCE as a hierarchical 'leader' or 'commander', he allowed.[83]

With regard to some of the conflictual situations in Eurasia, the UN might be able to do no more than non-committally to 'take note of' what other arrangements or agencies, especially the Russians in the CIS, might attempt to do by way of peacemaking.[84] It should at least try to gain Russia's acknowledgement that requests for UN blessing of peacekeeping missions in the area of the former Soviet Union are subject to 'the same guidelines' as such operations anywhere else.[85] Too direct a challenge to the dominant Russian/ CIS hand in the Caucasus and Central Asia, it is realistically feared in Washington and other Western capitals, could cause the Russian government to block American or European action in Haiti or in Bosnia if UN Security Council approval is sought. Regardless of the UN Organization's own peacemaking capabilities or lack thereof, it is now generally recognized, on both sides of the former Cold War divide, that for pragmatic-political reasons as well as for moral-legal ones the involvement of the UN in regional peacekeeping is virtually inescapable.

---

[82] Bruce Clark, 'Grachev Calls for Wider Co-operation on Security', *Financial Times*, 26 May 1994.

[83] Andrei V. Kozyrev, 'Russia and NATO: A Partnership for a United and Peaceful Europe', *NATO Review*, 42/4 (Aug. 1994), 3–6.

[84] Paul Lewis, 'Russia Seeking U.N. Backing for Caucasus Force', *New York Times*, 27 June 1994.

[85] Madeleine K. Albright, 'Realism and Idealism in American Foreign Policy Today', Commencement address, Kennedy School of Government, Harvard University, Cambridge, Mass., 8 June 1994, *US Department of State Dispatch*, 5/26 (27 June 1994), 434–7.

4. THE UN, REGIONAL ORGANIZATIONS, AND AN AGENDA FOR PEACE

As the foregoing analysis of past and recent cases of peace intervention has made apparent, new forms of inter-organizational co-operation for peace making purposes are becoming possible.[86] UN Secretary-General Boutros-Ghali's 1992 report to the Security Council, An Agenda for Peace, remains the locus classicus of the continuing discussion of global–regional relations in the field of peace and security.[87]

During the Cold War, Boutros-Ghali critically noted, 'regional organizations worked on occasion against resolving disputes in the manner foreseen in the Charter'. With the end of that conflict, they could more easily work together with the UN. Accepting that the UN Charter 'provides no precise definition of regional arrangements and agencies', he stressed that the Charter allows 'useful flexibility' for undertakings by state groupings. Relevant 'associations or entities' included 'treaty-based organizations' (created either before or after the founding of the UN), 'regional organizations for mutual security and defence', 'organizations for general regional development or for co-operation on a particular economic topic or function', and 'groups created to deal with a specific political, economic or social issue of current concern'. Clearly, the intent was to cast the widest possible net for future region-based partnership with the UN.

Praising 'a rich variety of complementary efforts', Boutros-Ghali argued against any standard or rigid framework. 'Just as no two regions or situations are the same, so the design of co-operative work and its division of labour must adapt to the realities of each case with flexibility and creativity.' In the post-Cold War 'new era of opportunity', regional arrangements or agencies could render great service in fulfilling the tasks highlighted elsewhere in An

---

[86] e.g. Alan K. Henrikson, Defining a New World Order: Toward a Practical Vision of Collective Action for International Peace and Security (Medford, Mass.: Fletcher School of Law and Diplomacy, Tufts University, 1991), 19–23, in which it is proposed, inter alia, that national peacekeeping units be designated for regional use, that base-sharing arrangements be negotiated, and that inter-regional organizational security ties be formed.

[87] See section VII of An Agenda for Peace, 'Co-operation with regional arrangements and organizations', from which subsequent quotations are taken. For the Secretary-General's early views regarding regionalism, see Boutros Boutros-Ghali, Contribution à l'étude des ententes régionales (Paris: A. Pedone, 1949).

Agenda for Peace specifically, those of preventive diplomacy, peacekeeping, peacemaking, and post-conflict peace-building. Such activities, however, must be 'undertaken in a manner consistent with the Purposes and Principles of the Charter', particularly if their relationships with the UN, especially the Security Council, were 'governed by Chapter VIII'. Under the Charter, he emphasized, the Security Council has, and will continue to have, 'primary responsibility' for maintaining international peace and security.

But regional organizations would have a larger role. Regional action 'as a matter of decentralization, delegation and co-operation with United Nations efforts could not only lighten the burden of the Council but also contribute to a deeper sense of participation, consensus and democratization in international affairs.' Implicitly, Boutros-Ghali confirmed the known fact that the UN was becoming overburdened and could not afford or otherwise manage to carry on all of the peace-operations that were necessary. He seemed also to acknowledge that the moral authority of the UN, particularly the Security Council after the Persian Gulf War, was in question and needed 'democratic', including multi-regional, buttressing. Regional arrangements and agencies, the Secretary-General clearly believed, could strengthen both the sinews and the sense of world community.

How could their contributions be facilitated? Boutros-Ghali suggested a number of possible ways, ranging from mere diplomatic communication with the UN through inter-organizational collaborative measures to actual UN-designation of a regional body to act on its behalf. 'Consultations', he noted, could do much to build international consensus on 'the nature of a problem' and also on 'the measures required to address it'. Members of regional organizations participating 'in complementary efforts with the United Nations in joint undertakings' might encourage other states, outside the region, to act in support. Should the Security Council choose—in accordance with the terms of Article 53(1) presumably—'to authorize a regional arrangement or organization to take the lead in addressing a crisis within its region', such an endorsement would 'lend the weight of the United Nations to the validity of the regional effort'.

The Secretary-General's September 1993 annual *Report on the Work of the Organization*, noting the enormous expansion that recently had taken place in the number and scope of peacekeeping operations, expressed regret over the difficulty in securing sufficient military observers and infantry. However it made no comprehensive proposal, involving an increased focus and reliance on regions, to solve what was coming to be known as 'The Crisis in Peacekeeping'.[88] In *Building Peace and Development*, his 1994 report, he described a meeting he had convened in New York on 1 August 1994 ('the first meeting of its kind') between himself and the heads of regional bodies. The purpose of this event was to 'assess' existing co-operation between the UN and regional organizations with a view to 'further enhancing' it. Those in attendance were the CIS, Commonwealth Secretariat, EU, LAS, NATO, OAU, OAS, OIC, and WEU. ECOWAS was invited as well, but was unable to attend. The participants, as Boutros-Ghali reported their views, were in broad agreement that 'primary responsibility for the maintenance of international peace and security' remained with the Security Council. At the same time, they acknowledged the desirability of 'decentralizing some tasks'. In the view of many delegations 'the key' to closer co-operation and co-ordination between the UN and regional organizations was 'a smooth and constant exchange of information on emerging crises at a sufficiently early stage'. Among the specific substantive issues discussed at the meeting were the training of peacekeeping personnel from regional organizations, co-ordination of command and control for joint peacekeeping operations, and co-ordination of the implementation and verification of sanctions under Chapter VII.[89]

In a public 'Beleaguered Are the Peacemakers' appeal, Boutros-Ghali summarized the UN case for increased help from and to regional organizations.[90] His reasoning proceeded by quick steps: 'The UN invented peacekeeping.' 'Peacekeeping today has become

---

[88] Boutros-Ghali, *Report on the Work of the Organization*, 66, 102, 103–4. See also Adam Roberts, *The Crisis in Peacekeeping*, Forsvarsstudier 2 (Oslo: Institutt for Forsvarsstudier, 1994).

[89] Boutros Boutros-Ghali, *Building Peace and Development 1994: Report on the Work of the Organization from the Forty-eighth to the Forty-ninth Session of the General Assembly* (New York: UN Department of Information, 1994), 257–8. Evidently pleased with this 'useful exchange of views', he expressed his 'intention to hold further meetings of this kind': Boutros Boutros-Ghali, 'Supplement to An Agenda for Peace: Position Paper of the Secretary-General on the occasion of the Fiftieth Anniversary of the United Nations', A/50/60-S/1995/1, 3 Jan. 1995, in *An Agenda for Peace 1995*, 2nd edn., with the new supplement and related UN documents (New York: UN Department of Public Information, 1995), 31.

[90] Boutros Boutros-Ghali, 'Beleaguered Are the Peacemakers', *New York Times*, 30 Oct. 1994. Subsequent quotations are from this text.

far more complicated.' 'These changes require greater involvement of regional organizations and arrangements.' Such groups can 'help ease the financial and material burdens' placed on the UN. They can 'provide special insights' into conflicts in their various regions. They also sometimes can 'respond more quickly militarily'. He insisted, however, that 'unity of command is essential' lest the different types of UN-authorized activity in a situation counteract each other. Thus the 'new regionalism' is a 'challenge', as Boutros-Ghali ambivalently called it. Regional entities could 'enhance the efficiency and effectiveness' of UN efforts for peace, and their involvement would further 'democratize' the international system. But the very features that made their involvement effective could make them seem 'threatening'. Regional involvement might in particular, raise old fears of 'hegemony' and 'intervention'. Therefore, methods of UN-regional co-operation must be improved, presumably on the basis of UN guidelines. 'We must take care that new regionalism does not become an alternative to multilateralism.' The resurgence of 'spheres of influence' and the 'resultant re-kindling of old regional hostilities'—implicitly, the Cold War—would deal 'a serious blow to collective security', the Secretary-General warned.

5. TOWARDS A GLOBAL–REGIONAL PEACEMAKING 'SYSTEM'

The arguments for better co-operation between the UN and regional organizations may now be drawn together, and also reconsidered in a broader context. The case here to be presented is threefold. Its purpose is to suggest the outlines of a comprehensive global–regional peacemaking 'system', or more practical working partnership between international bodies on a world and regional scale.

The first general reason for a more systemic approach is political. It arises from the fact that we are now witnessing both what might be termed 'a world-wide trend toward regionalism'—that is, the tightening of the world's focus on the concrete problems and prospects of nations and other social groups in their regional settings —and development in the environmental, demographic, technological, and other fields of a planetary consciousness. Ethnic and

other problems have come to the fore locally. Economic interdependence, mass migration, and universal telecommunication have
extended human contact globally. Regional and planetary
awarenesses are emerging at the same time.

The political challenge is to find the right vantages upon these
somewhat paradoxical regional and global tendencies. Wisdom
would seem to lie in a 'bifocal' perspective. Problems must be seen
both 'from the inside out' (by the inhabitants, residing in regions)
and 'from the outside in' (by diplomats located in metropolitan
capitals and at UN Headquarters).[91] There is no one, logically
central, privileged angle of vision upon international politics
anymore, as might have seemed to be the case in 1945 or even in
1989 and 1991. Not least of the important current changes is that
many non-Western societies, notably the Chinese and the Islamic
worlds, are beginning to project their own, competing designs upon
international relations.[92] Regions and regionalism, if viewed non-
centrally, might seem less incoherent and less incompatible with
traditional ideas of world order. And, as Secretary-General
Boutros-Ghali has suggested, regionalization, or decentralization,
can help bring further international 'democratization' and with it,
perhaps, greater stability to the world.

A second reason for finding new global–regional relationships is
broadly institutional, having to do less with intellectual perspective
than with organizations and procedures. It seems important not so
to emphasize the distinct personalities, or specialized roles, of the
OAS, OAU, NATO, or other regional or subregional entity that
this interferes with understanding of the vital function of the main
body, the 'trunk' of the world system. The Charter and the Organization of the United Nations provide the essential framework for
world co-operation. The 'dilemma of regionalism', a wise American
internationalist who served at the UN, Ernest Gross, once wrote, is
how 'to coalesce the parts without fragmenting the whole'.[93] The
entire assemblage, a kind of organism, must live as a unit.

Many proposals are being put forward today—some of them
occasioned by the UN's fiftieth anniversary in 1995—to bring

---

[91] Sahnoun, *Somalia*, p. xii.
[92] Cf. Samuel P. Huntington, 'The Clash of Civilizations?' *Foreign Affairs*, 72/3
(Summer 1993), 22–49.
[93] Ernest A. Gross, *The United Nations: Structure for Peace* (New York: Harper
& Brothers, 1962), 47.

regional organizations and the world organization into a closer relation. Certain of these ideas are too formalistic. Among them is the suggestion that regional organizations (e.g. the European Union) actually be eligible for permanent seats on the UN Security Council, alongside or instead of their constituent national governments. The 'current chairman or president of their supreme organs' would exercise their Security Council memberships.[94] The risk is that these regional components would be fused into the central skeletal system in such a way as either to unduly subordinate the regional organizations or to give them undue sway, depending on their strength relative to the UN.

A better answer would lie in multi-organizational 'networking', in greater or lesser proximity.[95] Its main purpose would be to share the knowledge of central and regional organizations in relatively informal ways. Some methods that have been suggested include: the frequent regional-rotation of holders of the non-permanent seats on the UN Security Council, perhaps to be expanded; regular regional organization–Security Council meetings to discuss issues pertinent to different regions; and the appointment of a high-ranking Secretariat member, acting as 'rapporteur or co-ordinator' for the Security Council, 'to serve as a focal point for greater flow of information and a feedback mechanism' through contacts with regional group chairmen at the UN.[96]

An implication of this model is that regional bodies and the central world institution no longer would have to be relied on solely or exclusively for performance of their own 'charter' tasks, narrowly and rigidly conceived. All organizations would be constantly adjusting while interacting. Through two-way (three-way, n-way) communication and the resulting reciprocal influencing that would occur, the peripheral and central international institutions would monitor, moderate, and even modify the essential processes of each

[94] Report of the 'Open-Ended Working Group on the Question of Equitable Representation on and Increase in the Membership of the Security Council', chaired by Ambassador Samuel Insanally, Permanent Representative of Guyana to the UN and President of the 48th General Assembly, 28 Feb. 1994; see pp. 7, 12, 28.
[95] This idea of 'networking' has been suggested by Sidney W. Witiuk. Multi-organizational networking could admit of some, if limited, formal connections between the UN and region-based bodies, e.g. the May 1993 UN–CSCE 'framework agreement'. On this relatively loose arrangement, see Wilhelm Höynck, 'CSCE Works to Develop Its Conflict Prevention Potential', NATO Review, 42/2 (Apr. 1994), 20.
[96] Report of the 'Open-Ended Working Group', 7, 17, 18.

other, altering many regional–universal interconnections. The whole 'system' would change. Some institutions might take on new roles, as ECOWAS did, and others might abandon old functions. ASEAN, for example, might assume more peace-and-security responsibility, through the ARF, while NATO, might become a more political and even through its contact with the UN and the EU, economic organization.

These lively, human, inter-organizational exchanges ought not to be conceived of as existing on different 'levels', in some structural-legal hierarchy. Primacy is not the issue. The ideal operating rule for the new partnership should be function, not form. Regional organizations and the UN can best work together on a kind of collegial basis—as 'fellow' organizations, to use John Galvin's expression in describing relations between the UN and NATO during the Persian Gulf conflict.[97] There should be no thought of 'subcontracting', as the UN–NATO relationship during the Bosnia conflict sometimes has been characterized. It might be noted that there can be subcontracting 'upward'—from regional groupings to the UN—as well as subcontracting 'downward'—from the UN to them.[98]

A possible consequence of a global–regional network might be provision for resources- or revenue-sharing between and among institutions—a kind of inter-organizational Lend-Lease, or 'swap' system. One or another international organization will get caught 'short' as political crises and security problems, often unpredictable, arise without adequate budgetary or material provision having been made for them.[99] There are, at bottom, just two kinds of institutions: those that have money (e.g. NATO and the European Union) and those that do not (e.g. most agencies of the UN system and also many Chapter VIII regional organizations). Arrangements

[97] General John R. Galvin, remarks at the Fletcher School of Law and Diplomacy, Tufts University, Medford, Mass., 16 Sept. 1992.

[98] Thomas G. Weiss, 'The United Nations and Civil Wars', *Washington Quarterly*, 17/4 (Fall 1994), 151, noting particularly the cases of Cambodia and Central America. Regional leaders in effect called upon the services of the UN.

[99] Although inter-organizational funds-sharing is not discussed in the Report by the Independent Advisory Group on UN Financing co-chaired by Shijuro Ogata and Paul Volcker (*Financing an Effective United Nations* (New York: Ford Foundation, 1993)), the group did consider 'borrowing' by the UN, though it rejected this idea in favour of increased national assessments, establishment of a larger revolving fund, and payment of more future costs of UN peacekeeping out of individual member countries' defence budgets.

could and should be negotiated for shifting assets to those institutions that most need and can best use them. It surely would be more 'cost-effective', for example, for Western governments and their organizations to subsidize the OAU's new Mechanism for Conflict Prevention, Management, and Resolution than to intervene themselves to try to maintain peace and security throughout Africa.[100] Even the UN-affiliated Bretton Woods institutions (World Bank and International Monetary Fund) might be called upon to support regional peace. Alvaro de Soto and a colleague have urged the establishment of a closer link between the UN and the Bretton Woods institutional group so as to introduce into peace-related operations 'the concept of rewards—the carrot'. At the very least, they propose, there ought to be enough flexibility to provide financial support for those reforms aimed at 'peace-related national governance'. Bank funding for the new National Civil Police in El Salvador is a case in point.[101] More controversial, but still conceivable, would be Western (even NATO) financial support (perhaps via the NACC) for Russian/CIS peacekeeping operations in parts of Eurasia.[102] Inter-organizational synergy has costs as well as rewards.

A third basic reason for a better, richer partnership between the UN family and international organizations involved in preserving regional peace and security is essentially a philosophical one. This is the argument of pluralism, for variety, but of variation acting within an overall world order. In the history of internationalist thought, the characteristics of civilization itself often have been assumed to derive from multiplicity—the Many in continual interplay within, and sometimes even working against, the One. The German historian Leopold von Ranke, in his 1833 essay on 'The Great Powers' (*Die Grossen Mächte*), likened the post-Napoleonic

[100] Lincoln P. Bloomfield, 'The Premature Burial of Global Law and Order: Looking Beyond the Three Cases from Hell', *Washington Quarterly*, 17/3 (Summer 1994), 155. Cf. the proposal of Mohamed Sahnoun for joint sponsorship by the UN and regional organizations of 'a monitoring system' in different parts of the world. Sahnoun, *Somalia*, xii.

[101] Alvaro de Soto and Graciana del Castillo, 'Obstacles to Peacebuilding', *Foreign Policy*, 94 (Spring 1994), 30. The need for broader help from the World Bank and IMF also is stressed in Erskine Childers, with Brian Urquhart, *Renewing the United Nations System* (Uppsala: Dag Hammarskjöld Foundation, 1994), 77–84, 197–8.

[102] Russia's Foreign Minister Andrei Kozyrev in fact has suggested this to NATO. Kozyrev, 'Russia and NATO,' 6.

order in Europe to a 'conversation'. A nation, like a single person, 'only feels happy', Ranke observed, 'when many-sided personalities, freely developed, meet on a higher common ground or indeed produce this very meeting-place by stimulating and complementing one another'.[103]

Human freedom on an international scale consists in, and also depends on, having a 'choice of venue' among a variety of decision-making structures and the solutions they can offer in different places. Secretary-General Boutros-Ghali's conception of global 'democratization' partakes of such a larger vision. So too does the thinking of Andrei Kokoshin who, when Deputy Director of the Institute of the USA and Canada in Moscow under the USSR, explained that, 'when searching for a new security structure to ensure stability, it would not be wise, even in Europe, for the Soviets to confine themselves to only one approach ... After all, given the discouraging historical experience in this area, the Soviet Union can hardly trust one universal security structure'.[104]

Taken together, these three general reasons—political, institutional, and philosophical—form a rationale for strongly supporting any serious attempt, such as that outlined by Boutros-Ghali in *An Agenda for Peace*, to bring the one, central international organization, the UN, into a functioning new partnership with the many regionally based ones. The new partners include regional alliances such as NATO as well as the growing list of Chapter VIII organizations—the OAS, OAU, and Arab League, now joined by the OSCE and, even more recently, the CIS. This broadly systemic goal, as the present chapter has argued, should be sought without unduly subordinating regionalism to globalism, for reasons of international political reality, needed organizational effectiveness, and the impulse of human freedom.

[103] The Great Powers (*Die Grossen Mächte*)', in Theodore von Laue, *Leopold Ranke: The Formative Years* (Princeton: Princeton UP, 1950), 218.

[104] Andrei A. Kokoshin, *The Evolving International Security System: A View From Moscow*, CNA Occasional Paper (Alexandria, Va.: Center for Naval Analyses, Dec. 1991), 27.

6

National Identity and the Revival of Regionalism

James Mayall

HISTORICALLY, nation and region have stood in much the same relationship to one another as actor and stage. The regions of the world, separated as much by history and culture as by oceans, deserts and mountains, provided the political space in which the drama of nation, state, and empire-building was enacted. Proximity frequently led to conflict over land, access to precious metals and other resources, trade routes, status, and religion. Proximity also made possible the dynastic and military alliances, the exchange of goods and services, and the diffusion of ideas, tastes, and values through which a modicum of security and welfare was provided and without which neither national cultures nor international society could have developed. The boundary between these separate regional worlds was seldom unambiguous, let alone impermeable; sometimes conflict across the line was deeply embedded—as in South-East Europe where the division between the Orthodox and Catholic worlds and between Christendom and Islam is often described by analogy to a geological 'faultline'. But, until the twentieth century, politics, like architecture, was constrained within a human scale.

The ground-plan of the modern world was laid down in the previous century. The consequences of European imperial expansion were far-reaching: for the first time all parts of the world were integrated within a single economy; and the wars of the great powers were also fought world-wide. As always, thought followed action—grand ideological and geopolitical theories were generated to explain what had happened. When European power was withdrawn in the mid-twentieth century, there was a predictable reaction. The concept of region ceased to be used in a purely descriptive sense, to denote a cultural or geographical area, and was increasingly invoked to support a political doctrine or a principle of international order.

From the start regionalism has had to overcome certain disadvantages in the market-place of political ideas. It is a concept of the middle ground, lacking the highminded appeal of cosmopolitanism and the atavistic warmth of nationalism. However, the defeat of fascism (under which the atavism finally drove out the warmth) and the rapid disintegration of the European empires created an organizational void in world politics. After 1945 an attempt was made to design an international order based on principles of co-operation rather than conflict. The intention was to reconcile rival claims and interests at the national, regional, and universal levels, but the East–West conflict quickly overshadowed this attempt. Nationalism and regionalism were not totally written out of the script, but they were undoubtedly subordinate. The Cold War, in both its military and ideological dimensions, was acted out on a global stage.

It is perhaps not surprising, therefore, that, the ending of the Cold War has been followed by both a resurgence of nationalism and a proliferation of regional projects and regionalist arguments. These developments prompt three questions. First, how have regionalism and nationalism been related, in theory and practice, since 1945? Second, how were they related, severally and together to wider conceptions of international order? And third, can they be accommodated within a reconstructed world order, or are they fundamentally antithetical doctrines?

1. TERMS AND DEFINITIONS

Answering these questions is not straightforward: the terms themselves are ambiguous and contested. It may be helpful, therefore, to begin by sketching the disputed terrain before turning to the way in which the disputes have been handled in practice.

There is no problem with the doctrine of nationalism itself. It merely states that the world is divided into nations and that each nation should have its own independent sovereign state. The difficulty arises from conflicting definitions of what constitutes a nation. Romantic historicists view it in primordial or essentialist terms. For them the origins of the nation, into which one is born, are known, yet lost in the mists of time. In effect, the nation has always existed, although it may well have lost its ancient independence to foreign conquerors. National identity is defined in cultural terms, most often by membership of an ethnic group speaking a common natural language. For romantics, the doctrine of national self-determination refers to the right of all such groups to reclaim their birthright, whether through the break-up of empires or by secession from an existing state.

By contrast, liberal pluralists, equate the nation with the political community. The nation is defined by the constitution and by citizenship. Ethnic and cultural identities are largely irrelevant, although some liberal thinkers, such as John Stuart Mill, have argued that, from a practical point of view, democracy is likely to prove fragile in countries where powerful ethnic communities compete to capture the state through the ballot box.[1] In recent times, liberals have tended to support the breaking up of empire through negotiation, but usually stop short of endorsing wars of national liberation (at least until they have been won) or secession from existing states. On the other hand, modern liberals are divided on the issue of the legitimacy of humanitarian intervention in cases where members of an ethnic or other minority have their fundamental human and civil rights systematically abused.

When we turn to the concept of region, the disputes may be less passionate, but are almost equally confusing. As a political doctrine regionalism is even more incoherent than nationalism since those who advocate regional solutions to political and economic problems do not merely differ on the meaning and implications of the concept, but are frequently pursuing contradictory projects. Consider the following examples. Some Euro-enthusiasts, have hinted at the possibility of transcending the state and nation by creating a wider federation and a regional political identity. Yet the federalists have been repeatedly frustrated by the continuing vitality of the national idea.[2] Scottish or Catalan nationalists are more likely to see regionalism as the doctrine which will justify granting them greater autonomy, and thus provide an escape route from the tyranny of the sovereign state. These and other such 'peripheral' nationalisms emphasize their own 'Europeanist' and 'international-

---

[1] J. S. Mill, *Utilitarianism, Liberty, Representative Government* (London: Dent, Everyman's Library, 1910, repr. 1957), ch. XVI.
[2] See James Mayall, *Nationalism and International Society* (Cambridge: CUP, 1990), 94–5.

ist' orientation but aim not for a single European identity but rather for a Europe of the regions. A further perspective is provided by the functionalists' appeal to regional criteria such as transport networks or migratory labour patterns to suggest that political frontiers somehow distort reality and hence unnecessarily reduce human welfare. But they are divided among themselves over the possible consequences of regionalism, in particular over the desirability of superseding the nation state with what Mitrany once dubbed the 'continental union'.[3]

Finally, some nationalisms, pan-Africanism and pan-Arabism for example, operate at the regional as well as the state level. In these cases the claim is that a regional political identity already exists, even if it does not require a surrender of sovereignty by existing national governments. Indeed when states endorse a solidarist ideology of this kind, they define it in a way which reasserts the primacy of the state in the event of any conflict between the national interest and any wider obligation.[4] This has been all too clearly reflected in groupings such as the Organization of African Unity or the League of Arab States.

The gap between these rival interpretations is one of kind not degree. However, not all of them command equal respect within the society of states. Since 1945 national and regional issues have been 'managed' in international politics pragmatically as they have arisen, rather than according to a preconceived doctrine. Conventional interpretations have emerged of both national self-determination and the role of regional organizations in international society. Let us consider how these orthodox interpretations came about.

2. REGIONALISM AND POST-WAR RECONSTRUCTION

The peacemakers in 1945 built upon the foundations of the League of Nations. Like the League, the UN was designed to provide security for a world of nation states, not to replace the state with a new form of political organization. However, it was not considered sufficient merely to return to the *status quo ante*. After the excesses

---

[3] David Mitrany, *A Working Peace System*: (Chicago: Quadrangle Books, 1966), 44–68.
[4] Mayall, *Nationalism and International Society*, 145–6.

of the Nazi period, nationalist doctrine was widely discredited amongst the major powers. The economic depression of the 1930s had proved that autarky was not a practical option for industrial societies. The war had then demonstrated the importance of standing military alliances in control of an extensive industrial infrastructure. The bombs dropped on Hiroshima and Nagasaki left little room for doubt that the separate state could not defend itself in a war taken to the limit. If the world was to survive and prosper it seemed that new forms of political and economic association would be necessary. Writers like E. H. Carr and John Herz attempted to map the contours of the new age, without, it must be said, clarifying how the problem of sovereignty was to be overcome.[5]

It was not immediately obvious that regionalism was the solution to the old problem of international insecurity, or the new one of economic interdependence. David Mitrany, the most important of the early functionalists, saw in a world of competitive regional powers all the dangers of the system of separate states magnified on to a larger scale.[6] His own solution—the ensnaring of the sovereign state in a web of transnational welfare activities—may have been unrealistic, but his charge against the dangers of regionalism has never been satisfactorily answered. In any case, in the immediate post-war period the preferred solutions were a revised form of collective security presided over by the five permanent members of the Security Council, and in the economic sphere the reconstruction and strengthening of an open world economy.

The UN charter established the primacy of the sovereign state and the inalienable right of all peoples to self-determination, without acknowledging the apparent contradiction between these two principles. Whatever the intellectuals might think, it seemed that governments believed that the best chance of building a new world order was by arranging a marriage between the individual, who would have his rights guaranteed, and the state which would be secure in its independence. The concept of guarantees for minorities, which had been a feature of the League, was omitted from the UN Charter.

Regionalism was not a central feature of this post-war design,

[5] E. H. Carr, *Nationalism and After* (London: Macmillan, 1945) and John Herz, *International Politics in the Atomic Age* (New York: Columbia UP, 1962).
[6] Mitrany, *A Working Peace System*.

but its claims had to be recognized if only as a corollary of the respect paid to state sovereignty. If states were sovereign, they had to be free to associate, for any co-operative or defensive purpose, provided that by so doing they did not prejudice the security or welfare of other states. Article 51 of the UN Charter acknowledged this right in matters of security by expressly permitting military alliances. Article 24 of the General Agreement of Tariffs and Trade (GATT)[7] similarly excluded customs unions and free-trade areas from the obligations of the non-discriminatory most favoured nation principle on which the system of liberal multilateralism was to be based. The vast majority of such associations were likely to be regional in character.

The outbreak of the Cold War ensured that these provisions of the new world order were given rapid prominence. It also served to freeze the political map in Europe and to confine state creation (and hence the application of the principle of national self-determination) to the former colonies of the European powers. The first consequence of the Cold War was the military division of the world into rival military blocs, organized on the one side through the North Atlantic Treaty Organization (NATO) and the regional alliances by means of which Western power was projected on a global scale, and on the other through the Warsaw Treaty Organization, which legitimized the subordination and military occupation of Eastern Europe by the Soviet Union. The global reach of Cold War antagonisms meant that the revised form of collective security was stillborn: it had assumed the continuation of the wartime alliance between the Soviet Union and the Western democracies, and could not survive the repeated use of the veto by one of the permanent members. But although the two sides confronted one another in Europe, by the 1960s it was clear that neither side could challenge the political and territorial dispensation that had emerged at the end of the Second World War.[8]

The national question, which had proved such a disruptive force in European politics after the break-up of the Habsburg and Otto-

---

[7] The GATT filled the gap when the charter of the proposed ITO failed to carry through the US Congress.

[8] This dispensation included communist, but non-aligned Yugoslavia, which, after its excommunication from the Comintern in 1948, was propped up by the West, as a kind of ideological no-man's land between East and West.

man empires, was pushed into the background. So long as the power and authority of the Soviet Union was unchallenged, it suited both sides to accept that the People's Republics (and Yugoslavia) rested on the exercise of self-determination, as was their acknowledged right under the UN charter.

Beyond Europe, the Cold War created an environment which favoured anti-colonial nationalism. Both superpowers opposed the continuation of the European empires, although the USA soon tempered its opposition to its strategic requirements for military bases. None the less, once India had been granted independence in 1947, the liquidation of the British, French, and Dutch empires was only a matter of time.

The UN provided the stage on which the anti-colonial struggle was internationalized. Despite unconvincing efforts by the imperial powers to deny the organization any role, as each new state was admitted to membership, it joined the chorus of ex-colonial states demanding the complete eradication of empire and its proscription. With the passage of General Assembly Resolution 1514 in 1960 they achieved their objective. This resolution condemned any delay in the granting of independence, even on the grounds that the population was unprepared to receive it.

It was thus the former colonial rather than the European states that established the orthodox interpretation of national self-determination in post-war international society. The consequences for the new world order are only now becoming apparent. In Europe, before the Cold War the national problem had arisen because ancient, and more important, politically self-conscious cultures were divided between different states. In Asia, and more particularly in Africa, imperialism had more often than not destroyed the old political order and created new territorial units that had not existed before. The political movements that were created to oppose colonial rule, and which eventually succeeded in gaining control of the colonial state, claimed to represent the nation; but in reality they mostly faced the need to create nations out of a heterogeneous group of peoples and cultures that had been thrown together under colonial administration.

Self-determination became a synonym for decolonization, the transfer of power within the frontiers laid down by the European powers. From the point of view of the West, this was an acceptable outcome, particularly as the political idiom employed by most of the new nationalists, at least during the early years of independence, was that of the liberal pluralists: the nation was evidently no more than the political community which they strove to create. There was no dissent from the Western democracies when the governments of the new would-be nations showed themselves as intransigent in the face of secessionist claims as the European powers had been during the nineteenth century.

Liberal democrats have generally leaned towards Lincoln's view that a minority should aim to transform itself into a majority by influencing public opinion, rather than by attempting to secede.[9] This allowed them to interpret the right of self-determination as arising from the break-up of empires, a once-and-for-all event in the past with no implications for the creation of new states in the future. In so doing, of course, they conveniently overlooked the uncomfortable fact that in deeply divided societies, public opinion is not swayed by argument but by historically embedded loyalties and structures.

This conventional understanding of a principle, which might otherwise have been highly subversive of the existing international order, was paradoxically reinforced by the nature of Third World regionalism. Pan-Asian sentiment was always weak, certainly when compared with the strength of local rivalries and the magnetic attraction of the two major world ideologies. Although not all Afro-Asian countries resisted the blandishments of the Western alliance system, the majority did. For most Asian states, the Non-aligned Movement, a loose coalition opposed to the blocs, upheld the sovereignty and territorial integrity of the new states, and rendered any tighter regional security arrangements superfluous. However, in Latin America, the Arab world, and Africa, for a variety of economic and ideological reasons, non-alignment and the attempt to assert a regional presence in world affairs went hand in hand.

Territorial identities competed with racial, linguistic, and religious loyalties for Arabs and Africans. By appealing in the name of pan-Arabism or pan-Africanism, over the heads of neighbouring conservative governments, radical nationalists, such as Nasser of Egypt and Nkrumah of Ghana, aimed to monopolize the political

---

[9] See Harry Beran, 'A Liberal Theory of Secession', *Political Studies*, 32 (1984), 21–31.

identity and command the loyalty of the newly liberated masses. It was a threat which the governments, many of which had indeed been co-opted by the Western powers as the radicals maintained, could ill afford to ignore. Both the League of Arab States and the Organization of African Unity claimed to represent a wider political community whose members shared a common identity and interest. In practice, both organizations captured the pan-national ideology for the separate states.

Before the withdrawal of European power, there had been much talk amongst Arab and African intellectuals of the artificial nature of the states created by European colonialism and of the need to redraw the political map. Such attitudes evaporated rapidly after independence. Sovereignty was regarded as too precious an inheritance to be easily transferred or pooled. In the face of the outside world, Africans and Arabs maintained common positions on issues of key interest to them, in particular confrontation with Israel and South Africa. But in relations amongst themselves they stood jealously on their rights and refused to transfer any power to a supranational authority. Indeed, the charters of both organizations echo in many respects the charter of the UN itself. The OAU Charter was drafted with help from the Organization of American States (OAS) which had itself traditionally combined territorial nationalism with a regional identity based on language, culture, and geopolitics.

In all three areas, then, political regionalism amounted to little more than a diplomatic concert for dealing with the outside world. Criteria for membership were geographical rather than ideological, although each organization was partly defined by a consensus on a major foreign-policy issue. Thus members of the OAU were required to confront South Africa, Cuba was suspended from membership of the OAS when its government embraced communism, and Egypt expelled from the Arab League after Sadat had made a separate peace with Israel. Regional organizations were also charged with settling disputes between neighbours. In this respect, however, the record of regional peacekeeping was not noticeably superior to that of the UN. Relatively few post-colonial states succeeded in creating conditions of security for their citizens; so it is not surprising that their regional organizations have failed to develop genuine security communities.

3. REGIONAL AND MULTILATERAL ALTERNATIVES TO ECONOMIC NATIONALISM

The Cold War also had a decisive, if indirect, impact on the development of economic regionalism. At the Bretton Woods and Havana Conferences, the central objective had been the restoration of an open liberal economy in which individual businesses would compete freely for markets and consumers have the widest possible choice. This objective was far from narrowly technical. The main danger was that governments would slip back into the economic nationalist policies which had led to massive trade diversion and distortion during the interwar period, and had helped to poison the political atmosphere. The programme of liberal multilateralism required the major trading currencies to be convertible and governments to refrain from discriminatory trading practices. It did not require economic co-operation at the regional level, although, as we have seen, in the case of free-trade areas and customs unions, it was to be permitted, presumably on the grounds that they could be shown to be 'trade creating' rather than 'trade diverting'.[10] However, the bias of the new economic order was towards universalism rather than regionalism.

This bias was reversed, partly because there was insufficient credit in the system to support currency convertibility in the short run, but also because, with the outbreak of the Cold War, there was pressure on the Western powers to find a long-run solution to the problem of European co-operation in order to strengthen the Atlantic Alliance. We cannot know whether the original six members of the EEC, and particularly France and Germany, would have persevered with such determination to promote European integration, in the absence of a threat from the East. But we do know that the US government made progress towards the dismantling of intra-European monetary and trade barriers a condition of Marshall Aid. The USA also welcomed the Treaty of Rome, even though Part IV (which established associate status for the former colonies of France, Belgium, and Italy) clearly contravened the GATT.

Stalin would have nothing to do with capitalist universalism. He regarded the Bretton Woods system and GATT as the economic

[10] The classic statement of this argument is Jacob Viner, *The Customs Union Issue* (New York: Carnegie Endowment for International Peace, 1950).

infrastructure of the Western Alliance and would not permit any member of the socialist bloc to participate. The USA and its allies overtly denied any linkage between their security and economic policies, but in practice the multilateral system was always more Western than universal. For the USA, the priority was to construct a security arch across the Atlantic: they were prepared to support any arrangement which would strengthen the European pillar on which this arch was to rest.

The political imperative, whether viewed from Washington, Bonn, or Paris, was how to resolve the German problem. If nothing was done there was no reason to suppose that, over time, Germany and France would not again confront one another, as they had already done three times since 1870. In that event the task of holding the Western Alliance together against the Soviet Union would be impossible. One favoured approach was to transcend the national states by creating a federated United States of Western Europe. The rejection of the proposal for a European Defence Force by the French National Assembly in 1954 blocked this option. This failure in turn led to the creation of the European Coal and Steel Community which signalled the decision to find an alternative, economic, route towards co-operation. In a sense, it was fortuitous that Article 24 of the GATT had already established a way in which regional integration and the multilateral trading order could be reconciled. However, its existence meant that the Treaty of Rome could consolidate the new regional approach, and thus promote Western strategic interests without damaging the wider attempt to entrench liberal multilateralism as a structural support of the new international order. In effect, both universalism (i.e. liberal multilateralism) and regionalism were to be used to combat the danger of a retreat towards competitive economic nationalism.

In the longer term, the contradictions between both regional and global, and national and regional, economic interests, resurfaced. Indeed, it seems extremely unlikely that a demonstration of the massive trade distortion caused by the Common Agricultural Policy (CAP) will be sufficient to bring about its total abandonment. During the early years of the European Community, the CAP was the linch-pin which held together the Franco-German Alliance. It had the effect of compensating French agriculture for opening the French market to German industry. No doubt, it no longer performs this crucial political function, but in the meantime powerful national interests have developed and want to see it perpetuated. For example, the revolt of French farmers in 1992, and their organized opposition to the Maastricht Treaty, and the completion of the Uruguay Round of GATT negotiations was linked to the proposed reform of the CAP.

I shall return to these long-term contradictions in the final section of this chapter. For the moment let us consider the implications of the European experience for the rest of the world, particularly the Third World. The most important of these was as a model. The West Europeans had evidently found a way of promoting and intensifying co-operation amongst themselves, without flouting international economic law and without sacrificing their national sovereignty. Since most developing countries were critically dependent on the Western powers for economic sustenance, and hence under considerable pressure to frame their economic policies in accordance with accepted international practice, while being extremely unwilling to surrender the sovereignty they had so recently acquired, the creation of free-trade areas and customs unions seemed to offer them a painless way forwards. Moreover, as Sydney Dell once argued from an economic point of view, Third World countries were more in need of integration than those in Western Europe. The latter all had developed industrial economies, with national markets which for the majority of goods were sufficiently large to allow the exploitation of optimal economies of scale. They also already enjoyed extensive trade amongst themselves. By contrast the markets of the former were limited twice over; even in populous countries, market size was constrained by very low per capita income, while many more were both poor and had small populations. Intra-regional trade was in most cases insignificant. In such circumstances, it was most unlikely that the investment, without which there could be no development, would be attracted from abroad, or even, where there were domestic savings to be tapped, locally, it followed that regional economic integration was a political necessity for development.[11]

The logic of this argument was widely accepted in the Third World, although at times it led to disputes about the nature and

[11] Sydney Dell, *Trade Blocs and Common Markets* (London: Constable, 1963).

boundaries of the regions to be integrated. For example, Kwame Nkrumah, who believed that the African continent should form both a single currency area and a common market, attempted to frustrate the putative efforts of the three former British colonies in East Africa to federate.[12] He need not have bothered: the internal tensions within Uganda, and between Tanzania and Kenya, were sufficient to scupper the project before it was launched, without external assistance. The East African Community, the purely economic organization which was established on the basis of the colonial East African Common Services Organization lasted into the 1970s. In the end, it too fell foul of the political conflicts between the three members governments and the doubtful validity of the model to East African circumstances. The numerous conflicts between the Kenyan and Tanzanian governments and the Ugandan dictator, Idi Amin, provided the immediate cause of the collapse, but by then the contradictions between Kenya's protocapitalist economic policies and Tanzania's experiments with collectivism had dealt the regional structure so many body blows that there was little hope of recovery.

The circumstances of the widespread collapse, or atrophy, of Third World regional-integration schemes differed from case to case, but the underlying reason—the poor fit between the imported model of regional integration and the circumstances in which it was applied—was very similar. Since it is not clear (at least to this author) that the weaknesses of the model are being adequately addressed in the revived enthusiasm for a regional approach to international order, it may be worth while to provide a brief sketch of them here.

There are political and economic weaknesses in the model. Both derive from the false analogy between Western Europe and the Third World. In Europe, although there were many economic obstacles to the free movement of goods and services across national borders, the political problem was more urgent and also, seemingly, more intractable. By the mid-twentieth century, the issues which dominated the political agenda in industrial societies, were, in any case, increasingly issues of political economy. It was because no purely political solution was available, that the Europeans agreed

[12] See Joseph Nye, *Pan-Africanism and East African Integration* (Cambridge, Mass.: Harvard UP, 1965).

to create, by economic means, a new kind of hybrid international body, something less than a state but more than an old-fashioned marriage-of-convenience alliance.

Third World countries face many political problems and threats, but the overwhelming constraints on their development are economic and environmental. Some of these lie far beyond their capabilities; others are the result of disastrous economic policies pursued in the past. The main point, however, is that effective regional co-operation requires a high, not a low, level of political commitment. Weak states often have strong, even dictatorial governments for whom the exercise of sovereign control means the ability to form the state in their own image, and to farm it in their own rather than the general interest. In many cases, control over the modern sector of the economy, however small that may be, is the only way the government has to establish its hold over society at large. The high level of military expenditure, on which many such governments depend, has after all, to be generated from somewhere. Even at the height of the Cold War, very few Third World governments could rely solely on free hand-outs from the superpowers and their allies. The issue of sovereignty, in relation to the increasing powers of the European Community in Brussels, is still hotly debated within Europe. In the Third World, to hand over the right to levy excise and customs duties, or licensing, to a regional body is deeply unattractive to most of those who exercise power.

The economic weaknesses in the model relate on the one hand to the existing pattern and level of intra-regional trade and on the other to the asymmetrical costs and benefits that are likely to result from regional integration. The six original members of the European Community, all had diversified industrial economies and depended on a complex division of labour amongst themselves (i.e. they exchanged manufactures, often of the same kind, rather than manufactures for raw materials or semi-processed goods) well before they agreed to integrate.

During the 1960s and 1970s most Third World states which attempted to establish regional integration schemes had competitive rather than complementary economies, in the sense that they mostly produced the same kind of goods—raw materials and tropical agricultural products—for sale to the industrial world in exchange for capital goods and manufactured commodities. Consequently, the level of intra-regional trade was generally very low (although certainly understated in the official statistics). Integration failed to occur because in most cases there was virtually nothing to integrate. Reducing a tariff on intra-regional trade was a symbolic and largely painless move, but achieved nothing because so little moved across regional borders in the first place.

The customs union/free-trade area model assumes the existence of a market economy in which both public and private enterprises engage in arm's-length pricing and free exchange. The government's role is meant to be limited to framing the rules under which commercial competition takes place and guaranteeing, through the law, that contracts are honoured. Conceptually, the model was a development within liberal economic theory. Its justification is that economic freedom within the Union will generate optimal long-run welfare gains. Liberals have never denied that, in the short run, there will be winners and losers from any change in the rules. Politically, this means that some way must be found to compensate (or at least appease) the losers, if they have a capability to disrupt the scheme.

Within Europe, a redistributive mechanism was developed in the shape of a strong regional fund through which resources could be channelled to depressed areas such as southern Italy and, with the enlargement of the Community in the mid-1970s, to whole countries such as Ireland. Without a mechanism of this kind, these areas would have been marginalized: left to itself, investment will flow to the centres of growth within countries and to the strongest national economies within the Union. The gains of trade would also go disproportionately to those enterprises located at the centre. This phenomenon is not peculiar to Europe: it is a necessary consequence of operating a free market. So long as the regional economy is expanding and the Union is perceived to be in the wider political and economic interest of the strongest member countries, they may grumble, but they will be willing in the end to foot the bill.

None of these conditions obtained in the Third World during the first phase of regional enthusiasm. In areas where all countries are poor, although not equally so, resentment will be fanned by the natural tendency of foreign investment to flow to the most attractive location, i.e. the country with the least underdeveloped infrastructure. It will be inflamed still further when industries from the relatively better-placed economies begin to displace those in poorer neighbouring countries.

In the East African case, which we used earlier to illustrate the poor survival record of Third World integration schemes, an attempt was made to deal with this problem through a transfer pricing system and an intra-regional investment policy. Under the former, the distribution of Community revenues was weighted in favour of the two poorer members—Tanzania and Uganda, while under the latter investment in specific industries was assigned to each country, again with a weighting in favour of the poorer members. The first of these policies led to complaints from Kenya about its equity and the second never worked. Leaving aside the political disputes between the three governments, the economic explanation is neither surprising nor complicated. It is that in regional unions where the members do not have already complementary economies, and where growth rates do not appear to be greatly affected by integration, the relatively less poor will have little incentive to share the pain with those even less fortunate than themselves.

Most Third World governments, where they were not entirely predatory, justified their policies during the Cold War era, in terms of nation-building. The most prevalent of these policies was import substitution. It was pursued partly for its own sake, and partly in a vain attempt to overcome the chronic shortage of foreign exchange, which quickly established itself as a defining characteristic of Third World status. Governments in all parts of the Third World flirted with regionalism on the European model, and talked loudly about the importance of South–South trade; but regionalism turned out to be a poor bulwark against their own nationalist aspirations and internecine rivalries, and an inadequate antidote to their comprehensive dependence on the industrial West.

There is a sense in which this conclusion is unduly negative. Not all Third World regional schemes were quite as unsuccessful as the account given here suggests. But where they both persisted and proved their utility, the explanation was often curiously paradoxical. In Europe, the customs union formula was adopted because it was available under GATT rules, and because it provided a way forward when more direct political co-operation was impossible. In the Third World, where regional organizations have taken root, the pursuit of economic integration has generally been a veneer, ignored in practice and sometimes in theory also.

Three examples may illustrate the point. The most successful of Third World organizations, ASEAN, has still not developed into an effective customs union and operates as a traditional, but informal, diplomatic concert for managing intra-regional problems and concerting policies towards the outside world. SADCC (now SADC), established after the Independence of Zimbabwe in 1980, has deliberately avoided commercial integration from fear of provoking intra-regional conflict of the East African kind. Yet it was founded with the explicit objective of building a regional economy capable of withstanding the magnetic, and destabilising pull of the South African economy. Member countries were assigned sectoral responsibilities for developing regional development plans, with an initial emphasis on infrastructure and professional services and standards. The organization—held together by a common, although uneven fear of South Africa—has operated successfully as a mechanism for co-ordinating and maximizing international aid into the region. Whether it can adapt itself to absorb a post-apartheid South Africa, now that its original political rationale has virtually collapsed, is uncertain. If it is to survive as an effective organization it will have to develop an approach to regional trade. This cannot be done without confronting the rival national sensibilities which SADC has so far been so careful to avoid offending.

In West Africa, ECOWAS, dealt with the same problem, which was rightly seen as having destroyed the East African Community, by adopting the customs union formula but projecting the removal of trade and other barriers so far into the future as to remove the issue from the immediate political agenda. As a regional economic organization, ECOWAS, has done little or nothing to reverse the disastrous economic plight of the region. Nor has it been able to contain the integration of the unofficial, as distinct from the official, economy through smuggling between the franc-zone member countries and their neighbours. Yet politically ECOWAS has survived and has provided the required cloak of legitimacy for a regional peacekeeping force in the Liberian Civil War. This operation may not have been an unqualified success, but at a time when neither the OAU nor the United Nations were willing to get involved, it has at least bought some time in which to check the slide into barbarism and anarchy and, optimistically, work out a viable political solution.

4. REGIONALISM AND NATIONALISM AFTER
THE COLD WAR

A summary of the argument should now provide us with an answer to the first two questions asked at the beginning of this chapter: how have regionalism and nationalism been related since 1945, and how were they related to wider conceptions of international order?

Since it was agreed that international reconstruction required both acknowledging the sovereignty of states and the right of all people to self-determination, a way had to be found of reconciling these two principles. In practice, the sovereignty of all existing states was guaranteed and the right of self-determination was confined to the colonies of the European powers. Except where they coincided with state boundaries, little attention was paid to ethnic claims. The post-war international order, unlike its predecessor, was also held to require an institutional support system to underpin the liberal economy, and to prevent countries backsliding into beggar-your-neighbour and other politically dangerous nationalist policies. Both liberal theory and the fact that the whole system rested on the bedrock principle of sovereignty, required a permissive attitude towards regional arrangements where these had neither an aggressive nor a discriminatory intent. But, the original bias of the proposed system was towards universal arrangements, collective security in the political sphere, and non-discriminatory multilateralism in the economic.

The Cold War reversed the priorities. Collective security was marginalized as a mechanism of international order and regionalism was elevated. In the first instance, this was seen as a means of strengthening the European side of the Atlantic Alliance against the threat from the East, and subsequently, as the result of a largely putative demonstration effect, over much of the non-communist world, as a strategy for promoting economic development and reducing Third World dependence on the West. Regionalism is widely held to have been successful in the first case, and a failure in the second. Within Europe, a large part of the explanation is that both the experience of the Second World War and the ideological confrontation between capitalism and communism which followed it, effectively froze the political map and encouraged, on both sides of the divide, visions of a political order which would transcend the national ideal. Within the Third World, where nationalism was associated with liberation from colonial rule, a large part of the explanation for failure was that, in practice if not in theory, regional arrangements challenged the national ambitions and aspirations of most post-colonial successor governments.

It remains to answer the final question: can nationalism and regionalism be accommodated within a reconstructed international order? In the final analysis, history will provide an answer to this question. The best that can be done here is to sketch some of the problems which will accompany any effort to reconcile these competing principles of order and some of the issues that will have to be confronted if the attempt is to appear at all credible.

Even this modest task must overcome an initial difficulty: what are the criteria by which the new order is to be judged? This is a more complex issue now than it appeared to be in 1945. Then, the architects of reconstruction were led by a self-confident power with clear ideas about what kind of political and economic order it wanted to achieve. The Americans wanted a liberal order, within which their own primacy would be acknowledged and the rest of the world would be as like the USA as possible. When that goal proved elusive, it settled for containment of the Soviet Union and ideological confrontation with communism wherever it spread.

The chaos created by the Second World War also cleaned the slate. No doubt it was not as clean as it appeared to be to the victors, but 1945 none the less constituted a break with the past, qualitively different from 1989. The end of the Cold War left only one superpower, and exposed the bankruptcy of the only alternative macroeconomic strategy to capitalism. But the USA was no longer self-confident about its world role, and its relative economic decline, no doubt greatly exaggerated by academics with a theory to peddle, is still real. The new world order is being debated on the hoof in most unpropitious circumstances.

Not only is the world economy in the deepest and most prolonged recession since the war, but the resurgent national question will not easily be settled by recourse to the kind of pragmatic compromise—colonial self-determination and opposition to all secession—that was adopted after 1945. It is ethnic nationalism and religious sectarianism, not discriminatory economic policies, that are currently tearing states apart in many parts of the world. If the state collapses, the warlords move in, as they have already done in

Bosnia, Somalia, parts of the former Soviet Union, and elsewhere. Where chaos is substituted for the anarchical society, talk of international co-operation, whether at the regional or global levels, is largely fantasy.

What then is to be done? If, hypothetically, there was a chance of designing a new international order from scratch, rather than having to deal with messy unforseen problems as and when they arise, what would it look like? It is not so difficult to answer the question in the abstract. Presumably most people of goodwill could accept that international arrangements should be designed to promote the security and welfare of the world's population. It is probably safe to assume also that agreement, in principle, could be reached on the need to safeguard the fundamental human rights which are already entrenched in theory in the Universal Declaration. It is when one tries to go beyond these broad, and perhaps pious, statements of principle, that the difficulties crowd in. After all, the problem is not what the ultimate objectives of international order should be; on this, my hypothetical consensus already echoes the existing UN Charter.

The problem is how best to pursue these agreed objectives in the new circumstances, and what role to assign respectively to the nation state (and its supporting nationalist ideology) and the region. If the objective is to provide security and welfare for people (and it is), it follows that their collective identities must also be acknowledged and protected.

There is nothing, in principle, to say that people cannot identify with, and express loyalty to, a region and its organizations. To some extent, they already do. As other chapters in this book have discussed, there has been a revival in regional awareness in various parts of the world, particularly Latin America and Asia. Moreover, for some commentators there are already signs of the emergence of a broader European identity albeit primarily at an élite level.[13]

Nevertheless, regionalism represents a weak, and emotionally thin form of identification, generally recognizable only at a distance from hearth and home. Pan-African or pan-Arab sentiment is likely to be more appealing in London, Paris, or New York than in Cairo, Lagos, or Maputo, just as ordinary (as opposed to Eurocratic)

---

[13] See e.g. William Wallace, *The Transformation of Western Europe* (London: Pinter for RIIA, 1990), esp. ch. 6.

Spaniards or Swedes are more likely to recognize themselves as members of a common civilization in Tokyo or Sumatra than in Madrid or Stockholm. Nations, as has often been pointed out, are ultimately inventions or, in Benedict Anderson's felicitous phrase, 'imagined communities'.[14] They gain their power over human beings because over time they come to form a deeply felt (if often consciously unrecognized or even repudiated) part of our imaginative and emotional lives. By contrast, regional organizations are mostly in their infancy. They are self-conscious constructs for managing specific political and economic problems, strong on administrative rationale of a Weberian kind, but short on the power to move people in the mass, or extract loyalty from them.

Indeed, in Western Europe, the very success of the Community in facilitating economic integration and thereby supporting a relative homogenization of products, 'life-styles', and tastes, has also led to a popular reaction. Ironically, at the same time that the newly liberated countries of Eastern Europe were looking forward to their eventual entry into the Community, the British, Danes, and French were agonizing over what was widely perceived as an excessive surrender of national sovereignty, and the way in which this was eroding cherished symbols of national identity. Even the Germans, faced with the economic and psychological costs of reunification, became more hesitant in their Euro-enthusiasm. While major doubts remained over whether governments were prepared to surrender their currencies to the ECU, despite the commitment of most of them to monetary union, at the popular level the reaction took the form of special interest protests—against the usurption of beer by wine, or the creation of Europe-wide standards which militate against farmers catering for local and particular tastes. The ruling that the British sausage was not a sausage in the true sense of the term, may strike the discerning consumer as, in the main, just; but the survival of the British fruit-growing industry has been purchased at the price of increasing the size of the Cox's orange pippin to meet EC standards and so substantially reducing its natural taste! Such national irritations are unlikely to resist the logic of economic advantage for long, but they may help to explain why regional organizations may be respected, but are unlikely to be greatly loved.

[14] Benedict Anderson, *Imagined Communities, Reflections on the Origins and Spread of Nationalism* (London: Verso, 2nd edn., 1992).

But if it is true that popular identities have not significantly shifted away from the national and towards the regional unit, it does not follow that all is well, even with the old and supposedly well-established national identities. It may well be that standing up to 'the threat from Brussels' is more a sign of weakness than of strength. The states of Western Europe, whose national identities were constructed only slowly between the sixteenth and nineteenth centuries, are under simultaneous attack from at least three directions. From above, the relentless progress of economic, and more particularly financial globalization, is undermining the claims of governments to excercise national control. From below, the reassertion of ethnic and local political identities is challenging the official monopoly of the symbols of national integration. From outside, the pressure of those trying to get in from the south and the east is testing the self-perception of societies as being based on citizenship rather than ancestry. In these circumstances, the question, what it is to be British or French, is becoming increasingly strident and desperate. And the German solution—a right of return under the *ius sanguinis* for anyone of German descent, regardless of whether they speak German, and the prolonged naturalization procedure which leaves many second-generation immigrants without citizenship—is hardly an improvement.

Many of the states in the Third World are facing an even more acute identity crisis. Although in East Asia, the authorities adopted traditional interventionist state and nation-building policies before embracing the open market, in most other regions the policies of import substitution and state-promoted development, around which nationalist claims were largely constructed, manifestly failed. However, the new international orthodoxy which demands of governments that they open up their markets to foreign competition and private investment while simultaneously embarking on democratic reform, runs the danger of putting the cart before the horse: the state is being rolled back before it has established a legitimate sphere of competence. Add to this, the fact that in the poorest parts of the world as much as 75 per cent of GDP is often derived from external assistance, that the professional élites frequently fail to return from training in Europe and North America, and that in some countries the average age of the population is as low as sixteen, and it is hardly suprising that governments find it hard to mobilize national support and are frequently at the mercy of sectarian or communal movements.

These challenges to the legitimacy of the state, which affect industrial and developing countries alike, are symptomatic of a more serious problem. The resurgence of ethnic nationalism which has been such a feature of the disintegration of the Soviet Union and its sphere of influence, is currently finding echoes in many other parts of the world from the Punjab to Quebec. It constitutes a direct challenge to international society because such groups attack the state, either as a result of the systematic abuse of their civil and political rights, or in order to assert their right to self-determination, in which case they are liable to finish up as victims of state terror just the same. The Cold War no longer provides a prudential excuse for inaction, but it is not at all clear what the international community (i.e. other states) should do.

What can then be done? As we have seen, it is unlikely that regionalism will come to represent an alternative locus of human identity. It should be viewed, at least in the first instance, not as an alternative doctrine to nationalism, but as a supplement to it. Regional organizations, in other words, should be designed not to replace the nation state and its command of the people's loyalties, but rather to help manage the inevitable problems that arise from the coexistence of competing national groups.

In thinking about the forms that such regional management might take, it may be useful to distinguish between 'normal' and 'abnormal' political conditions. By 'normal' is simply meant circumstances in which conflicts of interests and adjustments to changing political and economic forces can be accommodated within the framework of a regional organization and without resort to force. It seems possible, for example, that the relevant European organizations (i.e. the European Union, Council of Europe, and CSCE (now OSCE)) may be able to reduce the level of political instability arising from the resurgence of sub-national groups. It is no accident that the politically self-conscious but stateless ethnic groups in Europe—for example the Basques, Bretons, or Scots— have embraced the European Community, even if the route towards greater *regional* devolution within a larger and regional whole remains obscure. Certain steps which would support this view have already been taken. The Maastricht Treaty provides for a Committee of the Regions. There seems no reason in practice why this committee should not evolve in ways which would provide for a measure of representation at the European level for stateless national groups, even if, as a matter of principle, member states insist that the regions should be defined in economic terms rather than as units of popular affective identification. Perhaps of greatest significance at a time when European societies are having to adjust to the political fall-out from the collapse of communism, the Council of Europe and the OSCE have both recognized the importance of minority rights in the wider Europeans order. The criteria for membership of the Council of Europe consist of a proven commitment to multiparty democracy, the rule of law and the entrenchment of fundamental human rights, including minority rights. Since membership is desired by most European states and recognition can be withheld, in this instance the regional framework can in principle exercise a benign influence towards the reconciliation of ethnic and national conflicts at state level. The OSCE has gone further by establishing a Commissioner on Minorities, with powers of investigation and recommendation in countries where ethnic tensions threaten to explode into open conflict. To the extent that the resurgence of nationalism and nationalist conflict is world-wide, and not merely a European phenomenon, it must be hoped that regional organization will be able to evolve analogous techniques for containing its destructive impact.

Unhappily, it is not clear that under 'abnormal' conditions, that is when a state has already irrevocably broken down, or a new political and territorial dispensation is already being contested by force, regional management will be effective. The reason has less to do with the relative weakness of regional sentiment than with the structure of international society itself. The problem may conveniently be illustrated by reference to the topical debate concerning humanitarian intervention and coercive international efforts to protect oppressed groups trapped within the prison house of the sovereign state.

The political language in which the post-war international order was conceived, with its emphasis on human rights and resolutions passed by votes at the United Nations, belonged firmly within the vocabulary of Western democratic pluralism. But the central place in the scheme given to state sovereignty in turn ensured that it was a democracy of states only: authoritarian dictatorships were as able as liberal democracies to shelter behind the principle—a logical corollary of recognizing sovereignty—of non-interference in the internal affairs of other states. Both classical and modern liberals have differed over the legitimacy of humanitarian intervention. The post-war order, however, recognized only one cause for invoking the collective security provisions of the Charter: to deter or repel threats to international peace and security. Because the major states with global international interests and capabilities also had a power of veto within the Security Council, the ability of international society to provide even minimal security to its members was barely tested throughout the Cold War.

The absence of any effective case-law meant that it was difficult to argue coherently about the adequacy, or otherwise, of the central mechanism which had been intended to underwrite international peace and security. It is this which made experience of Operation Desert Storm central to the 'new world order' debate. The crisis, in which one member of the UN attacked and attempted to annex another, was tailor-made to test international resolve to prohibit war carried out for aggressive or foreign policy purposes. In this sense it was an old-fashioned and reasonably unambiguous crisis, which was handled effectively and within the spirit of the traditional society of states. There may have been those in the USA and other Western governments who wanted to continue the war until the Iraqi ruler, Saddam Hussein, was overthrown, but they knew that they could not hold on to the regional members of the coalition, who had provided vital backing for the relevant Security Council Resolutions, if they threatened the sovereignty and integrity of Iraq itself.

So far so good. However, the aftermath of the war raised two kinds of doubts about the adequacy of current arrangements and understandings. These doubts point in opposite directions. The first points, on pragmatic and prudential grounds, to the dangers of moving far from the existing conventions of the anarchical society. The second points to the artificial distinction between domestic and foreign affairs, and to the necessity of making some adjustments if the new world order is to have any chance of be an improvement on the old.

Even during the war, Western public opinion became agitated over the fact that Western lives were being put at risk to defend a state whose own government's human rights record was unimpressive. Potentially, far more damaging to the new world order, was the way in which, as soon as the war was over, Western governments appeared eager to walk away from the consequences of their policies.[15] They appealed to the Iraqi people to finish the job, and had to be forced by public outcry, to acknowledge that Iraq has a deeply divided society, and that those whose own frustrated national aspirations would prompt them to heed the message, would be brutally suppressed for their pains. In the end, the Western powers, acting with the connivance rather than under the authority of the Security Council in the Kurdish north, and more equivocally still in the Shi'ite south, effectively suspended Iraq's sovereignty from the air. From the Kurdish and Shi'ite point of view the idea of a safe haven secured by an air exclusion zone was presumably better than nothing. But as a defence of their most fundamental human rights it was precarious; and as a precedent for the new world order it is not encouraging. The national and religious crisis in Iraq is a far more typical post-Cold War challenge to international society than its invasion of Kuwait.

If humanitarian intervention is a problematic way of managing such problems, what of revising the idea of self-determination and the criteria for admission to international society? In answering this question it is tempting—and certainly fashionable—to invoke the concept of civil society. There have always been available two alternative views of what constitutes a nation, the exclusive ethnic group and the inclusive political community defined by citizenship and allegiance to the constitution. Only the latter conception, it will be argued, is capable of measuring up to reality, namely the fact that the vast majority of states are now (and will continue to be) multi-ethnic in composition. Also, only a nation-cum-political community will be able to tolerate diversity within civil society—and hence protect the human rights of its citizens—without regarding it as a form of treason and threat to the state. If this line of reasoning is accepted, then there is little for the international community to do. Certainly, it will not be required to recognize every tribal or ethnic group that claims the right of self-determination. The one departure from established practice which might be urged is the recognition of new states where the people have clearly demonstrated their desire to establish a political community with an entrenched and strongly defended civil society. Earlier (and more

[15] See James Mayall, 'Non-intervention, Self-determination and the New World Order', *International Affairs*, 67/3 (July 1991), 421–9.

principled) recognition of Lithuania and Slovenia, it has been claimed, would have increased the respect in which the international community is currently held.[16]

Nevertheless the temptation to argue in this way should be resisted. Not only are the criteria for distinguishing between legitimate claims to exercise the right of self-determination, i.e. in order to establish a plural democracy, and illegitimate ones on behalf of ethnic communities, unclear and question-begging, but there is no reason to believe that a commitment to democratic government can be secured by legislation or long-distance social engineering. It is true that national identities *can* be supported by a political culture which subordinates ethnicity to citizenship. Ethnic conflict has certainly not been eliminated from the political life of the USA, Britain, France, or indeed most other West European democracies, but equally ethnic origins clearly do not wholly define the 'imagined community' of these nations. But how are we to distinguish publicly—and before the event—between, say, the claim of the ethnically homogeneous Slovenes to establish a genuine representative democracy and Serbia's and Croatia's widely suspected ambition to expand their territory at their neighbours' expense, and to use the form of democratic government as a cover for systematic discrimination against ethnic minorities?

If there was a simple answer to this question, we should know about it. There is not. There seems, therefore, no alternative but to deal with the linked questions of when to recognize the right of self-determination, how to agree on state creation in a post-imperial world and when to intervene for humanitarian purposes on a case-by-case and even consequentialist basis. There is no escaping passing judgement in particular circumstances. The only fixed points are that international action should always aim at improving the security and welfare of the people at whom it is directed, rather than *merely* acting to cloak with respectability the foreign policies of the major powers; and that it should not be quixotic, lightly undertaken, without a serious attempt to estimate the dangers and foresee the consequences. These axioms apply as much in the field of international economic policy as they do in relation to the international response to political crises.

---

[16] See Tomaz Mastnak, 'Is the Nation-State Really Obsolete', *Times Literary Supplement*, 7 Aug. 1992.

It follows that the level—i.e. regional or global—at which the international community should be mobilized in particular cases is also a question for pragmatic judgement. Certain recent positions favoured by powerful states need to be treated with caution. For example, it is difficult not to sympathize with the view that the European Community's determination to discredit the nation state in its attempt to speed up the process of regional integration, led it to pay insufficient attention to national aspirations in Eastern and Central Europe. Since most countries in the area had their eyes firmly fixed on eventual entry to the Community, it had considerable political leverage. The Community may not have been able to do much to prevent the disaster which has now overwhelmed the region, but with hindsight it would obviously have been prudent to have placed as much emphasis on confidence-building measures amongst minorities as on the importance of having elected governments. As one Slovene critic has argued, there is not much point in unseating Leviathan merely to substitute a Behemoth in his place.[17]

Similarly, in the economic sphere the new enthusiasm for regionalism, which was spurred on by American frustration with progress towards global trade liberalization in the Uruguay Round, and short-run domestic pressures to relieve the trade deficit, provide grounds for concern. Amongst professional economists there is a vigorous debate about whether the current American policy of pursuing regional free-trade agreements is worth encouraging in its own right or only if it contributes to kick-starting the American economy out of recession and hence, indirectly, helps to overcome the obstacles to continued multilateral trade liberalization.[18] Whatever the merits of the technical arguments, from the point of view of international order, the only case for preferring regional to global economic arrangements is if it can be established that the creation of a more integrated regional market will not damage the world trading community as a whole. The prospect of three powerful competitive trade blocs attempting to shut each other out of their home markets has been reduced with the completion of the Uruguay Round and the creation of the new World Trade Organ-

---

[17] See Mastnak, 'Is the Nation State Really Obsolete'.
[18] A useful review of the arguments is contained in Jagdish Bhagwati, *Regionalism and Multilateralism: An Overview*, Paper delivered to World Bank Conference, Washington, DC, 2–3 Apr. 1992.

ization. However, whether world-wide liberalization can be sustained remains unclear. The alternative prospect is not only politically unattractive for the countries involved, but threatens to cut off peripheral areas. e.g. much of Africa, from the benefits of world trade altogether.

The Secretary-General of the United Nations has developed a parallel argument in relation to security. On his view, a principle of subsidiarity should apply to conflict management and peacekeeping. Attempts should be made to resolve civil conflicts within the country where they arise, after which they should be referred to the appropriate regional organization, and only if all such efforts fail, to the Security Council.[19] There is a compelling logic to this argument. If the numerous inter-ethnic conflicts that have arisen around the world in the aftermath of the Cold War, are all referred to the Security Council it will quickly exhaust the organizational capacity and financial resources of the United Nations. At the same time it is within the regions that the immediate spillover effects of such conflicts are most likely to be felt, particularly in the form of vastly increased refugee movements and appeals for asylum. Regionalism may not excite much passion as a political doctrine, but in most cases there should be a strong regional interest in containing the conflict at its source.

Even here there are dangers in placing too much faith in a hierarchically organized international order in which the United Nations acts as the security guarantor of last resort. The first is that regional intervention in local crises is likely to be fuelled by the special and partisan interests of neighbouring governments and the pressures to which they must respond. Opinions still differ about the wisdom of the European Community's recognition of Slovenia and Croatia, in view of the terrible civil war that erupted subsequently in Bosnia-Hercegovina. There can be little doubt that, in forcing its partners into line, the German government was responding to domestic pressures, notably from the resident Croatian community. How, it was asked, was it possible to deny the peoples of the former Yugoslavia the right of self-determination which had so recently been extended to East Germany?

A second danger in the regional approach to international order is that it threatens to marginalize the United Nations again just as

---

[19] For a fuller discussion, see Alan Henrikson's chapter.

there is an opportunity for it to play the central co-ordinating role in international society for which it was originally designed. Marginalization would occur if the UN became merely the defender of the Third World. In cases where the state breaks down and society disintegrates into brutal anarchy, there may be a case for reviving the idea of United Nations trusteeship.[20] Many but not all such breakdowns are likely to occur in the Third World. If this idea was to gain legitimacy it would therefore have to be divorced so far as possible from the national interests of particular powers.

Admittedly at present the omens for such a development are not good. The experience of the UN in Bosnia-Hercegovina and Somalia, where international intervention went further in the direction of humanitarian intervention than ever before does not suggest that the major powers are anxious to experiment any further with peacemaking as distinct from traditional peacekeeping. In neither case was the intervention unequivocally successful; and in both powerful voices can be heard to argue that the interventions were misplaced in the first place. A major reason given in support of this view is that where there is no peace to keep, UN military personnel cannot be impartial and cannot confine their activities to humanitarian relief. One conclusion that might be drawn from this observation is that when the moral case for intervention none the less proves irresistible, the United Nations must accept that strategic and political responsibility cannot be separated from humanitarian relief. However, the conclusion that is in fact increasingly drawn is that they should not be there at all. Perhaps, but if so, we must fervently hope that regional approaches to international co-operation will develop more strongly than the argument in this chapter has suggested likely.

[20] This idea was openly canvassed in the context of the Security Council's decision to intervene militarily to ensure the delivery of humanitarian assistance in Somalia.

PART II

7

Regionalism in Europe: Model or Exception?

William Wallace

'EUROPE' was a well-structured international region for forty years from 1950 to 1990: the very model of formal regional integration, which other groups of countries aspired to imitate. Other chapters in this volume talk of European integration as a 'model', an 'example', and a 'challenge' to other regional experiments; even of 'the demonstration effect' of successful European regionalism. The revival of the momentum of West European integration in the 1980s—the revision of the Treaty of Rome through the Single European Act, the '1992' single-market programme, moves towards the abolition of internal frontiers, progress even in the most sensitive fields of money, foreign policy, and defence—revived hopes in other regions that, in the 1990s, they might be able to follow the same path.

Looking back from the perspective of the post-Cold War era, however, the peculiar circumstances which favoured the creation of formal structures for regional integration in the western half of this half-continent after the Second World War, and which allowed and encouraged the informal economic and social integration which followed, are evident. West European integration was the product not only of a common culture and history, and of a particular geographical density, but also of a common disaster and predicament: the war and its aftermath, American hegemony and the Soviet threat. With all of Eastern Europe, and much of Central Europe, under Soviet domination, 'Europe' as an entity shrank to its western core.

The end of the Cold War, and the consequent widening of the idea of a 'united Europe', thus raised immense questions about the future of West European structures of integration which had until then been securely grounded within the Western Alliance. It also raised difficult questions about the balance and extent of Europe as a 'region', with governments of countries emerging from the socialist bloc proclaiming their 'European' character in order to bolster their claims for early accession to the European Community, and in many instances NATO as well. Regional integration in Europe, it emerges, has been subregional integration: the construction of institutional structures to combine the interests of a group of countries within a wider region. Seen from this perspective, the European Community should more accurately be compared in global terms with ASEAN than with APEC, with the Andean Pact than with the OAS.

One of the central features of this West European regional integration was the separation of politico-military issues—security in the strict sense—from politico-economic. The security order of the Cold War had made it possible for the economic integration of Western Europe to develop without directly confronting the most difficult issues of internal balance or of external foreign and security policy. The disorders which erupted to Western Europe's east and south-east in the early 1990s thus found the governments of Western Europe unprepared: too accustomed to following (or resisting) an American lead to be able to reconcile their own divergent assumptions or form a common response. The removal of the global overlay of superpower confrontation may well, as other chapters suggest, have provided a powerful stimulus to closer regionalism elsewhere.[1] But in Western Europe itself, the pattern for regional integration elsewhere and the original focus for the Cold War confrontation, the loss of the Cold War 'order' has reopened many of the awkward underlying questions of European balance which had for forty years been suspended, or even apparently resolved.

The European region which emerged from the Cold War was *not* however the same collection of nation states which had drifted from the 1914–18 European War to the European and World War of 1939–45.[2] Forty years of economic growth, accompanied by the

---

[1] The concept of 'overlay' is developed by Barry Buzan, *People, States and Fear* (London: Harvester Wheatsheaf, 1991), 19–21.

[2] The neo-realist argument put forward by John Mearsheimer ('Back to the Future: Instability in Europe after the Cold War', *International Security*, 15 (Summer 1990), 5–56) assumes that the processes of formal and informal integration within Western Europe over the past forty years has nevertheless left relations among states, and the definition of their national interests, unchanged; without

dismantling of barriers between national markets, had transformed the West European economy. Since the completion of the process of post-war reconstruction a further surge of industrial and financial innovation, accelerated by revolutions in communications and electronics, had integrated the regional economy.[3] Affluence, short distances, and improved communications had similarly transformed social communication across Western Europe, sweeping aside the border controls erected by nation states over the previous century.[4]

Social and economic integration within a geographically concentrated region had weakened national antagonisms. The impact of these largely informal processes on the Western European region in the 1970s and 1980s stands in sharp contrast to the experience of Eastern Europe during those decades, where authoritarian controls and economic stagnation helped to preserve national grievances and where the kind of hegemonic regionalism established by the Soviet Union through organizations such as the Warsaw Pact and Comecon, failed utterly to take root.

1. EUROPE AS THE WORLD ORDER: THE HISTORICAL LEGACY

The international state system which now covers the globe grew out of the regional order established in Europe after the defeat of the Counter-Reformation and the Habsburg bid for hegemony. The idea of Europe as a 'region' within a wider global system would have appeared absurd to European statesmen of the imperialist era before the First World War, when Europe accounted for nearly a third of the world's estimated population and the superiority of the European races was taken as self-evident. Consciousness of the distinctiveness of European regional interests developed in the

examining the evidence of extensive interpenetration of governments and political systems, which has transformed the context within which governments define and redefine their interests.

[3] See Albert Bressand and Kalypso Nicolaïdis, 'Regional Integration in a Networked World Economy'; and Margaret Sharp, 'Technology and the Dynamics of Integration', in William Wallace (ed.), *The Dynamics of European Integration* (London: Pinter, 1990).

[4] Federico Romero, 'Cross-Border Population Movements', and Bruno de Witte, 'Cultural Linkages', in Wallace (ed.), *The Dynamics of European Integration*.

course of the 1970s, as the pursuit of European *détente* became separated from the global superpower confrontation and institutionalized in the 'Helsinki Process' of the Conference on Security and Co-operation in Europe (CSCE). But the boundaries of that region were never clearly defined. The CSCE itself drew in much of the northern hemisphere, including the USSR, Canada, and the USA, but was designed to focus on stability within 'the European theatre'—itself a term open to several definitions, most ofen assumed to include the western USSR but not to extend east of the Urals.

European *détente* in the course of the 1970s and 1980s reopened the question of 'Europe', its geographical extent, and geopolitical significance. The mental maps of Western policy-makers slowly adjusted to the re-emergence of a degree of autonomy among Moscow's Warsaw Pact allies, and to the pleas of Czech, Polish, and Hungarian intellectuals to accept that their Central European cultures also belonged to 'the West'. The 'Europe' of the European Community, accepted as a natural region within relatively clear boundaries, became again Western Europe, rediscovering its eastern and south-eastern peripheries—though uncertain how far to draw them within its established structures for economic co-operation and security.[5]

Historical reference points from earlier European orders thus gradually re-emerged from under the artificial boundaries which the Cold War had imposed. Part of the confusion of European regional politics in the early 1990s, indeed, flowed from the proliferation of competing images of the past, with policy-makers uncertain which remained relevant, and publics swinging from old dreams to old nightmares—most acutely in the periphery itself, where myths and memories of Serbia, Macedonia, medieval Hungary, and post-Versailles Romania all challenged existing boundaries, with shadows of the Austro-Hungarian and Ottoman empires looming in the background.

The imagery of the Cold War was of a Europe divided into two halves: 'their' Europe and 'ours', held in stable tension by the

---

[5] See William Wallace, *The Transformation of Western Europe* (London: Pinter, 1990), ch. 2. The election of a Polish Pope in 1978, the heroic quality of the Solidarity strikes and demonstrations in 1980–1, and the discovery by Western European élites and media of sympathetic intellectual dissidents in Czechoslovakia, also contributed to this shift of perceptions of 'Europe'.

balance between the two alliances. In reality the political, economic, and demographic balance of Europe has been tilted towards a western core region—stretching from south-eastern England through the Low Countries and the Rhine valley, and on through Burgundy and southern Germany into northern Italy—for the past 1,000 years. Nineteenth- and early twentieth-century Eastern and South-Eastern Europe differed sharply from the industrializing states to the west, which were successfully imposing common languages and national identities on their populations. To the east of Berlin and Vienna lay peasant societies speaking a profusion of languages and dialects, under imperial rule, with German the prevailing language of the towns and of commerce.[6] Optimists among the élites of those countries emerging from socialist rule were speaking in 1989–90 of 'rejoining the West': implying that their states had been comparable to those of Western Europe in political and economic development before they were subordinated to Soviet rule. Hungary, Poland, the Baltic states had—it is true—been part of Western Christendom, but they had only experienced the edges of the 'Great Transformation' which swept across their Western neighbours before they were overtaken by war and subjugated by Soviet control.[7]

The seventeenth-century European system *was* primarily a West European system, with Sweden and Poland vying for dominance on its north-eastern borders, and Ottoman Turkey—a non-Christian power and therefore an outsider to the system—pressing hard on its south-east.[8] The concept of 'Christendom' as the basis for this

---

[6] Prague contained more German-speakers than Czechs throughout the first half of the nineteenth century, for instance, until industrialization brought floods of immigrants in from rural areas. Present-day Lvov, now in western Ukraine, was Lemberg, the capital of Austrian Galicia, where the language of command and higher administration remained German until the First World War. Kaliningrad, now stranded as a detached part of the Russian Federation surrounded by Polish and Lithuanian territory, was Königsberg, the city of Immanuel Kant and intellectual centre of German East Prussia.

[7] Karl Polanyi, *The Great Transformation: The Political and Economic Origins of Our Time* (Oxford, 1944), captures the immensity of this revolution with an acuteness of perspective which partly derived from his Hungarian origin; he had witnessed its progress across Eastern Europe as well as its impact on the West. Bohemia by this criterion was clearly part of the West by the first half of the twentieth century: highly urbanized and heavily industrialized, in sharp contrast to the peasant society of Slovakia which the Treaty of Trianon attached to it.

[8] Iver B. Neuman and Jennifer M. Welsh, 'The Other in European Self-definition: An Addendum to the Literature on International Society', *Review of International*

developing community of European societies and states gradually gave way during the following century to the more secular concept of 'the civilized world': 'the West', as opposed to the uncivilized and 'Asiatic' 'East'. Russia, a semi-Asiatic state outside the European order at the time the Westphalian system was constructed, thrust itself into eighteenth-century Europe by displacing first the Swedish empire and then Poland, by transferring its capital to its north-western coast, and by pursuing a deliberate policy of 'Westernization'.

The nineteenth-century European order succeeded in maintaining stability while accommodating substantial changes in the balance of power among its major states, and while adjusting to the spread of industrialization from west to east and to major shifts in the size and balance of populations. The diplomatic cohesion of the European 'powers', which faltered in the 1850s, was re-established after the achievement of German and Italian unification: co-operating on extra-European issues, bargaining to resolve conflicts of interest among 'the powers', co-operating to contain disorder on the European periphery.

The two 'central powers' of Prussia—imperial Germany from 1871—and Austria straddled the divide between the nation states of the West and the intermingled subject populations of the East. German political and cultural dominance was reinforced by the increasing dominance of the German economy, in terms of trade and investment—most markedly over Eastern and South-Eastern Europe, including Russia and Ottoman Turkey. But Germany was also the most important trading partner for the Nordic countries, the Low Countries, Switzerland, and Italy, and the second trade partner for Britain and France. 'Round Germany as a central support the rest of the European economy grouped itself,' John Maynard Keynes wrote in 1919, 'and on the prosperity and enterprise of Germany the prosperity of the rest of the continent mainly depended.'[9] Ottoman Turkey, in decline, was at times accepted as

Studies, 17/4 (Oct. 1991), 327–48. The 'otherness' of Turkey did not, however, prevent both France and England pursuing good relations with this enemy of the Habsburgs. Divisions among the 'Christian' powers, not only between Protestant and Catholic states but also between Catholic France and Catholic Austria, overrode papal and Habsburg calls for Chistendom to unite against the religious enemy. Protestants in Transylvania in turn accepted Turkish protection against the Habsburg-sponsored Counter-Reformation.

[9] J. M. Keynes, The Economic Consequences of the Peace (London: Macmillan, 1919), 14.

a 'country member' of this regional system useful in containing the rival ambitions of Austria and Russia. But at other times it was treated as a subject for the powers to consider 'the sick man of Europe', to be amputated from its European possessions one by one. The expansion of Europe spread also across the Mediterranean. Coastal Algeria became part of metropolitan France; incorporation shaded into empire along the rest of the southern littoral. European officials, traders, and tourists flocked through Alexandria and Cairo and extended European influence into the Ottoman territories of the Levant.

What had thus become a Europe-centred world order collapsed into general war in 1914. Three of the factors which brought the system down still resonate today: the problem of Germany, Europe's central power and strongest economy, then determined on expanding its influence further in Eastern and South-Eastern Europe; the instability of South-Eastern Europe itself, with competing ethnic and religious groups contesting the boundaries which the Western powers had drawn for them as the Turks were pushed back; and the political and economic weakness of Russia, compounded by its ambitions to play the role of a great power in Eastern and Central Europe.

The 1919 settlement sought to re-establish European order on the liberal basis of nation states. But Germany remained as too large a state for its neighbours, yet still with minorities beyond its borders; while the new and uncertain states of Eastern Europe, caught up in the politics of Franco-German rivalry, weakened by the impact of global economic recession on their largely agricultural economies, sank into authoritarianism. Revolutionary Russia, half-excluded from interwar European diplomacy, agreed out of a sense of vulnerability a pact with Germany in 1939; nevertheless, attacking in 1941, the German armies penetrated as far as Moscow and the Caucasus before they were driven back. The Russian–American confrontation which succeeded the Allied victory in 1945 left Russia in Germany's place, the dominant power in Eastern and East-Central Europe: dominant militarily, though economically so weak that it was able to plan for post-war reconstruction only on the basis of draconian political control.

The leaders of post-Cold War Europe are only one or two generations removed from the order which collapsed in 1914. Most of them grew up during the traumas of the Second World War and its aftermath. Many of the most awkward obstacles to the construc-

tion of a stable regional order across Western and Eastern Europe
lie in their memories and myths: hopes and fears frozen under the
Cold War, national ambitions nurtured under the blanket of socialist internationalism, to re-emerge as the superpowers withdraw.

2. THE COLD WAR ORDER: THE WORLD
WE HAVE LOST

For Western Europe, and for its American patron, protector, and
hegemon, the order which emerged out of the post-1945 confrontation was remarkably successful. It provided forty years of security
and rising prosperity. They regularly reaffirmed their commitment
to German reunification; but Germany's neighbours were happy
with its effective containment, while as the decades went by even
the population of West Germany began to feel comfortable with the
reality of division. They protested the harshness of Communist
Party rule under Soviet influence in Eastern and South-Eastern
Europe; but benefited from the stability which the two alliances
each imposed on their halves of the continent.

   This successful European regional order to which other pro-
moters of regional integration look is, of course, *not* Europe as a
whole but Western Europe—and not even Western Europe as a
whole, but those West European countries (at first a small core
group) which came together to form the European Communities.
The history of European integration is itself a contested area, with
its own myths and debunkers.[10] One of the central myths is that of
Western Europe as a 'civilian power', pursuing economic objectives
without the need for Clausewitzian power politics.[11] The central
reality was that West European integration was rooted in a wider
security framework, and constructed in large part around the
security dilemmas which faced France, the Low Countries, and a
divided Germany.

   West European integration began under American initiative, protection, and pressure. The Marshall Plan of March 1947 was conditional upon its European recipients co-operating closely to

   [10] See e.g. 'The Lives and Teachings of the European Saints', ch. 6 of Alan
Milward, *The European Rescue of the Nation State* (London: Routledge, 1992).
   [11] Hedley Bull, 'Civilian Power: A Contradiction in Terms?', *Journal of Common
Market Studies*, 21/1–2 (Sept.–Dec. 1982), 149–64.

distribute it, and agreeing to concert policies for economic reconstruction among them. Those which accepted registered that they were part of 'the West'; those, like Poland, which wavered before refusing recognized that they were from then on within the opposite camp. Enthusiasts within the USA—and within the US Administration—urged upon the Europeans they had liberated (or occupied) the project of a 'United States of Europe'. Failing that, they fell back on the idea of a customs union of all the sixteen European members of the Organization for European Economic Co-operation, the body set up to co-ordinate Marshall Plan assistance.[12] When the British Government, with its extra-European interests and aspirations, resisted, the Americans supported instead the integration of 'little Europe' which the French proposed and the Germans accepted.

Jean Monnet shared the American vision of a European federation: if possible with Britain included, if not to bring together a smaller group of states. Robert Schuman, French Foreign Minister in 1950, faced the more prosaic necessity of constructing a policy towards Germany that would satisfy American demands to rebuild West Germany as a bulwark against the Communist threat, but without laying France open again to an independent, industrially powerful, and eventually rearmed Germany. The Schuman Plan thus responded to both French and American security interests—as the Preamble to the ECSC Treaty makes clear, with its resolve to overcome 'age-old rivalries' and 'to create, by establishing an economic community, the basis for a broader and deeper community among peoples long divided by bloody conflicts'.[13]

The outbreak of the Korean War, a month after the Schuman Plan had been launched, made the choice more stark. American pressure for German rearmament to meet the apparent military threat from the east, barely five years after German power had been rolled back, made political and military integration appear the only way to contain a reviving Germany. But the plan for a European

---

[12] Robert Marjolin, *Memoirs 1911–1986* (London: Weidenfeld & Nicolson, 1989), 213: 'Originally, America's ambitions went very far . . . They imagined, somewhat naïvely, a Western Europe that would be an extension, as it were, of the USA in the old world, inspired by the same values, following the same policy'. See also Michael Hogan, *The Marshall Plan: America, Britain and the Reconstruction of Europe, 1947–1952* (Cambridge: CUP, 1987).

[13] Preamble to Treaty establishing the European Coal and Steel Community, Paris, Apr. 1951.

Defence Community collapsed in the face of British refusal, and French hesitations, to yield so central an aspect of sovereignty; to be replaced by the weaker Western European Union, placing constraints upon German weapons and procurement while placing the integration of West European defence firmly within the framework of the integrated Atlantic Alliance. Six American divisions in Germany, four British, and two French supported, but also counterbalanced, the planned twelve German divisions.

The 'relaunch' of West European integration through the two Treaties of Rome in 1957 was thus based upon an explicit separation of formal economic integration from the 'high politics' of foreign policy and security. Economic integration was a West European enterprise; security an Atlantic one. The golden years of West European integration, from 1958 to 1965, coincided with a period of continuing economic growth, with North America and Western Europe—the North Atlantic area—the focus of the world economy, and the OEEC transformed into a body closely paralleling NATO, the OECD.

From the American perspective the whole project of West European integration had to be seen within the wider framework of 'the West'. President Kennedy's 'Grand Design' for an Atlantic partnership, with an EEC enlarged through British and other accession forming the European pillar of a linked security and economic community, was countered by de Gaulle's insistence that security and economic integration must be brought together more closely within Western Europe alone.[14] The Commission's idealistic insistence that economic integration could be divorced from power politics, supported by the American academic theorists who shared its vision of 'upgrading the common interest' through redefining the context within which policies were made, led only to a sense of disillusion as broader issues of sovereignty and of high politics intervened.[15]

After de Gaulle's departure, the Hague summit of December 1969 relaunched the West European enterprise, as a specifically

[14] Alfred Grosser, *The Western Alliance: European-American Relations since 1945* (London: Macmillan, 1978), ch. 7. See also Pascaline Winand, *Eisenhower, Kennedy and the United States of Europe* (New York: St Martin's, 1993)

[15] Stanley Hoffmann, 'No Trumps, No Luck, No Will', in James Chace and Earl C. Ravenal, (eds.), *Atlantis Lost: US–European Relations after the Cold War* (sic) (New York: New York UP, 1976); Ernst Haas, 'Turbulent Fields and the Theory of Regional Integration', *International Organization* 30/2 (Spring 1976), 126–53.

civilian politico-economic structure. Negotiations for enlargement brought in Britain, Ireland, and Denmark in 1973. Again, the American response was to insist that such formal economic integration should be placed clearly within the context of Atlantic security integration. Henry Kissinger bluntly stated in the speech which launched the Nixon Administration's 'Year of Europe' that 'the political, military and economic issues in Atlantic relations are linked by reality, not by our choice nor for the tactical purpose of trading one off against the other.'[16] French and American grand designs clashed bitterly in the winter of 1973–4, in the wake of the October 1973 Arab–Israeli conflict and the subsequent oil embargo; to reach a renewed compromise in the NATO Ottawa Declaration of June 1974, accepting a modicum of West European co-operation on foreign policy while reaffirming the primacy of the Atlantic tie.

The image of West European regional integration in the 1960s and 1970s as a construct entire of itself, providing a model for other regions to follow, is thus to a substantial extent an illusion. Western Europe was a subregion within a wider Atlantic region: an Atlantic security community, committed to shared 'Western' values, within which the political, economic, and cultural influence of the USA on Western Europe was immense.[17]

All international regions are to some extent subjective: mental maps which emphasize some features and ignore others, tracing preferred links and boundaries.[18] The idea of an Atlantic community is a classic example of a mental map: resting on, and reinforcing, cultural ties, shared security interests, and economic links. The countries of North-Western Europe (most of all Britain and the Netherlands) adapted easily to this shift of perspective. West

[16] Secretary of State Henry Kissinger, Speech to Associated Press, New York, 23 Apr. 1973. See also William Wallace, 'Issue Linkage among Atlantic Governments', *International Affairs*, 52/2 (Apr. 1976), 163–79.

[17] Thomas A. Schwartz, *America's Germany: John J. Mcloy and the Federal Republic of Germany* (Cambridge, Mass.: Harvard UP, 1991). Louis Halle in *The Cold War as History* (London: Chatto & Windus, 1967) notes the emergence of the concept of 'the Atlantic bridge' and the hold which it gained on West European and North American imaginations. See also Karl Deutsch, *Political Community and the North Atlantic Area* (Princeton: Princeton UP, 1957).

[18] I have taken the concept of mental maps from Alan K. Henrikson, 'The Geographical "Mental Maps" of American Foreign Policy-makers', *International Political Science Review*, 1/4 (1980), 495–530. See also P. Gould and R. White, *Mental Maps* (Harmondsworth: Penguin, 1974).

Germans were unavoidably ambivalent, torn between their transatlantic sponsor—a country to which Germans had been emigrating (second in numbers only to Britons) for two and a half centuries—and their lost eastern territories. French politicians and public were even more ambivalent: valuing the American presence in Germany which guaranteed their security, resenting the displacement of French political and cultural influence by American, turning towards partnership with Germany as an alternative to the acceptance of Anglo-Saxon leadership, but, under de Gaulle from the early 1960s, also looking east to the other Europe for potential allies in containing a strengthening though still divided Germany.

In terms of the historical obstacles and the strength of the idea of the West European nation state, the formal integration of Western Europe has been remarkable enough. The European Economic Community completed the replacement of national tariffs by a customs union four years ahead of the twelve set out in the Rome Treaty, helped by strong and continuous economic growth which ensured that all member states and interests made relative gains. One detailed common policy, for agriculture, was agreed and implemented, transferring substantial authority in this specific field to Brussels. The French government, which saw a common agricultural policy as the essential counterweight to opening its industrial market to German competition, put all its weight behind this development, whilst at the same time blocking the Commission's 'supranational' ambitions in other areas. The Luxembourg 'crisis' of 1965–6, during which the French Government boycotted meetings of the Council of Ministers, ended with Commission hopes of moving to qualified majority voting sharply limited by the concession of the right for governments to veto decisions 'in areas of vital national interest'. The European Atomic Energy Authority, the parallel Community to the EEC intended to provide Western Europe with cheap and secure energy supplies, was blighted from the outset by French resistance to loss of national control in nuclear matters, civil or military.

The image of European integration which enthusiasts for 'European Union' and their American supporters conveyed to élites in other regions in the mid-1960s was of a supranational and enlightened administration emerging in Western Europe, 'beyond the nation state'.[19] The European Community which emerged into the 1970s was characterized much more by intergovernmental bargaining, by intermittent summits which developed into regular European Councils (of heads of state and government), by carefully crafted compromises rather than grand designs. When progress in formal integration revived in mid-1980s, with the successful negotiation and ratification of the Single European Act, some outside observers saw the years between 1967 and 1985 as a European 'dark ages' between the heroic classical era and the 1980s renaissance.[20]

Closer examination of the ebbs and flows of formal integration in Western Europe, however, throws up much more subtle patterns of light and shade. Economic integration in the early 1960s had made progress against the background of bitter Franco-American disputes over political and security issues. The Gaullist project for an independent *Europe des Patries* led only to the veto on British entry, the 1963 Franco-German Treaty (its clauses on foreign policy and defence co-operation blocked by Atlanticists in the Bundestag), and French withdrawal from the NATO integrated military structure. The 'relaunch' of the process of formal integration at the Hague Summit of 1969, after de Gaulle's departure, gave the Community a common budget, a loose and intergovernmental procedure for foreign policy consultations (European Political Co-operation—EPC), a commitment to enlargement, and an ambitious three-stage plan for Economic and Monetary Union (EMU) by 1980.

The widening US balance of payments deficit, and the consequent weakness of the US dollar, were motivating factors in German and Dutch acceptance of the French initiative for EMU. But the 'Nixon shocks' of August 1971 (delinking the dollar from gold and thus bringing to an end the Bretton Woods regime of fixed exchange rates) led to a period of international monetary instability which destroyed the EMU project before it had reached its second stage— and demonstrated the high interdependence between European regional economic integration and wider transatlantic economic relations. International recession made regional economic integ-

[19] The title of Ernst Haas's classic study, *Beyond the Nation State* (Stanford, Calif.: Stanford UP, 1964).

[20] Stanley Hoffmann, 'The European Community and 1992', *Foreign Affairs* 68/4–5 (Fall 1989), 27–47.

ration a much more painful process, with insufficient compensation from growth elsewhere for the restructuring which it entailed. Enlargement also made for a greater diversity of interests to be reconciled.

Nevertheless, the nine member states made slow progress in intensifying their co-operation. They committed themselves to a second round of enlargement, to bring in the Mediterranean countries emerging from authoritarian rule. They accepted the gradual encroachment of Community law over domestic legislation. They agreed to direct elections for the European Parliament in 1979: the first and still the only directly elected assembly above the level of the nation state. The French and German Governments launched a scaled-down version of EMU, the European Monetary System, to contain exchange-rate fluctuations within the European market. Foreign-policy co-operation made slow but definite progress. In the early 1980s the dossier on defence co-operation was also reopened, first through a Franco-German defence dialogue then through revival of the moribund Western European Union: distancing the West Europeans a little from the USA in the most sensitive areas of transatlantic relations, with German and British concern at the direction and quality of American leadership under a succession of four Presidents in eight years pulling their governments away from the assumption that the Atlantic commitment necessarily came first.[21]

3. THE RE-EMERGENCE OF THE WIDER EUROPE

It was de Gaulle who first reposited the mental map of Europe 'from the Atlantic to the Urals' after the building of the Berlin Wall in the course of his challenge to the American-led concept of the West. But it was the German government which did most to bring it back into the currency of West European discourse; responding

[21] Simon Nuttall, *European Political Co-operation* (Oxford: OUP, 1992); William Wallace, 'European Defence Cooperation: The Reopening Debate', *Survival* (Nov./Dec. 1984), 251–61. The underlying linkage between the Atlantic security framework and the EC structure of economic integration was evident in the process of Mediterranean enlargement. Several EC governments, most strongly the German, with the support of the US Administration, made it clear to the Spanish—the only non-NATO member applying—that accession to the Atlantic Alliance was a necessary part of its 'rejoining' of Europe.

to the Soviet invasion of Prague, which marked the collapse of de Gaulle's eastern strategy, by pursuing an *Ostpolitik* which accepted the boundaries and political and military dispositions of divided Europe in the hope of long-term transformation. Several factors came together in contributing to Western acceptance in 1972 of the long-standing Soviet proposal for a conference on European security: West Germany's need for a multilateral framework within which to pursue its strategy of *Wandel durch Annäherung*; the creation of European Political Co-operation, which from its first ministerial meeting in November 1970 focused its discussions on the Middle East and on the proposal for a European Security Conference; the established French interest in independent initiatives in East–West relations; and the US Government's preoccupation with Asia, which left it to its European allies to take the lead.[22]

The Helsinki Conference on Security and Co-operation in Europe, from 1972 to 1974, thus marked the point at which the lines between the two opposed alliances began again to blur, and the idea of a wider Europe to re-emerge. Conference diplomacy allowed each side to explore the nuances of attitude and interest within the other, with the 'European neutrals' actively engaged in the search for common ground. The Helsinki Declaration of 1975 granted the explicit recognition of post-1945 boundaries which the Soviet Union had sought, but delivered few of the concessions on trade and technological transfers for which the socialist states were hoping. In return the Warsaw Pact agreed to (and published in official newspapers as part of the Declaration) a statement on 'Respect for human rights and fundamental freedoms, including the freedom of thought, conscience, religion and belief' which set out the standards of behaviour towards their citizens which European states were expected to observe. 'Confidence-building measures' between the two alliances (involving for example mutual notification of troop movements and manœuvres), and proposals for further discussions on arms control, completed the package deal; with a commitment to periodic 'Review Conferences' on progress made towards implementing the provisions of the Declaration.

[22] In this section I am relying heavily on Marianne Hanson, 'The Conference on Security and Cooperation in Europe: The Evolution of a Code of Conduct in East–West Relations', D.Phil. thesis, Oxford University, 1992. On the evolution of West German foreign policy more generally, see Timothy Garton Ash, *In Europe's Name: Germany and the Divided Continent* (London: Cape, 1993).

None of the parties to the Helsinki Declaration appears to have anticipated the impact of its human rights clauses in encouraging intellectual opposition within Eastern Europe, in building informal links across the East–West divide, and in submitting the domestic policies of East European regimes to Western scrutiny. Even before the first Review Conference, at Belgrade in 1977, dissident groups and their leading figures were becoming familiar to Western publics. The Helsinki process, the growing visibility of dissidence, the evident weakness of the regimes of East-Central Europe and their efforts to differentiate themselves from the Soviet Union, all helped to transform the prevailing West European image of the socialist world from that of an alien monolithic bloc into one of European nations held back by authoritarian regimes.

The emergence of Solidarity in Poland, and the uneasy compromise eventually struck between the regime and Solidarity; the different compromise which evolved in Hungary, with a degree of economic reform and political liberalization; the prevarication of the Czech regime in dealing with its intellectual dissidents, who began to develop close links with Western Europe; the role of the Churches in supporting autonomous and dissident groups in these societies, underlined by the symbolic impact of the election of a Polish Pope—these marked out the three countries of Catholic East-Central Europe as closest to 'the West'. Part of the success of dissident groups within these countries was, indeed, to persuade Western Europe to 'reposition' them geographically: no longer as part of the East, but of Central Europe, which Milan Kundera defined as 'a part of the Latin West which has fallen under Russian domination . . . which lies geographically in the centre, culturally in the west and politically in the east.'[23]

The widening economic and technological gap between Western and Eastern Europe in the 1970s and 1980s also contributed to the re-emergence of a wider Europe, in four contrasting ways. First, the impact of Western radio and television—particularly television, as transmission and reception improved and as mass publics in Eastern Europe acquired their own TVs—was in many ways fundamental: undermining socialist regimes' control of the flow of information, giving their societies direct access to West European

---

[23] Quoted in Karl Schlögel, *Die Mitte liegt Ostwärts* (Berlin: Corso, 1986; my translation). On the broader developments in these three countries, see Timothy Garton Ash, *The Uses of Adversity* (Cambridge: Granta, 1989).

news, ideas, and consumer images. Almost the entire population of the German Democratic Republic could receive West German television by the mid-1980s, and watched it by settled preference. Here as in other ways geography matters. Austrian television was widely obtainable in Czechoslovakia and Hungary. West German programmes could be received in parts of Western Poland. Estonians watched Finnish programmes.[24] Further east and south-east illicit trade in videos and video machines entertained the élite without giving wider access to the masses.

Second, East European regimes were slow to accept the full implications of the wider revolution in communications which was sweeping the industrialized societies in the 1970s and 1980s: direct-dial telephone links and personal computers threatened to destroy their mechanisms of social control. Yet the logic of industrial modernization forced them partially to adapt. The peculiar situation of the GDR, partly subsidized by West Germany yet legitimated only by its commitment to an alternative economic and social model from that of West Germany, best demonstrates the contradictions: a separate German state which nevertheless hesitated to resist contacts with the other Germany and in which telephone calls between East and West rose from around a million in 1970 to over 40 million in 1987.[25] East European regimes in the 1980s *needed* direct communications with their Western neighbours, because trade with Western Europe—most of all, with West Germany—had become so important a factor in supporting and modernizing their faltering economies. But such links tied them more closely to Western Europe, and opened direct contacts between dissidents and Western journalists as well.

Third, East European regimes needed Western currency and encouragement of Western tourism was one of the surest ways to earn foreign exchange. Long before the formal barriers to east–west movement were eased in 1989–90, human movement across the short distances which divided West-Central from East-Central Europe had multiplied. In addition a shallower east–west flow of

[24] One of the first concessions the Estonian Communist Party made, in 1990, was to agree to publish Finnish TV schedules in the Estonian press. The two languages are of course mutually comprehensible.
[25] Richard Davy, 'The Central European Dimension', in Wallace, *The Dynamics of European Integration*, 148.

asylum-seekers and west–east flow of tourists lapped over the rest of Eastern Europe. West Germans were the most numerous visitors, accounting for over half of Western travellers in East European countries in 1987. Federal Germany was also the destination of most visitors and asylum-seekers from the East. Pre-Cold War patterns of interaction were re-emerging, in spite of continuing political obstacles. Viennese by the mid-1980s were travelling to Budapest to shop, with Hungarians in turn crossing the border in search of hard-currency bargains.[26]

Most paradoxical in its effect was the differential impact of technological and industrial change. Western Europe in the 1970s painfully adjusted to the revolutionary changes in industrial economies which stemmed from micro-electronics, advanced communications, and from the impact of these innovations on financial markets, in managerial style, marketing, and patterns of employment. The strains of industrial adjustment, during a period of slow growth, weighed down intergovernmental bargaining within the EC. Rising concern among industrialists and governments about the slow pace of adjustment and the institutional obstacles to innovation, in the face of dynamic Japanese growth and continuing American technological superiority, powerfully contributed to the impetus for further integration which led to the 1992 Programme and the Single European Act.[27]

But Eastern Europe had failed far more drastically. Clinging to a model of economic growth which stressed heavy industry and central control, with little sense of the need for constant innovation, the socialist economies found themselves more and more dependent on Western Europe for the advanced technology they saw they needed, and able to offer only low technology goods and primary products in exchange. Far from the heady hopes of the early 1960s that their economies might overtake the capitalist West, it was

[26] Davy, 'The Central European Dimension', 146–9. See also Norbert Ropers, *Der Tourismus zwischen West und Ost und seine politischen Implikationen* (Bonn: Gustav Stresemann Institut, 1988). Davy cites Austrian statistics that 450,000 Hungarians travelled to Austria from Hungary in 1987—out of a population of 10 million. When controls were partly lifted, in Apr. 1989, 200,000 Hungarians visited Austria in the first week.

[27] Bressand and Nicolaïdis, 'Regional Integration in a Networked World Economy', and Sharp, 'Technology and the Dynamics of Integration'. See also Wayne Sandholtz and John Zysman, '1992: Recasting the European Bargain', *World Politics*, 45/1 (Oct. 1989), 95–128.

becoming clear to the regimes of Eastern Europe by the late 1980s that they had little future except by making the most they could of their claim to form part of the European periphery, and by moving as close as they could to their Western neighbours.

4. A WIDER EUROPEAN REGIONAL ORDER?

The collapse of the socialist order in Eastern Europe took governments in Western Europe by surprise. The strategy of *Ostpolitik* had envisaged a gradual process of liberalization within socialist regimes, accompanied by step-by-step progress—over a further decade or two—in reducing troop levels and tension and in dismantling barriers to trade and to cross-border movement of people and finance. The underlying assumption had been that the states of East-Central Europe would gradually detach themselves from Soviet control and move towards closer association with Western Europe—with the Soviet Union itself remaining aloof.

Meanwhile, the strengthening of West European integration would continue within established security boundaries. Intense economic and social interaction across national boundaries, within an institutionalized regional political framework, had resolved the security dilemma within Western Europe through the development of a loose sense of political community; external security dilemmas were contained by the Atlantic Alliance and the Warsaw Pact. In 1989 the member governments of the EC were moving towards further amendment of the Treaty of Rome, with an intergovernmental conference envisaged for 1990–1 which would focus on revived plans for economic and monetary union and on further extensions or the Community's agenda. This would cover such consequences of intensified economic and social integration as co-operation against cross-border crime and financial fraud, common policy on entry and visa requirements for nationals of third countries, etc. In parallel to this the Commission President, Jacques Delors, proposed in January 1989 a reformulation of the association agreements with the largely neutral EFTA states to create a wider European Economic Area, acting on the assumption that the political inhibitions which had held these states back from full membership of a Community so closely associated with the 'Western' Alliance would continue to hold.[28]

Both the speed of change and its unexpected direction forced West European governments—as well as their American ally—into a succession of adjustments of policy, which never in the years between 1989 and 1993 attained the coherence of a strategy. Both the French and British Governments briefly expressed their resistance to any rapid unification of the two German states. As pressure for unification from within East Germany became unstoppable, the French and German Governments in April 1990 proposed that a second intergovernmental conference of EC member states should upgrade the loose mechanisms of European Political Co-operation and WEU into a commitment to a common foreign and security policy: to bind a united Germany more closely to its Western neighbours as Soviet forces withdrew and as its former eastern hinterland again offered alternative directions for policy. The American administration made clear its insistence that the Atlantic Alliance must remain the primary framework for West European security, and set in train with its partners a review of NATO objectives and strategy; while also beginning to consider what reductions in its 350,000 troops in Europe the transformed security situation now made possible.

The CSCE, the grouping with the widest membership among European states, had gained credibility and credit through its review process and the support this had given to those now moving from dissidence to government across East-Central Europe. A heads of government summit of its thirty-four member states in Paris in November 1990 (reduced from the original thirty-five by the unification of the two Germanies the previous month) agreed to strengthened procedures and new formal structures: a Secretariat in Prague, a Conflict Prevention Centre in Vienna, an Office for Democratic Institutions and Human Rights in Warsaw, and more regular meetings at official, ministerial, and even heads of government level. The new governments of East-Central and South-East-

[28] Of the six member states of EFTA in 1989, four—Switzerland, Austria, Sweden, and Finland—were politically neutral, and saw their neutral status as excluding membership of a Community with underlying political aims. Norway and Iceland were members of NATO, and held back more from concern for preserving their autonomy and identity, as small and peripheral countries. See Helen Wallace (ed.), *The Wider Western Europe: Reshaping the EC/EFTA Relationship* (London: Pinter, 1991).

ern Europe were at the same time making overtures to the Council of Europe, membership of which was seen as carrying the symbolic importance of acceptance into the 'club' of Western democracies; and to the European Community itself, which in a series of improvised responses developed a number of immediate programmes of assistance for these new *demandeurs*.[29]

Reinforcement of the CSCE, and more rapid progress in East–West negotiations on nuclear and conventional arms reduction, were based on the assumption that the two former 'blocs' would move closer together as relatively balanced groups and with the USA and the Soviet Union continuing to play leading roles. Disintegration in the east, first of the Warsaw Pact and the Council for Mutual Economic Assistance (CMEA, or Comecon) and then in the final months of 1991 of the Soviet Union itself, exposed more clearly than ever the underlying imbalance between Western and Eastern Europe, and the centrality of Western Europe's institutional structure to the re-establishment of any stable order across this wider Europe. One after another, every government west of the Soviet border—and after them, in 1991–2, the western republics of the former Soviet Union—declared their determination to secure eventual membership of the European Community and of NATO, as the only effective structures in assisting economic transformation and guaranteeing security.

The countries of Western Europe have thus been confronted with a succession of unwelcome, almost unanswerable questions. How far does 'our' Europe—defined either as a security community with a sense of common commitment and shared values, or as an economic community with a sense of common interests and shared benefits—extend? Does the easy confusion of 'Europe' with the European Community which grew up in Western Europe in the 1960s and 1970s, reinforced in the 1980s by further enlargement and the increasingly close association with the EC of the EFTA states, imply that the European Community should progressively extend its boundaries to incorporate all European countries—following the logic of Article 237 of the Treaty of Rome, which states that 'Any European State may apply to become a member of the

---

[29] At the beginning of 1989 the Commission of the EC had less than a dozen officials dealing with relations with the state-trading countries. By 1991 there were some hundreds, most in the 'Phare' Programme (an acronym retained from its first steps, directed to Poland and Hungary).

Community'? Or should the governments of Western Europe draw new boundaries between the rich West and the poor East to replace the old, taking in perhaps the Catholic countries of the former Habsburg empire but leaving the successors to the former Ottoman and Russian empires outside? What economic concessions and financial transfers should the strong economies of Western Europe now offer the weak economies of Eastern Europe, as an investment in future European stability; and which countries should be given priority in making such offers? What are Western Europe's security responsibilities for Eastern Europe? Are West European interests in this transformed world distinct from those of the USA, or should West European governments continue to see themselves as members of a 'Western' community under American leadership?

Western Europe's convenient dependence on the USA for politico-military leadership for the previous forty years had allowed its governments, individually and collectively, to avoid such awkward strategic issues. None of its governments proved capable during the rapid transition of 1989–93 of redefining its regional objectives, even of redefining the region as such. The French, while continuing to preserve a Gaullist challenge to American leadership, resisted both economic concessions and hopes of early enlargement, while clinging more closely to their transformed German partner. The Germans provided the largest public and private financial transfers to the East-Central European countries and to the Soviet Union/CIS, even while their economy was distorted by the costs of attempting a rapid economic transition in the new *Länder* of former East Germany. The EC Commission lacked the authority to redefine overall strategy; the WEU, still in the earliest stages of institutional strengthening, had no capacity to make a contribution. NATO, under American leadership, negotiated a 'New Strategic Concept' in the course of 1991, in response to the disappearance of its original *raison d'être*, only to agree and publish the document, at the Rome Summit of November 1991, a few weeks before the disintegration of the Soviet Union created a different and more complex set of security issues. America's dual external and budgetary deficits left its policy-makers no spare capacity for generous gestures to ease the instabilities of transition from socialism and Soviet control to a new European order. The USA looked determinedly to its West European allies to shoulder the costs of reconstruction in Eastern Europe, as it had shouldered the costs of reconstruction in Western Europe forty-five years before; while West European governments looked to their own faltering growth rates and public finances, and to their electorates' resistance to higher taxation, and concluded that they lacked the domestic basis needed for either grand gestures or grand strategy.

What emerged across this wider Europe in 1990–2 was a proliferation of overlapping institutions, without clearly defined roles. The ambiguous position of semi-European Russia, still militarily powerful but economically desperate, was compounded by the even more ambiguous position of the other former Soviet republics. Disintegration in Yugoslavia, the USSR, and Czechoslovakia had increased the CSCE to over fifty member states by early 1993, including several new central Asian members of this 'European' conference. German and American willingness to respond to East-Central European pressures for closer association with NATO led to the creation in 1991 of the NACC, which was then extended in rapid succession to the Soviet Union and to its successor states, to overlap substantially with the CSCE.[30] Creation of a consultative parliamentary assembly for the CSCE overlapped in membership and agenda with the long-established Assembly of the Council of Europe—an organization which was also expanding as former socialist states qualified through democratic elections for membership.

The European Community itself struggled to hold to an increasingly outmoded agenda through its twin intergovernmental conferences of 1991, agreeing in the December 1991 Maastricht Treaty to enlarge WEU and to 'develop it as the defence component of European Union and as a means to strengthen the European pillar of the Atlantic Alliance'.[31] Based on a German initiative, WEU in turn developed during 1992 its own security dialogue with the states west of the former Soviet border. The European Community, its member states struggling during 1992 to ratify the complex compromise among ill-defined national objectives which the Maastricht Treaty represented, signed 'Europe Agreements' first with the three 'Visegrad' countries of Poland, Hungary, and

---

[30] This was followed in 1993–4 by the Partnership for Peace initiative.

[31] *Declaration on Western European Union*, para. 3, annexe to *Treaty on European Union* (Brussels: European Communities, 1992). See also Anand Menon, Anthony Forster, and William Wallace, 'A Common European Defence?', *Survival*, 34/3 (Autumn 1992).

Czechoslovakia, and then with the two Balkan states of Bulgaria and Romania: combining grudging concessions on immediate access to West European markets with the distant promise of Community membership. Holding at bay applications for membership from Turkey, Cyprus, and Malta, the Community was preparing to open negotiations for early full membership—by 1995 or 1996—with Austria, Finland, and Sweden. And as the major organizations expanded in tasks and membership, so subregional groupings blossomed: the Visegrad three (later four), a caucus to improve its members' bargaining capacity with the EC as well as an interim mechanism for improving economic co-operation among them; the *Pentagonale*, an Italian initiative to build links with the states of the former Austro-Hungarian empire, which had grown in scope and numbers by early 1993 to include also Poland, Slovakia, Slovenia, and Croatia; informal groups for Baltic and Black Sea co-operation; and within the EC itself the Schengen Group of eight (originally five) countries attempting to move more rapidly to common policies on policing and border controls and the Franco-German 'Eurocorps' with its declared aspirations to form the nucleus for a future European army.

Such a confusion of organizations and objectives hardly suggests that the European region of the early 1990s offers an example for other international regions to follow. Western Europe's response to the re-emergence of the Eastern European periphery from behind the Iron Curtain has been marked by reluctance to face up to the broader issues at stake, even under the pressure of events and American demands. The external security challenge posed by the Iraqi invasion of Kuwait in 1990–1 saw America's European allies following a clear US lead, with WEU acting only as a convenient cover for naval co-operation in the Gulf. The fighting which broke out in Yugoslavia in the summer of 1991 (on what had been the borderline between Western and Eastern Europe) found West European governments entirely unprepared, in spite of intelligence warnings and planning papers prepared within their administrations. Neither the needs of East European economies nor intense pressures from the USA were sufficient to push the European Community into further opening of its agricultural markets, or towards a speedy completion of the long-delayed Uruguay Round of GATT.

In parallel with these external shocks, the deepening of integration within Western Europe had reached a point where the process had begun to challenge the familiar symbols of national statehood and identity, provoking a backlash among national publics against the Maastricht Treaty, even within the core states of France and Germany. The Commission and most member governments had seen the Intergovernmental Conferences of 1991 as further stages in the evolution of a process which had begun with the Treaties of Paris and Rome and moved forward through the 1969 Hague Summit, the decisions of successive European Councils, and the 1986 Single European Act. But formal integration is not a simple linear process, following a functional logic. Movement from common policies on food regulation and product safety to common policing and common currency takes governments from the margins of national autonomy to its core.[32]

The Maastricht agenda touched upon citizenship, border control, domestic order, foreign policy, defence, currency, domestic economic management, and taxation: issues at the heart of the idea of national sovereignty and the nation state. The transformation of Eastern Europe increased their sensitivity—bringing waves of asylum-seekers, raising expectations of financial transfers (and internal differences over burden sharing), externalizing the economic strains of German unification, calling on West European governments to share in the military response to the Yugoslav conflict. The logic of deeper and deeper integration, it was becoming clear, pushed states from intergovernmental co-operation towards federation. But the functional approach of West European institutions, their policy-making processes characterized by hierarchies of committees staffed by national and Commission officials focusing on the technical details rather than the broader political issues, had not prepared national publics for such a fundamental shift in the political landscape.[33]

[32] Anthony D. Smith, 'National Identity and the Idea of European Unity', *International Affairs*, 68/1 (Jan. 1992), 55–76. On the British dimension of these challenges to national sovereignty and identity, see William Wallace, 'Foreign Policy and National Identity in the United Kingdom', *International Affairs*, 67/1 (Jan. 1991), 65–80, and 'British Foreign Policy after the Cold War', *International Affairs*, 68/3 (July 1992), 423–42.

[33] Wolfgang Wessels, 'Administrative Interaction', in Wallace (ed.), *The Dynamics of European Integration*; Wessels, 'The EC Council: The Community's Decision-making Center', and Shirley Williams, 'Sovereignty and Accountability in the European Community', in Robert O. Keohane and Stanley Hoffmann (eds.), *The New European Community: Decisionmaking and Institutional Change* (Boulder, Colo.: Westview, 1991).

5. CONCLUSION: IS EUROPE STILL A MODEL?

Western Europe before 1990 offered an attractive model of formal economic integration, among a geographically concentrated group of countries contained within a stable and well-defined security framework. Europe after 1990 offers a much more sobering example for other regions to learn from. The established security community of Western Europe has not yet proved firm enough to extend that sense of mutual security beyond its borders, even to so familiar and close a country as Yugoslavia.[34] The absence of clear boundaries for the region, with peripheral claimants for participation and privilege stretching an increasing distance east and south-east, has thrown its established institutional structure into confusion and its future institutional cohesion into doubt. The dynamic economic, technological, and social forces which have pulled Western Europe together have also pulled Eastern Europe (and the countries around the Mediterranean) towards this prosperous and privileged core: a spreading periphery of would-be migrants, their countries clamouring for market access, investment, and financial transfers, their instability and insecurity threatening to spill over into wider disorder. The position of Germany further complicates the construction of a European order no longer dependent on American protection and leadership: as again Europe's central economy and most powerful conventional power, but acceptable neither to its own leaders and electorate as a regional leader nor to its less wealthy neighbours.

Political integration in Western Europe succeeded in large part because governments were able to separate the detailed bargaining over economic costs and benefits from the broader issues of high politics, security, and defence within which it was embedded. The threats which a partly integrated West European political system faces in the early 1990s are not sufficiently acute as to drive the member governments to unite further, but are sufficiently complex as to leave them baffled. None has been able to rouse its domestic publics, who have benefited so much from the prosperity which

---

[34] From the 1960s on, Yugoslavia was, after Spain, Italy, and Greece, the fourth most popular Mediterranean holiday destination for northern Europeans: in particular for British and German tourists. Its boundaries touch Italy and Austria; by train and motorway Slovenia and Croatia are both a short distance from southern Germany. There is a substantial Yugoslav population in Germany (mainly from Slovenia and Croatia), and smaller immigrant groups in France and Italy.

Atlantic security and West European integration have brought them, to support radical changes in existing policy, though there are many within all governments and regional organizations who appreciate that radical change may be unavoidable. Most would (at least tacitly) prefer the Americans to continue to provide leadership and see this as preferable either to the inherent tensions contained within the Franco-German relationship, or to an attempt to create a larger 'concert' of core countries, or to the eventual emergence, *faute de mieux*, of German leadership. Most, however, fear that American leadership will be more uncertain and intermittent, and American demands for others to carry the burden more insistent. It is easier to build and maintain regional order within a stable global order; and easier, perhaps, to build a regional order under the impetus of external pressures and external leadership than through agreement among the major regional powers, let alone through following the guidance of a (potentially hegemonic) power within the region itself.

8

Pacific Asia: The Development of Regional Dialogue

Rosemary Foot

THE end of the bipolar structure that has constrained international behaviour since 1945 has led, in concrete terms, to the conclusion of the ideological and strategic competition between the USA and former Soviet Union; the devaluation of military power and re-evaluation of economic strength; and the gradual integration of former 'enemy states' into a capitalist world economy. A further outcome has been increased attention to relations at the regional level as contacts between those governments and peoples previously distanced by Cold War attitudes and policies have grown in significance and number. In Pacific Asia,[1] the desire to continue the kind of stability that has helped generate impressive economic growth levels, together with the diminution of ideological tensions, has allowed economies such as the Chinese and Vietnamese to be increasingly integrated into region-wide economic networks. Moreover, the coming into being of the Single European Act in 1992, the establishment of a free-trade area in North America, the uncertainties over the final outcome to the Uruguay Round, and continuing economic tensions between the USA and Japan have also provided the spur to the development of a regional dialogue.

In the security realm, a focus on the region has emerged from an appreciation that the USA will continue to reduce its presence in the area, thus providing the opportunity for regional states—such as China and Japan—to emerge as leaders. This reduction in the American presence is coupled with the realization that certain outstanding problems, such as those concerning North and South Korea, and competing claims over the ownership of islands in the

---

[1] Pacific Asia is defined as those countries which border the western rim of the Pacific. The policies of the USA and the former Soviet Union are also discussed where relevant to the main themes of the chapter.

South and East China Seas, could further promote armaments spending or result in conflict with unsettling consequences. All such developments serve to turn attention to questions of regional security.

Nevertheless, the term 'regional dialogue' has been chosen in this chapter to signal that the security organization that is emerging amongst the states of Pacific Asia—the ASEAN Regional Forum— is based on consultation rather than on a formalistic process, as are those organizations that concentrate on economic relations, such as APEC. This chapter will first seek to explain why, to use Robert Scalapino's apt phrase and as we examine the post-1945 era, we have had little more than 'soft regionalism' in Pacific Asia, focusing on those political, strategic, and economic factors that have constrained the development of regional ties.[2] Attention will then be paid to recent regional and subregional initiatives to demonstrate the ways in which these constraints continue to operate as well as, more positively, to show the extent to which they are being overcome.

1. THE CONSTRAINTS ON REGIONAL CO-OPERATION

The literature on regionalism or regional integration in definitional terms stresses various forms of interdependence or interconnectedness. Affinities of language, religion, and culture, among others, together with geographical proximity are seen as objectively necessary conditions. Subjective elements involving consciousness of an area identity are also seen as vital since they lead actors to join together to deal collectively with external forces. This link between the internal and external has led some analysts to stress the identification of a common external threat, since this may act as a catalyst in the formation of regional frameworks.

(a) Threat perceptions in Pacific Asia

The consensus in the writings on Pacific Asia is that few if any of these attributes are present within the area.[3] To take first the matter

[2] Robert A. Scalapino, S. Sato, J. Wanadi, and S.-J. Han (eds.), *Asian Security Issues: Regional and Global* (Berkeley: Institute of East Asian Studies, University of California, 1988).

[3] One of the most forceful statements of this kind is made in Gerald Segal, *Rethinking the Pacific* (Oxford: OUP, 1990); for a more recent analysis, see also

of the external threat: there has not been a common threat perception in the region since 1945, and serious threats have been both internal to states as well as external. In structural terms, bipolarity has served well as a description of the regional division in Europe as exemplified by NATO and the Warsaw Pact. But despite the presence in East Asia of states divided along similar ideological lines—the two Vietnams, China, and Taiwan, and South and North Korea—the area has never been as comprehensively bipolar as Europe. The security order that was created in the Cold War era was built on an incomplete set of bilateral alliances, with the USA and, less stably, the Soviet Union at their respective hubs. But there was little in the way of horizontal linkage among alliance partners.

Moreover, the Soviet presence in the region was not strongly felt until the late 1960s and early 1970s, and then could be attributed as much to the deterioration in Sino-Soviet relations as to the Soviet determination to compete globally with the USA. The communist states and parties have shown little in the way of fraternal or bloc loyalty to one another; instead, violence and political tension have often affected their relationships. Chinese and Soviet pressure on the Vietminh to negotiate a ceasefire in 1954, Beijing's refusal to engage in 'united action' with Moscow in 1965 in order better to support Ho Chi Minh in his war against US forces (a decision that lost the Chinese Communist Party the sympathy of its Japanese counterpart), and the Sino-Soviet and Sino-Vietnamese wars, with their traditional and contemporary roots, demonstrate the inability of communists to work together in Asia. China's strategic shift from alliance with the Soviets in the 1950s, to a tacit anti-Soviet alignment with the USA in the 1970s, at a time when neither North Korea nor North Vietnam saw much evidence to support Beijing's view that Moscow was the more dangerous of the two superpowers, additionally confirms the limitations of the bipolar construct in East Asia.

Although the war between North and South Korea came to symbolize the Soviet–American Cold War confrontation, the conflict on the peninsula had a momentum of its own well before the North Koreans moved in strength across the 38th parallel, with some 100,000 Koreans losing their lives between 1945 and early

Kevin Clements (ed.), *Peace and Security in the Asia Pacific Region* (Tokyo: United Nations UP, 1993).

1950.[4] That bilateral momentum has remained in place. Even as it became apparent from the late 1950s that neither Beijing, Moscow, nor Washington would give support to their respective allies should they argue for a renewal of fighting, Seoul and Pyongyang continued to keep their forces in a high state of readiness. Some forty years after the outbreak of the Korean conflict, about 60 per cent of the North Korean land army remained close to the demilitarized zone and was reported to be in a position to fight high-intensity warfare for four months without resupply.[5] The Rangoon bombings in 1983, and the discovery of another tunnel beneath the DMZ in March 1990—allegedly wide enough to move a division of troops per hour[6]—give an intensity to that bilateral relationship not experienced, for example, by the two Germanies. In addition, the presence of a nuclear weapons dimension adds further levels of tension and fear to the relations between Pyongyang and Seoul,[7] and complicates any attempt at normalization of ties.

If the legacy of the war on the Korean peninsula continues to impose constraints in the current era, historical experiences have also impinged on relations elsewhere in the region. There is a historical dynamic to the Sino-Japanese relationship that renders more complex still the identification of the external threat in Pacific Asia. We frequently write of the impact of dealing with Hitler and the failure to confront Germany in the 1930s as having been the defining experiences for many Western politicians and as instrumental in shaping their policies and perceptions in the post-1945 period. The first forty years of the lives of China's gerontocracy—

[4] Bruce Cumings, *The Origins of the Korean War*, i and ii (Princeton: Princeton UP, 1981, 1990), and John Merrill, *Korea: The Peninsular Origins of the War* (Newark, Del.: University of Delaware Press, 1989).

[5] *Strategic Survey* (London: IISS, 1989–90), 149.

[6] *Far Eastern Economic Review (FEER)*, 15 Mar. 1990.

[7] Andrew Mack has outlined some of the reasons why North Korean could well have decided to acquire nuclear weapons. See his 'North Korea and the Bomb', *Foreign Policy*, 83 (summer 1991). Differences with the International Atomic Energy Authority (IAEA) over inspection led Pyongyang to announce in 1993 its intended withdrawal from the Non-Proliferation Treaty, a decision that it did not bring into effect. In Oct. 1994, the USA and North Korea signed a 'Framework Agreement' under which the United States would organize an international consortium to supply North Korea with light-water reactors. In exchange, Pyongyang agreed to halt construction of its graphite-type reactors, freeze other aspects of its nuclear programme, and allow IAEA inspection. For further details of this tortuous process, see *FEER*, 11 Mar. 1993, 24 June 1993, 12 May 1994, and 27 Oct. 1994.

including Deng Xiaoping—coincided with the peak of Japanese callousness and cruelty towards the Chinese, and it seems likely that this experience has affected their interpretations of Japanese actions in the more recent period. Although there is a grudging regard for Japan's technological prowess and a realization that Tokyo facilitates Beijing's access to advanced technology, this same ability applied to the military sphere makes Japan a formidable strategic competitor and potential enemy.[8] And while Japan has regarded China as the source of its cultural tradition and has made reference to its special relationship with and special understanding of China, it has also periodically derided Beijing for its episodes of internal instability and what it perceives as its backwardness. William Tow has described well these countervailing tendencies in the relationship, for while there remain many clear advantages to the sustenance of good political and economic ties, in the strategic realm China's nuclear capabilities are pitted against Japan's high technological base; its ambitions for a blue water navy against 'Tokyo's formidable maritime heritage and infrastructure'; and the 'more accurate and lethal Chinese nuclear ballistic missile submarines and land-based intermediate nuclear forces' compete with 'Japanese anti-missile and aerospace technology'.[9]

For Korea, too, and also for historical reasons, there is distrust of Japan, fuelled by the continuance of unfinished business with that country. Tokyo's development of its contacts with North Korea and the PRC in the 1950s, its negotiations with the Soviet Union in 1956 to end the state of war between the two countries, the treatment of Koreans in Japan, and the inability or unwillingness to account for or compensate those Koreans who were used as forced labour, combat forces, or as sex slaves during the Pacific War has served to alienate the two peoples. The misjudged Japanese attempt at normalizing its relations with North Korea, instead of being interpreted in the South as a contribution to Seoul's 'Nordpolitik' policy was depicted more often as Tokyo's way of keeping the peninsula divided, and economically weak, thus delaying its future economic challenge to Japan. Not surprisingly, therefore, there

    [8] For a recent discussion of the views of some Chinese researchers working on Japan, see Bonnie S. Glaser, 'China's Security Perceptions: Interests and Ambitions', *Asian Survey*, 33/3 (Mar. 1993), 257–9.
    [9] William Tow, 'Post-Cold War Security in East Asia', *Pacific Review*, 4/2 (1991), 101; and his 'Northeast Asia and International Security; Transforming Competition into Collaboration', *Australian Journal of International Affairs*, 46/1 (1992).

have never been any direct security ties between South Korea and Japan even though both have treaty links with Washington and American forces stationed on their territories. It will not be easy for them both to work together within a security structure in the future, despite greater willingness on Japan's part to express 'sincere remorse' and 'honest apologies' for the sufferings caused in the past.[10]

The role of Japan in Pacific Asia remains, then, problematical for the states of the area, adding complexity to the discussion of Japan as a future initiator of policy change or as a dominant actor in regional organization. Whereas from the 1950s West Germany was included in multilateral arrangements designed to rebuild a secure Western Europe, Japan, on the other hand, has been locked into a bilateral relationship with the USA, relatively isolated politically from other governments, and with little international or regional political status. One of the most gratifying developments in Western Europe has been the establishment of a security community among former enemy states (notably between France and West Germany)—that is, 'a group of states that do not expect, or prepare for, the use of military force in their relations with each other'.[11] In North-East Asia, such expectations do not seem to be in place; moreover, Beijing and Seoul, with the recent 'textbook' controversy in mind, have compared Japan unfavourably with Germany. Compared with Germany, the Chinese have argued, which had 'frankly admitted its responsibility' for the Second World War, Tokyo had 'often gone back on its word or prevaricated on some important issues, such as the responsibility for the Pacific War'.[12] This issue of war guilt has impinged more directly and enduringly on Japan's relations with Korea and China than it has on West Germany's relations with its neighbours. Furthermore, in the period since 1945, West German membership of NATO and the European Community has provided it with a bridge to help it move beyond its wartime history. Japan has never had such an institutional bridge;

[10] These phrases were used by Prime Minister Kaifu in 1990—definitely an advance over the Emperor's statement in 1984 in which he spoke of an 'unfortunate period in Japan–Korean relations'. *Asian Security, 1990–1* (London: Research Institute for Peace and Security, 1990), 137.

[11] Barry Buzan, 'New Patterns of Global Security in the Twenty-First Century', *International Affairs*, 67/3 (1991), 436.

[12] *BBC Monitoring Reports, Summary of World Broadcasts, (SWB)*, Far East, 900, 20 Oct. 1990.

it has never been part of a multilateral regional framework that would have helped soften its presence among former enemy states.[13] Thus, it still has no easy route from a dominant economic position to one that allows for a greater level of political participation.

South-East Asian peoples also suffered at Japanese hands, but threat perceptions in this area have reflected concerns about China, about Vietnam, and about domestic vulnerabilities too. The main security dilemma of the most significant subregional organization in South-East Asia, ASEAN, has not been primarily connected with Japan, but has related to member states' 'common vulnerability to internal threats aggravated by external predators taking advantage of a conflict-ridden regional environment'. Nevertheless, the rich diversity characteristic of the ASEAN states' experience has meant that, although they have all feared internal subversion and insurgency, there has been no agreement as to the prime source of the external threat.[14] A consequence of these factors has been the decision to retain the Five Power Defence Arrangement involving Britain, Australia, New Zealand, Malaysia, and Singapore; to establish bilateral defence treaties with the USA; and, on the part of some, to pledge commitment to non-alignment (although with a heavy pro-US slant to it). These factors further complicate a neat strategic depiction of this region as a whole.

(b) The diversity of Pacific Asia

The religious, political, demographic, and economic diversity of the region reinforces the complexity noted in the security realm. Not even the common Confucian tradition in North-East Asia can provide much in the way of bonding because that tradition has given way to cultural variation. The Chinese attachment to a single, supreme ruler contrasts with the Japanese penchant for the uncharismatic party-broker and emphasis on technically skilled bureaucrats, and again with the Korean toleration of bold and

---

[13] P. Polomka, 'U.S.–Japan: Beyond the Cold War', *Asian Perspective*, 14/1 (Spring–Summer 1990), 181.

[14] Michael Leifer, *ASEAN and the Security of South-East Asia* (London: Routledge, 1989) esp. 1–2. See also Amitav Acharya, 'A New Regional Order in South-East Asia: ASEAN in the Post-Cold War Era', *Adelphi Paper*, 279 (Aug. 1993).

assertive leadership.[15] South-East Asian countries are even more heterogeneous, understandably because Chinese, European, Indian, and Middle Eastern cultural influences have intersected here and have produced Buddhist, Catholic, and Islamic societies. Unlike in Western Europe, there are also a range of political systems in Pacific Asia, with democratic pluralism in its most developed form only having taken hold in Japan.

Economic divergence among the states of the area further complicates the search for a common agenda, and constrains moves towards advanced types of regional economic co-operation. The distance between Japan and its neighbours is not solely connected with its past imperialist policies, but is also determined by its place in the global economy—its membership in the Group of Seven, its trade, aid, and investment policies. The GNP of the NIEs and ASEAN in combination has recently stood at only one-third that of Japan. Within ASEAN itself, there are enormous differences in per capita income, with the average being at the end of the 1980s about $500 in Indonesia and $20,000 in Brunei.[16] If the vast range of wealth in the region has undercut attempts at integration, so too have the dominant patterns of post-war trade. For Japan and the NIEs, for example, that pattern has involved close links with the American and West European markets. And although there has been some diversification of trade links within and beyond the region in more recent times, for the 1980s, it was Japan's trade with the USA that showed the greatest increase, and for the NIEs the most striking feature of the 1980s was the growth of exports to America.[17]

[15] For further discussion of this point, see Lucian W. Pye, *Asian Power and Politics: The Cultural Dimensions of Authority* (Cambridge, Mass.: BelKnap Press, 1985).

[16] Kate Grosser and Brian Bridges, 'Economic Interdependence in East Asia: the Global Context', *Pacific Review*, 3/1 (1990), 2.

[17] Masahide Shibusawa, Zakaria Haji Ahmad, and Brian Bridges, *Pacific Asia in the 1990s* (London: 1992), 14–15. Note that from 1991 Japan's trade with Asia was larger than that with the USA, a development which needs careful interpretation, however. Many Japanese companies have shifted production facilities to Asia which has generated exports of plant and equipment. Output from those companies often ends up in the US market (see *FEER*, 9 June 1994). Intra-ASEAN trade has been insignificant: in 1988 for example it only represented 16.3 per cent of total trade: Marcus Noland, *Pacific Basin Developing Countries: Prospects for the Future* (Washington DC: Institute for International Economics, 1990), 140. See also Hans Christoph Rieger (ed.), *ASEAN Economic Cooperation: A Handbook* (Singapore: Institute for Southeast Asian Studies, 1991); and Ross Garnaut and Peter Drysdale

(c) Political fragility and leadership transition

A number of the political systems in this area have been or are politically fragile. Some leaderships see the political future as an unknown and relatively frightening prospect, others fear for their own political positions in the coming years.[18] Chinese leaders, given the demise of communism globally, the potential for a US-dominated unipolar world, and evidence of domestic unrest, have often reflected these fears.[19] Many analysts see political instability, or at least uncertainty as inevitable after Deng Xiaoping's death, for China has never properly tackled the problem of guaranteeing a smooth political transition, and there are few signs that it is doing so now. For other authors, problems within the society are viewed as a slow burning fuse. Michel Oksenberg has argued that there are 'several yawning gaps [that] now divide the Chinese polity', many with long historical roots, others having been exacerbated by China's opening to the West and its modernization policies.[20]

China has long had its divisions between the urban and rural, between the older and younger generations, between what Michael Hunt has labelled the 'populists' versus the 'cosmopolitans', but reform policies have sharpened these divisions.[21] Early populism sprang from a belief that China's salvation lay within its own borders and from a concern that foreigners left in their wake a demoralized people, economic disruption, and lawlessness. In the 1890s, Liang Qichao—a leading Chinese intellectual—complained that when Westerners wanted to conquer a country such as China: 'day after day they will criticize the corruption of that country's government, the disorder of its society, and the tyranny of its officials.'[22] Although Li Peng's allegation in September 1991 that the West desired to subjugate the Chinese people under a capitalist

---

(eds.), *Asia Pacific Regionalism: Readings in International Economic Relations* (Pymble, NSW, Aust.: Harper Educational Publishers, 1994).

[18] A point made in Polomka, 'U.S.–Japan: Beyond the Cold War', 179.

[19] For further discussion of these and additional points, see Kenneth Lieberthal, 'The Collapse of the Communist World and Mainland China's Foreign Affairs', *Issues and Studies* (Sept. 1992).

[20] Michel Oksenberg, 'The China Problem', *Foreign Affairs*, 70/3 (Summer 1991), 7. See also Kenneth Lieberthal, 'China's Political System in the 1990s', *Journal of Northeast Asian Studies*, 10/1 (Spring 1991).

[21] Michael H. Hunt, 'Chinese Foreign Relations in Historical Perspective', in H. Harding (ed.), *China's Foreign Relations in the 1980s* (Yale: Yale UP, 1984).

[22] Hunt, 'Chinese Foreign Relations', 23 and 28.

system through a strategy of 'peaceful evolution' seems to have been mostly dropped from Chinese propaganda after November 1992, such sentiments suggest that traditional suspicions of Western motives still have some currency among the leadership in Beijing.[23]

China, because of its relative homogeneity, is unlikely to suffer the deep ethnic tensions that we have witnessed in the former Soviet Union and in Russia. However, the leadership in Beijing since 1949 and to the current day has often suspected the loyalty of its national minorities. Many of China's minority peoples—such as the Kazakhs, the Kirghiz, and the Tadzhiks—have strong cross-border links, close ties of language and historical association across the northern frontier, and nationalist unrest since the 1950s is well documented in Chinese statements.[24] In August 1991, at the time of the failed coup against Gorbachev, China's Vice-President, Wang Zhen, chose to visit Xinjiang to urge the army 'unswervingly' to follow socialism and cling loyally to Marxism-Leninism-Mao Zedong thought.[25] In March 1992, in a special report by Xinjiang television, the head of the regional government, Tomur Dawamat, claimed that 'hostile forces both at home and abroad have stepped up their infiltration, subversion and sabotage'.[26] The fear is that Muslim separatists will be inspired to set up an independent state of East Turkestan, a development which in part explains China's decision to move rapidly to establish diplomatic relations with the newly independent Central Asian states. Similar fears exist with respect to Inner Mongolia where nationalism has been rising since the Mongolian Republic's elections in 1990, and where underground networks pressing for autonomy or independence have been active.[27] One possible implication of these developments is that internal security threats involving the control of China's periphery could absorb a large part of Beijing's energies in the next decade. Indeed, for some analysts problems of internal control and national unity are even more serious than that given the decentral-

[23] New York Times, 19 Sept. 1991, and Glaser, 'China's Security Perceptions', 260.
[24] Some examples are included in Allen S. Whiting and Gen. Sheng Shih-tsai, Sinkiang: Pawn or Pivot? (Michigan: Michigan State UP, 1958), 144; SWB, Far East, 5022, 26 Sept. 1975.
[25] FEER, 5 Sept. 1991.
[26] Guardian, 9 Mar. 1992.
[27] Glaser, 'China's Security Perceptions', 262–3.

ization of power that has taken place in the era of economic reform.[28]

The problems associated with leadership transition and the definition of a leadership role affect not only China but also North Korea and Vietnam. Although Kim Jong Il has apparently assumed power in Pyongyang after the lengthy rule of his father, Kim Il Sung, the long-term questions surrounding the succession remain open. A political power struggle in North Korea would mean fewer resources would be available to deal with regional questions and relations with Seoul. Political change in Japan and internal debates about its future global and regional leadership roles have also contributed to political uncertainty. Japan's transition, together with the uncertain advancement of political pluralism elsewhere in the region raises the possibility that several governments may be entering a period of domestic introspection rather than one where they can think creatively about regional concerns.

(d) Identifying with Pacific Asia

There is also little history among the major states with interests in the area and among those that are a geographical part of it of conceptualizing in regional terms. Although there has been no direct or acknowledged military confrontation between the USA and the Soviet Union in East Asia post-1945, their relations with Pacific Asia have predominantly been placed within the context of their global strategic confrontation. In the former Soviet Union, Gorbachev in 1986 lamented the fact that his country's approach to the region had been little more than the sum of bilateral ties with various countries. Similarly, US security arrangements in Pacific Asia have overwhelmingly been bilateral and not multilateral.

Japan, too, has not played an explicit regional role. For some of the reasons suggested earlier, and especially in the 1950s and 1960s, Tokyo has remained aloof from its neighbours, under the strategic umbrella of its US patron, with a stated commitment to separating economics from politics, and a determination to concen-

---

[28] Michael Yahuda, 'China's Future: Peaceful Evolution?', Paper presented at the British International Studies Association Conference, University College, Swansea, Dec. 1992; Gerald Segal, 'China Changes Shape: Regionalism and Foreign Policy', *Adelphi Paper*, 287 (Mar. 1994).

trate on its own economic development.[29] China similarly has had little in the way of a discernible regional policy and, moreover, not even a collective term for the countries of North-East Asia until the late 1980s.[30] As one analyst has noted, the PRC has had multiple identities since 1949—including as a member of the socialist bloc, the Third World, or quasi-ally of the USA—but has given no explicit definition of its place in Asia. Beijing has tended to approach relations with its neighbours on a bilateral basis, and on the basis of a set of global precepts that have involved the identification of the major threat and the formation of a united front to counter that threat (the USA in the 1950s and 1960s and the Soviet Union in the 1970s.)[31]

If we dwell somewhat longer on certain specific issues connected with security relations within the area, this may better demonstrate the impact that this inattention to regional policy has had. With respect to arms control, for example, agreements and decisions have been the result of unilateral, or at most bilateral arrangements.[32] In the Gorbachev era, Moscow agreed to cut some 120,000 troops along the Mongolian and Sino-Soviet border, a border that once had more Soviet forces stationed there than in the entire Eastern Europe. Since 1985, and not unrelated to the gradual normalization of ties with the former Soviet Union, the Chinese have demobilized about one-quarter of their total military forces, a decision that also contributed to the removal of about 100,000 troops from the northern border. But these moves were not the result of direct negotiation between Beijing and Moscow. It was only after the official normalization of relations in May 1989 that the two governments began a formal discussion of arms control and of confidence-building measures, discussions which culminated in April 1990 in the first official arms reduction agreement in Pacific Asia.[33]

[29] Tsuneo Akaha, 'Japan's Comprehensive Security Policy: A New East Asian Environment', *Asian Survey*, 31/4 (Apr. 1991), 325.

[30] Laura Newby, 'China and Northeast Asia: Global Politics on a Regional Stage?', Paper presented at Asian Studies Centre seminar series, St Antony's College, Oxford, Mar. 1992.

[31] Samuel S. Kim, 'China as a Regional Power', *Current History*, 91/566 (Sept. 1992); Steven I. Levine, 'China in Asia: The PRC as a Regional Power', H. Harding (ed.), *China's Foreign Relations*, 107.

[32] The Asian approach to arms control is considered in Gerald Segal (ed.), *Arms Control in Asia* (London: Macmillan, 1987).

[33] Gerald Segal, 'A New Order in Northeast Asia', *Arms Control Today*, 21/7 (Sept. 1991).

The USA, too, has steadily cut its forces in East Asia and reduced its nuclear arsenal—decisions that were of great consequence for relations between North and South Korea and for Washington's naval strategy. Yet neither policy emerged as a result of multilateral negotiations, but came out of domestic developments, developments in the former USSR, and shifts in America's bilateral relations with its allies in Asia.[34]

In the recent past, Gorbachev, together with the Australian Foreign Minister, Gareth Evans, and the Canadian Secretary of State for External Affairs, Joe Clark, were among those calling for the lifting of these efforts from the bilateral, unilateral, and informal levels to the more comprehensive and multilateral. The desire has been for a common security regime to be established in Asia to mirror that which emerged in Europe.[35] One argument has been that multilateralism contributes more powerfully to the construction of transparency, and to a security community, and that formal, legally binding agreements are generally more difficult to reverse.

These arguments in favour of formality and multilateralism may help to explain why so many of the unilateral initiatives concerning force reduction have invited suspicion and not approval. Soviet disarmament proposals were often depicted as converting a necessity into a virtue. When the CFE treaty was initialled, the attitude in Asia was not predominantly one of elation or a willingness to take this signing as further evidence that we were indeed in a new era of major power relations; the main fear was that European-based weaponry would be transferred east of the Urals. Quantitative restrictions in Chinese armed forces have similarly been greeted with suspicion, interpreted as representing a qualitative improvement

[34] William J. Crowe Jr. and Alan D. Rosenberg, 'Rethinking Security in the Pacific', *Foreign Affairs*, 70/2 (Spring 1991); US Department of Defense, *A Strategic Framework for the Asian Pacific Rim: Report to Congress, 1992* (Washington, DC, 1992). The Asian reaction to the nuclear initiative is discussed in *FEER*, 10 Oct. 1991. See also William T. Tow, 'Changing US Force Levels and Regional Security', in Colin McIness and Mark G. Rolls (eds.), *Post Cold War Security Issues in the Asia-Pacific Region* (Ilford, Essex: Frank Cass, 1994).

[35] Geoffrey Wiseman, 'Common Security in the Asia-Pacific Region', *Pacific Review*, 5/1 (1992), 43–4. Pessimism concerning the possibility of East Asian states building a multilateral organization of any kind (among states which 'have no modern experience of how to relate to each other on terms largely defined by the local dynamics of regional relations') is expressed in Barry Buzan and Gerald Segal, 'Rethinking Asian Security', *Survival*, 36/2 (summer 1994). A critique of the Buzan and Segal perspective has been provided by Kishore Mahbubani, 'The Pacific Impulse', *Survival*, 37/1 (Spring 1995).

and further evidence that China has moved beyond its 'people's war' doctrine and into a period where it more readily contemplates projecting conventional power beyond its land borders.[36]

2. THE DEVELOPMENT OF REGIONAL DIALOGUE

The portrait that has been painted of Pacific Asia in the post-1945 era has been made deliberately bleak and has emphasized the cleavages rather than the linkages within the region. The kinds of constraints outlined above clearly have served to prevent the development of formalized regional co-operation, but the analysis would be seriously incomplete if it neglected other countervailing processes that are at work. These processes have resulted from economic decisions taken in the 1960s and 1970s and from the developments in the global economic and strategic environments noted at the start of this chapter. Moreover, if the focus is shifted to the subregional level and if conceptions of regionalism are shed which implicitly have as their base the West European model, and, in addition, if we reflect on a West European experience that has also been fractious, and halting, and a process that in certain functional areas has lasted four decades, then we may increase our receptiveness to developments at the micro- and macro-regional levels in Pacific Asia.

(a) Subregional developments

In 1992, ASEAN celebrated twenty-five years of its existence. As an organization with no supranationality, it has survived in an area that has experienced high levels of violence and abrupt political change. No member of ASEAN has ever seriously contemplated withdrawal from the organization, and neither has expulsion of a member been considered. ASEAN governments continue to value the collegial style of decision-making and the benefits that have been derived from promoting intra-area security. The success of its dialogue arrangements with external partners, such as the European Community, the USA, and Japan, among others, has been instructive for other developing countries.

[36] FEER, 27 Feb. 1992.

Since 1991, the organization has begun a more vigorous attempt to define regional security objectives in the post-Cold War era, prompted in large part by a realization that the USA is unlikely to remain the prime or sole architect of the security order, where once it was.[37] At the fourth ASEAN summit in Singapore at the end of January 1992, a modest start was made with an agreement for ASEAN members regularly to discuss regional security issues at the annual Post-Ministerial Conference.[38] By 1993 the initiative had the support—with various degrees of enthusiasm—of Japan, the USA, South Korea, and China. Tokyo, as a prime mover in this scheme, promised that it would 'actively take part' in the attempts to 'develop a long-term vision regarding the future order of peace and security for their region' but sensibly said nothing to suggest that Japan was about to usurp ASEAN's leadership role on these questions. China, the other major state that ASEAN is interested in engaging, also pledged its support for 'discussions at annual ASEAN foreign ministers' meetings'.[39] It is clear, however, that Beijing still finds it premature to start building a more comprehensive regional security structure.[40] During Winston Lord's confirmation hearings in March 1993, the new US assistant secretary for East Asian and Pacific Affairs signalled a shift in emphasis from the Bush era: most notably, a greater willingness to participate in multilateral forums, specifically noting ASEAN's contribution to a process that could encourage the sharing of information, the easing of tensions, the resolution of disputes, and the fostering of confidence.[41] In May 1993, the Singapore summit pushed the security dialogue further with an attempt to draw up a security agenda, and in July 1994 the ASEAN six held the first meeting of the ASEAN Regional Forum, including the seven dialogue partners, plus China and Russia, and three observers—Vietnam, Laos, and Papua New Guinea. The first step towards the widening of ASEAN's membership has also been taken with Vietnam's accession to the Treaty of

[37] For a discussion of some of the security questions facing ASEAN, see Leszek Buszynski, 'ASEAN Security Dilemmas', *Survival*, 34/4 (Winter 1992–3), and of its developing security dialogue, see Andrew Mack and Pauline Kerr, 'The Evolving Security Discourse in Asia-Pacific', *Washington Quarterly* (forthcoming).

[38] *FEER*, 6 Feb. 1992.

[39] *Korea Herald*, 2 June 1993.

[40] See the report of Chinese Foreign Minister Qian Qichen's discussions in Tokyo, *SWB*, Far East, 1702, 31 May 1993.

[41] 'A New Pacific Community: Ten Goals for American Policy', opening statement at confirmation hearings for Ambassador Winston Lord, 31 Mar. 1993.

Amity and Co-operation, and Cambodia to follow should it also take this first step.

ASEAN member states have also turned their attention to economic relations. At the ASEAN summit in January 1992, the heads of government signed a 'Framework Agreement on Enhancing ASEAN Economic Co-operation', which commited the six to the establishment of a free-trade area within fifteen years. (Originally to begin in January 1993, its start date has been put back a year.) Opt-out clauses will undoubtedly be invoked and ASEAN will continue with its consensual method of decision-making which ensures that ASEAN only moves as fast as the slowest member. But this agreement reflects a desire to solidify and raise the level of their economic interaction, as well as an attempt to emulate regional trading patterns elsewhere in the world.[42]

In North-East Asia, there have also been notable developments in the security and economic realms. The high levels of tension that arose as a result of North Korea's threatened withdrawal from the Non-Proliferation Treaty, its previous adamant stand over inspection of nuclear facilities, and the indications that it does have a nuclear weapons capability, have served to focus much attention on the Korean peninsula in the post-Cold War era. Although North and South Korea are recognized as central actors in this process, there has been a clear understanding that other states, especially the USA, can affect the pace and the form of the dialogue between Pyongyang and Seoul and the resolution of the nuclear crisis. Japan, North and South Korea, the former Soviet Union, as well as the USA, have all made use of Beijing as an intermediary over a variety of issues concerning the two Koreas. From late 1988, North Korean and American diplomats for a time met on a regular basis in Beijing, and China's support was frequently elicited—not always successfully—to help restart the discussions over nuclear inspection.[43] The then South Korean foreign minister, Han Sung Joo, tried to institutionalize this, and threw his weight behind a more formal security dialogue in North-East Asia, envisaging a mini-CSCE for the area.[44]

[42] *FEER*, 6 Feb. 1992.

[43] Shin Junghyun, 'Changes in Relationship between the United States and North Korea: Outlook and Issues', *East Asian Review*, 4/1 (Spring 1992). Difficult though this process has been, one effect has been to highlight the multilateral aspects of this security problem.

[44] *SWB*, Far East, 1703, 1 June 1993.

These modest shifts in language and behaviour in North-East Asia in the security sphere have also been reflected in economic decision-making. To give one example, in February 1992 the Tumen River Area development programme—operating under UNDP auspices—held its inaugural meeting, involving delegates from North and South Korea, Japan, China, Russia, and Mongolia. This $30 billion trade and transport project, if it ever materializes, will include eleven harbours and a rail hub. The objective is to transform this backward region, which offers timber, minerals, oil, coal, and cheap labour, into an area to rival those further south, centring on China's Guangdong and Fujien provinces, Taiwan, and Hong Kong. Although the course of this project remains extremely uncertain, even more so as a result of the tensions involving Pyongyang, its contemplation reflects many of the features of the post-Cold War era: an attention to economic development and reform, a greater willingness by the divided states to be flexible concerning representation, and a closer association between nominally communist states and their capitalist neighbours.[45]

(b) Japan and Pacific Asia

Subregional developments suggest, therefore, sometimes a necessity, at other times a desire for a deepening of contact in the security and economic fields. Yet even beyond the subregional there is evidence to show that this thinking is being reflected in Pacific Asia as a whole. ASEAN may be taking the lead in the security realm but there is a desire to ensure that the USA remains engaged in some form in the region and that potential regional hegemons, such as China and Japan, are drawn into the dialogue. In terms of economic relations, there is a widespread, if still contested, belief that the economies of the area have begun to show signs of greater interdependence and that they themselves have become sources of economic growth and technological innovation.[46] Levels of intra-

[45] This project is described in some detail in *FEER*, 16 Jan. 1992. See also James P. Dorian, David Fridley, and Kristin Tressler, 'Multilateral Resource Cooperation among North East Asian Countries: Energy and Mineral Joint Venture Prospects', *Journal of North East Asian Studies*, 12/1 (Spring 1993).

[46] Such a process has been described in a recent OECD report as evidence of 'regionalization'; that is, an economic process in which trade and investment within a given region grow more rapidly than the region's trade and investment with the rest of the world. This could lead on to regional political co-operation and the

regional trade have risen steadily to some 45 per cent in 1994 and from 1991 Asia overtook the USA as Japan's largest export market. This is mainly a consequence of Japanese investment strategies, which have secured Japan a place as the largest single investor in such Pacific-Asian economies as South Korea, Indonesia, and Thailand, with China having become the dominant Asian investment partner from 1993. Moreover, this economic domination has been translated into influence on how firms work in the region and how firms react in order both to sell in the Japanese market and compete with Japanese firms elsewhere.[47]

In the late 1960s and 1970s, Tokyo mainly allocated its investment for the development of natural resources and of infrastructure to ensure that competitively priced raw materials would reach Japan. Subsequently, Tokyo shifted into manufacturing and the development of production processes in order to take advantage of low Asian labour costs for the production and assembling of finished goods or components. These flows from Japan have played an important role in spreading technological knowledge, capital, and marketing expertise with the result that, since the late 1980s, new patterns of FDI have begun to emerge with, for example, Thailand, Malaysia, and Indonesia each receiving investment from the four NIEs and ASEAN in turn investing in Vietnam and Burma. Thus, a hierarchy of development seems to be in place with Japan at the apex, followed by the NIEs, the remaining members of ASEAN, then China, Vietnam, and Burma. As Shibusawa *et al.* have forecast, 'a deeper and more stable pattern of regional specialization . . . may over time tie the developing countries of Pacific Asia more closely to Japan. In this sense, investment flows are the most important indicator of growing regional interdependence.'[48]

creation of institutions to provide 'governance structures' for managing this increased economic integration. See Albert Fishlow and Stephan Haggard, *The United States and the Regionalisation of the World Economy* (Paris: OECD, Apr. 1992). For a more tempered analysis, see Garnant and Drysdale (eds.), *Asia Pacific Regionalism*, pt. 5.

[47] 'Japan: Trade and Investment', *FEER*, 9 June 1994, and comment in n. 17. For discussion of trade, investment, and development assistance trends in the region see e.g. Christopher Howe, 'China, Japan and Economic Interdependence in the Asia Pacific Region', *China Quarterly*, 124 (Dec. 1990); Shibusawa *et al.*, *Pacific Asia*; Noland, *Pacific Basin Developing Countries*; Alan Bollard and David Mayes, 'Regionalism and the Pacific Rim', *Journal of Common Market Studies*, 30/2 (June 1992), esp. 208; and Garnant and Drysdale (eds.), *Asia Pacific Regionalism*.

[48] Shibusawa *et al. Pacific Asia* 17–18.

Not surprisingly, this hierarchy of development is being reflected in the movement of peoples. The changes in the labour market and wage differentials deriving from uneven levels of development have become strong inducements to migration, both legal and illegal.[49] For example, Japan remains an attractive port of call for workers throughout the region—not least because of high wage rates and steady demand that has led to the establishment of migrant labour communities able to facilitate the entry of newcomers to the country. With growing evidence that Malaysia and Thailand have also been suffering shortages of unskilled workers, Indonesians and Burmese have been on the move to these two countries. In turn, Malaysia has become a significant source of skilled labour to Singapore.[50]

(c) Macro-regional institutions

To some degree, this economic interconnectedness in which Japan plays a prominent economic but a politically invisible leadership role has taken institutional form in Pacific Asia. Because there is now widespread acceptance of the notion that there is a single global economy (rather than parallel if highly imbalanced socialist and capitalist economies) and because the commitment to central planning has been severely eroded, regional economic organizations now have a greater chance of being universal. Those that have emerged recognize in their membership the centrality of the US economy to Pacific Asia. They also include other less vital yet still important economic partners such as Australia and Canada. One author has pointed to the progression from the unofficial organizations such as PAFTAD and PBEC (Pacific Basin Economic Council), to the quasi-official such as PECC which is made up of academics, business people, and government officials operating in private capacities, to the organization APEC, formed in 1989 and involving Cabinet-level representatives in 1994 from eighteen states (or quasi-states) in the Asia-Pacific region.[51] At an APEC meeting in

[49] Nacy Viviani, 'The 1990s in the Region—Political/Strategic', in Stuart Harris and James Cotton (eds.), *The End of the Cold War in Northeast Asia* (Melbourne: Longman Cheshire, 1991), 251.

[50] Yoko Sellek, 'Illegal Foreign Migrant Workers in Japan: Change and Challenge in Japanese Society', in Judith M. Brown and Rosemary Foot (eds), *Migration: The Asian Experience* (London: St Antony's/Macmillan, 1994); *FEER*, 2 Apr. 1992.

[51] Harry Harding, 'The New Era in the Asia-Pacific Region: from Bipolarity to Multinodality', Paper presented to the conference on 'A Strategy for the 21st

November 1991 in Seoul, particularly notable for its introduction of three new members—China, Hong Kong, and Chinese Taipei— the APEC declaration described its objectives as, *inter alia*, to work to sustain the growth and development of the region; to develop and strengthen the open, multilateral trading system; and to reduce barriers to trade in goods and services and in investment. It also stated that member countries would co-operate in specific sectors such as energy, the environment, fisheries, tourism, transportation, and telecommunications.[52] At the 1993 summit, it was agreed to hold such meetings annually, and to discuss at ministerial level monetary and trade policies, and at the 1994 meeting to adopt a voluntary, non-binding investment code.[53] There is little enthusiasm, especially among the Asian members, to move towards formal integration or supranationalism, but the institution can be viewed as a 'consociational' body, one that might establish a 'set of regional economic norms and practices', and stand 'as an intermediate link between states (acting as economic units) and the international economy'.[54]

It is difficult to envisage APEC moving beyond this level of co-operation in the next few years, however, given the widely different levels of economic development, and the different kinds of trade regimes and political structures contained within it. Indeed, it is already apparent that there is a split between those, mainly Western states who would prefer a more formalistic body, and those, mainly Asian members, who prefer to maintain its consultative status. There are also difficult relationships to work out between APEC and NAFTA, and APEC and the East Asian Economic Caucus. Nevertheless, there is a logic to the retention of an organization such as APEC with its commitment to an open, multilateral trading

Century: The Development of International Relations Studies in China', Beijing, June 1991, 13. For an overview of APEC and a hard-headed view of the Nov. 1993 informal APEC summit in Seattle, see *FEER*, 9 June 1994; a more optimistic assessment of that summit is contained in C. Fred Bergsten, 'APEC and World Trade', *Foreign Affairs*, 73/3 (May/June 1994).

[52] *Korea Herald*, 15 Nov. 1991.

[53] Bergsten, 'APEC and World Trade', *FEER*, 12 May 1994 and 9 June 1994.

[54] Viviani, 'The 1990s', 254. Richard Higgott's interesting discussion of APEC includes the point that this institution represents 'tactical learning in which behaviour towards economic co-operation in the face of new circumstances has changed while . . . values and aims have remained largely unaltered'. See 'Economic Cooperation: Theoretical Opportunities and Practical Constraints', *Pacific Review*, 6/2 (1993), esp. 107.

system and its inclusion of the USA, still a vital economic partner for the export-orientated economies of East Asia. The US role remains significant in the security realm too if and when the region adjusts over time to a security order built not on bilateral and specific reciprocity but on multilateral, more diffuse reciprocity.[55]

3. CONCLUSION

The flexibility that has arisen from the removal of the constraints imposed by Soviet–American rivalry has exposed more starkly the fault lines and the diversity that lie within Pacific Asia. The uncertain future role of the USA, formerly the prime architect of the security and economic orders that existed in the area, reinforces the concerns about the consequences of these divisions. It is being questioned whether the USA will continue to act as a stabilizing power or will further retreat, and how punitively it will deal with its trading deficits with a number of East Asian States. These concerns about a possible US retreat remain, and in turn feed into a debate about Japan's and China's future leadership roles. In Tokyo's case, this debate is still affected by constraints operating in the domestic and foreign policy environments on the basis of a perceived inability to come to terms with its wartime past. Where Beijing is concerned there is a fear that it will be resistant to having its national concerns harnessed within multilateral frameworks that perforce lead to a diffusion of its power. More broadly, there is an outstanding question involving the manner in which domestic change in Pacific Asia will be managed, within the Communist states of the area in particular, but also elsewhere in the region.

Nevertheless, the same political concerns and the processes that have led to the dramatic economic transformation of the area also mutually reinforce a desire to respond creatively to the challenges of the post-Cold War era. Greater political flexibility has made concepts such as Pacific Asia more feasible than they were even a decade ago. This is reflected in the memberships of new institutions such as PECC and APEC. It is demonstrated too in the stress that

---

[55] John G. Ruggie, 'Multilateralism: The Anatomy of an Institution', *International Organization*, 46/3 (Summer 1992), 571–2. See also Buzan and Segal, 'Rethinking Asian Security', for a discussion of some of the obstacles to multilateralism in the region.

a subregional organization such as ASEAN has been giving to external security issues and in the initiatives it has taken to draw other regional states into a multilateral security dialogue. ASEAN throughout its existence has had a relatively modest, diplomacy-based security agenda; it now faces difficult problems of adjustment if it wishes to help extend a security community to the whole of Pacific Asia.

But ASEAN is not alone in facing such problems of adjustment, the success of which may well depend on whether, in determining the extent to which there is a broad security and economic consensus, the states of the region use that newly acquired information to engage in a process of reassurance and come together to respond with specific policies to the divergencies and disputes that are uncovered. The alternative is a retreat into a balance of power, 'beggar-thy-neighbour' approach in which arms merchants will be the primary benefactors.[56]

[56] For contrasting assessments of the prospects for the region, see Aaron L. Friedberg, 'Ripe for Rivalry: Prospects for Peace in a Multipolar Asia', and Richard K. Betts, 'Wealth, Power and Instability: East Asia and the United States after the Cold War', both in *International Security* 18/3 (Winter 1993/4).

9

Regionalism in the Americas

Andrew Hurrell

REGIONALISM in the Americas has historically meant two quite different things. In the first place, it has meant regional co-operation and attempted economic integration between the countries of Latin America. After more than a decade of disillusion, the 1980s saw a significant resurgence of this form of regionalism nowhere more so than in the *rapprochement* between Brazil and Argentina, whose historic rivalry had long been viewed as a defining feature of the international politics of the region. In the economic sphere, moves towards institutionalized economic co-operation gathered pace in the mid-1980s and proved far more resilient and successful than many predicted. These began with a series of bilateral economic agreements and were taken further by the creation of *Mercosur* in 1991 and by the creation in January 1995 of a common external tariff. In the security field, there has been a steady decline in levels of military spending in all of the countries of the Southern Cone, the successful negotiation and implementation of a series of arms-control and confidence-building measures, and a significant strengthening of the Tlatelolco nuclear weapons regime. Moreover, trends towards the growth of political *concertación*, the resolution or easing of historic border disputes and social conflict (in Central America most notably), declining levels of military spending, and the negotiation of free-trade agreements have not been limited to the Southern Cone, but have included, in one form or another, almost every part of Latin America.

The second form of regionalism covers the entire western hemisphere. Inter-American, or pan-American, regionalism has a long history again going back to the nineteenth century. In the course of

Parts of this chapter draw on arguments developed in an essay of the same name published in Abraham Lowenthal and Gregory Treverton (eds.), *Latin America in a New World* (Boulder, Colo.: Westview, 1994).

the century it developed an elaborate formal institutional structure in the Organization of American States and its related bodies. Moreover, this brand of regionalism also acquired a powerful new momentum in the late 1980s. First, there was the growth of institutionalized economic integration with the successful incorporation of Mexico into a North American Free Trade Area (NAFTA). Second, the launching of the Enterprise for the Americas Initiative (EAI), together with other US administration speeches, placed the question of a southward expansion of NAFTA firmly on the political agenda. Third, the period witnessed a deep and widespread shift in traditional patterns of inter-American relations, with improved relations and increased co-operation between the USA and its southern neighbours across a range of issues. This general trend towards convergence and co-operation, together with a possible southward expansion of NAFTA and the revitalization of the OAS, has raised the possibility of sustained hemispheric regional co-operation, perhaps even of some form of hemispheric community. The idea of a hemispheric community was given greater prominence by the Miami Summit of the Americas that took place in December 1994 and was attended by all the states of the hemisphere except Cuba. The Summit both upheld the importance of political democracy and agreed on the goal of a regional free trade area by 2005.

This chapter is divided into three parts. The first analyses the resurgence of subregional co-operation, concentrating on the evolution of relations between Brazil and Argentina and the formation of *Mercosur*. The second examines the factors that lie behind the successful negotiation of NAFTA and the trends that point towards the emergence of broader forms of hemispheric regionalism. The third section considers both the complex ways in which these two forms of regionalism are related and the limits that exist to the further consolidation of regionalism in the Americas.

1. LATIN AMERICAN REGIONALISM

In the early 1980s the prospects for regional co-operation in Latin America appeared extremely poor. The debt crisis that broke in 1982 led to the collapse of intra-regional trade flows and the further erosion of the already stagnant economic-integration schemes inherited from the integrationist wave of the 1960s, such as the Andean Pact, the Central American Common Market (CACM), and LAFTA (replaced by ALADI in 1980).[1] After an initial improvement in 1979–80 which had led to the signature of a series of agreements, relations between Brazil with Argentina fell back in the early 1980s.[2] Economic relations suffered from persistent trade imbalances with vocally expressed fears on the part of Argentinian industry of being swamped by Brazilian products. In addition, the Falklands/Malvinas War of 1982 was a worrying sign that the extreme 'territorial nationalism' in Argentina had not disappeared, that geopolitical thinking still dominated the minds of many in both countries, and that armed conflict might actually be possible within the region—a contingency that had seemed remote for most of the post-war period. Argentinian rearmament after the war fuelled fears that the region might be moving towards an arms race.

Indeed, many commentators were predicting that the region was becoming more conflictual and more like the rest of the developing world.[3] In the first place, the struggle for natural resources had, it was argued, drastically increased the stakes of many historical disputes: hydroelectric resources on the River Paraná between Brazil and Argentina, access to offshore oil, fishing, and seabed minerals in the case of Chile and Argentina (and, in many Latin American minds, Britain and Argentina); access to oil in the border disputes between Peru and Ecuador, Venezuela and Guyana, and Venezuela and Colombia. Second, the re-emergence of superpower rivalry in the Third World had increased the stakes and intensity of regional insecurity, above all in Central America. Third, many saw the overall decline of US hegemony and the virtual death by 1982

[1] For an excellent overview of integration efforts see Gordon Mace, 'Regional Integration in Latin America: A Long and Winding Road', *International Journal*, 43 (Summer 1988).

[2] On the 1980 agreements and the previous history of confrontation, see Andrew Hurrell, 'Brazil as a Regional Great Power: A Study in Ambivalence', in Iver B. Neumann (ed.), *Regional Great Powers in International Politics* (London: Macmillan, 1992).

[3] 'All this points to a new era of international politics in Latin America: an era characterized by power politics and realism during which the myth of regional unity will be replaced by rivalries among regional power': Mace, 'Regional Integration', 426. Trends towards increasing conflict are discussed (and rebutted) in Walter Little, 'International Conflict in Latin America', *International Affairs*, 63/4 (Autumn 1987).

of the Inter-American Military System as reducing the ability of Washington to maintain 'discipline' within its own sphere of influence. And finally, many noted the continued prevalence of extreme geopolitical thinking amongst the militaries of the Southern Cone and the fact that arms spending and the capabilities of national arms industries appeared to be increasing.

Yet these gloomy predictions proved ill-founded. The first moves towards regional co-operation were essentially political in nature. One example concerned regional attempts to secure peace in Central America with the creation of the Contadora Group (Mexico, Venezuela, Colombia, and Panama) and the Contadora Support Group, and the initiatives that led to the Esquipulas Agreement on regional democratization and pacification led by Costa Rica. Broader political consultation and co-ordination was promoted through such forums as the Group of Eight and its successor, the Rio Group.[4] But nowhere were the moves towards increased co-operation more evident than in the relationship between Brazil and Argentina. In November 1985 Presidents Sarney and Alfonsin signed an agreement which covered nuclear issues and energy co-operation and which set up a commission to examine future economic relations. In July 1986 the signature of the *Ata para a Integração* (Integration Act) established the Integration and Co-operation Programme (PICAB). Under PICAB twenty-four bilateral protocols were signed, followed by the Treaty of Integration and Co-operation in November 1988 and the Treaty of Integration, Co-operation and Development in August 1989. This envisaged the creation of a free-trade area between the two countries within a ten-year period.

In addition to the launching of agreements on economic co-operation the second half of the 1980s saw increased stability in the security relationship.[5] The failures of the Brazilian nuclear programme both increased the need for co-operation and reduced Argentinian fears of rapid and destabilizing Brazilian progress in this area. Brazil had much to gain from co-operating with Argentina's more advanced nuclear technology, whilst Argentina

[4] Membership of the Rio Group includes Argentina, Bolivia, Brazil, Chile, Colombia, Ecuador, Mexico, Paraguay, Peru, Uruguay, and Venezuela.

[5] For much of the 1970s security relations had been marked by suspicion and hostility with barely concealed nuclear rivalry and conflicts over the Itaipu hydroelectric project and influence in the 'buffer states' of Bolivia, Paraguay, and Uruguay.

realized that it no longer had to fear a rapid Brazilian push to acquire a nuclear weapons capability. Moreover, both countries continued through the 1980s to see the acquisition of technology in this area as important to their long-term development (and perhaps, at some later point, military) objectives and to view themselves as having a common position against attempts by outside powers to limit the proliferation of nuclear technology.

Increased mutual confidence on the nuclear question followed from a far greater degree of transparency. This was the most important result of the low-level technological co-operation that gradually expanded through the 1980s—for example the (not very successful) joint project to develop the CBA-123 executive aircraft. But it was also the result of greater public openness and more explicit confidence building measures. Thus Brazil gave Argentina prior notice of its public announcement in late 1987 of the existence of the secret so-called 'parallel' nuclear programme and of the functioning of a domestically built gas centrifuge enrichment facility. Most dramatically, confidence was enhanced by Sarney's visits to Argentina's nuclear facilities in 1987 and 1988, and Alfonsin's visit in 1988 to the hitherto officially unacknowledged Brazilian facility at Aramar.[6]

How should this *rapprochement* be explained? In the first place, increased co-operation between Brazil and Argentina reflected a convergence of foreign-policy interests and perspectives, born of common external pressures and of the erosion of alternative policy options. For much of the post-war period, major Latin American states tended towards a policy of constrained balancing: active efforts to diversify away from the USA but falling short of close and direct alignment with major US antagonists (both because of the high direct and indirect costs of such a move and because of the absence of a domestic constituency—except under conditions of social and nationalist radicalization). For countries such as Brazil (and to a lesser extent Argentina), diversification became the central principle of foreign policy. This involved the expansion of ties with Western Europe, Japan, and many parts of the Third World, and

---

[6] For details of the evolution of the nuclear relationship, see Monica Hirst and Héctor Eduardo Bocco, 'Cooperação nuclear e integração Brasil-Argentina', *Contexto Internacional*, 9 (1989). See also Thomas Guedes da Costa, 'A idéia de medidas de confiança mútua em uma visão brasileira', *Contexto Internacional*, 14/2 (1990).

also the emergence of a distinctly *tercermundisto* ('Third Worldist')
slant to foreign policy (the involvement of Mexico, Peru, Brazil,
and Cuba in the NIEO and the Third World movement).[7] Only
in rare cases (either out of necessity and or as a consequence
of revolutionary nationalist upheaval) would Latin American
countries run the risk of courting political or military support (as
opposed to economic exchanges) from the Soviet Union.

However, the grand (and always excessive) hopes of diversification were already wearing thin by the beginnings of the 1980s
and looked still less secure as the decade progressed. Moreover, as
the prospects for diversification waned, so the centrality of the USA
was reasserted—in terms of Washington's anti-communist crusade
in Central America, the region's renewed dependence on the USA as
a trade partner and as the dominant actor in the management of the
debt crisis, and the increasingly forceful US attempts to influence
Latin American policies on such issues as nuclear proliferation,
arms exports, and domestic investment and intellectual property
regimes. Thus as the strategy of constrained balancing and diversification proved to be ineffective, so Brazil and Argentina turned to
a second, and historically equally deep-rooted, possibility, namely
the formation of subregional alignments or coalitions—'group
power' of a more limited nature. Much of the explanation for the
'Latinamericanization' of foreign policy in the 1980s reflects both
the absence of the kinds of alternative options that Brazil and
Argentina had sought to develop in the 1970s and a common
rejection of US policy across a number of issues.

In Argentina foreign policy under Alfonsin was built around the
image of Argentina as a Western, non-aligned, and developing
country. Relations with Washington were strained as a result of
the lingering resentment over Washington's support of Britain in
1982 and persistent differences over the Central American crisis,
Argentina's strongly non-aligned stance, the management of the
debt crisis, and a range of trade and investment issues. In Brazil
there was a high level of continuity between the military period and
the New Republic, nowhere more so than in the continuation of the
frictions that had increasingly come to characterize US–Brazilian
relations since the mid-1970s. Under Sarney such friction centred

---

[7] See Andrew Hurrell, 'Latin America and the Third World', in R. J. O'Neill and
R. J. Vincent (eds.), *The West and the Third World* (London: Macmillan, 1991).

around debt management and Brazil's 1987 debt moratorium, trade issues (especially investment access and intellectual property rights in the informatics and pharmaceutical sectors), nuclear policy and arms exports, and environmental questions.

Increased regional co-operation was therefore born, at least in part, of the need to present a united front against a hostile world. The severity and uniformity of the economic crisis served to underline common interests and common perspectives between the two countries. The negative external environment re-emphasized the need to broaden and strengthen the regional market and to institutionalize the economic interdependence that had been growing through the 1970s, but which had fallen back so dramatically in the early 1980s. In addition, economic co-operation was also assisted at this stage by the convergence of heterodox economic policies domestically (the Cruzado Plan in Brazil and the Austral Plan in Argentina).

Second, power-political factors within the region worked to facilitate co-operation. On the one hand, there were continued tensions in the relationship between Argentina and Chile. On the other the concerns and threat perceptions of the Brazilian military moved progressively away from Argentina and towards the Amazon region. This reflected perceived fears of subversion seeping down from the Caribbean (Cuba, Grenada, Suriname), of a spillover of guerrilla violence from the Andean region, as well as the need to reassert control over the extremely rapid and increasingly disorderly development of the Brazilian Amazon. This trend has continued and discussions of national-defence planning and procurement policy have focused less and less on the possibility of interstate conflict with Argentina and ever more on the need to police borders in the North, to control flows of gold-miners, to counter *narcotrafficantes*, and to prevent the 'internationalization' of the Amazon region.

Third, regional co-operation was undoubtedly assisted by the process of democratization that was occurring in both countries (and throughout the region). Clearly harmony was not likely to be furthered by the existence of insecure military governments, heavily influenced by extreme and often paranoid geopolitical fears (e.g. that Brazil was building the Itaipu dam in order to threaten Buenos Aires with flooding) and, in the case of Argentina, inclined to use an aggressive foreign policy in order to buttress their declining political legitimacy. The move towards civilian rule has therefore been an important factor in the *rapprochement*. The Falklands/Malvinas fiasco led to the widespread discredit of military adventurism and to a radical loss of political support for the military. Democratization involved the (albeit incomplete) shift in political and bureaucratic power away from the military, both generally and, very importantly, in the management of regional foreign policy. (It is important to note that the foreign ministries (*Itamaraty* in Brazil and *San Martin* in Argentina) have been the dominant agencies in the whole process of political co-operation and economic integration.) Democratization also laid the political foundation for increased transparency on which more specific confidence building measures were later to be built.

Yet it very important to note that we are not dealing here with a 'democratic peace' between two well-consolidated democracies. The shared interests and perhaps shared identities of the two governments in the post-1985 period came rather from a common sense of *vulnerability*: the shared conviction that democracy was extremely fragile and that non-democratic forces were by no means out of the game (witness the military rebellions in Argentina). Hence the desire, especially apparent in Argentina, to use foreign policy as a means of protecting fragile and newly established democracies. It is very difficult to judge exactly how far democratization really mattered. First, there are clearly other factors pressing towards co-operation. Second, the Brazilian policy of improving relations with Argentina had first appeared in 1979–80 under a military government and there were significant elements of continuity between the military and civilian periods.[8] Third, the military remained politically powerful actors in both Brazil and Argentina— the persistence of so-called 'authoritarian enclaves'. Indeed, in Brazil their political role was explicitly recognized by the 1988 Constitution and the military successfully fought off proposals for a civilian minister of defence and for a parliamentary system that would make the five military ministers in the cabinet answerable to

[8] The 'Latin-americanization' of Brazilian policy had begun in the late 1970s and was not limited to relations with Argentina. It was also visible in Brazilian initiatives that led to the creation of the Amazon Pact in 1978; the increasingly common official statements proclaiming Brazil's Latin American identity; in the far more prominent Brazilian role in regional bodies; and in Brazil's policy of restoring relations with Cuba (which occurred in 1986).

Congress. Whilst the greater enthusiasm of the civilian élites and of President Sarney was crucial, it would have been unlikely to develop this far without general agreement of the military and without a parallel (albeit slower, more reluctant, and more grudging) shift in military thinking.

Despite these caveats, what is certainly clear is that the leading actors on both sides *believed* democratization to have been very important in redefining the interests of the two states and in reshaping their identities and their sense of common purpose. (But note this was a shared sense of common purpose between a limited group of politicians and government officials, rather than between political, let alone public, opinion more generally.) Indeed we can identify a sharp discursive break in the way in which co-operation is conceived: the constant iteration of a shared Latin American identity; the repeated emphasis that the emerging community was to be democratic; the way in which the agreements and presidential meetings explicitly sought to provide mutual support for the process of democratic consolidation. This was carried on both by language and symbols (e.g. the building of 'friendship bridges' or the inclusion of a commitment of Latin American integration in the 1988 Brazilian Constitution). It is also worth noting the differential treatment of undemocratic regimes in Paraguay and Chile (their exclusion from economic agreements and, in Brazil's case, the suspension of arms sales to Chile). There is, then, at this time a conscious attempt to talk a community or shared identity into existence.

Finally, it is worth stressing that liberal theories (both neo-functionalist and institutionalist) which see co-operation as a response to the problems generated by increased interdependence have little to say about the moves towards subregional co-operation that gathered pace in the second half of the 1980s. Indeed state-led co-operation was a response to *declining* levels of trade interdependence. Whilst it is true that by the late 1980s Brazilian and Argentinian businesses were investing in each other's countries the numbers and amounts were very small (around 250 firms and a total of $US86 million in 1982). Moreover, levels of social integration (tourism, educational exchanges) were also low.

The inauguration of Carlos Menem in Argentina in July 1989 and Fernando Collor in Brazil in March 1990 witnessed a significant effort to relaunch the somewhat flagging process of economic co-operation. In July 1990 they agreed to establish a full common market by the end of 1994.[9] In March 1991 the Treaty of Asunción creating *Mercosur* was signed between Brazil, Argentina, Paraguay, and Uruguay, entering into force in November 1991. As a result economic interdependence has continued to expand.[10] Trade has grown to far higher levels than most predicted. Intra-*Mercosur* trade increased from $US4.7 billion in 1991 to $US8.3 billion in 1993. By 1993 Brazil accounted for over 20 per cent of Argentinian trade (becoming the country's most important single trading partner), up from 10 per cent in 1989. More important given the common view of Argentina as marginal to Brazil's economic interests, Argentina's share of Brazilian trade rose from around 3.7 per cent in 1989 to over 13 per cent in 1993.

In addition, the expansion of economic relations has resulted in the formation of new interest groups and business interests favouring further integration. Equally, economic co-operation has provided the framework for an increase in the volume of institutionalized interaction between both bureaucracies and politicians. A further feature has been the conscious replication of the EU model in terms of drawing in congresses and politicians; and in emphasizing, at least rhetorically, that even when the content of the agreement has been economic, broader political goals, common interests, values, and principles have been at stake. Although much remains unfulfilled, the range of issues included in the co-operation agreements has been very wide.[11]

In the security field two developments have been especially notable. First, there has been significant progress on arms-control measures. Collor's formal renunciation of Brazil's parallel nuclear programme in September 1990 further enhanced the growing confidence between the two countries. The 1990 Declaration on a Common Nuclear Policy created a system of jointly monitored

---

[9] On the details of this process, see Sonia de Camargo, 'Caminhos que se juntam e se separam: Brasil e Argentina, uma visão comparativa', *Política e Estrategia*, 10/3 (1986); and Sonia de Camargo, 'Brasil e Argentina: A integração em questão', *Contexto Internacional*, 9 (1989).

[10] For a thorough assessment of economic integration, see Monica Hirst, 'Mercosur: Avances y Desafios en la Formación del Mercosur', in Roberto Bouzas *et al.*, *Los Procesos de Integración Economica en América Latina* (Buenos Aires: FLACSO, 1994).

[11] See Juan Mario Vacchino, 'Assessing Institutional Capacities', in Smith (ed.), *The Challenge of Integration*, 314–20.

safeguards and opened the way for full implementation of the Tlatelolco Regime (and in Argentina's case, eventually of the NPT). Finally, the Mendonca Agreement signed in September 1991 extended arms control to cover chemical and biological weapons. Second, it is important to highlight the low and declining level of military spending. 1990 to 1993 saw a decline in military spending in all three major states (Brazil to around 0.8 per cent of GNP, Argentina to around 2 per cent, and Chile to 3.5 per cent). Latin American arms imports fell from around 8 per cent of the world total in 1981 to 6.5 per cent in 1987, to 3.8 per cent in 1991. Latin American arms exports declined from 0.46 per cent of world total in 1981, to 1.5 per cent in 1987, to 0.37 per cent in 1991 and, in all three states, there has been increased willingness to accept tighter export controls. In part these trends can be taken as a secure indicator of declining levels of threat perception, but they also reflect the seriousness of the financial crisis and the decline of military-related industrialization as a result of privatization and economic liberalization.[12]

The forces at work in this recent period are more complex. There is, for example, more scope for neo-functionalist accounts that highlight the increased role of civil servants and technical élites and the creation of interest-group coalitions favouring integration. The network of binational working groups established under the 1986 agreements had acquired a degree of bureaucratic autonomy (and insulation from the ongoing political and institutional crisis in Brazil). Not only was the habit of consultation growing but a small group of officials were able to push the integration agenda forward and to work together to try and find solutions to problems (especially the recurrent trade imbalance). Moreover, the institutionalization of visits, exchanges by presidents and officials was leading to a broader 'habit of communication' of the kind that has been so important within Europe. Although the shared sense of vulnerable new democracies is less visible in this phase, the domestic process of democratization remains important. In Argentina, for example, the foreign ministry was able to secure a progressively greater role in

[12] For a detailed study of these trends, see Jorge Heine and Claudio Fuentes, 'La Reforma del Estado y la Defensa Nacional en America Latina', Paper prepared for SSRC conference on Economic Liberalization and Political Democratization, Rio de Janeiro, 24–6 July 1994. See also Augusto Varas and Isaac Caro (eds.), *Medidas de Confianza Mutua en América Latina* (Santiago: FLACSO, 1994).

'security' affairs and, with the backing of Menem, to force the military to accept a series of unpalatable decisions on weapons and nuclear policy.

Yet significant weight still needs to be given to the 'outside-in' pressures. The renewed efforts at economic integration need to be understood against a set of shared and widely held perceptions of the external environment: that economic multilateralism and the GATT framework was under threat and that a three-bloc world was emerging; that the end of the Cold War was leading to the 'marginalization' of the region; that the success of US military power in the Gulf signalled a 'unipolar moment' in which there was little choice but to come to terms with the realities of US power; and that economic globalization had undercut the viability of existing economic policies.

Partly as a result of this shared view of the international system, the relaunch of economic co-operation under Collor and Menem continued to be based on a convergence of both domestic economic policies and foreign policy. The foreign policy of both governments shifted strikingly towards improved relations with the USA and a strong (re)assertion of their country's 'Western' character. In Argentina, the new government stressed the need for a more pragmatic policy, concentrating on relations with Europe, parts of Latin America, and, above all, the USA. In Brazil, Collor's rhetoric of modernization encompassed a revised picture of Brazil's place in the world, with the denunciation of *terceiromundismo* and the talk of Brazil as an aspiring member of the First World (actually the revival of an old and recurring image). Great emphasis was placed on the rehabilitation of relations with the USA, and on measures to promote this, including: the symbolic decommissioning of the parallel nuclear programme, the agreement to an arms-export regime, the easing of the informatics regime, the decision to place intellectual property-rights legislation before Congress, the dramatic shift of policy on Amazon and environmental policy.

These developments were, in turn, reflections of a still more important change: the questioning of existing economic models based on import substitution, high tariffs, and a large role for the state. Latin American leaders had increasingly lost faith with the kinds of inwardly orientated development policies and on the schemes for self-reliance and autonomy that characterized so much earlier Third World thinking. More and more governments embraced economic liberalism—placing greater reliance on market mechanisms, seeking to restructure and reduce the role of the state, and laying greater emphasis on integration in world markets. This shift fed into regional policy in a number of ways. First, its most important impact has been to make the region more outward-looking and more dependent on the international economy at precisely the time when the overall pattern of international relations was in a state of great flux and uncertainty. It increased Latin American interests in the continued existence of a more or less open, multilateral world economy. But it also altered the options when global multilateralism appeared to be under threat, increasing the importance of regional and subregional economic liberalization. Second, the fact that both Brazil and Argentina were moving together (if still unequally) towards economic liberalization provided a potentially more promising basis for subregional economic co-operation than old-style ECLA prescriptions. Thus the specific character of integration changes significantly in this phase: away from balanced, sector-specific agreements based on specific reciprocity of the kind that had dominated the 1986–9 period (with a heavy focus on the capital-goods sector); and towards generalized, linear, and automatic reductions in levels of protection.

Thus, as with the movement towards democratization in the mid-1980s, definitions of interests shifted significantly in this period in ways that facilitated co-operation. External pressure has certainly played a role in this shift: direct external pressure from both states and multilateral agencies and the increasing tendency to make economic assistance conditional upon moves towards economic and political liberalization. The embracing of new economic 'ideas' is not simply a matter of greater enlightenment and rationality and the spread of economic and political 'models' cannot be understood outside the political structures and patterns of unequal power within which they are transmitted and promoted. Moreover, neo-realists can also highlight the continued hegemonic 'policing role' of the USA in forcing change in precisely those areas that had previously been central to Brazilian–Argentinian rivalry. Thus it is extremely difficult to explain the parallel shift in nuclear policy, missile technology, or arms exports without reference to the consistent pressure applied by Washington.

But direct external pressure has been only one factor behind these changes. On the one hand, the causes are partly to be found in purely domestic developments: the discredit and failure of previous development policies built around import substitution in which wide-ranging subsidy programmes and extensive direct state involvement in industry had played a major role; the increased recognition of the need for effective stabilization; the analytically distinct but temporally interconnected, fiscal, political, and institutional crises of the state; and the realization that successful economic modernization could prove electorally popular. On the other hand, these changes in economic policy are impossible to understand without reference to the critical impact of both the debt crisis and broader structural changes in the global economy: the increased pace of the globalization of markets and production, and the dramatically increased rate of technological change. This has led to a powerful Latin American *perception* that dynamic economies are internationalized economies; that growth depends on successful participation in the world economy; that increased foreign investment is central to the effective transfer of modern technology; and that the increased rate of technological change has undermined projects that aim at nationally based and autonomous technological development.

This sea-change in economic thinking and the deep-rooted moves towards trade liberalization have been important not just within *Mercosur* but throughout the region. They lay at the heart of the revival of the Central American Common Market, CARICOM, and the Andean Pact, as well as an increasing number of other free-trade agreements: Chile–Mexico (1991); Colombia–Venezuela (1992); Mexico, Costa Rica, El Salvador, Guatamala, Honduras, and Nicaragua (1992); the Group of Three (Colombia, Mexico, Venezuela 1993); and Chile–Venezuela (1993).

2. HEMISPHERIC REGIONALISM

There are three areas around which the revival of hemispheric regionalism needs to be considered. First, the process which led to the creation of the North American Free Trade Area (NAFTA). The decision to make a North American Free Trade Area an objective of US trade policy goes back to the Trade Agreements Act of 1979. One notable step was the successful negotiation of the US–Canadian free-trade agreement in 1988. In 1985 the USA and

Mexico signed an agreement on subsidy disputes. In July 1986 Mexico joined the GATT and in November 1987 the USA and Mexico signed a Framework Agreement which provided mechanisms both for the resolution of trade disputes and for the process of bilateral trade liberalization. In June 1990 President Salinas formally requested negotiations on a free-trade agreement and in August 1992 a draft treaty was agreed and initialled by the two sides.

NAFTA is politically significant in a number of ways: first, because it is not simply, or indeed primarily, about trade, but rather covers a wide range of issues covering investment rules, liberalization of the service sector, intellectual property rights, as well as establishing a variety of dispute-settlement procedures; second because, following Clinton's electoral victory in late 1992, 'side agreements' were signed on labour protection and environmental co-operation, thereby broadening the range of the agreement (and demonstrating the influence of pressure groups); third, because the disparities of income between Mexico and its northern neighbours make it an unprecedented example of 'North–South regionalism'; and finally because it marks a decisive shift in Mexico's international position towards incorporation with North America.[13]

Second, the idea that the North American Free Trade Area might extend further south was given prominence by Bush's Enterprise Initiative for the Americas speech of 27 June 1990. This pointed to a hemispheric free-trade area as a long-term objective. This would include both bilateral negotiations and agreements with the various subregional trade groupings within Latin America, a process which subsequently began with the negotiation of a series of loose framework agreements. The Initiative also spoke of the importance of debt reduction and rescheduling, but placed heavy emphasis on encouraging foreign investment, both by continuing economic reforms within the countries of Latin America and by the creation of a multilateral investment fund. Again it is worth stressing just how dramatically the picture has changed. As Roberto Bouzas and Jaime

---

[13] NAFTA has generated a large literature. But see esp. Nora Lustig et al., North American Free Trade: Assessing the Impact (Washington: Brookings Institution, 1992); Peter H. Smith (ed.), The Challenge of Integration: Europe and the Americas (New Brunswick, NJ: Transaction Publishers, 1993); Victor Bulmer-Thomas et al., Mexico and the North American Free Trade Agreement: Who will benefit? (London: Macmillan/ILAS, 1994).

Ros note, a decade ago the idea of a hemispheric free-trade agreement would have been regarded as too eccentric even to merit consideration or discussion.[14]

The third area in which inter-American regionalism has been revived concerns the OAS. The prospects for the OAS in the late 1970s and early 1980s appeared dim. The OAS was paralysed by the deep divisions that existed between the USA and Latin America over the crisis in Central America. In addition the Falklands/Malvinas represented, for many commentators, the last nail in the coffin of the Inter-American Military System. Yet the salience of the Organization has increased dramatically in the early 1990s. Although its role in the field of traditional peace security remains somewhat limited, it has adopted a much more forceful position with regard to the support of democracy. Indeed, many now see the effective collective defence of democracy as forming the heart of a renewed and strengthened inter-American political and military system.[15]

In June 1991 OAS foreign ministers approved the so-called Santiago Commitment which promised firm support for democracy and resolved that any 'sudden or irregular interruption of the democratic political institutional process' of any one of them would result in the calling of an emergency meeting of foreign ministers. Subsequently, the OAS sought to develop a co-ordinated response to democratic challenges, including the Haitian coup in September 1991 and subsequent attempts to restore President Aristide, the so-called *autogolpe* or 'palace coup' by President Fujimori in Peru in April 1992, and the Guatamalan coup in September 1993.[16] In addition, participation in elections and political activity has become a more central element of Latin American international human

---

[14] Roberto Bouzas and Jaime Ros, 'The North–South Variety of Economic Integration: Issues and Prospects', Paper presented to 'Economic Integration in the Western Hemisphere', University of Notre Dame, 17/18 Apr. 1993.

[15] See e.g. The Inter-American Dialogue, *Convergence and Continuity: The Americas in 1993* (Washington, DC: Aspen Institute, 1992).

[16] See Carl Kaysen, Robert A. Pastor, and Laura W. Reed (eds.), *Collective Responses to Regional Problems: The Case of Latin America and the Caribbean* (Cambridge, Mass.: American Academy of Arts and Sciences, 1994), esp. Richard J. Bloomfield, 'Making the Western Hemisphere Safe for Democracy? The OAS Defense of Democracy Regime'. For a recent argument that democratic entitlement is moving from a moral prescription to an international legal obligation, see Thomas Franck, 'The Emerging Right to Democratic Governance', *American Journal of International Law*, 86/1 (Jan. 1992).

rights law and the international monitoring of elections has become more widespread and accepted.[17]

How are these developments to be explained? Let us look in turn at the policies and attitudes of the major players:

(a) USA

US interest in regionalism in the Americas has grown significantly over the past five years. The first cluster of reasons are economic. As Andrew Wyatt-Walter's chapter analyses in more detail, US trade policy shifted significantly in the mid-1980s with the decision to push ahead with further multilateral trade negotiations but at the same time to strengthen and safeguard the US policy by broadening the range of US options.[18] On the one hand, this involved increased determination to use US power to force unilateral concessions from those countries whose trade policies were deemed to be contrary to US interests: most visibly in the form of investigations and retaliatory measures under section 301 of the 1974 Trade Act and its super 301 successor. On the other this involved the growth of bilateral trade agreements with Israel in 1985 and with Canada in 1988. These were intended to exert pressure on the EC and Japan and carried the implication that, if the Uruguay Round broke down, such measures would become the central thrust of US trade policy rather than an adjunct to it.[19] Structured free-trade agreements offer the USA both economic benefits (market access, the ability to ensure compliance with a favourable investment regime, and adequate patent protection, and a means to promote microeconomic adjustment and increased international competitiveness) and a political framework for the effective management of other issues (drugs, migration, environment).

This change was reinforced by the rhetoric of growing trends

[17] Art. 5 of the OAS Charter establishes the duty of members to promote 'the effective exercise of representative democracy' and the 5 June 1991 resolution on Haiti states that the principles of the organization 'require the political representation of [member] states to be based on the effective exercise of representative democracy'. See Franck, 'The Emerging Right', 65–6, and Tom Farer, 'The United States as Guarantor of Democracy in the Caribbean Basin: Is There a Legal Way', *Human Rights Quarterly*, 10 (1988).

[18] For an overview of this subject, see I. M. Destler, *American Trade Politics* (New York: Twentieth Century Fund, 2nd edn., 1992).

[19] See Jeffrey J. Schott, 'More Free Trade Areas?', *Policy Analyses in International Economics*, 27 (May 1989).

towards exclusive regionalism in other parts of the world. The *image* of 'Fortress Europe' and the growing *perception* of Japan as an increasingly hostile and antagonistic competitor undoubtedly contributed to the refocusing of US attention on Mexico (and to a much lesser extent the rest of Latin America). Moreover, these fears were reinforced by increasing disenchantment with the GATT and with the difficulty of securing key US objectives during the Uruguay Round, especially trade in services, intellectual property rights, and agricultural trade. Finally, the economic upturn and return of confidence that has taken place in most parts of Latin America since 1990 has led to renewed attention to the potential for US economic interests in the region (which accounts for around $US75 billion of US exports and has become a target for portfolio investment).

Second, both the Bush and Clinton administrations came to at least partially accept the argument that the USA needs to develop a more assertive regionalist policy because of the interdependencies that have developed on such issues as drugs, migration, and the environment. The notion that regionalism can be viewed as a response by states to the problems of interdependence has some purchase as an explanation of the new regionalism in Latin America, but principally in terms of US–Mexican relations. Indeed the US–Mexican relationship conforms quite closely to the image of complex interdependence in which the density of cross-border interdependence has created problems that demand common management. Economic interdependence is already at a high level and moves to create formal economic regional arrangements came on the back of high levels of trade, a sustained period of unilateral Mexican trade liberalization, and a high degree of integration of cross-border production arrangements. In addition, migration has led to a high degree of human interdependence, which dramatically increases Washington's stake in the continued economic development and political stability of Mexico, and which has begun to have an impact on identity and social and economic values in Mexico (and arguably parts of the USA, especially California).[20] Ecological interdependence, in particular in the border regions, is well established and the process of negotiating NAFTA illustrated the diffi-

[20] Around 10 per cent of the US population is of hispanic descent and Mexican and Central American immigrants are becoming one of the largest population groups in California. See Abraham F. Lowenthal and Katrina Burgess (eds.), *The California–Mexico Connection* (Stanford, Calif.: Stanford UP, 1993).

culty of preventing discussions of economic integration from spilling over into the environmental field. If 'security' is defined quite broadly, then it is evident that security factors have played an important background role in North American regionalism.

Third, the regionalist option is strengthened by the fact that it can be deployed, albeit in various ways, by both liberals and conservatives and can be readily accommodated into both the declining hegemony thesis and the idea of the USA as the world hegemon of the post-Cold War world. For the declining hegemony school, Latin America becomes the refuge from an increasingly hostile world. For the hegemony-resurgent school, Latin America is a test of the US ability to give concrete embodiment to its still diffuse vision of a New World Order, to act decisively in support of its values, and to assert its authority over recalcitrant or delinquent states.

This leads to the fourth factor pressing for an expansion of US interests within the region, namely ideology. US–Latin American policy has long been marked by a heavy ideological component and it is important to note the historically deep-rooted tendency to engage in democratic crusading, whether of the liberal Wilsonian variety (visible under both Carter and Clinton) or of the conservative variety that formed such an important element of policy during the Reagan years.[21] Whilst the Cold War certainly influenced their character, such objectives pre-dated the Cold War and have reappeared in the post-1989 period.[22]

The final factor influencing US regional policy concerns domestic politics. There are few other areas of the world in which a wider range of domestic actors, domestic political interests, and domestic pressure groups and lobbies are involved. From Cuban groups pressing for the end to Castro's rule in Cuba, to labour unions and

[21] See Thomas Carothers, *In the Name of Democracy: US Policy Towards Latin America in the Reagan Years* (Berkeley and Los Angeles: University of California Press, 1991); and Abraham Lowenthal (ed.), *Exporting Democracy: The United States and Latin America* (Baltimore: Johns Hopkins UP, 1991).

[22] In marked contrast to the early 1980s (and brought about primarily by the collapse of communism in Europe) the USA has been far more willing to concede linkages between economic management and democratization, and to make the promotion of democracy and good governance a more central criterion of both official aid policies and the lending policies of the multilateral funding institutions. These changes are catalogued and analysed in Joan Nelson, *Encouraging Democracy* (Washington, DC: Overseas Development Council, 1992), esp. 10–25.

environmental groups arguing for the inclusion of workers' rights and environmental protection in the NAFTA, to the transnational networks involved in the promotion of human rights and democracy, regional and domestic politics are deeply interwoven. Indeed, this interpenetration helps to explain why traditional realist definitions of national interest have been the exception in defining US policy towards the region.

(b) Canada

Canadian foreign policy had traditionally laid great emphasis on both economic and political multilateralism (especially the UN system). It had also sought to build up extra-regional relations (with Europe and the Commonwealth) and to develop an active policy of 'middle-powermanship' as a way of balancing the power of the USA and of protecting its economic and cultural autonomy. Historically, relations with Latin America had been minimal. However, since the mid-1980s the turn towards the region has become ever more pronounced. As Andrew Wyatt-Walter's chapter argues, economic defensiveness has been a central element in the story: first, seeking an FTA with the USA as a means of countering the growth of US protectionism and trade unilateralism; second, joining the US–Mexican FTA negotiations for fear that exclusion would undermine the benefits of its own FTA with the USA.

Yet other significant factors have been at work.[23] First, the Central American crisis of the 1980s had a powerful impact on Canadian public opinion, involving substantial NGO mobilization and pressure on the Canadian government to adopt a more visible policy. Second, the shift away from authoritarian governments in Latin America increased the perceived shared values and interests. Third, the decision of Caribbean countries to join the OAS diluted its previous dominance by the USA on the one hand and Latin American states on the other. And finally, once Canada had committed itself to a FTA with the USA, traditional realist logic combined with Canada's fondness for

[23] See H. P. Klepak (ed.), *Canada and Latin American Security* (Quebec: Méridien, 1993) and James Rochlin, *Discovering the Americas: The Evolution of Canadian Foreign Policy towards Latin America* (Vancouver: UBS Press, 1994), esp. Pt. III.

multilateralism to press Ottawa to expand relations to the south and to tie down the USA within an overlapping set of hemispheric institutions. Thus, in addition to NAFTA, Canada joined the OAS in 1990; almost immediately became involved in OAS efforts to support democracy in the region and in debates over the reform and revival of the security role of the organization; participated in the UN Observer Mission in Central America; and significantly expanded its diplomatic presence in Mexico and South America.

(c) Mexico

Of the three central players in the NAFTA story, the shift in Mexican policy has been the most dramatic, representing a major departure in the history of the country's foreign policy. For Mexico, the perceived costs of failing to modernize its economy gradually came to outweigh long-standing fears that freer trade with the USA would impose unacceptable adjustment costs (especially in manufacturing and agriculture), and would undermine the traditional quest to preserve national autonomy that has been so central to Mexican foreign policy.

As in so many parts of the region, external shocks (and especially the 1982 debt crisis), the perceived failures and limits of inward-orientated development, growing pressure from the institutional financial institutions, and fears of political and economic marginalization pressed the Mexican government towards economic liberalization and the adoption of broadly market-liberal economic policies. Externally these changes led to Mexico's entry into the GATT in 1986 and its subsequent Framework Agreement with the USA. But they also reinforced the importance of maintaining access to the critical US market and underlined the attractions of a bilateral free-trade agreements with the USA. FTAs offer the prospect of maintaining and guaranteeing market access to the region's most important market and escaping the growth of US protectionist measures (both countervailing duties and anti-dumping investigations on regional exports to the USA and Section 301 investigations on their own trade and investment regimes).

Yet, whilst Mexico was subject to the same generalized pressures for change, it is extremely important to underline the distinctiveness of the Mexican case.[24] Above all, Mexico's geopolitical position meant that the USA was forced to give significant attention to Mexico. Thus the asymmetry of the overall relationship is at least partially balanced by the need of the USA to find solutions to such non-traditional security concerns as drugs, migration, and the environment. Here at least interdependence is more than an empty slogan and it is this structure of interdependence that helps to explain the underlying political logic of NAFTA. (Although even in the case of US–Mexican relations interdependence is only one part of the story.) For the USA, the agreement offered: political stability in Mexico; continued access to the Mexican market and to Mexican oil; a political framework for managing the problems of drugs, migration, and the environment; the use of Mexico as a means of improving the competitiveness of US industry; and finally a regional fall-back should the GATT Uruguay Round negotiations collapse. For the Salinas government in Mexico, NAFTA involved accepting Washington's economic agenda in return for guaranteed access to the US market; a legal, regulatory, and institutional framework to tame Washington's aggressive unilateralism; and the increased attractiveness of Mexico to foreign investment (hopefully diverting investment from other Latin American countries).

However, this kind of negotiating model of NAFTA needs to be broadened to include domestic factors. On the one hand, the reform process in Mexico was initiated and led by the Mexican state and the relative strength and coherence of the Mexican state was a central characteristic of the NAFTA negotiations themselves.[25] On the other, the agreement was central to Salinas's *domestic* economic and political strategy. It provided a way of securing external support and reinforcement for his market-liberal reforms and of insulating his liberalization policies from the vagaries of the Mexican political system. Moreover, economic success and external recog-

---

[24] On the debates over how the shift in Mexican policy should be explained, see Manuel Pastor and Carol Wise, 'Mexico's Free Trade Policy', *International Organization*, 48/3 (Summer 1994).

[25] Miles Kahler has referred to the 'orthodox paradox': that successfully reducing the role of government in the economy and giving greater play to market forces, depends on the coherence of the state and may even involve strengthening the role of the state. See Miles Kahler, 'Orthodoxy and Its Alternatives: Explaining Approaches to Stabilization and Adjustment', in Joan Nelson (ed.), *Economic Crisis and Policy Choice* (Princeton: Princeton UP, 1990).

nition of that success was also a way of gaining a degree of external legitimacy for Mexico's less than wholly convincing democratic credentials.

(d) The rest of Latin America

The need to find a new basis for relations with Washington has led to a recasting of policy across a wide range of issues. From support for USA action against Iraq, to policies on arms production and nuclear proliferation, to the promotion of democracy, Latin American and US policies have moved far more closely into line. Although the debate on hemispheric regionalism is undoubtedly concerned with trade and economic issues, these questions form only one part of a broader rethinking of relations with the USA which has important strategic and geopolitical implications and whose institutional consolidation would amount to the creation of a new hemispheric order. This is well illustrated by the ease with which the Latin American debate slips between discussion of free-trade blocs on the one hand and the much broader issue of 'international insertion' or 'alliances within a new international order' on the other.[26]

How is this shift to be explained? Explanations that focus on the growth of interdependence are of little value. There are certainly elements of interdependence that have played a role in pressing Latin American governments to rethink attitudes to the USA. The growing perception that narcotics were not simply a problem for the USA but rather threatened both producing and consuming countries provides a good example. But in general there is a striking contrast between the reality of complex interdependence between the USA and Mexico and the relatively low levels of interdependence between the USA and much of South America. Thus what is most striking is the way in which the scramble for inclusion in bloc regionalism on the part of South America is a political response to the relatively low, and in some cases, *declining* levels of interdependence between North and South America.[27]

[26] Thus it is profoundly misleading to suggest that there is no strategic or geopolitical dimension to trade arrangements in the region. For such a view see John Whalley, 'CUSTA and NAFTA: Can WHFTA Be Far Behind?' *Journal of Common Market Studies*, 30/2 (June 1992).

[27] As Albert Fishlow argues, 'Rather than the culmination of decades of increasing economic integration, they [moves to hemispheric co-operation] represent an

For many commentators ideological convergence built around the values of political democracy and market liberalism forms a central part of the explanation. Yet whilst such convergence is indeed significant, it is important to investigate both the changing structure of material incentives on which this convergence has come to rest and to track the changing character of US hegemony. Given the undoubted improvements in US–Latin American relations, the dominant political discourse has tended to jettison the language of hegemony in favour of 'partnership' and 'co-operation'. Yet neither partnership nor co-operation are incompatible with continued US hegemony.[28]

Much of the shift in Latin American attitudes to the USA can be explained by the growing awareness of the limits to subregional alignment. In other words, the relatively weak states of Latin America have shifted from a strategy of *constrained balancing* or *diversification* in the 1970s, then to one of *subregional alignment* in the 1980s, and eventually to one of *bandwagoning* with Washington, preferably of *institutionalized bandwagoning*: because, even if successful, the economic bases of subregional integration were limited; because the political viability of such co-operation was undercut by Mexico's 'defection' (as well as by the failure of the potentially most promising weapon, the formation of an effective debtors cartel in the 1980s);[29] because the consolidation of NAFTA threatened countries such as Brazil and Argentina with substantial economic costs in the form of trade and investment diversion and

attempt to reverse a decade of weakening ties and economic depression': 'Regionalization: A New Direction for the World Economy', Paper presented to the Latin American Studies Association, Los Angeles, 21–5 Sept. 1992, 13–14. For a broader review of North–South interdependence, see John Ravenhill, 'The North–South Balance of Power', *International Affairs*, 66/4 (Oct. 1990).

[28] For an argument that hegemonic and coercive control is giving way to a genuine partnership, see Augusto Varas, 'From Coercion to Partnership: A New Paradigm for Security Cooperation in the Western Hemisphere', in Jonathan Hartlyn, Lars Shoultz, and Augusto Varas (eds.), *The United States and Latin America in the 1990s* (Chapel Hill, NC: University of North Carolina Press, 1992). See also the review article by Mark Peceny, 'The Inter-American System as a Liberal "Pacific Union"?', *Latin American Research Review*, 29/3 (1994).

[29] Indeed the Mexican case has consistently demonstrated the attractions of 'defection' by an individual country from a strategy of group negotiations with the USA, both during the negotiations over debt rescheduling and, more recently, over trade.

the loss of export markets;[30] because of the need to maintain investor confidence in order not to jeopardize the high levels of capital inflows that have been a feature of the early 1990s; and because of other material benefits (for example, involvement in multilateral peacekeeping operations is often attractive to Latin American militaries as a way of developing a more 'professional' role and of facilitating equipment modernization).

As we have already seen, to this neo-realist logic must be added the changes that have followed from the shift to market-liberal economic policies and the altered foreign-policy preferences to which this has given rise. The changed character of Latin American foreign economic policy goals and the importance of the USA as a major export market (especially for manufactured and non-traditional goods) explains *why* the USA has become so important and also why there is a strong incentive to prevent friction on non-economic issues from disrupting economic relations. It also explains *how* many previous sources of friction have been over-come. The gradual implementation of market-liberal policies has removed many of the previous sources of friction that existed between the USA and Latin America. Thus much of the bitterness in US–Brazilian relations in the 1980s focused on economic friction and, in particular, on attempts by the USA to alter Brazilian policies over trade and investment issues and over intellectual property rights (most notably in the pharmaceutical and informatics sectors). Not only are alternatives to the USA perceived as not readily apparent, but to many in Latin America the 'lessons' of the 1980s suggested that direct opposition to Washington was both costly and counter-productive. Proponents of this view highlight, for example, the dismal record of dissenting strategies on debt, or the extent to which Brazilian refusal to fall into line on trade and investment issues served only to provoke costly and ultimately fruitless conflict with Washington.

Although buttressed by shared ideological beliefs, realignment with the USA, then, needs to be viewed both in terms of changing

[30] For an evaluation of the impact of NAFTA on South America, see Roberto Bouzas, 'US–Mercosur Free Trade', in Sylvia Saborio *et al.*, *The Premise and the Promise: Free Trade in the Americas* (Washington, DC: Overseas Development Council, 1992), esp. 262–4; and E. V. K. Fitzgerald, 'The Impact of NAFTA on Latin American Economies', in Bulmer-Thomas *et al.*, *Mexico and the North American Free Trade Agreement*.

external incentives and as the product of changes in social and economic power within Latin American societies and of the emergence of new sets of political coalitions around the project of 'conservative economic modernization'.

3. THE LIMITS OF REGIONALISM

Taken together all these developments undoubtedly point in a generally 'liberal' direction: certainly not towards unalloyed peace and harmony, but arguably towards pacification, political convergence, and economic co-operation/integration. At both the subregional (micro-regional) and hemispheric (macro-regional) levels, therefore, we see relatively high levels of institutionalization—arguably stronger than in any other part of the world outside Europe—combined with a low demand security environment and with growing (although unevenly distributed) economic interaction.

Yet the relationship between these different forms of regionalism has been neither stable nor static and, in one form or another, has become the dominant issue on Latin America's foreign-policy agenda. Although relations with the USA have dramatically altered throughout the region (with the exception of Cuba), attitudes towards hemispheric regionalism vary. Mexico has of course already moved decisively towards integration with North America. Chile was the first South American state to request membership of NAFTA and, at least up until mid-1994, made no secret of its coolness towards subregional integration.[31] Moreover, the period from 1992 to 1994 saw significant differences of approach between Argentina and Brazil—sufficiently marked to raise doubts over their political commitment to *Mercosur*.

The Menem government in Argentina has made no secret of the priority that it attached to improving and intensifying relations with the USA and Western Europe. It consistently tried to distance itself from Argentina's previous non-aligned or 'Third Worldist' foreign policies and has sought to underscore this rejection through

[31] In early 1994 Chile announced that it intended to seek closer relations (although not membership) with *Mercosur*. This was a result of the economic losses that would follow the completion of a Common External Tariff by *Mercosur* as well as growing doubts over the likelihood of an early expansion of NAFTA.

a series of very visible and dramatic policy changes—what one might call the foreign policy of grand gestures: hence the decision to reject its previous 'non-aligned' voting record in the UN and to offer firm and consistent support to the USA and the 'West'; to send ships to the Gulf in support of the US/UN action against Iraq and, more recently, to the Caribbean in support of US action against Haiti; to reverse its policy on sensitive technologies with its cancellation of the Condor missile project and its decision to join the MCTR and to move towards membership of the NPT. Buenos Aires has also laid emphasis on improving relations with Western Europe, cultivating military relations with NATO (widely seen as the only security club worth trying to join) and building bridges with Britain over the Falklands/Malvinas dispute. These changes lay at the heart of foreign minister Di Tella's notorious statement that Argentina wanted a 'carnal relationship' with Washington and his policy of using exaggerated symbols to underscore the shift in Argentinian policy and to overcome Argentina's negative and unreliable image.[32]

Within the hemisphere Argentina has laid great emphasis on improving inter-American co-operation and reviving the OAS. There has been a good deal of talk about the outmodedness of traditional concepts of sovereignty and of the self-defeating nature of earlier Third World notions of autonomy. Argentina has played a leading role in giving greater teeth to the OAS's charter commitment to democracy and, in a further striking rejection of earlier thinking, has supported the use of coercion to restore democratic regimes. It has also semi-officially floated ideas for developing a doctrine of 'co-operative security' in the region, involving more active conflict prevention and the creation of multinational forces for the maintenance and restoration of peace. But, on the other side, the *relative* position of relations with Brazil and *Mercosur* has declined very significantly and there has been much debate in Buenos Aires as to why the country should give a higher priority to membership of NAFTA.

Instrumental logic and changing external incentives explain a good deal of the shift in Argentinian foreign policy: symbolic (and extreme) pro-American policies in order to underline the change in the country's foreign and domestic policies, and to bolster market

[32] Roberto Russell, 'Los ejes estructurantes de la política exterior Argentina', *America Latina/Internacional*, 1/2 (1994).

confidence (especially given the degree to which the Cavallo economic reforms remain very highly dependent on a continued inflow of foreign capital). Yet these changes also involved the politics of identity: the reassertion of Argentina's Western, European identity and scepticism of the possibility of meaningful or cohesive Latin American regionalism.

Brazilian policy towards hemispheric regionalism, by contrast, has been more ambiguous, and the elements of continuity far more pronounced. Foreign-policy statements have continued to lay great emphasis on the idea of 'universalism' and of the country as a 'global trader' whose fundamental interests lie in global multilateralism. Whilst Brazilian governments have certainly learnt the lessons of confrontation with the USA and whilst fear of exclusion from regional developments has forced Brazil to participate even when opposed (for example over the role of the OAS in promoting democracy), its attitude towards both Washington and tighter hemispheric integration has remained lukewarm. In marked contrast to other countries in the region, there still appears to be a belief that Brazil has (or should have) a broader range of international options; that geopolitical realities means that the USA is not really interested in incorporating most of South America into a regional bloc; and that, in any case, Brazil is large enough to negotiate effectively with Washington on the terms of their economic and political relationship. Thus whilst it is certainly true that Brazil has been unable to resist the need to redefine and improve its relations with Washington, it has also sought to maintain its freedom of action by strengthening the viability of subregional options. This logic would explain the Brazilian decision in October 1992 to launch its so-called 'Amazonian initiative' and the announcement by President Franco in October 1993 of the proposal to expand *Mercosur* into a South American Free Trade Area.

Yet, even if Latin American countries decide to press for ever closer hemispheric regional co-operation, they would face two major sets of obstacles. First, beneath the new rhetoric of convergence and co-operation, lie a number of dilemmas that would, at a minimum, complicate the process of regional institution building. In the economic field, the agenda for any southward expansion of NAFTA has already been well established by the USA and future agreements would almost certainly cover the full range of 'intrusive' trade-related provisions (investment liberalization, intellectual property protection, liberalization of trade in services), as well as further pressure for the broader adoption of market-liberal policies. Moreover, NAFTA's rules of origin and dispute-settlement procedures would not necessarily be either acceptable or economically rational for other Latin American countries. Finally, despite its rhetorical support for maintaining relations with South America, a southward expansion of NAFTA is not in Mexico's interest, given the benefits of positioning itself as the unique place to invest for exports both north (via NAFTA) and south (via a network of bilateral FTAs).

The Mexican financial crisis of early 1995, to which the Clinton administration was forced to respond with a $US40 billion emergency rescue package, has also undoubtedly tarnished the image of Mexico as the 'model' to which the rest of the region should aspire. The collapse of the peso has undermined the assumption that NAFTA would make economic reform irreversible and would guarantee continued investor confidence. It has also exposed the underlying political fragility of the country. The new president, Ernesto Zedillo, has been weakened by the scale of the currency crisis and Mexico's very visible dependence on US assistance; by being forced to implement a stringent package of budget cuts, tax rises and wage restrictions; by continued dissension and scandals within the ranks of the ruling party; and by the continued challenge from the Zapatista rebels in the south of the country. Mexico thus highlights the deeply ambiguous relationship between the logic of economic liberalization on the one hand, and that of political liberalization on the other.

In the political sphere, whilst the emphasis on the value of democracy and the importance of the collective defence of democracy may well reflect genuinely shared values, this does not necessarily translate into practical co-operation. Thus there may still be considerable room for divergence over the best ways for democracy to be defended, as well as over the costs of collective action. In the case of Haiti, for example, there is considerable Latin American unease over the possibility of being pressed to allow the USA an easy 'exit-strategy' by taking over the long-term stabilization of the country. There are also differences over the limits to the 'new interventionism' and continued doubts over the legitimization of military intervention. Consensus over the coercive enforcement of shared norms remains uncertain—with scepticism especially marked in Colombia, Mexico, and Brazil. Such scepticism reflects the still deep gulf between, what one might call *consensual solidarism* on the one hand and *coercive solidarism* on the other. Moreover, the outbreak of fighting in late January 1995 between Peru and Ecuador and the rise of tension between Venezuela and Colombia indicate that, outside the southern cone, historic border disputes have not wholly disappeared and suggest that regional security co-operation may well face greater challenges in the second half of the 1990s.

Perhaps most important is the continuing tension between the US desire to maintain its autonomy and independence of decision on the one hand, and the Latin American desire for institutionalized multilateral co-operation on the other. Although the Clinton administration has certainly come to value the legitimacy that follows from the endorsement of the UN or regional bodies such as the OAS, it has been as reluctant as its predecessors to allow international institutions to restrict its freedom of manœuvre. Even those Latin American states that are keenest to promote more permissive understandings of intervention perceive the need to subject such intervention to the formal legal requirements of the OAS and to a consistent and credible set of criteria. In the economic field, the Latin American fear is that increased liberalization on their part will not be met by a consistent willingness on the part of the USA to forgo protectionism and economic unilateralism.

It is indeed perfectly possible that Washington will believe that it can achieve it political and economic objectives without accepting multilateral constraints on its own freedom and without making regionalism or the construction of new economic arrangements a high priority. After all, if Latin American states are already altering policies in ways which conform to US interests and if deviations from US preferences can be adequately dealt with on a bilateral level, why negotiate a free-trade agreement? Hegemony, in other words, may well make institutionalized regionalism unnecessary.

This leads to the second, and ultimately decisive, set of limits. Although there is certainly room for creative statesmanship on the part of Latin American governments (particularly at a time when the exact definition of US interests in many areas is uncertain), the response of Washington is by far the most important factor that will decide how far and how fast hemispheric regionalism proceeds. Here there are a number of significant factors which work against

US promotion of a cohesive and broadly based regionalism in the Americas.

In the first place, overall US foreign-policy interests do not point towards the creation of a close, exclusivist regional bloc. The growth of US economic regionalism and of a regionalist 'option' has been a response to progressive disenchantment with the global trading system and to the perceived unfair behaviour of major trading partners. But this has been balanced by the strongly multilateral nature of US trade and investment interests and the unwillingness to spur economic regionalism in other parts of the world. Moreover, too decisive a move towards regional blocs would risk cutting the USA off from the most dynamic world markets and would favour less efficient Latin American producers in a number of sectors over their more efficient Asian counterparts, thereby eroding the long-term competitiveness of US industry. As a result, the initiative on NAFTA has been followed by a renewed emphasis on relations with the Asia-Pacific region and the development of APEC.[33]

Second, US involvement is likely to be limited to those parts of the region in which its interests are most directly engaged. This would include Mexico, Central America, the Caribbean, and, perhaps, the Northern tier of Andean countries. The concentration of economic interests in Mexico is already very marked and, as we have seen, economic interdependence is already at a high level. Moreover, it is in this area that threats from so-called 'new security issues' (such as drug trafficking, environmental degradation, migration, and refugees) are most directly felt. Thus, even if US interests are constrained *geographically*, it will become ever harder to limit the *scope and range* of US involvement: because of the nature of the problems facing this region; because of the ever-deeper integration of the region's economies and societies; and because of the range of domestic interests and groups involved in

---

[33] NAFTA is misnamed in that future accessions to the agreement are neither politically nor legally limited to the Americas (unlike the case of the EC). The accession clause to the NAFTA treaty (Art. 2205) does not make reference to the Americas and allows for extra-continental applications for membership. The freedom for the USA to negotiate NAFTA-like agreements with third parties without the consent of Mexico and Canada underwrites Washington's predominant voice in determining the ways in which NAFTA might be extended. For a discussion of the problems of accession, see Laurence Whitehead, 'Requisites for Admission', in Smith, *The Challenge of Integration*.

the formulation of US policy. In such a situation, for example, it becomes harder for the USA to support economic reform in Mexico, but to try and downplay environmental factors or political reform; or, in the case of Haiti, to try and deal with the immediate problem of refugees, but without seeking to restructure the political complexion of the state from which they are coming. Such deepening involvement in Mexico, Central America, and the Caribbean further reduces the scope for more far-reaching regionalist arrangements with the rest of Latin America. The Mexican crisis of early 1995 may well strengthen institutionalized co-operation between Mexico and the USA (perhaps by creating monetary or financial-support mechanisms). But the high level of Congressional opposition to the rescue package also exposed the lack of political support for an engaged and activist policy in the region.

Hemispheric regionalism is of growing importance to Latin America and, to a lesser extent, to the USA, and is likely to remain so. There is much to be gained by regional co-operation and there are some issues, such as migration, transborder pollution, or the drug issue, that can only be effectively addressed on a region-wide basis. But, even in the economic field, the southward expansion of free-trade arrangements is likely to remain somewhat patchy and *ad hoc*, and to take place over a lengthy period of time. The chances of a cohesive and exclusive regional bloc in the Americas are reduced by the balance of US interests and concerns in which both globalism and regionalism will continue to be present; by the continuing ambiguities of US–Latin American relations across a range of issues; by the greater pluralism of the international system, even if the full impact of that pluralism has yet to work itself out (particularly in terms of European and Japanese foreign policies); by the emergence and consolidation of global markets for production, finance, and technology; and by the growth of global issues which cannot be contained within a purely regional framework.

Such a scenario would suggest space for a variety of regional arrangements, some hemispheric, some subregional. This would reflect the differentiation of US interests across different issues and with different Latin American states. It would also reflect the heterogeneity of the region and the variation and complexity of Latin American foreign-policy concerns. But the European example suggests that 'alphabet soup regionalism' in which many different bodies seek to assume responsibility for different areas of policy, can easily become a source of weakness and not of strength, and that the meshing of different regionalisms is in practice far from simple. For South America the worst of all possible worlds would be one in which the USA was unwilling to commit itself clearly to the region, but where protracted uncertainty about its future intentions towards the region worked to complicate, if not undermine, the recent successes in strengthening subregional co-operation and economic integration.

10

Regional Organizations in the
Arab Middle East

Charles Tripp

DURING the 1980s a number of regional organizations were created in the Middle East, involving the governments of most of the
Arab states and giving the impression of a renewed interest in and
a commitment to regionalism among the governments involved. In
1981, in the east of the Arab world, the Gulf Co-operation Council
(GCC) was established, bringing six of the Arab states of the Gulf
into a single regional organization. This was followed in 1989, in
the west of the Arab world, by the creation of the Arab Maghreb
Union (*Union du Maghreb arabe* or UMA) which grouped together
five Arab states of the North African littoral. Almost simultaneously a third organization, the Arab Co-operation Council
(ACC) sprang into existence, linking four Arab countries which
could only loosely be said to constitute a 'subregion' of the Middle
East, but which nevertheless deployed all the familiar rhetoric and
rationales of regionalism to justify its establishment.

In other words, the founders of all three organizations laid great
emphasis on the need for economic co-operation and suggested that
it made sense for states situated geographically in close, or fairly
close proximity to each other to group together into a single bloc.
Such statements were often phrased in terms of the economic
security of the member states, making direct or indirect reference to
the existence of other powerful and possibly predatory trading
blocs in the world. It was, therefore, a relatively easy transition to
insert statements about other, non-economic aspects of security
into the regionalist discourse, without suggesting that these groupings necessarily constituted military alliances in the traditional
sense of the term. Equally, there were suggestions—delicately
phrased, for reasons examined below—that the countries formed
a cultural and historical community which gave their grouping

greater meaning and which lent to geographical regionalism a certain socio-political rationale.

In short, the emergence of various regional organizations in the Middle East has been associated with forms of public justification no different in type from those witnessed elsewhere in the world. In fact, at times the rhetoric has been so similar as to suggest that a certain model of presentation is being consciously adopted. Wherever this occurs, the question which must arise is whether the easily imitated style of public rationale corresponds to the real reasons for the various states' involvement in these organizations. It will be those reasons, after all,which will determine the fate of the relevant organizations and will thus indicate, in the Middle East as elsewhere, what the substance of regionalism may be. Now that some years have passed since the initial foundation of the regional organizations mentioned above, it should be possible to come to some preliminary conclusions about their nature and thus about the nature of the phenomenon of regionalism itself among the Arab states of the Middle East.

In the Arab world, 'regionalism' has had a rather chequered history, largely because of the ambiguity of the term in Arab political discourse. During the heyday of Arab nationalism, newly gained independence from British and French tutelage led many nationalists to believe that their ideal of a single Arab nation state was imminently realizable. Anything which worked towards this end, was, therefore, regarded as laudable and anything which appeared to delay or complicate the task was seen as being in some way connected with the pernicious designs of the recently departed imperialists. In this context 'regionalism' (*al-Iqlimiyya*) was contrasted with 'nationalism' (*al-Qawmiyya*)—the latter being the only acceptable object of an Arab's political endeavours and the former being highly suspect, suggesting an acceptance of the subdivisions of the Arab world and the privileging of particular states' interests over the putative interests of the Arab nation as a whole.

However, in practice, experience tended to show that the local concerns of regimes became the driving force of Arab politics. Arab nationalist rhetoric lived on, but effective organization and political activity took place on a more parochial level, whether within a given state, or in that state's immediate regional environment. Disillusionment with the record of self-proclaimed Arab nationalists and preoccupation with political survival concentrated the minds of many on specific states' interests. Identities and interests appropriate to these states began to make themselves felt and acknowledgement of this fact of life began to be heard, even in unexpected quarters.[1] It was nevertheless noticeable that, almost without exception, those who voiced either state-specific concerns or who advocated the establishment of region-specific organizations felt obliged to add the rider that this would not harm the greater 'Arab nation's' interest, nor was it intended to create further divisions among the people of the Arab world. Be that as it may, by the 1980s, it seemed to be possible for Arab governments openly to voice these concerns, however qualified in their public discourse, and to base their diplomacy on projects aimed at enhancing their security through the establishment of avowedly region-specific organizations.

This preoccupation with security, ultimately of the governing apparatus, but also of the resources available to it, lends to the Middle Eastern experience of regionalism features that are to be found elsewhere in the world. The resources in question may be the territory of the state, its military capability, or its economic potential. These attributes allow the government to amplify its power and to extend its reach and influence, domestically and in the environment of the state it rules. In this sense, therefore, regionalism in the Middle East has come to mean the effort to make the most of a state's regional environment. This may take the form of seeking to neutralize potentially troublesome neighbours by including them in a particular organization, intending to hold them accountable to a set of rules which will allow the emergence of a certain regional order. Alternatively, it may be the grouping together of states in a deterrent alliance, in order to face up to a commonly perceived regional, or indeed extra-regional threat. Such a menace may take the form of a potential military danger, clearly identified. It might also take the form of a perceived threat to the security of a particular form of political order. It could, equally, be a threat on the economic level, in the sense that the states concerned might see their options narrowing in the future, or might believe

---

[1] See e.g. Saddam Hussein's speech at the Amman Summit of 1987, when he urged his fellow heads of state to recognize the fact that 'we are a number of countries, each with its own concerns, problems and circumstances, which are usually similar, but sometimes different': Radio Baghdad, 8 Nov. 1987, *BBC Summary of World Broadcasts* (SWB) Middle East (ME), 11 Nov. 1987 A/4–9.

that only by forming some kind of regional cartel or trading bloc will they survive similar moves elsewhere in the world.

Consequently, regionalism in the Middle East, in so far as it has manifested itself in the establishment of regional organizations, has been motivated largely by fears of existing or developing dangers to the security of regimes. The fact that such organizations have often been described and lauded in the more positive language of mutual co-operation for development has been due to a strategy of legitimation, rather than to the motives for their establishment. It is worth, therefore, examining briefly the experience of regionalism in the Middle East. This is important, since recent Middle Eastern history is rich in examples of regional organizations designed to enhance the security of their members. However, the profusion, variety, and duration of these organizations, taken together with the visible insecurity and instability which has, sometimes dramatically, characterized the international relations of the Middle East at the same time, should alert one to some of the problems involved. It should also make one look more closely at the reasons for their construction and the consequent dynamics of the organizations in question. One must ask whether the forms which these organizations took, the concerns of their members and their effectiveness, or lack of it, tell one something about the underlying political preoccupations of those involved. This may, in turn, be useful in seeking to understand the potential, and the limitations of more recently created regional organizations in the Middle East.

1. REGIONALISM: PAST EXPERIENCES

A glance at the forms of regional organization which have emerged in the Middle East since 1945 will show that such organizations have primarily been concerned with security, broadly defined. They have, for the most part, been established to allow the governments involved to preserve an existing political order within and between their countries. In some cases, this has been due to a perceived military danger which has been assumed to threaten all the states involved. Another motive, often operating jointly with the foregoing, has been the fear of potentially disruptive political developments in the region which might destabilize the politics of the states concerned by endangering the various regimes. At times, these fears have produced alliances and regional organizations which have been initially inspired by outside powers, notably Great Britain and the USA, and which were designed to answer not simply regional concerns about security, but also those of the Western powers. Other organizations, however, have been wholly the product of local concerns, reflecting in their justifications and their structures regional-specific fears and local patterns of politics.

The most obvious regional organization, spanning the entire Middle East and incorporating all of the Arab states, is the Arab League. Initially set up in 1945 by Egypt, Iraq, Saudi Arabia, Transjordan, Syria, Lebanon, and Yemen, it grew into an organization which now includes all the Arab states. The original impulses behind the creation of the Arab League were various. The immediate concerns had to do with ensuring a French withdrawal from Syria and the Lebanon and with the attempt to prevent the establishment of a Jewish state in Palestine. However, also at work was the suspicion each of the governments of the founding states had of the other that, under the flag of Arab unity, the hegemonic designs of one ruler or another would be realized. Thus, the Arab League was created somewhat paradoxically as an expression of Arab unity, but one which guaranteed the independence and sovereignty of each of the Arab states. The latter point was crucial at the time, not simply because of the fear that one or other Arab government would try to 'hijack' the organization for its own ends, but also to reassure the Lebanese that the departure of the French would not mean the immediate disappearance of Lebanon into a Greater Syria.[2]

In some respects, therefore, the Arab League has come to epitomise a specific problem of regionalism in the Middle East. That is, the public justification and 'culture' of the organization have been largely explained in terms of the goals of Arab nationalism: the breaking down of regional divisions in the Arab world and the establishment of a single Arab state, coterminous with the lands inhabited by the Arab nation. At the same time, however, the Arab League has become the forum in which the great battles of what has been call the 'Arab cold wars' have been fought.[3] These battles have

---

[2] Y. Porath, *In Search of Arab Unity 1930–1945* (London, Frank Cass, 1986), 257–90.

[3] See e.g. M. Kerr, *The Arab Cold War 1958–1967* (Oxford: OUP for RIIA, 1967).

been pre-eminently between governments which have sought to use the Arab League to extend their own interests and reinforce their own security at the expense of others.

The conflicts were at their sharpest in the 1950s and the 1960s, when the League tended to be divided between those governments which styled themselves as 'progressive' and those which were seen as 'conservative'. The fact that both sides tended to justify their activities with reference to their own allegedly uniquely correct understanding of the interests and welfare of the 'Arab nation' merely added bitterness to the argument. In the 1970s and 1980s, the divide tended to revolve around different Arab governments' attitudes to Israel and, specifically, to Egypt's signing of a peace treaty with Israel. This resulted in Egypt's expulsion from the League for ten years, until attitudes towards Israel, and towards the indispensability of Egypt itself, among the other Arab governments led to Egypt's readmission in 1989. The apparent harmony of the Arab states was short-lived. In 1990, the mixed reactions of the Arab states to Iraq's invasion and annexation of its fellow League member Kuwait led to the inability of the League itself to take any effective action. And the initiation of the Middle East peace process in 1992 has not perceptibly enhanced the desire for co-operation among member states.

These are just some of the major issues which have divided members of the Arab League. They have not been the only items on the agenda of the organization. Unsurprisingly, however, the most contentious issues have also been those where the fundamental interests of the regimes of the member states have been at stake. In the much less sensitive areas of educational and cultural co-operation, a more harmonious atmosphere has tended to prevail.[4] In matters of economic co-operation, the degree of agreement has tended to be in inverse proportion to the centrality of the economic issues being debated. This is probably not surprising in an organization which is, after all, a gathering of independent, sovereign states, each with their individual conceptions of national interest. This is the political reality which no amount of appeals to Arab unity or Arab nationalism can dispel.

Thus, although it does act as a forum for discussion among the Arab states, as a regional organization it has proved to be largely

---

[4] See the essays by F. Burgat, M. Ben Hammed, and M. Mansouri in M. Flory and P. S. Agate (eds.), *Le Système regional arabe* (Paris: CNRS, 1989), 199–272.

ineffectual in matters of major importance. In some respects, the problem appears to stem firstly, from the fact that there is no agreement on what the 'Arab interest' may comprise and, secondly, there is as yet no agreed procedure for establishing what that interest may be in any specific case. None of the Arab heads of state who claim to represent their countries in the councils of the Arab League has been democratically elected and, consequently, there is no particular reason why their views on the 'interests of the Arab nation' should be privileged over others. Indeed, it has been their very insecurity on this score which has increased the sharpness of their disputes and added to the depth of divisions within the Arab world.

Preoccupations of this kind led to the rise and fall of another form of regional organization in the Arab world during the 1950s and 1960s. This was the United Arab Republic, formed between Egypt and Syria in 1958. Under the terms of its constitution, the two countries were to form equal parts of a unitary state. In fact, as might have been supposed, the UAR was dominated by the Egyptian partner which, under the authoritarian direction of President Gamal Abd al-Nasir (Nasser), increasingly treated Syria as a province of Egypt. This was to lead eventually in 1961 to the secession of Syria, since powerful sectors of Syrian society had come to resent the fact that the interests of Nasser had so obviously come to dominate the union, at the expense of their own interests. The detailed history of the UAR should not detain us here, but there are a number of aspects of this regional organization which are worth highlighting since they are to recur in relation to other regional organizations in the Middle East.[5]

First, the UAR was both established and dissolved essentially by *coups d'état*, carried out by small, unrepresentative, but powerful cliques in Syria. Despite the fact that the union was presented to the public as a first step on the road to realizing the alleged dream of Arab unity, very few people had been consulted and it was, consequently, impossible to establish what degree of enthusiasm might have existed for the adventure. Secondly, and relatedly, the coups which both set up and destroyed the organization were motivated by very specific fears on the part of particular groupings in Syria. In 1958, these fears revolved around the suspected ambitions of the

[5] For the best discussion of the events leading up to the formation of the UAR, see P. Seale, *The Struggle for Syria* (London: IB Tauris, 1986), 186 ff.

Syrian Communist Party, on the one hand, and of Hashemite Iraq, on the other. The Egypt of Nasser appeared, at the time, to be an effective counterweight to both of these threats and, therefore, the idea of unity appealed to a wide range of political actors in Syria. By 1961, many of these same actors had realized that the subordination they had tried to avoid was likely to emanate from Egypt itself: not only had Syria become effectively a province of the Egyptian administration, but Nasser's socialist and nationalizing measures were now being applied to Syrian agricultural and commercial interests. Lastly, the formation of the union served to alarm and to alienate other states in the region which feared that the coming together of Egypt and Syria was the prelude of a more ambitious Nasserist project of bringing greater and greater segments of the Middle East under his control.

The establishment of this particular regional organization, therefore, can be seen to illustrate a number of general features which have characterized others in the Middle East. First, its public rationales—the enhancement of the Arab nationalist ideal of unity and the advancement of regional co-operation for economic development—had little to do with the fundamental reasons for its establishment, or its dissolution. These stemmed from the fears and ambitions of small numbers of people, well situated, largely because of their control of the security forces, to act in the name of their state. Secondly, the organization itself inevitably became the instrument of the most powerful forces within it. Thus, it may have retained the appearance of a regional organization, but the underlying reality was the interest of the government of Egypt, personified by Nasser. Whilst those interests appeared to coincide with a significant number of well-placed Syrians, some semblance of regional co-operation and collegiality could be preserved. Increasingly, however, the dictatorial methods which were the hallmark of Nasser's political order made themselves felt. These methods determined the direction of command within the organization, as well as the effective structure of the organization itself, regardless of the constitutional provisions underpinning its formation. Thirdly, this particular regional organization was seen as a threat by all the other governments in the region which either disagreed with Nasser's political agenda, or which failed to subordinate their own concerns to his influence.

During the 1950s, with the extension of the Cold War to the

Middle East, a number of regional organizations were proposed by or established with the aid of the USA and Great Britain. These were primarily concerned with questions of military security, and were specifically aimed at countering the perceived threat from the USSR. In the Arab world, at least, all such organizations were marked by a number of fundamental flaws which eventually led to their dissolution. In the first place, whilst the USSR incontrovertibly came high on the list of threats to British and American interests in the Middle East, this view could not be shared by many of the Arab states at the time. On the contrary, their governments tended to regard the major threats as coming either from Israel or from other Arab states. In both regards, the aid which the USSR could offer was seen as being potentially more useful than that which was offered by the Western powers. The latter were still seen as being unregenerate imperialists, responsible for the creation of the state of Israel. Consequently, for newly established regimes in recently independent countries, too close an association with the West was not simply irksome, but tended also to undermine the legitimacy of the regime in question. As a result, organizations such as the Baghdad Pact (later to become the Central Treaty Organization, CENTO) were not only short-lived and ineffective, but may also have contributed to the destabilization of those governments which adhered to it.[6]

2. PRESENT FORMS

A rather more successful regional organization, established at the suggestion and on the advice of the British, has been the United Arab Emirates. The union had been intended to group together all the small Gulf states—Bahrain, Qatar, and the seven Trucial States—to enable them to protect themselves once the British withdrew from the Persian Gulf in 1971. In the event, the ruling houses of Bahrain and Qatar saw no particular reason to tie themselves to

---

[6] The Baghdad Pact was a defence pact set up in 1955 which linked Turkey, Iran, Iraq, and Great Britain, supported by the USA. It was vehemently opposed by Nasser in Egypt, and consequently by many Arab nationalists across the Middle East who looked to him for leadership. See E. Monroe, *Britain's Moment in the Middle East 1914–1956* (London: Chatto & Windus, 1963), 180–9; and Richard L. Jasse, 'The Baghdad Pact: Cold War or Colonialism', *Middle East Studies*, 27 (Jan. 1991), 140–56.

a federation with other rulers who could not be expected to share
their own concerns. To outsiders it may have appeared that
the interests of these rulers would be more or less identical but
clearly this was not the case, at least at the time the UAE was
formed.[7]

However, the rulers of the small Trucial States did see some
advantage in forming a federation. In the first place, the smaller and
poorer members could see that they would benefit from the relative
wealth of Abu Dhabi, the largest and richest of the UAE. As far as
Abu Dhabi was concerned, the attachment of the other statès, even
if it did imply some financial obligations, would at least give Abu
Dhabi itself greater weight in the region. The fear, as always, was
that, as soon as British protection ended, powerful regional states,
notably Saudi Arabia or Iran, would inexorably move first to
influence, then to dominate, and, possibly, eventually take over
their smaller and weaker neighbours. Despite the differences which
have occasionally erupted among the rulers of the seven Emirates,
the belief that they enjoy more freedom of action and security as
part of the UAE than as separate small states has kept the federation together.

The reasons for that cohesion are as significant as the reasons for
the collapse of the UAR a decade or so earlier. First, the specific
interests of the ruling houses can be taken to be broadly similar, if
not identical in all respects. Secondly, the informal understandings
which exist amongst all members of the UAE in what is essentially
a small society mean that severe divergences of interest are likely to
be noticed immediately. Thirdly, none of the parties which entered
into this regional organization appears to have done so with any of
the illusions which have characterized other regionalist endeavours.
The Union, like power itself, rests unashamedly with the ruling
families of the seven members of the federation, making the limits
of their co-operation more clear-cut. There exists a more or less
accepted hierarchy amongst the rulers, largely based on their relative wealth. This makes it unlikely that the corrosive effects of
sensed exploitation or unfair advantage will take hold, even if some
of the members may occasionally resent Abu Dhabi's pre-eminence.

In many respects, it was this experience of co-operation within a
flexible framework, based on similar concerns and informal styles

[7] F. Heard-Bey, *From Trucial States to United Arab Emirates* (London: Longman,
1982), 341–70.

of political behaviour which encouraged the emergence of the Gulf Co-operation Council in 1981. This organization brought together Saudi Arabia, Kuwait, Bahrain, Qatar, the UAE, and Oman into a pact ostensibly aimed at economic co-operation, but in fact established to enhance the internal and external security of the states concerned.[8] In Iran, the Islamic Republic had been established in 1979 as a result of the revolution which had overthrown the Shah. Fired by their success and inspired by their mission, Iran's leaders had immediately begun to call for similar revolutions elsewhere in the region. In 1980, partly as a result of the regional instability caused by these events, Iraq invaded Iran and the two states were thereafter locked in war with one another.

For the oil-rich but vulnerable monarchies of the Gulf, the war and Iranian enmity seemed to threaten both their military security and their internal security. Given the structures of their societies and their states, there was not a great deal that the members of the GCC could do—or, as it proved, were willing to do—to enhance their military security. However, they could and did take steps to enhance their internal security. This was the area in which the enmity of Iran was most likely to manifest itself and this was also the area in which the ruling élites of the GCC states had long been most proficient. As the experience of the following decade proved, internal security co-operation was the area of the most effective regional co-operation between the GCC states. Not only were there some notable successes for the security and intelligence organs of some of the states, but this appeared to be the area in which formal commitments or accords corresponded most closely with effective, informal patterns of behaviour.[9]

In other spheres, co-operation was less effective and, indeed, practically non-existent. On the economic front, despite the early talk of regional co-operation for economic development, the economies of these oil-rich states were structured in such a way that meaningful co-operation was more or less precluded. In the first place, an infinitesimal proportion of the economic activities of these states was taken up with trade with each other. All of them import

[8] E. Webman, 'The Gulf States', in C. Legum et al. (eds.), Middle East Contemporary Survey, v. 1980–1981 (New York: Holmes & Meier, 1982), 458–65.

[9] J. W. Twinham, 'The Gulf Co-operation Council', in C. F. Doran and S. W. Buck (eds.), The Gulf, Energy and Global Security (Boulder, Colo.: Lynne Rienner, 1983), 113–15.

goods and labour from outside the region. Similarly, their sole, if very substantial export—oil—naturally goes to consumer states outside the region. Consequently, there was very little substance to back up talk of regional economic co-operation. Secondly, each government was jealous of its own schemes for development and embarked upon these without any consultation with other members of the GCC. It was evident that they saw no obligation to consult the other members on such domestic matters and, furthermore, to have taken on board the priorities of others might have been assumed by domestic constituencies to have been a form of unjust neglect.[10] In political orders built upon networks of patronage, this is a dangerous sentiment to encourage. Lastly, even in the area of their major export, oil, there was no particular co-operation amongst the GCC states. Saudi Arabia tried to give the lead to all of the OPEC states, including, of course, the GCC oil producers, such as Kuwait and the UAE. However, by the 1990s the latter two, in particular, were increasingly dismissive of the OPEC quota system and were determined to pursue their own production targets, regardless of other OPEC or GCC members' concerns.[11]

On questions of defence co-operation, the inadequacy of the GCC as a regional organization was even more evident. During the eight years of the Iran–Iraq war, there had been disagreement amongst the GCC members about the seriousness of the military threat which they faced from Iran. The 'overspill' of the war, in fact, scarcely touched them. When it did, in the shape of increasing Iranian attacks on Kuwaiti shipping towards the end of the war, the Kuwaiti government essentially called in the protection of outside powers. This underlined the fact that the GCC states themselves, whatever provision they had been making for their own individual defence during the war years, had singularly failed to create any form of effective regional defence force. The gesture in this direction—the ambitiously named Peninsula Shield—was a force of less than 10,000 men whose significance was largely symbolic. Some of the rulers of the GCC states had spent lavishly on the procurement of weapons for their own national armed forces, but had done little to give teeth to regional defence co-operation and had indeed shied away from the logistical and personnel implications of making such

---

[10] Twinham, 'The Gulf Co-operation Council', 109–13.
[11] *International Herald Tribune*, 4 Dec. 1989; *Financial Times*, 22 Feb. 1990.

a defence capability effective.[12] In August 1990, when Iraq invaded Kuwait, the weakness of the GCC as a regional security organization was all too obvious.

Despite the limitations of the GCC, it appeared to other states in the Arab world that it did represent an attempt by a group of states to build on common concerns and to address problems specific to the region in question. There was, after all, no denying the proximity and vulnerability of the Gulf states to the Iran–Iraq conflict. It was also noticeable that, following the hopes and disillusionment which had characterized most of the moves at pan-Arab co-operation during the previous three decades, by the mid-1980s it had become possible for governments to talk of region-specific concerns, without bringing down on their heads the full weight of Arab nationalist criticism. Considerations such as these may have contributed to the revival, in 1989, of the old idea of Maghrebi union. In February 1989, at a summit of heads of state in Marrakesh, the *Union du Maghreb arabe* (UMA) was founded, comprising the five North African states of Mauritania, Morocco, Algeria, Tunisia, and Libya. There had been a number of abortive attempts in previous decades to institutionalize various schemes for forms of integration between the Arab states of North Africa. These had either become moribund through the lack of commitment on the part of the members, or else had ended in recriminations and acrimony. In 1989, however, in the shape of UMA, the idea of regional co-operation among the states of the Maghreb appeared to take on institutional form.[13]

The incentives for the creation of the UMA in 1989 were economic, as well as political, in so far as these two spheres can be separated. The governments of all the countries involved were concerned about their ability to control and protect their economies from externally generated shocks. They were also concerned, as ever, about the possibility that severe conflicts of interest among and between each other might have the capacity to damage the security of each regime. In the economic sphere, there was evidently some concern in Morocco, Algeria, and Tunisia, in particular, that the growing unity and protectionism of the European Community

[12] D. Gold, 'The Gulf States', in I. Rabinovich and H. Shaked (eds.), *Middle East Contemporary Survey*, ix. 1984–1985 (Tel Aviv: Tel Aviv University, 1987), 380–2.

[13] See A. Aghrout and K. Sutton, 'Regional Economic Union in the Maghreb', *Journal of Modern Asian Studies*, 28/1 (1990), 115–39.

would permanently turn the terms of trade against them. The view from North Africa was that a powerful economic bloc was forming on the other side of the Mediterranean and that, unless the Maghrebi states co-operated with one another, they would remain vulnerable to the overwhelming economic power of the EC.

In the political sphere, there appear to have been a number of considerations at work. The UMA seemed to provide a framework for cementing the newly restored relations between Morocco and Algeria. Hitherto, the dispute over sovereignty in the Western Sahara and over Algerian help for the guerrilla movement, Polisario, had soured and eventually had led to the break in diplomatic relations between the two states. The UMA, by bringing all the North African states (except Egypt) into a single organization, seemed also to provide a framework for the 'taming' of Libya's leader, Muammar Qadhafi. The latter had tried—and failed—any number of ill-considered 'unity' schemes during the previous twenty years with other Maghreb states. However, these had, as often as not, been aimed specifically at excluding or forming an alliance against one or more of the others. The idea of including Libya in a regional organization which included all the other states, therefore, was due to a commonly seen desire in regional organizations to include the unpredictable or maverick state within a collective framework as a means of controlling, or at least monitoring its government's behaviour.

As is often the case, the reality of the UMA proved considerably less spectacular than the rhetoric of its foundation and the ambitions spelled out in the 'unity project' had suggested. In the first place, the possibilities for economic co-operation were not immediately apparent. Trade amongst the five states of the UMA in 1988 constituted a mere 4.5 per cent of their total trade.[14] Furthermore, the pattern of their trade with the EC (accounting for some 75 per cent) seemed to suggest that they were more likely to be competing against each other. Any move to co-operate or to organize joint negotiating positions would have to encounter possible opposition from powerful economic constituencies in some of the states. It was also evident that the forms of their economies were very different: Morocco and Tunisia had more or less liberal economic regimes, with very substantial private sectors in agriculture, industry, and

---

[14] Aghrout and Sutton, 125–6.

services. The economy of Algeria was dominated by a state sector seeking to deal with the difficult social, economic, and political legacies of state-subsidized inefficiency. In Libya, the economy was almost wholly in the hands of the state, with only recently instituted moves to hand such sectors as retailing back to the private sector, as a means of compensating for a decade of state-supervised chaos and shortages.

On the political front, despite the talk of co-ordination and co-operation, little of substance was achieved. Either the governments of the five countries were preoccupied with internal political upheavals, as was the case increasingly with Algeria, or they simply disagreed with one another on major issues. Thus, the second UMA summit, planned for September 1989 in Tripoli was postponed to January 1990 and moved to Tunis. Reportedly, this was due to the distraction of Qadhafi whose attention had shifted elsewhere. When it did take place in Tunis, the Mauritanian President stayed away, ostensibly for personal reasons, but more probably because of renewed conflict over the Western Sahara and disagreements with Morocco. This issue appeared to dominate the summit and, despite talk in the final communiqué about examining defence co-ordination and co-operation, nothing was achieved and various intra-Maghreb grievances were aired.[15]

A similar pattern appears to have been followed at subsequent UMA summits. King Hassan of Morocco stayed away from the March 1991 summit in Libya and Qadhafi stayed away from the September 1991 summit in Casablanca. At the latter meeting, it was agreed that UMA summit decisions should no longer be reached by consensus, but that simple majority would suffice. This was probably in part a reaction to the paralysis which afflicted the UMA at the time of the Iraqi invasion of Kuwait. Reflecting the chaos in the Arab League, the five states of the UMA were unable to take a joint decision on the crisis. Instead, each government reacted individually and, in some cases, with a good deal of inconsistency and the UMA itself proved worthless as a forum for co-ordination or mediation.[16] Perhaps not surprisingly, discussions between the UMA and southern European governments on the creation of a Mediterranean security framework along the lines of

---

[15] *Le Monde*, 16 Jan. 1990; P. Hiett, 'The Maghreb–Summit Hitches', *Middle East International*, 2 Feb. 1990.
[16] F. Soudan, 'Maghreb: Le Miroir brisé', *Jeune Afrique*, 22 Aug. 1990, 52–3.

the CSCE have also produced few results. By 1992, the UMA appeared to have achieved little and to have become, as had so many regional 'organizations' before it, nothing more than a forum which the rulers of the states concerned could use as part of their own unilateral diplomatic strategies. It had acquired little institutional reality and seemed to materialize only at periodic summit meetings between the rulers.[17]

A regional organization of even less substance appeared suddenly and, perhaps not by chance, at the same time as the UMA was created. This was the short-lived Arab Co-operation Council (ACC) formed between Egypt, Jordan, Iraq, and the then Yemen Arab Republic. Reiterating the now familiar rhetoric of co-operation for economic development, the leaders of the four states met in Egypt at much the same time as the Marrakesh summit was laying the groundwork for the UMA and declared that they, too, were forming a regional organization aimed at promoting trade and prosperity amongst their countries. Little groundwork had been done before the foundation of this organization. Furthermore, the patterns of trade between the four suggested that they had a long way to go before anything like a meaningful economic trading bloc could be established.

The impression gained, however, is that the ACC was a strategic ploy on the part of its members, each of which was pursuing its own ends. As far as Egypt was concerned, it was important that the relationship with Iraq, established during the Iran–Iraq war, be maintained. Not only was this potentially profitable for the Egyptian arms industry, but it would also serve to contain Syria at a time when an old pattern of Egyptian–Syrian rivalry for influence in the Levant was beginning to re-emerge. There may also have been a consideration, on the part of Egypt's rulers, that it was important to bring Iraq into some form of alliance or bloc in order to moderate its behaviour in the region following the end of the Iraq–Iran war. For Iraq, a similar anti-Syrian motive was undoubtedly present: the notion that Syria was now encircled by an apparently pro-Iraqi alliance was an attractive one for Saddam Hussein. It is also possible that he saw the ACC as a means of encircling Saudi Arabia in the other direction. The Iraqi leader had always resented the fact that Iraq had been excluded from the GCC, since

[17] For a somewhat more positive view of the UMA, see Claire Spencer, 'The Maghreb in the 1990s', *Adelphi Paper*, 274 (London: IISS, 1993).

he saw this as a natural forum in which Iraq could exercise its leadership. He was also feeling more specifically aggrieved at the oil-rich Gulf states as the cost of the debt Iraq had run up with them during the eight-year war with Iran began to take its toll on Iraq's post-war recovery plans.

In the event, this sense of injury came to dominate Saddam Hussein's strategic thinking and led to the invasion of Kuwait in the summer of 1990. The Iraqi leader may have been pleased by the attitude of his fellow ACC members, Jordan and Yemen, since they both sought to prevent the international retribution which was to follow Iraq's act of violence. However, the leading role which Egypt played in the organization and implementation of this retribution demonstrated how flimsy an affair the ACC had been. It was evident from President Mubarak's remarks in August 1990 that he felt personally betrayed by Saddam Hussein.[18] The implication was that a very personal bond of trust between two rulers had been broken. Furthermore, as the crisis deepened and as the ambivalence of the Yemeni and Jordanian governments increased, similar language about the betrayal of personal trust was used in relation to them as well. In short, the Gulf crisis showed up in graphic form the way in which the language of regionalism and regional organizations had come to be accepted as a legitimating vocabulary for much more specific regime-centred interests and strategies. Where once the language of pan-Arabism had been used to disguise and legitimate state-based ambitions and concerns, so now the language of regional co-operation was being used to confer a kind of authority on the regional policies and goals of various rulers.

3. EXPLAINING REGIONALISM IN THE MIDDLE EAST

When seeking to explain regionalism in the Middle East, it is perhaps useful to understand that the forms it has taken in the present and in the recent past have been shaped by a combination of external and internal forces. That is, the impulse to come together into a single regional grouping has often come from developments and potential threats external to the states in question.

---

[18] President Mubarak's news conference, broadcast on Arab Republic of Egypt Radio, Cairo, 8 Aug. 1990, *BBC SWB/ME*, 10 Aug. 1990 A/7–12.

Equally, the response to such threats, in the shape of the regional organization itself, has been of external inspiration and has, for that reason, taken on an institutional form which promises to order the relationships between the rulers of the states concerned in a dramatically different way than heretofore. In such situations, the cure, if pursued wholeheartedly, may be seen as worse than the malady, even though the latter is regarded as real enough. Thus, where both the initial impulse and the forms of the response are so obviously externally inspired, the indigenous ordering of politics may transform or thwart the whole enterprise, adapting it to the underlying concerns of domestic politics in the relevant states. These might have produced the demand for some kind of concerted response in the first place, but would find the regionalist framework ultimately difficult to accept as a means of mediating power.

In explaining regionalism in the Middle East, therefore, it is worth thinking of four of the factors which recur in the analysis of the impulses for the renewed interest in regionalism and which also occur in the Middle East, but with certain specificities characteristic of the politics of the states involved—specificities which also set limits on the degree of regional integration which can be expected. These four factors are, broadly speaking, first, the influence of external impulses to suggest regionalism as a particular kind of response to certain forms of common problem; secondly, the question of political interdependence and the role it plays in suggesting the identity of appropriate states for a regional grouping; thirdly, the economic considerations of the governments concerned and the degree to which regional co-operation in this sphere is seen as an effective way of maximizing benefits; lastly, the question of security of a non-economic kind is one which has suggested various kinds of response, including that of regional co-operation. In all of these areas, there has clearly been a belief among governments of most of the Arab states in the Middle East during the 1980s that a regionalist response, generally understood, might be an effective way of dealing with the challenges they face. Once embarked upon, however, the implications of such a response for the interests and normal ways of proceeding of particular regimes have often proved to be too radical. As a result, the regionalist impulse has been transformed and adapted to suit these more pressing interests. The effect has been to paralyse and often to bypass the regional organizations themselves. Even where they continue to maintain a formal existence, the impression more often than not is that the real business of responding to external challenges, of shaping political alliances, of managing the economy, and of handling security is being conducted elsewhere. In short, the way in which regionalism has been mediated through the politics of the Middle Eastern states must throw into some doubt the substantive nature of regionalism in the area.

As far as external impulses are concerned, it is as well to bear in mind the associations and values which the language of regional co-operation has come to possess in the discourse of international politics. It has become, in some respects, an authoritative norm, encouraged by the dominant powers in the international order. To be seen to be working for regionally co-operative goals, to be making compromises over particular nationalist or state-based agendas, and to enter into some kind of institutional framework which promises to guarantee the order thereby worked out are all regarded as praiseworthy endeavours in two senses. First, these efforts are taken to confer a kind of responsibility upon states seeking the approval of the major powers. Such states are seeking favourable trading status, material benefits, or military assistance and adherence to a regional organization can lead to their requests and their arguments being taken more seriously than if they were acting individually. For the weaker and smaller states of the Middle East, this is clearly something of an advantage. Secondly, the ways in which adherence to such organizations has been portrayed in domestic political debate would suggest that it is also seen as a legitimizing device within the states concerned. Not only is it often suggested that these organizations are likely to produce untold benefits for the populations of the states concerned, but it appears to be yet another device whereby the unelected rulers of these states seek to reinforce their claim to speak for and to represent their people. Precisely because there are these other purposes involved in the appearance of various forms of regionalism in the Middle East, one should be wary of assigning too much effective weight to the resulting organizations.

It is true that governments in the Middle East, no less than governments elsewhere, desire a regionally secure environment and have come to see some purpose in making the most of whatever degree of interdependence may exist between their countries and others in the region. However, experience has tended to show that what may appear to be a good basis for reciprocity, has proved to excite suspicions on both sides that an unequal deal is being struck. This seems to be exacerbated by the authoritarian governing styles of most Middle Eastern governments. Rulers who are loath to make significant compromises with domestic constituencies, do not appear to be particularly willing to make compromises with neighbouring states. It remains to be seen whether the moves—albeit partial—towards greater democracy in parts of the Arab Middle East will substantially change this picture. Given the very partial and patchy nature of the democratization process, it seems unlikely to have any significant impact on regional co-operation, at least in the short term.

A recent example of the mismatch between stated intentions and the actuality of regional power can be seen in the results of the Damascus Declaration of 1991. In the wake of the liberation of Kuwait, the Arab members of the anti-Iraqi alliance (Egypt, Syria, and the seven states of the GCC) indicated in a declaration issued in Damascus in March 1991 that they would thenceforth co-operate in reinforcing the security of the Gulf states. The core of the idea appeared to be that Egypt and Syria would supply sufficient numbers of troops to create an effective deterrent force in the Gulf, whilst the oil-rich Gulf states would reward Egypt and Syria handsomely for their efforts. Despite repeated appeals to the 'spirit of the Damascus Declaration' during the following year or so, nothing substantial materialized. So disillusioned did Egypt and Syria become that they withdrew their forces from the Gulf. For their part, the Gulf states themselves pursued quite different paths to enhance their security: they entered into bilateral defence co-operation agreements with the USA, the UK, and France and spent lavishly on acquiring new weapons systems from these same states.[19]

This experience leads one to suspect that the political interdependence which made so much sense to the external parties as the foundation for regional co-operation and order, meant something rather different to the states of the region itself. Thus, the rhetoric of regionalism, apparently in evidence in the spring of 1991, could not long survive the more pressing preoccupations of the regimes in question. One of these preoccupations—and a telling one for the future of Arab regional organizations—was that allowing Egypt

[19] C. Tripp, 'The Gulf States and Iraq', *Survival*, 34/3 (Autumn 1992), 44–51.

and Syria effectively to take charge of a large part of the external defence of the Gulf states would give them undue influence over the Gulf states' domestic and regional priorities. In short, the fear existed in the Gulf states that troops from other Arab states, once installed in sufficient numbers in the Gulf, would give the relevant governments the opportunity to intervene in the political direction of these states. This was not an unfounded fear. Indeed, it refers back to the distinctive form of interdependence which exists in the Arab world. This could be described as 'political interdependence'. Far from being the basis for effective regional co-operation, it has been the cause of lasting mutual suspicion.

Such fears were at their most extreme during the years when Arab nationalism appeared to the dominant ideology of the Middle East. However, they still survive in the suspicion that many Arab governments have that other Arab governments may try to speak to their subjects directly, seeking to bend them to their will. It was a suspicion resuscitated in a dramatic form during the Gulf crisis, when Saddam Hussein tried precisely such a tactic in an attempt to escape from his predicament. Even without such a blatant use of the tactic, however, it is this lingering apprehension which causes many Arab regimes to fear for the permeability of their societies and their politics to the influences of other Arab regimes. This is perhaps understandable in a world where the title to rule remains largely disputed and where the claims of governments to represent their people are so blatantly without foundation. Inevitably, in such circumstances, structures of regional co-operation may appear to resemble structures for regional intervention. For those governments fearful of the implications of this for their own control and sovereignty, the answer has been to deprive the structures or organizations themselves of any institutional solidity. Indeed, this could be said to be a distinctive feature of regional organizations in the Arab Middle East and, as such, it is but a reflection of the internal organization of power within the states themselves.

This latter feature has lain behind the weakness of most of the regional organizations set up in the Middle East and will continue to undermine future regional structures for as long as the governments concerned refuse to submit themselves to any institutional order in their domestic environments. To invest an institution with power, to encourage the growth of institutional memory, to establish impersonal norms of political behaviour, and to submit to the rule of law, regardless of the outcome for one's own political survival, would be to go against the practice of most of the Middle Eastern states. Highly personalized political regimes, founded on patronage and on the principle that the ruler should never be systematically answerable to the ruled, cannot contemplate with equanimity the establishment of a system which would inevitably entail their destruction.

In the setting of domestic politics, this outcome has been avoided by the majority of the governments of the Arab states, although some have found it politic to maintain some semblance of institutional structure, in the form of political parties, national assemblies, and so forth. When people begin to take these structures seriously and seek to use them to indict the record of government, or simply to question its competence, the outcome has often been violent. The authoritarian impulse has been quick to emerge once the institutions threaten to take on a life of their own. In the regional sphere, there has been no less of a show of adherence to 'frameworks for co-operation', to regional organizations, and to all the formality, procedures, and etiquette which have come to be associated with international organizations. However, the underlying reality has remained the jealousy guarded preserve of the ruler's power. This is no more likely to be given away to a regional organization than it would be to a rival organization within the state itself.

In part for similar reasons, the third element in considerations of regional co-operation, economic co-operation, has not been as great as the rhetoric and the proclaimed intentions have suggested it should be. Indeed, the prospect of economic interdependence forming the basis of significant regional organizations is slight. In part, this is due to the patterns of trade within the Middle East. The percentage of external trade devoted to trade with other Middle Eastern states is extremely small and generally concerns areas of peripheral concern to the economies of the states involved. There is, consequently, little incentive for governments to become involved in regulating a sphere of activity which is so small a part of their preoccupations. However, there is another reason for the weakness of a possible economic basis for regional co-operation. This is connected to the problems of weak institutions and authoritarian, often arbitrary government. The private sector in the majority of Middle Eastern states is politically weak, even if it can command considerable economic resources. In general, these resources will not be able to come near to matching the resources controlled by government.[20]

More to the point, the weakness of the civil society, of which the private entrepreneurs form a part, as well as the prevalence of patronage as a condition for economic success, make these groups and their interests wholly subordinate to the ruling regime. Below the restricted level of government, therefore, there exist few of the organic interconnections which might encourage regionalism. Instead, the business sector takes its lead from the government, encouraged more often than not to see its interests in wholly individual, rather then collective terms. As a result, initiatives for regional co-operation come exclusively from the restricted circles of the rulers. Indeed, any other source of political initiative would be regarded by those rulers with the utmost suspicion and would either be stifled or appropriated by them. Consequently, it will be the ruler's agenda which will determine the shape and the substance of any regional organization—and such an organization will only take on the appearance of life when animated by the concerted activity of the rulers concerned.[21]

Naturally, there are some issues which concern these rulers more than others and, consequently, there will be occasions when concerted action can produce effective regional co-operation. In particular, this appears to have been the case in matters of regime security, where a number of regimes have perceived a broadly analogous threat to their survival—a threat, moreover, which they see little profit in themselves exploiting at the expense of their neighbours and which is taken to threaten them all in similar ways. Such has been the case among the governments of the GCC in the sphere of internal security when faced by the kind of challenge represented by the radical Islamic protest movements or by secular opposition in the form of nationalists, republicans, and democrats. It has also been suggested that similar concerns about the threat to internal security posed by their respective Islamic radical or protest movements may draw three members of the UMA—Morocco, Algeria, and Tunisia—together into a close working alliance, involv-

---

[20] Y. Sayigh, 'A New Framework for Complementarity among the Arab Economies', in I. Ibrahim (ed.), *Arab Resources* (London: Croom Helm, 1983), 147–67; by the same author see also, *The Arab Economy* (Oxford: OUP, 1982).

[21] This has been precisely the pattern of behaviour of the ACC, the UMA, and is also one of the more obvious characteristics of the GCC.

ing shared intelligence and internal security co-operation. In both cases, the existence of a regional organization does not necessarily facilitate co-operation of a kind that might take place in any event, but it does provide a form of publicly justifiable, legitimating cover for these preoccupations which remain so close the rulers' hearts. It must be here that any prospects for the success of regional co-operation will stand or fall, but such co-operation will depend upon the enthusiasm and political survival of the regimes concerned.

In the Middle East, as in other parts of the world, the impulse to regionalism, in the sense of creating collective organizations to deal with common problems, stems from a mixture of factors, both external and internal. The problems for which regionalist organizations are seeking to provide solutions, are in part a result of an international balance of power which Middle Eastern states, like their counterparts elsewhere in much of Asia, Africa, and Latin America, feel is tilted against them. In part, however, the problems lie a good deal closer to home and have to do with regional imbalances of power and threats to the security of regimes. Regionalism seemed to provide a useful international language, as well as, initially, a model of collective organization which might allow the governments of these states to address these problems satisfactorily.

However, it became clear from the moment of their inception that regional organizations, if taken seriously as mechanisms for collective decision-making, would provide a threat to these same regimes as radical as that of the various forms of menace to which they were ostensibly a response. Consequently, the limits on regionalism rapidly became apparent. These limits have stemmed in large part from the ways in which domestic politics in these states have been organized and are thus shaped by the preoccupations of the regimes concerned. Chief amongst these preoccupations is the refusal to share power with those who are not in some way obligated to the regime. This authoritarian and ultimately clannish impulse has rendered ineffective many of the institutions of the state, whatever their degree of formal definition. Equally, it has served to neutralize any regional organization which might demand that its members renounce even a portion of their jealously guarded sovereignty. The refusal to yield such powers to domestic institutions clearly bodes ill for the attempt by regional organizations to acquire the kinds of powers which would give substance to regionalism. In the absence of such substance the suspicion must remain that the rhetoric of regionalism is being used as a disguise for the active pursuit of other, more state-centred concerns, even if these are being pursued bilaterally in association with other like-minded regimes.

4. CONCLUSIONS

As far as regionalism in the Middle East is concerned, the prospects for grandiose, region-wide organizations which assume incremental growth of the institutional basis for co-operation would appear to be meagre. Not only will the purposes of the organization become vaguer the larger the number of states included within it, but also the fierce mistrust of institutions as repositories of real power would deprive any such organization of effective command. In the Middle East, as in other regions of the world, there are many subregions, based on socio-economic links, geographical proximity, common security concerns, and similar political-cultural formations. As an example, the GCC has managed to endure because it has brought together a number of states which share three of the four above features and thus form a relatively coherent subregion. The ACC evaporated largely because its member states shared none of them. For much the same reasons, the organization envisaged by the Damascus Declaration stood little chance of emerging. However, whilst it may be true that the GCC has endured, it is harder to say with any certainty what it has achieved, beyond that which its member states have achieved bilaterally.

Given the structure and the priorities of most Middle Eastern regimes, the prospects of bilateral, sometimes multilateral, but generally *ad hoc* and informal agreements would appear to be better than those for effective regional institutions. Among Middle Eastern states themselves, these agreements may often be achieved within the apparent framework of a regional organization. However, the latter is likely to be little more than a legitimating cover for the more pressing concerns of the regimes. It would be the material manifestation of a discourse in which 'regionalism' itself has come to take on a positive value, and may, for that reason, be claimed to be serving ends rather different from those which the governments in question may be pursuing in their strategies of regional co-operation.

Thus, the public rationale may bear little relationship to the actual forms of bilateral, or multilateral co-operation which take place. The important consideration, however, is that these forms of co-operation should be occurring at the initiative and under the complete control of the regimes concerned. In some cases, as in bilateral agreements concluded with powers from outside the region itself, the public rationale of the apparent regional organization might seem to conflict with the conclusion of such pacts. However, precisely because the organization in question will never have as much substance as the governments which claim to have adhered to it, its existence will not be an obstacle to the single-minded pursuit of a specific regime's interests.

This situation is likely to persist as long as the governments of most of the Arab states in the Middle East maintain themselves in the way to which they have become accustomed, avoiding the systematic answerability which the formulation of collective goals through institutional procedures would imply. As long as this remains the case in domestic politics in the Middle East, it would seem that, in regional politics, 'regionalism' will remain a largely symbolic issue. It may give rise to various formal organizations. However, it cannot be assumed that the channels of real interest, power, or action will follow those suggested by these formal organizations. On the contrary, they may be serving purposes quite other than those professed by their creators—purposes which, if revealed, would demonstrate the insubstantial nature of most of these organizations.

11

Conclusion: Regionalism and International Order?

Andrew Hurrell and Louise Fawcett

TRADITIONAL understandings of international order have come under increasing challenge. The conceptions of order that emerged within the classic European state system were largely concerned with elaborating limited rules of coexistence between states. Order was to be constructed around the mutual recognition of sovereignty and aimed at the creation of certain minimalist rules, under-standings, and institutions designed to limit the inevitable conflict that was to be expected within a pluralist and fragmented political system. In the course of the century, however, such views have been challenged by more far-reaching, maximalist conceptions of order involving more extensive schemes of co-operation to safeguard peace and security, to promote economic development, to solve common problems, and to sustain common values. The end of the Cold War has witnessed a further expansion of the normative ambitions of international society. Order is increasingly held to involve the creation of rules that affect very deeply the domestic structures and organization of states, that invest individuals and groups within states with rights and duties, and which seek to embody some notion of a common good (human rights, democra-tization, the environment, the construction of more elaborate and intrusive interstate security orders).

This switch can be characterized in different ways: in terms of Terry Nardin's distinction between a practical association on the one hand and a purposive association on the other; or Hedley Bull's distinction between pluralist and solidarist conceptions of international society; or the distinction drawn by many inter-national lawyers such as Richard Falk or Antonio Cassese be-tween a Westphalian model of international law and a UN Charter model.[1] There are three principal reasons why this shift has occurred. First, because the goal of minimal order has become less and less adequate given the range and seriousness of the problems and challenges facing international society. Second, because the growth of interdependence and the degree to which individual societies depend on each other for security, prosperity, and their ability to control their environment mean that the legitimacy of governments now depends on their capacity to meet a vastly increased range of needs, claims, and demands. And third, because of the emergence of an albeit still very fragile cosmopolitan moral consciousness that demands that greater attention be paid to questions of individual and collective human rights, and to the promotion of certain minimum standards of human welfare throughout the world.

This concluding chapter seeks to draw together some of the principal implications of the resurgence of regionalism for international order. It will look first at the claims of those who argue that that regional co-operation and regionalist arrangements can provide the most effective framework for order and stability *within a particular region*. It will then consider the relationship between increasing regionalism and the promotion of order *between regions* at the global level.

1. THE PROVISION OF REGIONAL ORDER

There are the five ways in which it is argued that regionalism and regional organizations can contribute positively to the provision of order and stability within a particular region.[2]

In the first place, changes in the international system have shifted the burden of responsibility for regional order firmly onto the states of that region. As earlier chapters have argued, regionalism has become more relevant and more important because of the

---

[1] Terry Nardin, *Law, Morality and the Relations between States* (Princeton: Princeton UP, 1983); Hedley Bull, The Anarchical Society (London: Macmillan, 1977); and Antonio Cassese, *International Law in a Divided World* (Oxford: OUP, 1986).

[2] For earlier, but still important, discussions of regionalism and order see Inis Claude, *Swords into Plowshares: The Problems and Progress of International Organizations* (New York: Random House, 1956); Joseph S. Nye, *Peace in Parts: Integration and Conflict in Regional Organisations* (Boston: Little, Brown & Co., 1971); Bull, *The Anarchical Society*, esp. ch. 11.

'regionalization' of international security. In contrast with the era of European colonialism and with the Cold War years, the pressures on great powers to develop a global role and to exploit regional conflicts as part of some broader power political competition have declined very significantly. This shift in the interests and ambitions of major powers has led to a 'decentralization' of international security. As a result the causes of instability have less to do with the meddling and intervention of outside powers, exposing instead the importance of intra-regional or domestic dynamics and requiring that they be understood and addressed on their own terms.[3]

Moreover, if outside powers today have less incentive to intervene nefariously, they also have less interest in assisting with the resolution of regional conflicts. Accordingly, states within a particular region will have little alternative but to look to their own security and to seek co-operative regional solutions. Thus regional organizations are likely to have the greater incentives to work towards promoting peace and security, the greater appreciation of the dangers of instability, and perhaps also the greater understanding of the causes and nature of regional security problems. For the optimists, this may in turn help to overcome the dilemmas of all collective security systems: the difficulty of persuading states to define their national interest in terms of a collective whole; to forsake the temptation to free-ride on the efforts of others; and to bear the costs of collective action. These costs may be economic, for example, agreeing to redistributive mechanisms to relieve poverty or starvation. Or they may be military, reflecting the fact that effective alliances depend on the shared perception of belonging to a 'community of fate'.

This trend towards regionalization has been reinforced by the nature of security challenges. In the post-Cold War international system many of the most pressing security threats do not derive from power political challenges to the *status quo* to which, as realists have long argued, states will respond with such traditional strategies as increasing defence, reinforcing deterrence, or constructing alliances. Many contemporary security threats derive not

[3] This has been the theme of much recent writing on post-Cold War security. See e.g. Patrick M. Cronin (ed.), *From Globalism to Regionalism* (Washington, DC: National Defense University, 1993); and Michael T. Klare and Daniel C. Thomas (eds.), *World Security: Challenges for a New Century* (New York: St Martin's Press, 1994).

from strength but from weakness: from the absence of political legitimacy or the failure of states to provide minimal conditions of order within their borders; from the way in which domestic instability can spill into the international arena; and from the incapacity of weak states to form viable building-blocks of a stable regional order, or to contribute towards the resolution of broader common purposes. The consequences of these failures, it is argued, are likely to be felt most acutely within a particular region, and will therefore press local states to seek solutions.

A second contribution of regional organizations relates to their role as providers of international legitimacy: especially important today because the extent to which international co-operation depends on ever greater degrees of intrusion into what was previously the exclusive domestic jurisdiction of states. Thus in the security field definitions of 'threats to international peace and security' have moved away from the prevention of classic interstate conflict to include civil wars, internal disintegration, humanitarian catastrophes, and even the failure to protect democracy and human rights. The traditional peacekeeping roles of both the UN and regional bodies have been expanded to include far-reaching attempts at peacemaking and even state-building/reconstruction. Thus, not only has there been a revival in the ambitions of regional organizations to act as collective security systems, but there is increasing emphasis on the need for 'co-operative security' which seeks to prevent conflict, to tackle the sources of conflict, and to promote reassurance rather than deterrence or containment.[4] In the economic field, as interdependence grows 'deeper', so more intrusive forms of management are required. Thus we have witnessed what many see as an inevitable move away from negotiations on trade issues towards the elaboration of international rules covering investment regimes, intellectual property rights, environmental protection, and industrial policy.

Third, regionalist supporters argue that it is easier to negotiate effective agreements regionally. For liberal institutionalist theorists this has much to do with the benefits of smaller numbers; with the

---

[4] On the expansion in the definition of security to be promoted by collective security systems, see Andrew Hurrell, 'Collective Security and International Order Revisited', *International Relations*, 11/1 (Apr. 1992). On the concept of co-operative security, see Janne E. Nolan (ed.), *Global Engagement: Cooperation and Security in the 21st Century* (Washington, DC: Brookings Institution, 1994), esp. ch. 1, 'The Concept of Co-operative Security'.

greater sense of consensus and common interest than is possible at the global level; and with the greater scope at the regional level for isolating a manageable negotiating agenda in which all states have an interest and which is broad enough for productive issue-linkage but not too broad to impede effective bargaining. The same conclusion can be reached by neo-realists who stress the benefits of inequality and the role of hegemony in underpinning international institutions. Thus, whilst it may be true that the decline in US hegemony and the absence of other purposeful great powers is detrimental to multilateralism at the global level, the existence of unequal power within regions still provides scope for the provision of effective, hegemonically led structures of order.

Fourth, liberals have traditionally argued that increasing regional economic integration would inhibit the outbreak of conflict and increase the incentives for managing it: first, by increasing the material costs of armed conflict, and second, by providing the framework within which new collective identities and new forms of institutionalized co-operation can emerge. Although not necessarily limited to the regional level, processes of deep integration and the emergence of new security communities are nevertheless more likely to occur where geographical proximity, high levels of regional interdependence, and a shared history and common cultural traditions are present.

Finally, as we have seen in earlier chapters, regionalism may contribute towards order to the extent that it represents a way of mitigating ethnic, nationalist, or communal conflict. Many such conflicts arise from the clash between the persistence, revival, or invention of ethnic or nationalist identities on the one hand, and the exclusivist claims to political authority represented by the state and the state system on the other. If national or ethnic identities themselves cannot be wished away and do not disappear as a consequence of greater economic development or enlightenment (as both liberals and marxists have often predicted), then perhaps the historic link between sovereignty and self-determination can be broken and the struggle for the control of states can cease to be a game in which the winner takes all.

On this view regionalism provides one way in which responses to demands for self-determination can be broadened and in which minorities and stateless groups can find a secure place and a meas-

ure of representation within a larger political community.[5] It is for
these reasons that the regionalist road to a 'new medieval' order is
seen as providing the basis for a more stable order in the many
regions where diffuse and changing identities can never be made to
fit neatly within the boundaries of the state system. The emergence
of new kinds of regional polities can make two kinds of contribution: first, by allowing sovereignty to be 'unpacked' and par-
celled out, both up to regional institutions and down to subregional
bodies; and second, by institutionalizing at the regional level
(through regional bodies and through strict criteria for admission)
a commitment to multiparty democracy, the rule of law, and the
entrenchment of fundamental human rights. Such strategies represent a potentially promising means of mitigating what are widely
perceived to be the dangers of excessive fragmentation implicit in
the doctrine of self-determination and constructing a broader and
more encompassing order, albeit one that is very different from
traditional interstate arrangements.[6]

Yet, whilst these arguments may well be important in particular
cases, the chapters in this book make it clear that regionalism offers
no panacea and that there can be no automatic presumption in
favour of the advantages of regionalism.

In the first place, the natural advantages of letting regional states
assume primary responsibility can be questioned. It is not clear that
the balance of interests and incentives will automatically press
regional states to take up the burden of responsibility for regional
security. The complications of regional politics may on the contrary
make it far harder for regional bodies to embark on risky and
politically divisive action. Historic involvement and partisan interests may undermine the possibility of even-handed action at the
regional level and make regional states unacceptable as inter-
locteurs and mediators. The EC, for example, has been viewed by
the Bosnian Serbs as irredeemably partisan, undermining its role as
a potential peace-broker.

[5] This idea is developed in Michael Keating, *State and Regional Nationalism*
(Hemel Hempstead: Harvester Wheatsheaf, 1988).
[6] The danger of excessive fragmentation is stressed by Boutros-Ghali: 'Yet if every
ethnic, religious or linguistic group claimed statehood, there would be no limit to the
fragmentation, and peace, security and economic well-being for all would become
ever more difficult to achieve': Boutros-Ghali, *An Agenda for Peace*, repr. in Adam
Roberts and Benedict Kingsbury (eds.), *United Nations, Divided World* (Oxford:
OUP, 2nd edn., 1993), 474.

Action requiring involvement in the domestic affairs of their neighbours is likely to prove especially problematic. This is unsurprising given the extent to which, as James Mayall points out, much regionalist activity has been devised to strengthen and protect existing state structures and to secure the position of dominant state élites. Hence the traditional refusal of the OAU to become involved in claims for self-determination and to support secession movements, or the reluctance of ASEAN to become involved in issues that affect domestic politics of a member state. Even in the Americas where the centrality of democratic governance has been reaffirmed as a regional norm, the OAS was still unable to agree a position on coercive intervention in Haiti and it was left to the local hegemon to orchestrate a non-regionally based multilateral action.

Moreover, even if a common interest is perceived, it may be extremely difficult to forge a common policy in the face of conflicting interests, competing prescriptions, and collective action problems between member states. The use of military power in response to security challenges whose origins lie in civil wars, ethnic conflict, or state collapse raises very troubling questions as to the true nature of state interests and the precise objectives being sought. As a result it is not surprising that contemporary security threats tend not to cement regional (and other) alliances as in the past, but rather to place enormous strain on regional cohesion and consensus. Indeed, for the cynic one of the attractions of working through regional organizations is precisely because it represents a politically useful way of *appearing* to do something, knowing that either inaction and the lowest common denominator principle are the most likely outcomes.

Second, the provision of legitimacy is in practice far from simple and the difficult trade-off between effectiveness and legitimacy bedevils institutions at both the global and regional level. One problem concerns the scope and size of regionalist groupings. On the one hand, political legitimacy presses towards inclusiveness, towards involving all the members of a region. On the other, effectiveness depends on restricting effective decision-making to a small number of states that have both the capability and willingness to act. One increasingly common solution is to resort to diplomatic 'contact groups' or to *ad hoc* coalitions dominated by a smaller number of states with the power and interests to take effective action, but embedded within a regional grouping. Yet, although undeniably useful, this road opens up the possibility of a hierarchy of membership and threatens to replicate within the region many of the issues of legitimacy and accountability that currently affect the workings of the UN Security Council.

Moreover, even strongly institutionalized regional bodies may lack the power, and especially the military power, to act effectively and may have to rely on extra-regional assistance. Thus the limited resources of African states opened the way for external involvement in Somalia and Rwanda. More strikingly, the failures of the EC over the former Yugoslavia expose the hollowness of the notion of Europe as a 'civilian power' and the fragility of existing mechanisms for European defence co-operation.[7] Finally, effectiveness may well depend on the willingness of the locally dominant power to take the lead. Yet deferring to the local major power in the interests of effectiveness becomes all too easily a cover for the institutionalization of regional hegemony—the role of the USA within the Caribbean or the Nigerian-led ECOWAS intervention in the Liberian civil war provide two contemporary examples. Yet hegemonic regionalism, even if buttressed by shared values and shared interests, has always raised questions of long-term political sustainability.

A third, and related, difficulty concerns the relationship between different sets of regional groupings. As the chapters in this book have repeatedly emphasized, central to the contemporary politics of regionalism is the tension between different conceptions of the 'region' and between different regional groupings. As William Wallace's chapter underlined, this has been a central characteristic of recent European experience. But this sort of overlap is found in every region and perhaps inevitably so. Different forms of regionalism compete and coexist in virtually every part of the world, just as regional organizations coexist with the UN or regional economic

---

[7] Although the EU possesses significant political power and high levels of economic power, member states were forced to look to NATO rather than to WEU for effective military options—because of NATO's reputation for effectiveness, its proven military structure, its collectively owned assets (such as headquarters, planning capabilities, standing naval forces, and early warning aircraft), and its political clout (including as it does three of the five members of the Security Council). The Bosnian experience illustrates both the difficulties of adapting NATO's military capabilities to the requirements of peacekeeping/peacemaking, and the very serious problems of achieving effective co-ordination between different institutions.

groupings will have to work within the newly formed World Trade Organization. Yet whilst the proliferation of regional bodies may well be an understandable solution to regional political problems and may answer to genuine needs and ambitions, it undoubtedly increases the problems of effective co-ordination.[8]

Fourth, there is no obvious case for believing that it is necessarily easier to create and sustain effective institutions at the regional level. The arguments of both neo-realists and neo-liberal institutionalists can be deployed at both regional and global levels. On the one hand, the problem of large numbers can complicate effective institution-building in large and diverse regions. On the other, multilateralism, the emergence of coalitions, and the dominance of a small number of major players (such as the USA, the EC, and Japan within the GATT) have in the past helped to facilitate the creation and maintenance of non-regionally based institutions. Equally, whilst the existence of a common culture may well contribute to regional co-operation, it can also contribute to non-regionally based institutions, such as NATO or the economic institutions within the OECD world. There is no automatic reason why security communities should be predominantly regional. Moreover, as the phenomenon of civil wars reminds us, neither neighbourhood, common culture, nor dense societal interdependencies are sufficient to guarantee stability and solidarity.

Finally, it is very easy to exaggerate the security role of regional institutions. Once conflict between the major states of a region has diminished and potential overlapping interests have been identified, then institutions can play an important role. In many cases their primary role lies in cementing or consolidating *rapprochement*, in helping to prevent back-sliding, but rarely in making the initial break-through. As the Cambodian or Middle Eastern peace processes suggest, this is likely to follow from changes within the structure of conflict itself, combined with the intervention of powerful external powers. Where conflict between major regional powers is intense, regionalism remains marginal. Compare, for example, region-building in South Asia where the continuing conflict between Pakistan and India has continued to undermine efforts at regional co-operation with the situation in Latin America where the *rapprochement* between Brazil and Argentina laid the ground-

[8] This theme is developed for the case of Europe in Edward Mortimer, 'European Security After the Cold War', *Adelphi Paper*, 271 (Summer 1992), 66.

work for subsequent and extensive schemes of regional co-operation. Similarly as different Arab states move towards an accommodation with Israel, the chances of effective co-operation
increase—one thinks in particular of the possibilities inherent in the
sort of functional co-operation suggested by an Israel–Jordan–
Palestine grouping.

2. REGIONALISM AND GLOBAL ORDER

There is a long tradition in Western thinking on international
relations that has seen regionalism and, in particular, regional
spheres of influence, as providing a framework for global order.
This tradition has stressed the benefits for global order that follow
from a world made up of a relatively small number of cohesive and
clearly defined regional units, each dominated by a great power. On
the one hand, great powers are said to sustain order by 'policing'
the relations between the states of their particular sphere or region.
On the other hand, spheres of influence enhance global order to the
extent that they lay down clear ground rules about the acceptable
limits of both power-political rivalry and mercantilist economic
competition. Amongst practioners, Churchill's advocacy of regionalism is well known, as is the role of spheres of influence in
Kissinger's thinking on *détente*.[9]

These classical conceptions of the relationship between regionalism and international order are of limited (but perhaps growing)
relevance today: because the contemporary development of regionalism has occurred against the background of a powerful parallel trend towards globalization; because of the interpenetration of
economic interests across regions; because of the global nature of
US interests; because of the resilience and increasing importance
of non-regional institutions; and because of marked absence of
great powers, with Russia weakened, China preoccupied with economic modernization, and Germany and Japan still heavily conditioned by post-war patterns of foreign-policy behaviour. The

---

[9] For an excellent discussion of these claims, see Paul Keal, *Unspoken Rules and
Superpower Dominance* (London: Macmillan, 1983), esp. ch. 8. Such arguments
have been usually, but not always, limited to the West. For a developing country
perspective (perhaps unsurprisingly Indian), see Rajni Kothari, *Footsteps into the
Future: Diagnosis of the Present World and a Design for an Alternative* (New Delhi:
Longman, 1974).

complexity of regionalist patterns visible today cannot therefore be easily equated with traditional notions of great powers and spheres of influence.[10]

Nevertheless the relationship between regionalism and the broader balance of power remains important. The point is not that a classical balance of power order could ever be sufficient to deal with the challenges facing contemporary international society. But rather that a stable and agreed set of understandings between the major powers and some recognition of the regional special interests of those powers are likely to remain inevitable and necessary under-pinnings of all international institutions, whether global or re-gional. For these institutions to ignore this would be to undermine their effectiveness and, as so often in the past, to court irrelevance. Moreover, these questions could become more central if, as writers such as Kenneth Waltz predict, states such as Germany, Japan, Russia, and China do come to see themselves as great powers in the classic mould and to lay increasing weight on claims for special rights within particular regions and for the acknowledgement of those claims by others.[11]

Particularly in the early post-war period, the issue of inter-national order was couched in terms of a clear choice between globalism on the one hand and regionalism on the other. Yet, as earlier chapters of this book have argued, this idea of a simple choice between regionalism and globalism is not especially helpful

[10] For some commentators it is precisely the differences between contemporary regional organization such as the EC and classical great powers that are crucial. On this view, regional groupings will be so preoccupied with the management of internal affairs that they will no longer be able to act in the aggressive power-seeking manner of sovereign states. This pacific tendency would be strengthened by the liberal character of their political arrangements and by the extent to which integra-tion does not result in a fully blown superstate but instead in a neo-medieval arrangement of multiple identities and overlapping levels of authority. Such group-ing would be inner-directed and would find it extremely difficult to harness the power to engage in aggressive, outer-directed foreign policy. See Paul Taylor, *International Organization in the Modern World: The Regional and Global Process* (London: Pinter, 1993), 5–6 and 43–4.

[11] This problem is already re-emerging in the difficulties faced by both the UN and regional bodies in reconciling the still very strong US tendency towards unilateralism in its dealings with the Caribbean and Russia's increasingly explicit claims for special interests in the 'Near Abroad'. See Maxim Shashenkov, 'Russian Peacekeep-ing in the "Near Abroad" ', *Survival*, 36/3 (Fall 1994). On the 'inevitable' re-emergence of Germany and Japan as great powers, see Kenneth N. Waltz, 'The Emerging Structure of International Politics', *International Security*, 18/2 (autumn 1993).

nor indeed relevant. Institutionalization is taking place at both regional and global levels. The issue is not about which level should have primacy but how they can be related together and how they may reinforce each other, or come into conflict. On one side of the argument, we find a recurrent liberal vision of a productive partnership and of the neat interlocking of regional political, security, or economic co-operation within an overarching global order—'inter-regional globalism' to use Alan Henrikson's phrase. This image suggests a form of global subsidiarity in which different institutions and organizational expertise, and different domains of jurisdiction and authority are deployed according to the nature of the issue.

In the security field, as Alan Henrikson examines in his chapter, the period since 1989 has seen renewed calls for a revised and more effective partnership between global and regional organizations. The rationale for such a partnership is clear. The UN is heavily overburdened. Regional organizations and regional coalitions can therefore contribute significantly to burden-sharing, providing special experience and knowledge of particular problems; greater legitimacy within the region; greater awareness of local sensitivities; and a greater willingness to deploy resources and to bear the cost. In turn, regional organizations simply cannot do without the UN: first, because of its unrivalled political legitimacy; and second, because it represents the best framework for extra-regional involvement in those cases where regional states lack either the capacity or political neutrality to respond effectively to security challenges. The failure to contain the civil war in Yugoslavia suggests just how regional organizations can fail if they are not backed by the global jurisdiction and legitimacy of the United Nations.[12]

Yet the obstacles to effective co-operation remain very considerable. Involving both the UN and regional bodies may add to political legitimacy (as in the cases of Kuwait, Yugoslavia, or Haiti), but it also increases the difficulties of co-ordination. This involves practical problems, for example, of the command and control of enforcement action or the feasibility of sharing sensitive intelligence. But it may also open up serious political problems involving conflicting assessments of both the nature of the conflict and the

[12] Andrew Bennett and Joseph Lepgold, 'Reinventing Collective Security after the Cold War and the Gulf Conflict', *Political Science Quarterly*, 108/2 (1993), 231.

prescriptions and plans for ending it. In addition, although arguments about the primacy of regional vs. global organizations may well by outdated, the choice of institutional venue and the decision over which grouping plays the dominant role remain highly politicized issues with important practical consequences. The tendency of major powers to give priority to whichever institutional level provides the most flexible multilateral cover has by no means wholly disappeared.

The economic version of this idea sees regional integration as a stepping-stone to further global liberalization and views open regionalism as fully compatible with economic multilateralism. Regionalism permits differential levels of integration and institutionalization according to the degree of economic development and interdependence. On the one hand, it is easier to tackle the agenda of deep integration amongst like-minded countries, with common economic and political structures. On the other, economic regionalism can serve as a way of furthering the liberal agenda, both by way of example and through its use as a bargaining tool in global negotiations. Thus, supporters of US regional policy have claimed that NAFTA and APEC helped to secure completion of the Uruguay Round and continue to be compatible with the future workings of the World Trade Organization.[13]

But, again, there remain difficulties in achieving a happy marriage between globalism and regionalism. Andrew Wyatt-Walter's chapter argued that, thus far, the new economic regionalism has not proved incompatible with multilateral arrangements: because of the strength of pressures for globalization; because the growing regionalist 'turn' in US policy is still balanced by a commitment to multilateralism; because of the resilience and longevity and 'institutional stickiness' of existing multilateral institutions; because of the strength of market-liberal economic ideas and the prevalence of market-liberal economic policies which pay at least lip-service to the goal of global multilateralism; because of the balance of domestic coalitions both within the EC and the USA.

Yet, as his chapter also argues, it is far from clear that this mutually reinforcing relationship can be expected to endure. First, it was to a great extent the product of a particular set of historical

[13] For a clear example of this argument, see C. Fred Bergsten, 'APEC and World Trade: A Force for Worldwide Liberalization', *Foreign Affairs*, 73/3 (May–June 1994).

circumstances in which there was a close relationship between economic relationships and Cold War security structures. Second, the use of bilateralism or regionalism to try and maximize short-term advantage can all too easily lead to a spiral of tit-for-tat discrimination, and can damage overall prospects for stable multi-lateral order as those excluded from bilateral or regionalist arrange-ments respond by adopting similar measures. Third, regionalism can allow scope for protectionist lobbies to increase their power and legitimacy. Within the USA the narrow passage of NAFTA and the defeat of further fast-track negotiating authority provide evi-dence for those who see a continued decline of the free-trade coalition within the USA. Within the EC a great deal will depend on the ways in which further expansion affects the balance of power between free-trade and protectionist interests. There remain, then, good grounds for concern that regionalism might develop a cumu-lative momentum that will undermine the effectiveness of economic multilateralism and that regionalist economic arrangements are bound to take on an increasingly inward-looking and protectionist attitude. Underlying these fears is the belief that a world of regional blocs, far from engendering restraint, would tend to see all conflicts in zero-sum terms. The dominant picture would not be one of careful and restrained diplomacy but of head-to-head confronta-tion in which all issues are seen in zero-sum terms and in which antagonist images reinforce each other.[14]

A third important example concerns human rights and democra-tization. For many people human rights are inherently universal, concerned with protecting and furthering the dignity and worth of all human beings. Certainly the human rights regime that has emerged in the period since the Second World War is global in at least two senses: first, that the individual and collective rights defined in the increasing number of international legal instruments are indeed held to apply to all human beings; and second, that the UN plays a central role in the process of standard-setting, as well as in the promotion and protection of human rights.[15] Regional bodies

[14] This notion lay at the heart of David Mitrany's *Working Peace System*. For Mitrany, the great danger of regional or 'continental' blocs was that they would merely replicate interstate conflict on a larger scale.

[15] For an up-to-date survey of the UN's roles, see Tom J. Farer and Felice Gaer, 'The UN and Human Rights: At the End of the Beginning', in Roberts and Kingsbury (eds.), *United Nations, Divided World*.

enter into the story principally in terms of implementation—'the local carriers of a global message' to use John Vincent's apt phrase.[16] The rights themselves are universal, but their practical implementation will be more effective if devolved to the regional level. Thus we have seen a variety of regional human rights regimes in Europe, the Americas, Africa, and the Arab world with differing degrees of institutionalization (especially in terms of enforcement) and, within the limits of global standards, some acknowledgement of cultural differences. As with co-operation more generally, so it is argued that greater social, political, and economic homogeneity will make it easier to implement human rights at the regional level and make the inevitably increased intrusion into domestic affairs politically easier to accept.

Yet the line between global promulgation and regional implementation is a problematic one. It is hardly surprising that regional human rights frameworks, and regional groupings more generally, have served as vehicles for the promotion of conflicting conceptions of human rights and conflicting views as to how those rights should be promoted. Some of these conflicts are of long standing, such as the clash between the Western liberal emphasis on individual rights and the greater stress placed by many in Asia or Africa on the rights of groups or of society as a whole.[17] Others have appeared more recently, resulting in particular from the expansion of the human rights agenda in the 1990s to include the promotion of political democracy and 'good governance'. In many parts of the world these debates have been central to the emergence of greater regional awareness: what it is to be part of Europe, the Americas, or Asia? How it is that 'we' are to be differentiated from 'them'? Perhaps the most powerful contemporary example concerns Asian regionalism where the growth of an Asian regional indentity—some would even call it an Asian 'worldview'—and of Asian regional co-operation has come to involve an increasingly overt challenge to US and European understandings of human rights and democracy, the role for the coercive enforcement and differing forms of 'conditionality', and the relationship between human rights and

[16] R. J. Vincent, *Human Rights and International Relations* (Cambridge: CUP, 1986), 101.

[17] These and other difficulties are examined in Vincent, *Human Rights*, esp. chs. 4, 5, and 6. See also Jack Donelly, *Universal Human Rights in Theory and Practice* (Ithaca, NY: Cornell UP, 1989), esp. ch. 3.

political democracy on the one hand and efficient economic development on the other.[18]

Thus, far from slotting nicely into a neat pattern of global subsidiarity, regionalism and regional co-operation may form the political framework for conflict over the definition of human rights and over the means by which they should be enforced internationally. At the extreme, regionalism could come to reflect and embody different and conflicting 'civilizations' to take up Samuel Huntingdon's gloomy vision of the future. In this way, then, regionalism may become the framework for the articulation and promotion of challenges to global values.

The difficulty of making firm generalizations about the relationship between regionalism and international order reflects the broader complexities of the current regionalist debate with which this book has sought to grapple. First, what are the underlying factors that explain the resurgence of regionalism? To what extent can new or revived regionalist schemes be explained in terms of the old logic of states, power politics, hegemony, and the dynamics of anarchy; or to what extent do they reflect the imperatives of economic interdependence, globalization, and their accompanying logics of transformation, of co-operation, and of community? The traditional view that regionalism is driven by state policies and state imperatives is challenged by those who see the new regionalism as a reflection of increasing economic and social integration in which new actors, new social complexes, and new forms of identity are emerging both above and below the existing territorial state. Existing theories of International Relations have found it difficult to provide an explanation for the place of regionalism in a world of sovereign states. Neither the dismissiveness and scepticism of the realists (often shared by radical structuralists), nor the optimism, even utopianism, of many liberals enable us to capture the essence of regionalism: something more than traditionally conceived narrow national interests, yet less than pure internationalism, while also containing the promise or potential for fundamental changes in the character of the international system.

Second, how resilient is the new regionalism? Several of the

---

[18] For Asian government perspectives, see Bilahari Kausikan, 'Asia's Different Standard', *Foreign Policy*, 92 (Fall 1993); Robert Bartley *et al.*, *Democracy and Capitalism: Asian and American Perspectives* (Singapore: Institute of Southeast Asian Studies, 1993).

chapters in this book have painted a somewhat sombre view of the long-term prospects. The commitment of many regional organizations to greater unity has been rightly brought into question and their overall record remains patchy. Despite the emergence of 'North–South regionalism', there is still a gap between the impressive advances made by the structures of regional co-operation in the industrialized Western world (especially Europe and North America) and the far more mixed situation in many parts of the developing world. In the developing world many regional organizations are still seen as being more committed to rhetoric than action, the modest successes of organizations like SAARC, SADC, or ECOWAS notwithstanding. Broad-ranging economic treaties, such as the one mooted by the OAU, are of little more than symbolic value. Other, potentially far more significant groupings, such as APEC, are only gradually moving away from being debating clubs, still having to cover the difficulties of reaching consensus with general statements of good intentions.[19] Moreover, the relationship between increased economic regionalization and formal institutionalization remains, in the case of APEC, very much an open one. Perhaps most strikingly, in the Middle East the three most recent regional creations, the Arab Maghreb Union, Arab Co-operation Council, and Gulf Co-operation Council bodies have all disappointed expectations and indicated the great difficulties of forging any common policy in that region. One thing is clear: the current interest in regional co-operation and the parallel proliferation of regional bodies will not, in itself, secure a place for regionalism in the new world order. If in Europe regionalism is here to stay, despite the attendant difficulties, it is still difficult to predict its future in other areas.

Yet there are also a number of reasons to be optimistic and to agree with Bhagwati's comment: 'That the current rise of regionalism is likely to endure and gain in strength seems probable: History is unlikely to repeat itself.'[20] In Latin America subregional co-operation appears to be more firmly established today than at any time in the past. In Asia ASEAN appears to have institutionalized both the 'habit of co-operation' and the sense of belonging to a

[19] Robert A. Manning and Paula Stern, 'The Myth of the Pacific Community', *Foreign Affairs*, 75/6 (Nov./Dec. 1994).

[20] Jagdish Bhagwati, *The World Trading System at Risk* (Princeton: Princeton UP, 1991), 71.

well-established region in which economic and societal regionalization has grown apace. In southern Africa and the Middle East the end of apartheid and the success of the peace process open new possibilities. Indeed some have described the regional consequences of the Middle East peace process as epochal, comparable in impact to those produced by the end of the Cold War, and predicted that a settlement, and the creation of a stable regional environment, will provide the vital spur to greater integration.[21] Of course, it would be naïve to overlook the immense challenges facing the success of regionalism in large parts of the less developed 'non-Western' world. Yet the argument that interdependence remains a theme more applicable to Western politics than to other regions of the world is no longer valid. In this sense there is clearly something new about the new regionalism.

Third, what is the relationship between different forms of regionalism? As this book has argued, the relationship between macro- and micro-regional schemes and between regional and broader global initiatives are two of the most important questions, affecting regionalism in almost every part of the world. In the Americas, the possibility of an expanded NAFTA affects the prospects of subregional economic groupings such as *Mercosur*. For some South American countries, like Chile and Colombia, there is the dilemma of whether promoting local pacts or joining a US-led trade bloc offers the better option and of whether subregional co-operation should be seen merely as a stepping-stone to membership of NAFTA. The question 'which regionalism is best' is also relevant in the East Asian context, with geographically limited groupings such as ASEAN and the EAEC having to compete with broader visions of an Asia-Pacific community. The same tensions have also affected Europe (although here the attractions of EU membership have tended to undermine most alternatives) and the Middle East. With trading blocs and CSCEs joining the range of regionalist options, it is difficult for many countries to devise a rational policy towards regional co-operation. And for some developing countries in particular, given the weakness of regional groupings, reliance on global institutions may remain the more attractive and feasible option.

---

[21] Phebe Marr, 'The United States, Europe and the Middle East: An Uneasy Triangle', *Middle East Journal* 48/2 (Spring 1994), 223.

That arch-regional sceptic, Hedley Bull, once noted the growing tendency of states 'to seek to integrate themselves in large units',[22] a tendency which has greatly accelerated since his death in 1985. The chapters in this book, in different ways, have sought to describe and explain this tendency and suggest some tentative conclusions about the new regionalism in a changing world order. It may well be premature to suggest that regionalism should be considered as a 'metaphor for our time'.[23] Indeed, one clear conclusion that has emerged from this book is that whatever grounds for optimism there may be about the future of regionalism, it is far from being a 'unified concept' and hence far from being the organizing principle for any new global system.[24] At best it can be argued that regionalism may come to constitute one of many pillars supporting an evolving international order.

[22] Hedley Bull, *The Anarchical Society* 264.
[23] W. W. Rostow, 'The Coming Age of Regionalism', *Encounter*, 74/5 (June 1990), 3.
[24] See Robert D. Hormats, 'Making Regionalism Safe', *Foreign Affairs*, 72/3 (Mar.–Apr. 1994), 100.

SELECT BIBLIOGRAPHY

ACHARYA, AMITAV, 'A New Regional Order in South-East Asia: ASEAN in the Post-Cold War Era', *Adelphi Paper*, 279 (Aug. 1993).

AKINDELE, R. A., *The Organization and Promotion of World Peace: A Study of Universal–Regional Relationships* (Toronto: University of Toronto Press, 1976).

ALAGAPPA, MUTHIAH, 'Regionalism and the Quest for Security: ASEAN and the Cambodian Conflict', *Journal of International Affairs*, 46/2 (Winter 1993).

ANDEMICAEL, BERHANYKUN (ed.), *Regionalism and the United Nations* (Dobbs Ferry, NY: Oceana Publications for UNITAR, 1979).

ARCHER, CLIVE, *International Organizations* (London: Routledge, 2nd edn., 1992).

BHAGWATI, JAGDISH, *The World Trading System at Risk* (Princeton: Princeton UP, 1991).

BUZAN, BARRY, *People, States and Fear* (London: Harvester Wheatsheaf, 1991).

BULL, HEDLEY, *The Anarchical Society*, (London: Macmillan, 1977).

BULMER-THOMAS, VICTOR, NIKKI CRASKE, and MONICA SERRANO, *Mexico and the North American Free Trade Agreement: Who will Benefit?* (London: Macmillan, 1994).

CASSESE, ANTONIO (ed.), *United Nations Peace-keeping: Legal Essays* (Alphen aan den Rijn: Sijthoff & Noordhoff, 1978).

CANTORI, LOUIS J., and STEVEN L. SPIEGEL, *The International Relations of Regions: A Comparative Approach* (Englewood Cliffs, NJ: Prentice-Hall, 1970).

CLAWSON, ROBERT W. (ed.), *East–West Rivalry in the Third World: Security Issues and Regional Perspectives* (Wilmington, Del.: Scholarly Resources, 1986).

CLEMENTS, KEVIN (ed.), *Peace and Security in the Asia Pacific Region* (Tokyo: United Nations UP, 1993).

DESTLER, I. M., *American Trade Politics* (New York: Twentieth Century Fund, 2nd edn., 1992).

DEUTSCH, KARL, SIDNEY A. BURRELL, and ROBERT A. KANN, *Political Community in the North Atlantic Area* (Princeton: Princeton UP, 1958).

FISHLOW, ALBERT, and STEPHAN HAGGARD, *The United States and the Regionalisation of the World Economy* (Paris: OECD, Mar. 1992).

FRANKEL, JEFFREY A., and MILES KAHLER (eds.), *Regionalism and Rivalry. Japan and the United States in Pacific Asia* (Chicago: University of Chicago Press, 1993).

GARNAUT, ROSS, and PETER DRYSDALE (eds.), *Asia Pacific Regionalism: Readings in International Economic Relations* (Pymble, NSW, Aust.: Harper Educational Publishers, 1994).

GEORGE, STEPHEN, *Politics and Policy in the European Community* (Oxford: OUP, 1991).

GRUNWALD, JOSEPH, MIGUEL S. WIONCZEK, and MARTIN CARNOY, *Latin American Economic Integration and US Policy* (Washington: Brookings Institution, 1972).

HAAS, ERNST, 'The Challenge of Regionalism', *International Organization*, 12/4 (Autumn 1958).

—— *The Obsolesence of Regional Integration Theory* (Berkeley, Calif.: Institute of International Studies, 1975).

HART, JEFFREY A., *Rival Capitalists: International Competitiveness in the United States, Japan, and Western Europe*. (Ithaca, NY: Cornell UP, 1992).

HARTLYN, JONATHAN, LARS SCHOULTZ, and AUGUSTO VARAS (eds.), *The United States and Latin America in the 1990s* (Chapel Hill, NC: University of North Carolina Press, 1992).

JACKSON, JOHN H., *The World Trading System: Law and Policy of International Relations* (Cambridge, Mass.: MIT Press, 1989).

KHATRI, SHRIDKAR K., 'A Decade of South Asian Regionalism', *Contemporary South Asia*, 1/1 (1992).

KEOHANE, ROBERT O., *International Institutions and State Power* (Boulder, Colo.: Westview, 1989).

—— and STANLEY HOFFMANN (eds.), *The New European Community. Decisionmaking and Institutional Change* (Boulder, Colo.: Westview, 1991).

LEIFER, MICHAEL, *ASEAN and the Security of South-East Asia* (London: Routledge, 1989).

LISTER, FREDERICK, 'The Role of International Organizations in the 1990s and beyond', *International Relations*, 10/2 (Nov. 1990).

LOWENTHAL, ABRAHAM F., and GREGORY TREVERTON (eds.), *Latin America in a New World* (Boulder, Colo.: Westview, 1994).

LUSTIG, NORA, BARRY P. BOSWORTH, and ROBERT Z. LAWRENCE, *North American Free Trade: Assessing the Impact* (Washington: Brookings Institution, 1992).

MACFARLANE, S. NEIL, and THOMAS G. WEISS, 'Regional Organizations and Regional Security', *Security Studies*, 2/1 (Fall 1992).

McINESS, COLIN, and MARK G. ROLLS (eds.), *Post Cold War Security Issues in the Asia-Pacific Region* (Ilford, Essex: Frank Cass, 1994).

MAYALL, JAMES, *Nationalism and International Society* (Cambridge: Cambridge UP, 1990).

MIALL, HUGH (ed.), *Redefining Europe: New Patterns of Conflict and Cooperation* (London: Pinter for RIIA, 1994).

MILWARD, ALAN, *The European Rescue of the Nation-State* (London: Routledge, 1992).

MITRANY, DAVID, *A Working Peace System* (London: Royal Institute of International Affairs, 1943).

NEUMANN, IVER B. (ed.), *Regional Great Powers in International Politics* (London: Macmillan, 1992).

—— 'A Region-Building Approach to Northern Europe', *Review of International Studies*, 20/1 (1994).

NOLAN, JANNE E. (ed.), *Global Engagement: Cooperation and Security in the 21st Century* (Washington, DC: Brookings Institution, 1994).

NOLFO, ENNIO DI (ed.), *The Atlantic Pact Forty Years Later: A Historical Reappraisal* (Berlin: Walter de Gruyter, 1991).

NYE, JOSEPH S., *International Regionalism: Readings* (Boston: Little, Brown & Co., 1968).

—— *Peace in Parts: Integration and Conflict in Regional Organization* (Boston: Little, Brown & Co., 1971).

O'BRIEN, RICHARD (ed.), *Finance and the International Economy* (Oxford: OUP/*Amex Bank Review*, 1991).

OYE, KENNETH, A., *Economic Discrimination and Political Exchange* (Princeton: Princeton UP, 1992).

PALMER, NORMAN D., *The New Regionalism in Asia and the Pacific* (Lexington, Mass.: Lexington Books, 1991).

PENTLAND, CHARLES, *International Theory and European Integration* (London, Faber & Faber, 1973).

ROBERTS, ADAM, and BENEDICT KINGSBURY (eds.), *United Nations, Divided World* (Oxford: Clarendon Press, 2nd end., 1993).

ROBSON, PETER, 'The New Regionalism and the Developing Countries', *Journal of Common Market Studies*, 31/3 (1993).

ROSECRANCE, RICHARD, 'Regionalism and the Post-Cold War Era', *International Journal*, 46 (Summer 1991).

ROSTOW, W. W., 'The Coming Age of Regionalism', *Encounter*, 74/5, (1990).

RUSSETT, BRUCE, *International Regions and the International System* (Chicago: Rand NcNally, 1967).

—— *Grasping the Democratic Peace* (Princeton: Princeton UP, 1993).

SCALAPINO, ROBERT A., S. SATO, J. WANADI, and S.-J. HAN (eds.), *Asian Security Issues: Regional and Global* (Berkeley: Institute of East Asian Studies, University of California, 1988).

SEGAL, GERALD, *Rethinking the Pacific* (Oxford: OUP, 1990).

SMITH, PETER H. (ed.), *The Challenge of Integration: Europe and the Americas* (New Brunswick, NJ: Transaction Publishers, 1992).

TAYLOR, PAUL, *International Organization in the Modern World: The Regional and Global Process* (London: Pinter, 1993).

THUROW, LESTER, *Head to Head: The Coming Economic Battle among Japan, Europe and America* (London: Nicholas Brealey, 1992).

TOW, WILLIAM, *Subregional Security Cooperation in the Third World* (Boulder, Colo.: Lynne Rienner, 1990).

TSOUKALIS, LOUKAS, *The New European Economy. The Politics and Economics of Integration* (Oxford: OUP, 2nd edn., 1993).

WALLACE, WILLIAM (ed.), *The Dynamics of European Integration* (London: Pinter for RIIA, 1990).

—— *The Transformation of Western Europe* (London: Pinter for RIIA, 1990).

WALTERS, F. P., *A History of the League of Nations*, 2 vols. (London: OUP, 1952).

WALT, STEPHEN M., *The Origins of Alliances* (Ithaca, NY: Cornell UP, 1987).

INDEX

network of world trade 102, 103,
104
reunification 220, 222
and a wider Europe 214–15
Gilpin, Robert 26
globalization 1, 6
metaphor of 54–5, 74, 75–7, 111
and regionalism 3, 19, 55–8, 319–
20
and structural independence 53–8
in trade and investment patterns
114
Gorbachev, Mikhail 18, 20, 238, 239,
240
Gross, Ernest 164
Guyana 252

Haas, E. B. 14, 60
Haiti 144–7, 159, 278, 281, 315
hegemony:
decline in US 93–4, 268, 313
and regionalism 50–3, 313
Henrikson, Alan 5–6, 19, 320
Herz, John 173
history of regionalism 10–17
Ho Chi Minh 230
Hoffmann, Stanley 12
human rights 322–4
Hurrell, Andrew 5, 6, 20

IAEA (International Atomic Energy
Agency) 153
identity, see national identity; regional
identity
Ikenberry, John 68
'imagined communities' 189, 195
India 32, 50
Indonesia 245
institutionalist theory 61–4, 73, 258
interdependence, and regionalism 58–
66
International Atomic Energy Agency
(IAEA) 153
international co-operation, and the end
of the Cold War 18–20
International Relations theories 5, 12,
37, 71, 324
international system, decentralization
of the 20–3
investment, see foreign direct
investment (FDI)
Iraq 193–4, 224, 272, 276, 295
and the ACC 298–9

and the Arab League 288
Ismay, Lord 141
Israel 288, 291, 318

Japan 4, 51, 234
and the ASEAN 242
and China 231–2
economic power 94, 235
and economic regionalism 91, 92
FDI (foreign direct investment) 95,
105, 106–8, 245
and Korea 232–3, 243
and Latin America 254
money and finance 110, 111, 112
network of world trade 102, 103,
104
politics 235, 238
regional trade patterns 98–101, 114
role in Asia Pacific 233–4, 238–9,
244–6, 248
and the United States 85, 233, 234
and the world economy 117

Kennedy, John F. 210
Kenya 181, 184
Keohane, Robert 54, 61–2
Keynes, John Maynard 206
Kissinger, Henry 211, 318
Koh, Tommy 123–4
Kokoshin, Andrei 168
Korea 153, 228, 230–1, 234–5
and Japan 232–3
North Korea 153, 228, 230–1, 236,
243, 244
South Korea 228, 230–1, 242, 243,
244, 245
and US arms control 240
Kothari, Rajni 27
Krugman, Paul 94
Kuwait 288, 295, 299

labour migration, in Asia Pacific 246
LAS, see League of Arab States
Latin America 250, 251–63, 317–18
democratization 29, 69, 257–8,
260–1, 262
economic regionalism 25–6, 87–8,
97, 261–2
fear of 'Africanization' 22
and hemispheric regionalism 263–6,
270–5
and the limits of regionalism 275–82
and neo-realism 49

Lightning Source UK Ltd.
Milton Keynes UK
UKOW050611130112

185263UK00001B/29/A